The Word and the Sword

Studies in Social Discontinuity

General Editor Charles Tilly, The New School for Social Research

Studies in Social Discontinuity began in 1972 under the imprint of Academic Press. In its first 15 years, 53 titles were published in the series, including important volumes in the areas of historical sociology, political economy, and social history.

Revived in 1989 by Basil Blackwell, the series will continue to include volumes emphasizing social changes and non-Western historical experience as well as translations of major works.

Published:

The Perilous Frontier
Nomadic Empires and China
Thomas J. Barfield

Regents and Rebels
The Revolutionary World of an Eighteenth-Century Dutch City
Wayne Ph. te Brake

Coffee, Contention, and Change
in the Making of Modern Brazil
Mauricio Font

Nascent Proletarians
Class Formation in Post-Revolutionary France
Michael P. Hanagan

Social Evolutionism
A Critical History
Stephen K. Sanderson

Coercion, Capital, and European States
AD 990–1990
Charles Tilly

In preparation:

Modern French Anti-Semitism
A Political History
Pierre Birnbaum

Rites of Revolt
The War of the Demoiselles in Ariège, France (1829–1831)
Peter Sahlins

The Word and the Sword

How Techniques of Information and Violence Have Shaped our World

LEONARD M. DUDLEY

BLACKWELL
Publishers

Basil Blackwell, Inc.
3 Cambridge Center
Cambridge, Massachusetts 02142, USA

Basil Blackwell Ltd
108 Cowley Road, Oxford, OX4 1JF, UK

Library of Congress Cataloging in Publication Data

Dudley, Leonard, 1943–
    The word and the sword : how techniques of information and violence have shaped our world / Leonard M. Dudley.
        p.   cm. – (Studies in social discontinuity)
    Includes bibliographical references and index.
    ISBN 1-55786-246-X
    1. State, The.   2. Communication and traffic – History.
    3. Military history.   4. Taxation – History.   5. World history.
    I. Title.   II. Series: Studies in social discontinuity (Basil Blackwell Publisher)
    JC325.D83   1991
    355'.009 – dc20   90-28297
                                                                        CIP

British Library Cataloguing in Publication Data

A CIP catalogue record for this book is available from the British Library.

Typeset in 10½ on 12pt Ehrhardt
by DEKR Corporation
Printed in the USA
by Edwards Brothers, Ann Arbor, MI

Contents

Editor's Preface

Studies in Social Discontinuity present historically grounded analyses of important social transformations, ruptures, conflicts, and contradictions. Although we of Basil Blackwell interpret that mission broadly, leave room for many points of view, and absolve authors of any responsibility for propaganda on behalf of our intellectual program, the series as a whole demonstrates the relevance of well-crafted historical work for the understanding of contemporary social structures and processes. Books in the series pursue one or more of four varieties of historical analysis: (1) using evidence from past times and places systematically to identify regularities in processes and structures that transcend those particular times and places; (2) reconstructing critical episodes in the past for the light they shed on important eras, peoples, or social phenomena; (3) tracing the origins or previous phases of significant social processes that continue into our own time; (4) examining the ways that social action at a given point in time lays down residues that limit the possibilities of subsequent social action.

The fourth theme is at once the least familiar and the most general. Social analysts have trouble seeing that history matters precisely because social interaction takes place in well-defined times and places, and occurs within constraints offered by those times and places, producing social relations and artifacts that are themselves located in space–time and whose existence and distribution constrain subsequent social interaction. The construction of a city in a given place and time affects urban growth in adjacent areas and subsequent times. Where and when industrialization occurs affects how it occurs. Initial visions of victory announce a war's likely outcomes. A person's successive migrations have cumulative effects on his or her subsequent mobility through such simple matters as the presence or absence of information about new opportunities in different places and the presence or absence of social ties to possible destinations. A population's previous experience with wars, Baby Booms, and migrations haunts it in the form of bulging or empty cohorts and unequal numbers of the sexes. All these are profoundly historical matters, even when they occur in the present; time and place are of their essence. They form the essential subject matter of Studies in Social Discontinuity.

Edward Shorter, Stanley Holwitz, and I plotted the Studies in Social Discontinuity in 1970–71; the first book, William Christian's *Person and God in a Spanish Valley*, appeared in 1972. Over the years, Academic Press published more than 50 titles in the series. But during the early 1980s publication slowed, then ceased. In 1988, happily, Basil Blackwell agreed to revive the Studies under my editorship. Leonard Dudley's *The Word and the Sword* continues a great tradition.

Dudley dares. In a day when technology and technological determinism both have bad odors, he dares to chronicle the effects of major technical innovations on large blocks of human experience. He does it with gusto, throwing out bold conjectures and quick syntheses like glittering tokens from a *Mardi Gras* float. His is not a book of dense description, of plodding footnotes, of swollen appendices, of worried qualifications. It is a book to make us think, and rethink.

Dudley's technological determinism has refreshing vim. It carries a reader along compelled to attend, if not always to agree. Like William McNeill, Dudley is a gifted simplifier. His central thesis is straightforward: in all of human history eight technical innovations – four military, four in the field of communications broadly defined – marked and caused the major transitions in the character of social life. Military and informational technologies make all the difference, he argues, because they "are the glue that holds a state together." (He might have added: and, paradoxically, the *plastic* that blows states apart.) Innovations providing new economies of scale in either regard rapidly promote agglomeration, which in turn transforms human existence. The eight innovations? Writing, printing, mass media, and integrated circuits; metal weapons, artillery, steam transport, and heavy cavalry. While considering his information innovations the obvious choices for primacy, Dudley explicity gives the military innovations on his list priority over chariots, crossbows, longbows, rifles, rifled cannons, machine guns, submarines, airplanes, tanks, nuclear weapons, and ballistic missiles. He makes the implicit claim that these innovations mattered more than nuclear power, more than cultivated potatoes, more than wage-labor, more than paved roads, more than paper money, more than the joint-stock corporation, more than the factory, more than monotheistic religion, among the other claimants to be world-shaping inventions. He traces the early appearance of cities to writing rather than *vice versa*. Enthusiasts for these rival candidates will find they face a formidable advocate.

On the whole, Dudley's epochal inventions encouraged – he would probably say caused – great increases in the scale of human organization. Heavy cavalry and integrated circuits stand as interesting exceptions to the main trends; cavalry, by his account, actually decreased the optimum scale of land armies as integrated circuits reduced the optimum scale of production. Heavy cavalry contributed to the Roman Empire's collapse, he argues, precisely because it reduced the advantage of territorially extensive states over smaller ones. Integrated circuits, he continues, are now facilitating Japan's increasing mastery over the United States. To the extent that he is right, anyone who frets about the collapse of American power had better start thinking about new technologies to restore it.

Let us cheer Dudley's insistence on military and informational innovations, not to mention their connections. The two contrast interestingly, with military innovations such as the devastating introduction of artillery typically arriving as dramatic events while informational changes typically transform life increment by increment, but incessantly. Both, nevertheless, call attention to the way that a history written as great leaders, grand nations, and global ideologies neglects the inexorable effects of logistics, the sheer effort consumed by the mounting of armies and states under varying technical conditions. His dramatic analyses of decline in Rome and the United States will force us to reevaluate standard ideas about national survival.

Dudley presents his theses in a series of eight relatively independent historical essays, each treating an era and a political process in which one of the eight innovations played, in his view, the crucial role. Each essay is illuminating and exciting in its own right. Cumulatively, the essays present an extraordinary panorama of technology in history. Others will have to decide whether apparently contrary cases such as the occasional rise of great naval powers having small land bases and puny armies – Phoenicia and the Dutch Republic come to mind – challenge Dudley's bold generalization. In the meantime, *The Word and the Sword* will delight readers, stimulate students, and incite scholars to rethink their evidence.

CHARLES TILLY

Preface

This book is about systematic changes in state power – the power to control territory and the power to tax. Each chapter tells a story, focusing on a short period of history during which an innovation altered the relations between superior and subordinate. The result in each case was a discontinuity – revolution, war, the expansion or the collapse of empires – as territorial boundaries and levels of taxation adjusted to the shock. Over the course of the book, the scene changes from the dry soil of the Euphrates valley, to a walled town in medieval France, to the flight deck of the aircraft carrier *Nimitz*. Each of these stories is complete in itself; together, they describe how we got where we are and suggest where we might be going.

Although the book is about technology, it makes no mention of the wheel, the sailing ship, the airplane, the automobile, or the atomic bomb. Although it is about revolution, it has nothing to say about the American Revolution, the French Revolution, or even the Industrial Revolution. Although it is about empire, it fails to discuss the British Empire, and it deals with the Roman and American empires only in their dying phases. Although it is about warfare, it neglects the Napoleonic Wars, the American Civil War, and the Second World War. The reason for these apparent omissions is that the political units that have been chosen – whether villages, towns, or empires – are the first examples of the impact of eight remarkable innovations in informational and military techniques. The rest of the history of the state may be viewed as sets of variations on these themes.

The origins of this book date back three decades, to the time when, as a fascinated teenager, I pored over H. G. Wells's *Outline of History*. More recently, the structure of a possible monograph took form as I followed the lines of synthesis proposed by William H. McNeill in *The Rise of the West* and Fernand Braudel in *Civilization and Capitalism: 15th–18th Century*. The idea that key historical events may be explained by changes in the capacity of superiors in a hierarchy to control their subordinates was suggested by a seminar that Jean Tirole presented at the University of Montreal in 1986.*

Although there have been many excellent individual studies of innovations in military or communications technology, few have attempted to combine these two types of developments systematically. What was missing in most previous analyses of historical patterns, it occurred to me, was a means of integrating the conquest of territory and the willingness of citizens to pay taxes. At the heart of this book is the concept of *interlocking hierarchies* – the insight that the soldier and the tax collector are interdependent, and that the extent of their joint success determines the fortunes of states.

.   Leonard M. Dudley

---

*Jean Tirole, "Hierarchies and bureaucracies: on the role of collusion in organizations," *Journal of Law, Economics and Organization*, 2 (1986), pp. 181–214.

Acknowledgments

I would like to thank Roger Blockley, Alexander Demandt, Arther Ferrill, Paul Hohenberg, William McNeill, Joel Mokyr, Larry Neal, Douglass North, Mancur Olson, Jean Tirole, and Gordon Tullock for taking the time to comment on individual chapters of the manuscript. Ulrich Blum introduced me to the German school of spatial economists and collaborated on an article that forms the basis of the chapter on Renaissance France. George Grantham read and commented on this same chapter. He and his colleagues at McGill University, along with Stanley Winer and his colleagues at Carleton University, allowed me to expose the theoretical underpinnings of the manuscript to expert criticism. Jean-Jacques Rosa and his graduate students at the Institut d'Études Politiques of Paris gave me a chance to subject the manuscript in its entirety to detailed criticism over a three-week period in the spring of 1990.

My colleagues and former colleagues Reuven Brenner, Abraham Hollander, Claude Montmarquette, Pierre Lasserre, Pierre Perron, François Vaillancourt, and Kimon Valaskakis made many constructive suggestions and offered their encouragement during the four years of preparation of this book. Jan Kowalski as a visiting professor read and criticized the chapter on the Russian Revolutions. Marcel Leibovici of the history department at the University of Montreal provided valuable help for the first two chapters on ancient Mesopotamia. I also wish to thank Elizabeth Johnson as the editor who first read the manuscript and conscientiously supervised its evaluation. The criticisms of Charles Tilly and a second, anonymous referee were greatly appreciated.

I owe a debt of gratitude to Ramzy Yelda who, first as an undergraduate and later as a graduate student, helped with the references and maps and criticized the successive versions of the manuscript.

The following works contain maps that were particularly useful in the preparation of the figures that begin each chapter:

G. Barraclough (ed.), *The Times Atlas of World History*, rev. ed. (Hammond, 1984).

H. C. Darby, and H. Fullard (eds), *The New Cambridge Modern History Atlas* (Cambridge University Press, 1978).

S. N. Kramer, *Cradle of Civilization* (Time-Life Books, 1967).

M. E. L. Mallowan *Early Mesopotamia and Iran* (McGraw-Hill, 1965).

R. R. Sellman *An Outline Atlas of World History* (St Martin's Press, 1970).

The following figures have been reproduced with kind permission:

Figure 1.2: I. J. Gelb, *A Study of Writing* (University of Chicago Press, 1963).

Figure 1.3: L. Cottrell, *Reading the Past* (Crowell-Collier, 1971).

Figure 2.2: The Trustees of the British Museum, London.

Figure 2.3: The Ancient Art and Architecture Collection — Ronald Sheridan's Photo-Library.

Figure 2.4: Giraudon, Paris: Musee de Louvre, Paris.

The preparation of a book such as this requires access to a truly encyclopedic amount of information. Although I have not cited the *Encyclopedia Britannica* in the text, I should mention that it proved an invaluable source for filling in the gaps between the accounts to be found in individual specialized studies.

Introduction

In each period of history, the patterns detected by observers have differed. The idea to be explored in this book is that history has been shaped by a number of great waves, each of which swept away much of what lay in its path. These waves brought sharp changes in society's ability to reward and punish and so perturbed the existing structure of social relationships. At any one time, observers looking back concentrated on the effects of the latest wave, in which they themselves were caught up. Most failed to notice that overlying all of these developments was a meta-pattern of which each successive wave was a part. Since informational and military scale economies are the glue that holds a society together, a revolution in these technologies will alter the optimal boundaries and levels of government intervention of the typical state. From the beginning of historical records, there have been eight such revolutions, four affecting information processing and four the application of violence. Each merits detailed study.

Late summer is the traditional period for holiday travel in Europe. The month of August, 1989 was hot and dry – ideal vacation weather. Nevertheless, Hungarian border police were disturbed to find large numbers of tourists from neighboring Communist countries exploring the regions near the frontier with Austria. Typical was the Shulte family from East Berlin who abandoned the small Trabant automobile they had saved 16 years to buy and fled through a field of tall corn toward the border.[1] Also typical were Holgar and Andreas, two 23-year-old electricians from Leipzig who turned over all of their belongings to an anti-Communist passer from West Germany, and set out for the border point he had indicated to them. Just as they were about to cross into Austria, they were confronted by two armed Hungarian guards with a dog. Holgar meekly turned himself in, but Andreas desperately ran toward what remained of the barbed-wire barrier.[2]

Three months earlier, the Hungarian government, anxious to improve its relations with the West, had begun to tear down the fencing along a 240 km section of the Iron Curtain that had separated Eastern and Western Europe for four decades.[3] As the news of this possible escape route spread, hundreds and then thousands of East Germans, along with smaller numbers of Romanians and members of other nationalities, flocked to the border area. When the East Berlin regime of Erich Honecker protested, the Hungarian authorities promised to crack down, preventing any Eastern-bloc tourists without exit visas from crossing into Austria. The Shulte family and Andreas managed to escape, but Hungarian border patrols turned back thousands of other East Germans, stamping their passports to show that they had tried to flee.

Yet the exodus continued. Finally, in early September, after weeks of intense Western diplomatic pressure, Hungary agreed not to detain those East Germans who wished to cross into Austria. The moderate flow then turned into a torrent. Each week, many thousands of East Germans who had been unable to express themselves politically at home displayed their dislike of the Honecker regime by voting with their feet. Since the Bonn government recognized all East Germans as German citizens, it was compelled to organize special trains to transport the refugees from Austria to camps in Bavaria. Most of the emigrants were under 30 years of age, and almost all had vocational or professional training.[4] They were the young elite of the most prosperous state in Eastern Europe.

The events along the Hungarian border in the late summer of 1989 caught Western observers by surprise. Although there was some speculation about these developments, most commentators limited their attention to the immediate effects of the mass emigration on West Germany. Yet the situation in late September was clearly unstable. The orthodox Marxist regime of East Berlin could not sit by passively as its most promising young workers fled abroad. Nor could the citizens of other Eastern-bloc countries fail to observe what was happening in the German Democratic Republic. But why were these events occurring? And how might one foresee what their outcome would be?

PATTERNS OF THE PAST

Recorded events are like debris scattered across a beach by the receding tide. At first glance, the objects left behind seem to be scattered randomly; but a closer look reveals what appear to be patterns. Near the high-water mark, inland, the records are few, their characters faded. But toward the sea, the objects deposited on the sand become more numerous. The traces of separate waves can be distinguished with increasing ease. Along the water's edge, the individual events are plentiful: here there is life and activity, glistening in the freshness of the present. Beyond, seaward, the sand is still submerged, hidden beneath the ocean's dark surface. But as each wave retreats, it leaves behind a new set of deposits and exposes more of the beach previously concealed.

People have long been fascinated with these seeming patterns in the sand. Properly interpreted, they might explain how we got here – and where we are going. Those who have had the most to say about the meaning of the debris are the priests, epic poets, political philosophers, and historians who have combed the beach over the past five millennia. It has been they who have observed, collected, and interpreted the records of the past, searching for order in what to the inexperienced eye appeared to be the fruit of hazard.

The explanations offered have been as varied as the observers. In some of the first historical texts, priests and religious scholars reported the suffering of those on whom the gods had inflicted punishment. For example, the flood story of Sumer, written long before the biblical tale of Noah, suggests a link between human actions and natural calamities. It tells of a decision by the gods to destroy sinful mankind. Only a pious and god-fearing man named Ziusudra is warned in time to save himself and his family. When, after seven days and seven nights, the flood waters recede, the grateful hero sacrifices to the sun god. He in turn is rewarded with "life like (that of) a god" in the land where the sun rises.[5] By implication, those who wish to avoid divine retribution must appease the gods by following their directives – or those of their earthly representatives.

At a somewhat later period, epic poets recited the exploits of heroes who fought battles and undertook long voyages. They too had a lesson to transmit: by using courage and strength, men could hope to overcome the obstacles that fate placed in their way. Herodotus, writing in fifth-century BC Athens, picked up this theme. In the outcome of the Persian Wars, he saw a triumph of civilization over barbarism. Still later, at the time of the Roman Empire, however, historians were less sanguine. From Tacitus to Aurelius Victor, they perceived the internal danger from challenges to imperial power by ambitious generals and the external threat from ever-stronger coalitions of barbarian tribes.

By the first centuries of the modern era, it was the political philosophers who dominated the discussion. Niccolo Machiavelli formulated a set of recommendations for a prince who would unite the petty states of Italy into a larger unit. Using cunning and strength, the prince would persuade his subjects to support him and proceed to defeat his rivals. The political philosophers of the seventeenth and eighteenth centuries saw a different pattern. Hobbes, Locke, and Rousseau compared an initial state of nature with a later society in which a social contract transferred power to a single individual or a set of representatives. This approach revealed a new awareness of a collective identity among the individual members of a state.

Writers of the nineteenth century emphasized the irresistible rise of liberal capitalism. Writing in the middle decades of the century, Karl Marx stressed the manner in which the emergence of market relationships between capital and labor had destroyed the institutions of feudalism. He predicted that tensions between the new social classes would lead to revolution. As the century drew to a close, however, no such upheaval had occurred. Across Western Europe new institutions had been formed to allow individuals greater access to political decision-making. The English liberal historian, Lord Acton, could view European, British, and American history as a unified whole, showing the ultimate rise of constitutional liberty.[6]

In the first decades of the present century, the liberal ideal faded. The nations of Europe were drawn into a period of intense competition in which individual freedoms were submitted to the needs of the collectivity. At the same time, recently uncovered archaeological evidence showed that Western European civilization was but one of many that had arisen over the previous millennia. Looking back, the German historian Oswald Spengler argued that each civilization went through a life-cycle of birth, expansion, maturity, and inevitable decline. Western civilization, he felt, had entered the final phase of such a cycle.[7]

Arnold Toynbee too found traces of cycles, detecting 21 civilizations of which Western Latin Christendom was among the latest. Unlike Spengler, however, he believed that decline was not inevitable: a civilization's fate depended on its capacity to respond to challenges.[8] By mid-century, it was clear that not only had Western civilization and its Russian satellite civilization survived but also that its two major powers with their alternative forms of government together dominated the world. William H. McNeill explained this dramatic rise of one of the world's major regions at the expense of the others as the culmination of a long process of diffusion of new ideas.[9]

Then, in the early 1970s, observers began to detect major changes in both the structure of Western society and its place relative to non-European societies, particularly those of Asia. Daniel Bell and Alvin Toffler argued that Western societies were in the midst of a post-industrial or information revolution comparable in its impact to the agricultural and industrial revolutions of earlier periods.[10] For other observers, the most recent developments are an extension of a second industrial revolution that began a century ago.[11] Recently Paul Kennedy detected a 500-year pattern of military expansion and decline linked to a state's economic capacity.[12] Because of a fall in their share of world production, the political and military positions of the United States and the Soviet Union were gradually being eroded.

In each period of history, it would seem, the patterns detected have differed. Some observers have seen a trend toward expansion, while others have noted decline. Some have detected a trend of submission to the state, while others have remarked a rise in the importance of the individual. It is the thesis of this book that each of these different points of view is nevertheless correct. However, to reconcile these apparent contradictions – and in so doing better understand where we have come from and where we might be going – an additional analytical step is required.

A tidal wave is an unusually high ocean swell set off by an earthquake. The idea to be explored here is that history has been shaped by a number of such great waves, each of which swept away much of what lay in its path. These waves, it will be argued, brought sharp changes in society's ability to reward and punish and so perturbed the existing structure of social relationships. At any one time, observers looking back concentrated on the effects of the latest swell, in which they themselves were caught up. Most failed to notice that overlying all of these developments was a meta-pattern of which each successive wave formed a part.

To explain tidal waves, one must explore the nature of the earthquakes that set them off. Rather than look at normal periods when societies were flourishing, this study will focus on the abnormal times when the existing order seemed to be coming apart. It is during these periods in which the waves of change were striking with their greatest force that the overall pattern is most easily detected. The shocks, it will be argued, came in the form of revolutions in informational and military technology – critical innovations that transformed the way people interact.

THE LIMITS TO STATE POWER

One of the ever-fascinating aspects of human behavior is the richness of our social groupings. In approximate order of increasing size, there are the family, the neighborhood, the tribe, the labor union, the firm, the political party, and the religious group, to name only a few. The most complex and most pervasive of these social groupings is the autonomous political unit or state. Consequently, when a revolution in technology changes the capacity of people to control other people, the social group that is likely to be the most profoundly affected is the state.

From the United States to Mauritius, there are two fundamental characteristics of a state: a recognized right to use force over a specified area, and a recognized power to levy taxes within the limits of this territory. A political unit such as a village, a town, a province, or a colony that does not have these characteristics will necessarily be a sub-unit of a larger state. Sometimes the formal boundaries of a state may differ from the actual limits to the power of its ruling group. In medieval Europe or present-day Lebanon, for example, one may find the ruler's control confined to only a sub-area of the nominal political unit. In such cases, this study will focus its attention on the real limits to the controlling group's authority.

When a major technological shock occurs, it will tend to affect the margins of these two basic powers of the state. The limit to the exercise of force, the territorial boundary, might be termed the *external margin* of the state. Except for political units whose borders are on broad expanses of water, the point at which one jurisdiction's right to exercise military power ends is also the point at which another's right to use force begins. Any shock that changes what one state considers its optimal boundary is therefore likely to set off a series of disturbances and conflicts. Here, then, is a possible explanation for many of the international conflicts that have occurred over the millennia. For example, from the mid-nineteenth to the mid-twentieth centuries, there occurred a series of wars and scrambles for territory around the world. A series of shocks appeared to have disturbed the optimal external margin for a large number of countries.

Within a given territory, the share of total income that is raised through taxes constitutes the limit to the state's fiscal power. This boundary between public and private allocation of a community's resources may be thought of as the *internal margin* of a state's power. Any extension of this margin would entail the confiscation of additional revenue from the political unit's citizens. It may be seen, therefore, that a shock that alters the optimal position of this internal limit to state power will trigger internal conflicts within individual countries. Such a disturbance, for example, may help explain the revolutions that have shaken the internal structure of states around the world from the sixteenth century to the present.

What is it that determines the limits to a state's external and internal power? This question is perhaps most easily answered in the case of the territorial boundary. Military control of remote territory depends on technology. The ruler of a state faced with a rebellion by the inhabitants of an outlying region must consider not only the probability of victory but also its cost. If both sides use the same military technology, the ruler will attempt to put down the revolt by sending a larger force than that controlled by the rebels. The crucial factor for him will be the expected cost of an enemy casualty for his larger army relative to the expected cost of a casualty for the smaller opposing army when the two bodies engage in combat.

If the anticipated costs of a casualty to the enemy are about the same for both sides regardless of the relative sizes of two opposing armies, then there will be no economies of scale in military technology. Accordingly, the cost of controlling territory will be high. When it is expensive for a ruler to control territory, states will tend to be small. This, for example, was the situation in the Middle Ages, when armed combat tended to be a series of contests between individual horsemen and the losing side could retreat behind stout castle walls that were expensive to penetrate.

However, if up to a certain size, a large army generally has a lower cost of inflicting a casualty than a smaller force, one could say that military scale economies exist. A central authority maintaining a standing force of the optimal size could then control a wide territory around its capital, defeating any opposition in detail. The casualties it suffered would be light relative to those inflicted on its opponents. By the sixteenth century, for example, effective individual firearms and artillery permitted the kings of Europe to subdue rebellious nobles at a moderate cost. Defeating their opponents on the battlefield with superior numbers of disciplined troops and denying them the security of their castles, the Renaissance monarchs were able to maintain the royal power over extended territories.

The other margin, the limit to the share of a state's income that may be seized in the form of taxes, also depends upon technology. If migration is possible, one may view the state as a network, in which membership is voluntary. The ideology of a society, as discussed by North, may be viewed as a set of protocols – codes of precedence and interaction – for such a network.[13] In return for his dues or taxes, each person who belongs to the community receives the right to interact with other members using the facilities of the network. Thus the level at which taxes may be set depends on the gains that the individual derives from the community relative to his best alternative. Taxes may be raised to the point at which citizens are indifferent between remaining within the network and undergoing the effort of establishing themselves elsewhere.

The gains to the individual from network membership will tend to increase in turn with the economies of scale in information processing. For example, in a nomadic agricultural society, such scale economies are likely to be slight and the gains to network membership accordingly small. Large-scale organization will therefore be unnecessary, each family or clan being able to do as well on its own. However, in a complex urban society, where the information technology permits large-scale organization, there will be considerable benefits to network membership. Some or all of these gains may be extracted from the members in the form of taxes. Thus, the capacity of the fiscal system to generate tax receipts will depend on the technology for storing, reproducing, and transmitting information.

Informational and military scale economies, then, are the glue that holds a state together.[14] The introduction of new types of mortar and bricks will tend to alter the size and internal structure of houses that are built. In the same way, it is conceivable that new techniques for processing information or for applying violence will alter the boundaries and levels of government intervention in the typical state. On the one hand, an increase or decrease in scale economies of information processing will change the willingness of citizens to pay taxes. On the other hand, an increase or decrease in military scale economies will alter the cost of controlling territory. Each of these types of innovation constitutes a class of wave which, sweeping across the beach of history, will wash away existing institutions. In the process, state borders will change and the situation of the individual relative to the collectivity be transformed.

EIGHT KEY INNOVATIONS

Over the millennia, there have been numerous innovations in both informational and military technology. Which ones have been important enough to reshape social and political institutions? To assure that sufficient information on boundaries and tax levels is available, the analysis will be limited to the historical period; that is, to the past 5,000 years, for which written records exist. In the case of informational scale economies, the task is then relatively easy. The key innovations have been few and their impact on information processing profound: writing, printing, the mass media (mass circulation newspapers, motion pictures, radio, and television), and the integrated circuit must each be studied in detail. Other possible candidates, such as the alphabet and paper, had relatively less important effects on the cost of storing, reproducing, and distributing information .

Writing, printing, and the mass media all tended to increase informational scale economies. For example, it is much more difficult to teach a person to both talk and write than simply to talk. Therefore, with writing, the cost of storing the first bits of information in standardized form increased sharply. However, as human memory is both fallible and severely limited in capacity, the cost of accurate, permanent storage of additional data was much less expensive with writing than with oral methods. Writing replaced the scattered recollections of individuals with the centralized storage of large amounts of information.

With printing, the cost of the first copy increased further, but that of additional copies fell dramatically. Informational scale economies therefore rose again. For printed information to reach beyond the small elite trained to read Latin, however, further changes were necessary. A standardized written form of the vernacular or spoken languages had to be developed and the ability to read had to be extended to the general population.[15] With the development of mass media, national information networks penetrated deeper into society, thereby yielding increased benefits to each individual. Part of these benefits could then be taxed away so as to provide a vast additional flow of public revenues.

Recently, however, the availability of increasingly powerful, miniaturized integrated circuits, or microchips, at ever-lower relative prices has greatly reduced the expense of producing and distributing the first copy of a set of information. The cost of small-scale information processing has therefore fallen much more sharply than that of large-scale systems, thereby reducing the advantages of great organizations.

In the case of military technology, the choice of the key innovations is more difficult. Certainly metal weapons, heavy cavalry, gunpowder, and the steam engine would appear to be likely candidates. Where, however, do the chariot, the crossbow, the longbow, the rifle, the rifled cannon, the machine-gun, the submarine, the airplane, the tank, nuclear weapons, and the ballistic missile fit into the overall picture?

With regard to innovations whose primary effect was on land warfare, the chariot seems to have been effective against undisciplined troops or as a means of harassing trained foot soldiers. Otherwise, it did little to change the nature of warfare. As for the crossbow, the longbow, the rifle, the rifled cannon, the machine-gun, and the tank, all had important effects on military tactics and strategy. However, in none of these cases was the optimal size of an army greatly affected. For example, despite the introduction of the machine-gun and tank, the German armies on the western front in the First and Second World Wars were of the same order of magnitude as the German force occupying France in late 1870.[16]

In the case of the airplane and the submarine, although these innovations have played important auxiliary roles in recent conflicts, they have rarely been decisive. As for nuclear weapons, they have been used on only one occasion, and had only a marginal impact on the outcome of that struggle. Similarly, the ballistic missile has to date had only a slight effect on the size of military formations.

In analyzing the possible roles of the four remaining innovations in generating historical discontinuities, there is some justification in confining one's attention to land warfare. Heavy cavalry, of course, had little effect on naval combat. As for the other three innovations – metal arms, gunpowder, and the steam engine – their effect on scale economies in naval warfare was on the whole similar to their impact on land battles: the size of the optimal fighting force increased. Another consideration is that the effect of each of these three new technologies on naval warfare occurred *after* their impact on land combat. The battle of Salamis, for example, occurred two millennia after the application of metal weapons in Sumerian warfare, the defeat of the Spanish Armada over a century after the use of field artillery at Formigny and Castillon, and Jutland half a century after the crucial impact of steam transport at Sadowa.

Three of the four key military innovations – metal weapons, artillery, and steam transport – tended to increase the optimal size of a field army. The effect was most evident in the case of bronze and iron weapons. Since Egypt long remained isolated from military developments elsewhere in the Near East, Egyptian monuments from the late fourth and the third millennia BC provide some idea of the nature of proto-historic armed conflict. Although the Egyptians of the Old Kingdom were familiar with the short thrusting spear and shield, there are battle scenes that depict soldiers armed only with the mace, without protective armor or shield, fighting a series of individual combats.[17] Scale economies appear to have been slight.

However, with the development of bronze and iron armaments, it became possible to form a shield wall of infantrymen, armed with shock weapons such as the sword and the long spear with socketed head and protected by body armor, helmet, and large, reinforced shield. Sumerian monuments depict a line of such heavy infantrymen advancing in tight formation.[18] By enveloping or penetrating the enemy line, a large force of these disciplined foot soldiers was generally able to inflict more casualties on a smaller force than it suffered in return.

Two other inventions also served to increase the size of the optimal field army. In the later Middle Ages, the development of artillery firing iron-reinforced and cast-iron projectiles sharply lowered the cost of penetrating static defenses behind which a small force could take refuge. And in the nineteenth century, the establishment of rail and telegraph networks greatly reduced the cost of assembling, supplying, and coordinating very large numbers of soldiers.

The exception among the most important military innovations was heavy cavalry. The combination of the heavy horse, able to carry armor for itself and its rider, with the saddle and stirrup, providing a stable platform for shock combat, made it possible to penetrate the infantry shield wall. However, since there were few gains to coordination of shock cavalry combat, a large force was generally unable to inflict more casualties than it incurred. As a result, military scale economies fell.

Each of these eight innovations was revolutionary, introducing either a new way of dealing with information or a new means of organizing the application of violence. Each required a restructuring of the basic ways in which people interact socially. And each was sufficiently important to warrant detailed study in its historical context.

TECHNOLOGICAL DETERMINISM?

One final issue remains. The proposed approach sounds suspiciously like technological determinism; that is, the position that all human social relationships are determined ultimately by technology. Indeed, since the study is to be limited to a small number of cases of innovations in communications and military techniques, it would appear to be an extreme example of this oft-criticized doctrine. Can one possibly justify the use of such a simplistic approach to explain historical causality?

The answer, obviously, is no. In the chapters that follow, every effort will be made to indicate how new technologies themselves developed as a consequence of social conditions at certain moments in history. Examining technological change in the nineteenth century, Paul David showed how key innovations were to a great extent predetermined by previous short-sighted decisions taken to solve current production problems.[19] Extending this idea, Richard Nelson and Sidney Winter have proposed an evolutionary theory of technical progress.[20] At a given moment, an organization such as a firm has a set of routines that it uses to produce, set prices, allocate management time, and improve its information. Its success in the competition for scarce resources depends on its ability to adapt these routines in the face of uncertainty. However, the organization's capacity to evolve is itself determined by routines it has set up previously.

This study may be seen as an application of this evolutionary theory of technical change to political institutions. It is recognized that technology, population growth, and political structures are mutually determined. Yet in a given region, the direction of possible change at any particular moment is to a great extent circumscribed by geographical factors and by the sum of past events. It is then the response of this complex system to unpredictable shocks that determines historical change. It would be impractical, however, to give equal weight to each of these possible elements in the eight historical studies that have been chosen. In what follows, therefore, the effect of such factors as geography and demographic change will be duly noted and assessed. But in each case, the principal focus will be on the latest of a series of technological improvements and on the discontinuous transformation of social patterns that accompanied the diffusion of these innovations.

In the case of Eastern Europe during the summer of 1989, something triggered a series of population movements. To understand the importance of what was occurring and what its possible effects might be, one must go back in time, traveling south-east to the two great rivers of Mesopotamia.

NOTES

1 *Newsweek*, August 28, 1989, p. 22.
2 *Newsweek*, September 18, 1989, p. 34.
3 *Time*, September 11, 1989, p. 32.
4 *Time*, September 25, 1989, p. 22.
5 Helmer Ringgren, *Religions of the Ancient Near East*, tr. John Sturdy (The Westminster Press, 1973), p. 23.
6 William H. McNeill, *Mythistory and Other Essays* (University of Chicago Press, 1986), p. 122.
7 Oswald Spengler, *The Decline of the West* (Allen and Unwin, 1926).
8 Arnold J. Toynbee, *A Study of History*, revised and abridged (Oxford University Press, 1972).
9 William H. McNeill, *The Rise of the West: A History of the Human Community* (University of Chicago Press, 1963).
10 Daniel Bell, *The Coming of Post-Industrial Society* (Basic Books, 1973); Alvin Toffler, *The Third Wave* (William Morrow and Co., 1980).
11 See Douglass C. North, *Structure and Change in Economic History* (Norton, 1981), p. 67; James R. Beniger, *The Control Revolution: Technological and Economic Origins of the Information Society* (Harvard University Press, 1986), p. 427.
12 Paul Kennedy, *The Rise and Fall of the Great Powers* (Random House, 1987).
13 North, *Structure and Change in Economic History*, pp. 45–9.
14 See Mancur Olson, "Toward a more general theory of government structure," *American Economic Review, Papers and Proceedings*, 76 (1986), pp. 120–5.
15 Elizabeth L. Eisenstein, *The Printing Press as an Agent of Change* (Cambridge University Press, 1979), pp. 126–8.
16 Larry H. Addington, *The Patterns of War since the Eighteenth Century* (Indiana University Press, 1984); R. Ernest Dupuy and Trevor N. Dupuy, *The Encyclopedia of Military History from 3500 BC to the Present*, 2nd edn (Harper and Row, 1986), pp. 931, 1057.
17 Richard Humble, *Warfare in the Ancient World* (Cassell, 1980), pp. 36–7.
18 Ibid., p. 19.

19 Paul David, *Technological Choice, Innovation and Economic Growth* (Cambridge University Press, 1975), p. 4.
20 Richard R. Nelson and Sidney G. Winter, *An Evolutionary Theory of Economic Change* (Harvard University Press, 1982), p. 14ff; Richard R. Nelson, *Understanding Technical Change as an Evolutionary Process* (North-Holland, 1987), p. 21.

I

Ziggurats in the Sand

Why did the first cities appear in Sumer between 3500 and 3000 BC? Some have argued that a natural disaster forced the inhabitants of many small communities to come together in larger political units. Others have suggested that cities arose because of the crowding that followed population growth. However, the process occurred over too long a period to be explained as an ecological adaptation and over too short a period to be accounted for by demographic pressure. Excavations at the site of the city of Uruk indicate that during this time interval, the Sumerians developed the first system for recording information by the use of phonetically coded symbols. By the end of the fourth millennium BC, some of the earlier small agricultural communities had grown to become temple-states, with populations of over 10,000 inhabitants, administered by an elite of priests and scribes. These sets of evidence appear to be linked: writing seems to have led to the rise of cities by increasing the optimal size of social information networks.

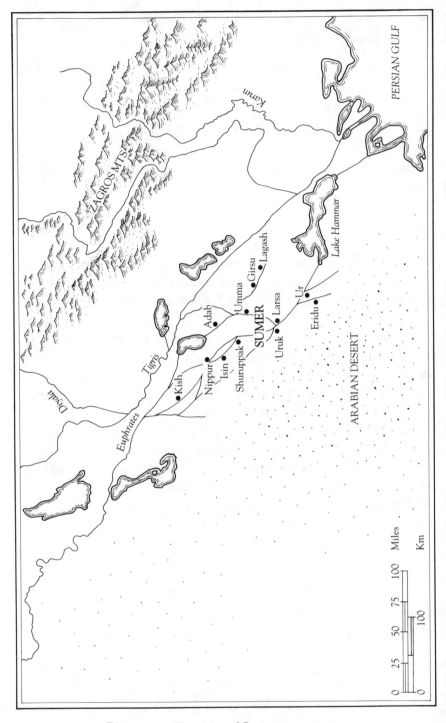

Figure 1.1 The cities of Sumer, ca. 3000 BC.

(*Source*: Samuel N. Kramer, *Cradle of Civilization*, Time-Life Books, New York, 1967, p. 38.)

An armed river-steamer was to carry the boundary commission south-east from Baghdad down the Tigris river. However, one of the group's members, William Kennett Loftus, boldly decided to set out on horseback with his friend, H. A. Churchill. They would accompany the party's pack animals and their mounted escort, crossing the desert and marshes between the lower Tigris and Euphrates rivers to the head of the Persian Gulf. Loftus was particularly keen to see the ruins of Warka, reputed to be the birthplace of the biblical patriarch Abraham. As yet no Europeans had visited this site, which lay 7 km inland from the banks of the lower Euphrates and was accessible only in the driest winter months.[1]

To their astonishment, at Warka, Loftus and his companion found a vast field of ruins almost 10 km in circumference on an elevated tract of desert soil. They discovered traces of a mighty rampart 13 m high that had once surrounded a city. The site contained three massive layered temples, or ziggurats, built by a people whose identity was unknown. It had evidently been occupied continuously for hundreds or perhaps thousands of years and then abandoned. No life of any kind was observable for kilometers around. In fact, the local Arabs shunned the site, holding it to be a place of evil spirits; none would dare pass the night there.[2]

The year was 1850. Loftus was the geological member of a quadripartite commission made up of representatives from Britain, Russia, the Ottoman Empire, and Persia sent out to resolve a boundary dispute between the latter two states. He was sufficiently impressed by what he discovered at Warka to request funds to make some small-scale excavations. However, the size of the site was so great that when he returned on two subsequent occasions, he and his party could do no more than literally scratch the surface. He guessed that he had found the city of Ur. It was not until three-quarters of a century later, in 1924, that the first of a series of German expeditions began the systematic excavation of Warka.[3] It was learned that the original name of the city was Uruk, known in the Old Testament as Erech.

The archaeological evidence that these expeditions uncovered was of the greatest significance. It revealed that between 5,000 and 6,000 years ago, Warka and the surrounding region were the site of one of the most profound changes that human societies have experienced – the rise of cities. Because the transformation occurred gradually over the course of more than a dozen generations, few of those who experienced it may have even been aware that it was happening. Nevertheless, it is evident from the standpoint of the twentieth century, that the cumulative effect of these changes constituted a discontinuous and irreversible change in the way people lived and worked.

To put these developments into perspective, in the late fourth millennium BC, most of the population of the Americas still lived by hunting animals and gathering wild fruits and vegetables. Only in Mexico were people beginning to form agricultural communities to raise corn. At that time, Europe was covered by forests interspersed with small farming settlements whose inhabitants grew grain on rain-watered land. Yet in certain parts of the Middle East, south and east Asia, and north-eastern Africa, more complex agricultural communities practicing irrigation had arisen.

One of these areas was southern Iraq, whose situation until the middle of the fourth millennium BC had been similar to that of the other more advanced regions. The land bordering the marshlands formed by the Tigris and Euphrates rivers before they empty into the Persian Gulf was known as Sumer. Its inhabitants lived in villages whose houses were built of rectangular bricks baked from the mud of the river banks. They had learned to make pottery of a green shade, decorated with intricate geometric patterns. In the larger communities, they had built small temples of a rectangular design similar to that of their houses.

By the end of the fourth millennium BC, however, some of these communities had grown sufficiently in size and in population density to be called cities. One obvious change that had occurred in the intervening period was in architecture. At the centers of the first Sumerian cities were massive temples built on limestone foundations that raised them above the level of the flood plain. Another and more profound difference between these two periods was in the social fabric. Within the new highly structured urban societies, the division of labor was carried to a far greater extent than in the earlier village economies. Increases in productivity permitted agricultural workers to provide a substantial food surplus that could be used to feed many new groups within the society. There were classes of skilled artisans who produced textiles, metal-ware, jewelry, and new types of pottery, and traders who exchanged these goods with peoples in distant lands. At the same time, a new class of scribes was taking the first steps toward the systematic accumulation of knowledge in permanent form.

The prehistoric villages of Sumer had shared a common characteristic with communities in other parts of the world. Since the beginning of human social groupings, men and women had almost always interacted with people they knew and who knew them, if not by name then at least by sight. Any strangers were likely to be enemies and were therefore to be avoided. Within the new Sumerian cities, however, a typical resident might in his daily life come across hundreds or even thousands of people he did not know. Yet the presence of these strangers had become as necessary to assure his own well-being as that of his own family. All were bound together by an invisible web of exchanges.

This phenomenon – the coming together in a small area of a large number of people who participate in a complex system of specialized activities with people they may not know – is called civilization. That it first occurred in Sumer in the late fourth millennium BC is now generally accepted. Why and how it occurred at this place and time are questions that are worth exploring.

THE TWO RIVERS

To understand how the first cities emerged, it is necessary to have some idea of the geography of Lower Mesopotamia. Sumer occupied an area of about the size of Denmark on the flood plain of the lower Tigris and Euphrates rivers (see figure 1.1). As this region received fewer than 20 cm of precipitation per year, rain-watered agriculture of the type practiced in certain other parts of the Middle East was not possible.[4] However, the rivers overflowed every spring, permitting crops to be grown in the fertile alluvial soil along their banks. To increase agricultural production, all that was required was to find a means of transferring water from the rivers themselves to the desert land stretching beyond their banks.

Protecting the Mesopotamian plain were deserts to the south and west and mountains to the north and east. However, as there were passes through these mountains, the area was highly susceptible to attack from outside.[5] By the middle of the fourth millennium BC the area was dominated by a people who called themselves Sumerians. On the basis of linguistic evidence, some scholars have suggested that the Sumerians were recently arrived invaders who had come through these mountain passes from Iran to the north-east. Mingling with the indigenous population, they eventually formed a relatively homogeneous group that spoke the Sumerian language.[6] However, other researchers have argued that since the archaeological evidence shows no indication of a sudden change in living conditions during the proto-historic period (the period immediately prior to the first written records), the Sumerians must have long inhabited this region.[7] Whatever the true origin of this group, it was during their period of dominance that the first cities emerged.

The Kinship Boundary

In addition to an understanding of the geography and recent history of Sumer, it is essential to have some idea of how the society of this region was organized. It is useful to distinguish two boundaries or margins that indicate the limits to certain types of human social behavior. One of these limits, the territorial boundary of a political unit, indicates the amount of territory that can be controlled from a single point. It might be termed the *external margin* of the state. The other limit is that which separates public from private activities within a single community. It might be called the *internal margin* of the state.

In Sumer by the early fourth millennium BC, the channels made by the lower Euphrates river, as it meandered its way to the south-east toward the sea, were dotted with small agricultural communities. The majority of these settlements occupied an area of a hectare – the size of two football fields – or less. Even the largest measured only slightly over ten hectares, and with a population density estimated at 125 people per hectare, had fewer than 2,000 inhabitants.[8] One may surmise that each community's members would generally belong to a few related families.[9] In the terminology of Parsons, the pre-Sumerian settlements could be classed as "advanced primitive;" that is, status within the kinship group had begun to be differentiated, some families being recognized to have higher social positions than others.[10]

These families derived their incomes from agriculture – principally from grains such as barley and flax. The date palm was also an important food source.[11] The sparse rainfall that the region received was insufficient to permit crops to be grown. However, some 2,000–3,000 years earlier, it had been discovered that channels cut into the soil to bring water from the rivers could permit agriculture even in the driest regions.[12] The banks of the lower Euphrates and Tigris were therefore irrigated by means of local systems of dikes and canals that allowed the alluvial soils along the rivers' edges to be farmed.[13] Other techniques that were known to the region were the working of pure copper, pottery, and the use of bricks made with dried mud from the river banks for construction.

One of the key dimensions in defining a society is the number of people who belong to the same political community. More precisely, what is important is the number of individuals who can be called upon to share the cost of goods such as irrigation canals that provide benefit to the entire community. The difficulty with these small agricultural villages was that there were relatively few people to bear the burden of such projects. As Cottrell observed, "if mankind had been forced to live perpetually in these small self-supporting communities, each producing just sufficient to feed its members, the great civilizations of the ancient world would not have arisen."[14] It was only through cooperation of large numbers of people that a surplus of food could be produced sufficient to feed the number of workers required for large public investment projects.

In Lower Mesopotamia, the population had expanded to the limits of the food supply that the cultivated land along the river banks could produce. However, the land farther back from the river was potentially extremely fertile if some way could be found to supply it with water. To support a larger population on this territory, it would be necessary to form larger political units, in which the costs of collective goods such as irrigation canals could be shared among a greater number of citizens. But to do so, it would be necessary to bring together people who not only were unrelated but also might never know one another. In other words, what has been described here as the community's external margin had to be pushed beyond the boundary of kinship.

Irrigation and Social Organization

A second boundary separates different types of human behavior within a given community. The division between individual and collective activity may be referred to as the society's *internal margin*. To make more efficient use of the soil and thereby support a larger population, it would be necessary to build new feeder canals and irrigation ditches. In addition, continual care would be necessary to avoid excessive salinization of the intensively irrigated soil and weakening of the dikes.[15] That the physical labor involved in building and maintaining the extensions to the irrigation system was difficult and monotonous was only part of the problem. The community's leaders would also have to convince their followers to devote part of their energies to projects that would provide direct benefits to people other than themselves or their kinsmen. In order to push the external margin beyond the kinship boundary, therefore, it was necessary to assure some kind of redistributive mechanism by which those who gained from the new public works projects could compensate those who had done the actual labor.

The principal difficulty is that irrigation canals have some of the characteristics of what economists define as public goods. These are commodities such as defense and the protection of property rights, which tend to be provided in insufficient quantity by people acting independently. The market mechanism breaks down in this case because once the good has been made available to some individuals, it costs very little to provide it to an additional consumer and because it is expensive to prevent the latter from benefiting from the good's availability. In the case of irrigation projects, once water has been brought to one plot of land distant from the river banks, it costs very little to make it available to neighboring plots. Moreover, once the canal is built, it may prove difficult to prevent those occupying land along its edges from appropriating water for their crops.

If individual initiative could not be counted upon to finance an extensive network of irrigation canals, how could such a project be organized? One option is collective action through the existing political structure. It has been suggested that proto-historic Mesopotamia was organized politically along democratic lines. According to Jacobsen, "the indications which we have, point to a form of government in which the normal run of public affairs was handled by a council of elders but ultimate sovereignty resided in a general assembly comprising all members – or, perhaps better, all adult free men – of the community."[16] This assembly would be called upon to settle conflicts within the community. It would also decide on major questions such as how to defend the city in case of outside attack. Only in periods of crisis, might it decide to grant supreme authority, kingship, to one of its members, and then just for a limited period. Within the community, most land was probably held privately, in the names of families rather than individuals.[17] However, the temple would also have land whose produce was at its disposal.[18]

The council of elders was not only the executive organ for the community, but also its principal store of information. In the absence of written records, the information available to the community would be limited to that remembered by its oldest constituents. In all likelihood, such an assembly functioned by consensus, under a presiding officer of the same status as its members.[19] Accordingly, its decisions could probably be blocked by a minority of these members whenever some group felt that its interests were not being sufficiently taken into account. A representative assembly would therefore be handicapped in coordinating any activity such as the construction and maintenance of irrigation canals in which the benefits would be dispersed unequally among the community's residents. Moreover, since the council itself would probably have no permanent existence, its members dedicating only a fraction of their time to its activities, it would be ill-equipped to assure the day-to-day administration of such a complicated social activity. In short, the two-level hierarchy of follower and leader was inadequate for coordinating large-scale cooperative activities.

What was the alternative? Since it was unlikely that the private landholders acting either individually or collectively would spontaneously provide labor and resources for the public works program, expansion of the area under cultivation would require the intervention of some other authority. Now the Mesopotamian village had one or more full-time employees who were engaged in the production of services for the entire community; namely, the priests who served in the temple. Moreover, these individuals were probably among the most knowledgeable and best-informed members of the community. It is not surprising, then, that the task of organizing the surveillance of the canals and dikes seems to have fallen initially to this social group.

The question raised by the excavations at Uruk is why the first cities appeared at the time and place that they did; namely, in southern Iraq in the second half of the fourth millennium BC. Careful study of the archaeological records has yielded a first set of evidence. Around 4000 BC, the communities of Sumer were small in terms of population and apparently decentralized in their power structure. Information storage, based largely on human memory, was also dispersed. However, the potential gains to an innovation that permitted more efficient centralized information processing were great. Large-scale irrigation projects would expand the area under cultivation and allow an increase in the population that could be supported.

THE DEVELOPMENT OF WRITING

One of the questions which has long interested historians is where writing was first invented. The weight of the archaeological evidence supports the hypothesis that this innovation originated in Mesopotamia with the Sumerians.[20] How was writing discovered? Although no one can be sure, a plausible explanation is that it arose from the needs of an administrative group within the Sumerian community. Management of an extensive public works program required the storage and transmission of large amounts of information. Workers had to be organized and sent out to do specific tasks. To some extent, each landholder could be obliged to offer services on a part-time basis. However, major works would also require full-time laborers whose subsistence would have to be organized. To state the problem in the simplest terms, food to feed these workers and their families had to be collected by force or threat of force from the rest of the society and distributed to those engaged in public works.

Compulsory redistribution of resources by collective decision is by definition taxation. In its simplest form, pillage, the transfer of assets from one group to another by force without recompense, is a process that is probably as old as humanity. Although administratively simple, it has one major disadvantage: if too much of current income is taxed away, the household may be unable to maintain its level of production and the tax stream will eventually dry up. Pillage was therefore unsuited to the financing of a long-term project such as an irrigation system.

Periodic taxation, by which a part of a household's regular flow of income is confiscated for purposes determined by a political unit's decision-makers in return for collective services, is a more recent development. It is also one that is considerably more difficult to administer once the community has expanded beyond the kinship group. Toynbee argued that to administer the irrigation system once it had exceeded a certain size, the temple priests needed some sort of book-keeping device.[21] Some way had to be found to record permanently who had paid what in the form of taxes to the temple.

The evidence comes from level IV of the excavations at Uruk.[22] One way to identify who had sent given objects, such as pieces of cloth, was for the sender to tag his shipment with a sign that others recognized as corresponding to him. The heads of important families therefore had cylinder seals made with which they could mark clay or gypsum tags on objects that they sent to other people. The difficulty with these tags was that since they conveyed no information about the contents of the shipment, they could not be used for purposes of verification.

Denise Schmandt-Besserat showed that two- and three-dimensional clay tokens of different geometric shapes had been in use throughout the Middle East since the ninth millennium BC for representing transactions.[23] However, it is clear that the users of these tokens attributed the names of objects or ideas rather than *sounds* to these tokens. They therefore cannot be considered a form of writing.[24] In the fourth millennium, it was discovered that if the counters were enclosed in a clay sphere or *bulla* marked with the sender's seal, it was possible to identify both the sender and the number of objects being sent. The *bullae* found at Susa were perhaps used as bills of lading.

The disadvantage of this method of recording information was that in order to verify the number of objects, the *bulla* had to be broken and the tokens counted. Some alternative means had therefore to be found if the information were to be used more than once. The solution found was to inscribe marks on the outside of the clay sphere which conveyed the shapes of the tokens inside. However, once the meaning of the symbols on the exterior of the *bullae* came to be generally known, the tokens themselves became superfluous. The *bullae* were therefore replaced by clay tablets marked with the sender's seal and the symbols for the number of objects sent.

As Gelb pointed out, however, the new clay tags were still not an entirely satisfactory solution to the identification problem. If the tag became detached from the object, there was no means of knowing what type of good had been sent. It was therefore impossible to use this system to maintain a permanent record of transactions involving multiple commodities. Another problem was that only the wealthier members of the society had cylinder seals. As a result, transactions with other citizens could not be recorded by this method.[25]

Logographic Records

The solution to the identification problem came in two series of steps: first, the creation of logographic records, and second, the development of phonetic symbols. In an initial step, written signs for the objects sent were added to the tags. Additional signs were quickly conceived to identify the senders. As a result, the cylinder seals were no longer necessary except in

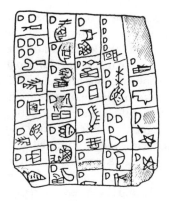 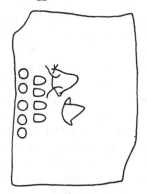

Figure 1.2   A ledger tablet from Uruk.
(*Source*: I. J. Gelb, *A Study of Writing*, University of Chicago Press, Chicago, 1963, p. 64.)

those cases in which the sender's identity had to be certified.[26] This important development meant that records could be transmitted and stored independently from the objects they represented, whether or not the originators had cylinder seals. Figure 1.2, for example, displays the two sides of a ledger tablet from Uruk. The face illustrated on the right indicates that 54 oxen and cows were sent. The other face of the tablet breaks this number down by individual, each frame indicating a certain number of animals along with the name of the corresponding person.

This first stage in the development of writing is known as logography. As the example illustrates, it consists in attributing a standardized written symbol to each word to be recorded. From the point of view of the history of the state, it is undoubtedly a key step, since it for the first time allowed complex sets of information to exist separately from the fallible memories of human beings and to be transmitted other than orally. Although it was difficult to find symbols to represent many parts of speech, the meaning of most ideas could usually be inferred from the context. Even today, the Chinese written language is to a great extent logographic. From the earliest times, however, the Chinese have used word signs to represent syllables. Thus Chinese, like Sumerian, is known as a logo-syllabic language.

The Phonetization Breakthrough

The difficulty with a purely logographic system is that no matter how elaborate it is, there is a limit to the number of things that it can express conveniently.[27] There was one area in particular in which the logographic system proved inadequate; namely, in recording human names. In a city of many thousands of inhabitants, the number of different names, including identification of paternity and place of origin, would necessarily be large.[28] If a different symbol were to be found for each piece of information, the resulting number of characters would soon become unmanageable. Some more compact system for recording human names had to be found.

The solution was to break the name into smaller phonetic parts – syllables – and to assign a symbol to each syllable. In this way it was possible to represent a large number of names with a limited set of characters. Often the symbols used were existing characters that were already being used to represent one-syllable words. For example, the symbol for "arrow," pronounced *ti* in Sumerian, would be used to represent the syllable *ti* in other words, such as the word for life.

This second step in the development of writing, known as phonetization, assigns a symbol to a sound, rather than to an object or idea. Although it was conceivable to apply the principle of phonetization by syllables to all Sumerian words, in practice the written language retained a large number of the original logographic symbols. For this reason, Sumerian is known as a logo-syllabic language.

Over the following centuries, further steps were taken to accelerate the writing process. It was found that the characters could be written more rapidly if the original pictographs were rotated counter-clockwise by 90 degrees. Since the symbols were written in clay by means of a stylus of reed, metal, wood, or bone, it proved faster and neater to impress the characters into the surface of the clay rather than to scratch them. Moreover, because curved lines were difficult to impress into clay, it was necessary to simplify the original rounded figures into a set of wedge-shaped horizontal, vertical, or oblique marks.[29] This script, which was later adopted by the Babylonians and Assyrians, became known as cuneiform from the Latin *cuneus*, "wedge," and *forma*, "shape" (see figure 1.3).

A New Information-processing System

The result of these efforts was the development of a new information-processing system. Such a system has several essential components. One of these is a means of storing information. The previous oral system, based on what individuals could remember, had been to a great extent limited by the capacity of the human brain for learning and retaining information. Now, with clay tablets, there was virtually no limit to either the amount that could be stored or the length of time it could be kept without deterioration.

Another characteristic of an information system is the means by which

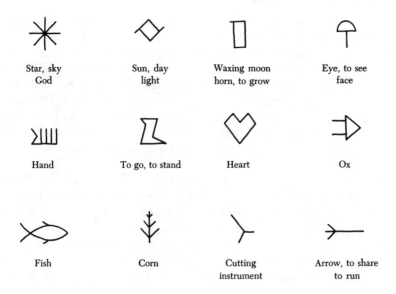

| Star, sky God | Sun, day light | Waxing moon horn, to grow | Eye, to see face |

| Hand | To go, to stand | Heart | Ox |

| Fish | Corn | Cutting instrument | Arrow, to share to run |

MEANING OF SIGN	FIRST POSITION	LATER POSITION	EARLY BABYLONIAN	ASSYRIAN
Bird				
Fish				
Ox				

Figure 1.3   The evolution of writing, from pictograph to cuneiform.
(*Source*: L. Cottrell, *Reading the Past*, Crowell-Collier, 1971, p. 97.)

messages are reproduced. The earlier oral system had the advantage of rapid low-cost reproduction. A single person could transmit information simultaneously in hundreds or even thousands of copies, depending on the number of people who were within hearing distance of his voice. With writing, since each copy had to be hand-written, the cost of reproducing a message was in effect equal to the original cost of acquiring it. Because of this sharp increase in the cost of reproduction, a writing-based information system would therefore necessarily be more centralized than an oral-based system. Information would be concentrated at a single node where the original records were stored.

Finally, there is the question of the cost and speed of distributing information. Under an oral system, anyone who understood the language of a person speaking could acquire the message transmitted cheaply and rapidly, if not always accurately. As a result, the existing stock of information could circulate widely among all members of a community. However, the logo-syllabic system developed by the Sumerians, with several hundred different symbols, was sufficiently complex that only a small fraction of the total population could ever hope to master it. Direct access to the large quantities of additional information made possible by the development of writing would therefore be limited to a literate elite.

In the second half of the fourth millennium, then, the Sumerians were able to develop a powerful new information system based on phonetically coded written symbols. Whereas the previous oral information system had been decentralized and accessible to all of the population, the new written system would necessarily be centralized and accessible only to an elite. From Sumer, writing spread to Egypt at a time when Mesopotamian influence was strong.[30] In addition to Sumerian and Egyptian, there are five other logo-syllabic systems for which one could claim independent development; namely, Proto-Elamite and Proto-Indic to the east of Sumer, Cretan and Hittite in the Mediterranean, and Chinese.[31] However, all seem to have been developed subsequent to the appearance of writing in Sumer.

THE ORIGIN OF BUREAUCRACY

In the late fourth millennium BC, at the same time that writing was being introduced, the *internal margin* between individual and collective decision-making in Sumerian communities underwent a fundamental transformation. It is at Uruk that the earliest traces of the new organizational structure may be observed.[32] It was there, in the inter-war years of this century, that excavations reached the levels corresponding to the development of writing.[33]

One of the most remarkable features of the first written documents is that their subject matter was entirely economic in nature. As the example in figure 1.2 indicated, they were records prepared by the temple scribes to indicate quantities of agricultural products such as cows and barley. Literary writings and historical documents apparently did not appear until several centuries later.[34] Initially, with most land in the hands of the important families, the transactions recorded would probably have been payments of taxes or gifts to the temples. Since it was the temples that managed the extensive new irrigation systems, however, they undoubtedly retained a share of the land reclaimed. In practice, therefore, as the irrigated terrain managed by the religious bureaucracy grew, an increasing share of these transactions became internal transfers within the temple economy.

It is not difficult to see, however, that the introduction of writing greatly changed the scope for tax collection and the management of large land-holdings. In a society without records, tax collection was liable to be arbitrary, depending on the relative powers of the collector and the tax-payer. The ability to transmit information in written form meant that criteria for the collecting of levies or rents could be applied uniformly by a number of officials. Even more important was the capacity of written records to greatly increase the accuracy of information storage. If tax rates were set carefully and maintained consistently over time, it would be possible for the authorities to extract a steady stream of revenues without destroying their income base.

The excavations at Uruk indicate that this period saw the emergence of a new category of workers specialized in the treatment of written information; that is, the first bureaucracy. The German sociologist, Max Weber, was one of the first to define the nature of a bureaucracy. In *Wirtschaft und Gesellschaft*, published in 1922, he described the characteristics of a "rational legal authority":

1 A continuous organization of official functions bound by rules.
2 A specified sphere of competence.
3 The organization of offices follows the principle of hierarchy.
4 Only persons who have demonstrated an adequate technical training are eligible for appointment.
5 There exists complete separation of the property belonging to the organization and the personal property of the official.
6 There is a complete absence of appropriation of his official position by the incumbent.[35]

A bureaucracy, then, is a permanent hierarchically structured organization that engages employees to carry out specific functions.

Since the archaeological records that have survived from the first centuries of the Sumerian cities are almost all temple documents, more is known about this institution than about any other element of Sumerian society.[36] The temple's employees were organized into several categories, each with specific functions. The priests directed the communities' ritual activities but also filled important secular roles such as flood control. There was also a class of scribes or record-keepers who collected taxes, managed the stores of goods, supervised the redistributive activities such as the provision of assistance to widows, orphans, the elderly, and the handicapped. The temple scribes set up their own set of equivalences or accounting prices to express the relative values of the different goods and services they managed.[37] A further group was made up of skilled workers who engaged in textile and metal-working crafts. Finally, there were the unskilled laborers, who maintained the temples and the canals, worked the temple lands, and served the other categories of workers. Some of this labor was provided on a corvée basis from households outside of the temple structure.[38]

It is also clear that these four groups were not of the same status. The priests were the principals in this structure, while the two classes of workers were their agents. Between was the supervisory and administrative class of scribes. Thus there is every indication that the Sumerian temple officials comprised a hierarchically structured bureaucracy, as defined by Weber.

Could such an administrative structure have existed before the invention of writing? Weber himself evidently did not think so. An additional characteristic of a bureaucracy, in his opinion, was:

7 Administrative acts, decisions, and rules are formulated and recorded in writing.[39]

In managing any organization with more than two levels of agents, the principal difficulty is the separation of official from personal interests, as captured in Weber's fifth point. Written documents not only enabled the temple authorities to extract income from the community's members. They also permitted them to verify whether the amounts reported by the lower officials corresponded to the quantities paid by the taxpayers or sharecroppers and to the amounts actually on hand in the temple storehouses. One of the main reasons why a large bureaucracy had not been possible previously was the potential problem of corruption when the leaders could not observe the behavior of their appointed officials. Although writing by no means eliminated the potential for corruption, it meant that an efficiently run bureaucracy could limit the extent of potential abuses.

By permitting more accurate verification of what could not be seen directly, writing made possible a degree of complexity in social organization that was impossible with oral methods of communication supplemented by human memory. It has been suggested that the introduction of writing also affected the thought patterns of those who came into contact with it. By far the bulk of all Sumerian documents that have been recovered are lists, i.e. tables of information in matrix form that have no counterpart in everyday speech. The existence of these written lists, it has been argued, encouraged the classification of information into categories. Since any system of classification is bound to be arbitrary, exploration of the limits of existing categories may have led to the advancement of knowledge.[40] The cultural differences between Mediterranean societies and those of the Middle East – for example, in the degree of acceptance of authority – might then be explained by differences in the systems of writing used; that is, in the means of communication.[41]

The question which must be asked, however, is whether variations in forms of communication were not a cause but a result of differences in social structure. It is at least plausible that once the principle of writing became known, the changes made in adapting it to each language reflected the needs of specific societies. Thus a centralized society organized around an irrigation system would need a system that could be understood by an administrative elite. A pictograph-based system with its hundreds of characters would be adequate. More decentralized communities, based on individual trading initiatives, might develop a simpler form, more readily learned by a large fraction of the population. Even the dominant presence of lists among Sumerian documents may reflect more the specific needs of an elaborate redistributive organization than the effect of the communications system on ways of thinking.

Regardless of the way in which the initial idea was eventually used, it may be suggested that written documents made possible the extraction of a much greater share of the total income of a large community than had previously been possible. In a political unit of more than a few hundred inhabitants, the share of total resources that could be effectively channeled into public uses would therefore have risen sharply.

The Role of the Temple

It was in the temples of the new cities of Sumer that the procedures of bureaucratic organization were first applied. In the earlier villages, the role of the temple had been primarily ritual. Each community had its own god, the shrine being the god's house. The priests' primary responsibility was to direct the celebration of the cult of the god.[42] Gradually, however, the temple also came to play an increasingly important administrative role within the Sumerian community. Both the Tigris and Euphrates rivers had low gradients, high silt content, and a substantial seasonal variance in their flow. As a result, floods were frequent and the rivers continually changed their course.[43] Moreover, because of the scanty rainfall, land at any distance from the rivers' edges could be cultivated only by means of a large-scale and complex irrigation system. To manage the community's water resources, some centralized authority was necessary. For the community to grow, it had to consume more scarce water. The administrative functions of the temple must therefore necessarily increase.

As the margin of cultivation was extended by means of large-scale irrigation projects, it was found that a considerably greater food surplus could be obtained than had previously been available. Increasingly, the activities of the temple were directed toward the appropriation and distribution of this surplus. The temple officials oversaw a system of rationing of the basic staple foods, part of the excess being reserved for widows, orphans, and the handicapped.[44] The priests also directed long-distance trade in order to acquire wood, metals, and other products not found in the river valleys. In the Sumerian city-state, therefore, the temple was not simply the site used for religious activities; it was also "the center of economic and commercial activity."[45]

Important though it was, the temple did not monopolize economic activity in the early Sumerian city-state. The production and trade of pottery and fish most likely remained in private hands.[46] An earlier generation of researchers asserted that Sumer possessed "neither market places nor a functioning market system of any description."[47] However, more recent research casts strong doubt on this position.[48] It would appear that the temple economy coexisted with a private exchange economy which was never eliminated, although its relative importance may have varied over the centuries. Land in the preliterate village communities had been largely in private hands. Later, however, as the cities expanded by reclaiming land through irrigation under the direction of the religious officials, it is probable that the temples themselves retained title to at least a part of the new holdings. Over time, therefore, the religious institutions gradually became major landholders. An important part of the agricultural population comprised serfs or sharecroppers on temple land. In addition to these two classes of holdings, there were also small plots where the poor could raise their crops and nomads and shepherds could graze their flocks.[49]

Although there is no way of knowing the exact breakdown among these three groups of landholders, in all probability, however, the temples were the largest property owners. In the words of Jacobsen:

"Central in the city state was the city, and central in the city was the temple of the city god. The temple of the city god was usually the greatest landowner in the state, and it cultivated its extensive holdings by means of serfs and sharecroppers.

Other temples belonging to the city god's spouse, to their divine children, and to deities associated with the chief god similarly had large land holdings."[50]

It has been argued that the greater part of the land nevertheless remained in private hands or in those of secular authorities.[51] However, the period referred to by those scholars who take the latter position is considerably later than that studied in the present chapter; namely, the late fourth and early third millennia BC. In this period, before the growth of population brought the city-states into protracted conflict, the temples dominated political and social life. The temple authorities served as intermediaries between the general population and the gods of the city, who were considered to be the ultimate owners of the land. The position of "king" in the sense of a permanent secular authority did not appear until later in the third millennium.[52] By about 2500 BC, the middle of this millennium, the introduction of bronze weapons would lead to the rise of a class of professional soldiers. The power of this new group would inevitably conflict with that of the priesthood.

To the extent that the lands of the city were owned by the temple, taxation was not necessary. The serfs who cultivated the land would be required to furnish a certain share of their production to the temple. Such transactions may therefore be considered internal to the public sector. However, the existence of private holdings would require a system of compulsory transactions between private landholders and the temple – that is, taxation. To assure that the cost of building and maintaining the canal system and other public works was shared among all who benefited therefrom, the owners of private land would be required to contribute goods and services to the temple and to the projects organized by it.[53]

Territorial Expansion

The introduction of writing and the emergence of the complex hierarchically structured administrative organization centered in the temple coincided with a change in the *external margin* or territorial boundary of the Sumerian state. During the millennium prior to 2700 BC, the size of the typical political unit in Sumer progressed from that of a large village to that of a city with surrounding villages. How important were these changes in population? In the early centuries of the fourth millennium BC, the largest communities measured only slightly over 10 hectares, with a population of under 2,000 people.[54] Yet only a few hundred years later, by the year 3100 BC, there stood on the Sumerian plain cities whose size was an order of magnitude greater than that of their predecessors. One of these cities, Uruk, measured 100 hectares and had a population of over 10,000 people.[55] Over the following centuries, Uruk continued to grow. In the year 2700 BC, it had attained a population of 40,000–50,000 people.[56]

Another indication of an increase in the size of political units is offered by archaeological evidence of an increase in the size of public buildings. At the end of the prehistoric period, prior to the invention of writing, the largest buildings in Sumer were of the size of a rectangular temple discovered at Eridu which measured 25 × 13 m.[57] However, by the middle centuries of the period under discussion, around 3100 BC, the Sumerians at Uruk had built a temple covering 14 times this area, measuring 80 × 50 m.[58] Finally, dating from the period 3200–2600 BC, also at Uruk, correspond the remains of a temple with walls painted white. A remarkable new architectural feature had been introduced: the temple was built on a massive platform whose sides slope inward. It was the prototype of the Sumerian ziggurat – the massive layered temples on terraces that were to characterize Sumerian society at its peak in the middle and late third millennium.[59] This last set of evidence therefore suggests that over the thousand years prior to 2700 BC, there was a substantial increase in the size of the units of political organization in Sumer.

THE FIRST COMPLEX SOCIETIES

It is clear that the late fourth and early third millennia BC were a period of profound change in many aspects of Sumerian society. Initially, communities had been small, with populations of at most 1,000–2,000 inhabitants. Collective decision-making had been reserved for a limited number of critical situations, with major decisions being taken jointly by the heads of families. Then, over the period studied, the Sumerians developed a new communications technology, based upon permanent written records. At the same time that these events were occurring, some of the Sumerian communities grew to become cities with tens of thousands of residents. Within their new borders, these extended communities moved increasingly toward collective decision-making, with the temple as the focus of power. What was the relationship between these different developments?

If one wishes to explain major changes in social patterns, there are several possible approaches. One possibility is to focus on environmental change; that is, on modifications in the physical setting that force people to adapt. A rise in average temperatures such as occurred at the end of the last ice age, for example, could alter the types of plants and animals living in a given region. Another approach is to concentrate on demographic change, a modification in the numbers of people who live in a given setting.

For example, an increase in a region's population could give rise to new patterns of social organization. Yet another possibility is to examine technological change, an extension in the body of knowledge that people use in interacting with one another and in reacting to their physical environment. The discovery of a new means of transport, for example, could permit the dispersal of a given population over a larger area.

Of course, these different factors may interact with one another. For instance, environmental change could trigger other developments: a decrease in rainfall might cause people to seek other means of watering crops, leading to the discovery of irrigation and subsequent demographic growth. Or a change in population density may lead to the discovery of a new technology that in turn affects the environment: population pressure could lead hunter-gatherers to plant their own seeds, which could cause soil depletion. However, it is important to an understanding of the evolution of social groupings to be able to identify the principal directions of causality. Was the rise of civilization caused primarily by environmental change, by demographic factors, or by the development of new technology?

Explanations that fall into each of these categories have been proposed for the origin of complex societies in Sumer in the fourth millennium BC. The environmental or adaptationist approach was used by Gibson to explain the rapid growth of Uruk and Kish between 3300 and 3000 BC.[60] He argued that the entire eastern branch of the Euphrates in northern Sumer lost its water at the beginning of this period. The growth of southern cities was then necessary in order to absorb the thousands of people whose land had been made uninhabitable.

While this adaptationist hypothesis may account for fluctuations in the size of individual states over relatively short periods, it is difficult to see how it can explain a generalized long-term trend toward larger political units. Not only did rapid urbanization in southern Mesopotamia precede the environmental change mentioned by Gibson, but also the cities of Sumer continued to grow for four or five centuries after this event occurred. Before the north–south population shift, Uruk had already grown from about 10 hectares to a size of 70 hectares.[61] While the city grew to 100 hectares by about 3100 BC, following the shock mentioned by Gibson, it continued to increase rapidly in population, reaching a maximum area of 400 hectares around 2800 BC.[62] In short, while the adaptation of existing population to environmental change may explain part of the demographic growth of southern Sumer between 3300 and 3100 BC, it cannot provide a satisfactory explanation for the origins of urbanization in this region.

The demographic approach too has been offered to explain the rise of the first cities. Carneiro argued that as population rises toward the carrying capacity of a given environment, conflict necessarily increases in intensity.[63] This conflict in turn affects the structure of society. In an open setting, defeated groups may emigrate and so avoid exploitation. However, in a circumscribed environment, where migration is precluded, losers cannot escape the conditions imposed on them by victors. Complex social structures of exploiters and exploited appear and statehood is achieved.

Here again, the proposed model fails to fit the events of urbanization in Mesopotamia. It predicts that increasing conflict should accompany the rise of cities. Yet before 2800 BC, there is no evidence of the defensive walls that are a sure sign of warfare. Moreover, in the legends and written records that date from the period of rapid urban growth, peace is the rule.[64] Those who hold to the demographic argument might reply that complex societies did not exist in Mesopotamia prior to the third millennium.[65] However, this position is surely untenable, as is demonstrated by the existence of massive temple complexes at Uruk by 3100 AD, with attached living quarters for specialized personnel.[66]

It might be argued that the evidence presented in this chapter simply confirms the view proposed by Boserup, Brenner and others that population density has an impact on social structures.[67] Indeed, as Mumford has argued, the pressure of demographic growth was undoubtedly a major factor in leading the temple priests of Sumer to experiment in new ways of storing information.[68] Such a position, however, overlooks the fact that the pressure of population on resources has been a recurring, if not a constant, theme in human experience. Yet major changes in social structure, such as the appearance of the first cities, have been rare. Communities as large as Uruk in the immediate prehistoric period had existed for at least four millennia. In Palestine, for example, Jericho had reached a size of around 2,000 inhabitants prior to 7350 BC.[69] Why did population pressure not lead to the formation of larger communities earlier?

Another possible explanation for the emergence of cities at the time and place where they first appeared lies in the discovery of a new technology that allowed given resources to produce food for a greater number of people. If so, then, what were the crucial innovations and how were they linked to the rise of the first cities? A generation or two ago, Wittfogel and other scholars identified irrigation as the primary causal factor in the rise of complex social institutions.[70] However, it is now known that irrigation had been practiced for thousands of years before the first cities appeared.[71] Though large-scale irrigation was necessary for producing the food surpluses on which the Sumerian urban societies were based, some other element was evidently missing prior to the late fourth millennium.

Writing and the Rise of Cities

Another possible explanation for the rise of complex societies is the discovery of writing. Could it be the introduction of phonetically coded symbols used to represent spoken sounds that enabled Sumer, at least temporarily, to cope with population pressure by means other than by famine, disease, or emigration? The idea of a link between writing and the rise of cities is not new.[72] What is unclear in many previous studies, however, is the exact nature of the causal relationship between writing and urban society. Why, for example, if this hypothesis is correct, should the innovation in communications have favored an increase in the size and degree of centralization of organizations? Could it not have permitted a more efficient use of decentralized transactions among literate individuals?

Perhaps because of the difficulty of proving historical causality, at least in this case, some observers hesitate to go beyond the notion of coincidence of the two developments. The scholar of writing, Ignace J. Gelb, observed that writing appeared in the ancient world at a time "characterized by a simultaneous growth of all those elements which together make for what we usually call civilization."[73] If civilization is defined by the presence of higher forms of culture, the relation between writing and civilization becomes almost a tautology. David Diringer declared that "without writing, culture, which has been defined as a communicable intelligence, would not exist (except, perhaps, in a form so rudimentary as to be virtually unrecognizable)."[74]

For still other researchers, writing is a precondition for civilization: without it, complex urban societies could not exist. Talcott Parsons argued that the availability of written documents served to increase social stability. As an example, he offered the case of a contractual agreement between two individuals that "need not depend on the fallible memories of the parties or witnesses but can be written and made available for verification as need arises." According to Parsons, such stability is a major condition for increasing the extent and complexity of many components of social organization.[75] The difficulty with this argument is that the period which followed the introduction of writing was not characterized by the stabilization of societal relationships. Rather it was witness to an acceleration in the rate of social change that has continued virtually unchecked until the present time. Indeed, instead of an instrument for maintaining stability, writing was a catalyst for social change.

More generally, what is missing in previous studies is an analysis of the precise manner in which writing led to the great changes in social behavior that are implied by the term civilization. How was the increased capacity to store and transmit information which writing made possible related to changes in the size and structure of communities? Another shortcoming in previous studies is their neglect of the impact of writing on the division between private and public decision-making. The rise of the first cities in Sumer coincided with a remarkable increase in collective decision-making at the level of the city, at the expense of decisions taken by the clan or family. Was there a relationship between the two developments?

The Community as Information Network

Stripped down to its bare essentials, a community may be viewed as a group of individuals who acquire, store, and exchange information; that is, a community is an information network. The value of group membership to each individual then depends on the usefulness of the information that he obtains as a result of interacting with his neighbors. Only if the value of what he gains is greater than what he could obtain on his own outside the community is social membership desirable. The greater the economies from centralized information processing, the more he will be willing to contribute to the social group rather than be deprived of its benefits. In part, therefore, the community is based on consent – the willingness of individuals to give up part of their income in order to obtain the advantages of belonging to a social network.

However, the community is also based on constraint. Although each person may be willing to pay some positive amount for the benefits of membership in society, he will only do so under threat of some penalty. Such a penalty could involve a reduction in his wealth, or temporary or permanent exclusion from the community. Therefore, the social group must have some means to enforce payment of its membership dues, as well as compliance with its other rules. In addition, the society must be able to dissuade those from outside from appropriating the wealth of its members. The success of the community in raising taxes will therefore depend on the technology available to it to assure control of its territory.

During the period under discussion, military technology changed very little in Sumer; however, the technology for processing information clearly underwent a complete transformation. In the early Sumerian communities, each family was relatively self-sufficient, maintaining its own limited irrigation channels, and producing most of its own food and clothing. Membership of a larger group, the village, was of value primarily for the protection it offered from external attack and, in addition, as a means of access to the skills of craftsmen such as potters. Yet it was not the collective goods themselves – security and the services of a market – that were the essential contribution of the community. Rather it was the knowledge of how to produce them from individual efforts and distribute them in a generally acceptable way that was the value of community membership. If the village failed to grow much beyond several hundred people, it was because, with information storage limited by human memory, there was little to be gained by adding further members. Without some means of integrating the information that individuals held, the addition of extra population would simply increase the time required for making collective decisions without any compensating gain.

The evidence from Sumer suggests that the invention of writing permitted a population increase by raising the total area of land that could be cultivated. Writing reduced the degree of asymmetry in available information between administrators and those who worked for them, enabling more effective monitoring of subordinates. The new information system therefore raised the number of individuals whose activities could be effectively coordinated, permitting the construction of large-scale public works projects such as extended irrigation canal networks. As water became available at considerable distances from the rivers' edges, more land could be brought under cultivation.

However, the adoption of the new communications medium affected not only the size of Sumer's population but also its organizational structure. The increasing degree of centralization of Sumerian urban life may be explained in part by the cost of storing, reproducing, and distributing written information. Compared with verbal communication, it was expensive to make the first record of a piece of information and virtually as costly to duplicate it. Moreover, even when reproduced, such documents were expensive to distribute, since it was necessary to train people to understand them. Accordingly, access to the new technology was rationed according to the priority of the individual. It circulated only within a restricted group who had learned to read and write. Writing made possible for the first time the existence of a category of workers specialized in the manipulation of information. These hierarchically structured elites were the first bureaucracies.

Once the administrative hierarchy for supervising an irrigation system had been established, it cost relatively little to apply it to additional territory outside the limits of the original villages. Instead of growing by the replication of identical villages, therefore, Sumer experienced a great expansion of its largest centers. The emergence of cities may therefore be explained by an increase in the economies of scale in information processing due to the introduction of writing. As a result of the impact of writing on the structure of the community's information network, the maximum optimal size of the political unit rose from the scale of a large village to that of a small city. In other words, the territorial limit or *external margin* of the typical political unit shifted outward.

Because a surplus of food was available only within the new urban information network, it could be taxed away by the administrative class. As long as income levels of urban workers after taxes and rents were kept at least as high as those of laborers in the traditional villages, there would be no incentive to abandon the city. The surplus obtained in this way could then be used to feed the new bureaucracy, along with other new classes of workers. The result was that a larger share of the community's resources came to be allocated by means of a public bureaucracy rather than by individuals and families. The society's *internal margin* had shifted in favor of collective action.

In short, by increasing the size of the optimal information network, the new technology of writing allowed Sumerian societies to produce more food from given resources. As a result of large-scale irrigation, the new urban communities were able to produce a food surplus that could be used to finance the activities characteristic of civilization. Although the development of writing was undoubtedly stimulated by the pressure of population upon resources, the emergence of large complex communities – what McNeill has called the "breakthrough to civilization"[76] – would appear to have occurred in Sumer before other areas of human settlement because the Sumerians were the first to discover a means of codifying the individual phonetic components of speech.

On Writing and Hierarchy as Necessary Conditions for Complex Societies

The hypothesis that hierarchies based on written communications were necessary for the development of complex societies has been criticized on empirical grounds. One argument that has been made is that the Incas in pre-Columbian South America created a highly structured urban society without the use of written records.[77] However, the Incas did have a substitute for writing: the knotted cords or quipus that they used to store and transmit information. These cords were used for conserving quantities under a decimal system and also as a mnemonic device for recording other types of data by a special category of people who memorized information. The cost of recording a unit of data with the quipus was comparable to that with writing. However, the retrieval of that information required the intermediation of a specific individual who knew what the knots meant. Therefore, the cost of reproducing and transmitting data was much higher than with writing. The Inca information system consequently was less complex than that of the Sumerians but required greater centralization.

In building their empire, the Incas had access to a military technology that was unavailable to the Sumerians in the predynastic period (prior to 2800 BC): bronze weapons. With superior armaments, one would expect the Incas to have controlled a larger territory than the Sumerians. This was indeed the case: the Incas ruled over a territory stretching from Ecuador to Chile, whereas the early Sumerian states were confined to the land surrounding their temple. But because of their simpler information system with greater scale economies, the Incas would also be expected to have had a less complex and more highly centralized social organization than the Sumerians. This also seems to have been the case. In accord with the bias of the Incas' information system toward quantitative information in decimal form, their empire was divided arbitrarily into units of 100, 500, 1,000, 5,000, and 10,000 taxpayers. The rulers' main concern was to extract taxes from each ethnic group. No group was allowed to keep more than was required to maintain its population.

This rigidity made it difficult for the Inca society to withstand a shock without collapsing. In 1525, following the death of its ruler, the empire endured seven years of civil war. The new emperor, Atahuallpa, had barely finished his victory celebration before the arrival of a Spanish expedition. With fewer than 200 European followers, Francisco Pizzarro seized control of the summit of the hierarchy and killed the emperor. Because of its excessively simplified and rigid social structure, the Inca information network could not adapt to a shock that knocked out its most important node. The empire had existed for less than a century, whereas the Sumerian civilization flourished over a period of almost two millennia. It is questionable, therefore, whether the Inca society constituted a civilization of a complexity comparable to that of the Sumerians.

Another criticism of the hypothesis of writing-based bureaucracies as a necessary condition for civilization is that in the region of Sumer itself there is no archaeological evidence of hierarchical social structures. For the period prior to 2800 BC, the distribution of items reflecting status, such as stone mace-heads or beveled-rim bowls, is not correlated with site size as it would be, it has been suggested, under a centrally organized system.[78]

One should realize, however, that the absence of a spatial hierarchy of wealth does not necessarily mean the absence of social hierarchy within each separate political unit. Intense competition among states for territorial domination would not begin until the middle centuries of the third millennium BC. For several centuries, the extension of irrigation enabled Sumer to support a steadily growing population on a given territory. By the conversion of desert into farmland, villages were able to grow into towns and towns into cities without coming into conflict with one another. It was only when the available resources of water and irrigable land had become fully exploited that the gains of one state necessarily meant losses to another. It was in the ensuing conflict, in which some states were able to impose their authority over others, that a spatial hierarchy of inhabited sites emerged.

WRITING AND THE EMERGENCE OF CIVILIZATION

The ruins that Loftus discovered in the sand at Warka are striking evidence of a fundamental change in the structure of societies. In the second half of the fourth millennium BC, in what is today southern Iraq, large numbers of people who did not know one another began to cooperate in complex networks of exchanges. It may be seen that this development, the emergence of civilization, had three components: first, an innovation that changed the capacity of a community to process information; second, a change in bureaucratic structures that permitted the innovation to be exploited; and, finally, a shift in two boundaries or margins that characterize social information networks.

The hypothesis proposed here is that the innovation which changed the rules of the game in Sumer in the late fourth millennium was writing. Compared with the traditional oral communication system, writing made possible the efficient storage of much larger amounts of information. However, since the cost of reproducing that information was much higher than under the oral system, centralization of data concerning a large number of people became imperative. Because hundreds of symbols had to be mastered, the primary distribution of information in its new written form was limited to a relatively small part of the population who had learned the new techniques.

Writing made possible for the first time the transmission and permanent storage of large quantities of information. It thereby permitted a given decision-maker who had access to the new skills to be better informed about the activities of a greater number of people than was ever possible previously. In this way, the innovation led to a reduction in the asymmetry of information that characterizes any hierarchical relationship, enabling the principal to keep better informed about the activities of his agents.

To handle this new technology, it was necessary to create a specialized profession: the scribe or intermediary in the processing of information. As a result, the mechanism for political control became more complex. Instead of the schematically simple structure of leaders and followers that had characterized earlier agricultural societies, the new system involved a layer of literate scribes in an intermediate position between the other two groups of actors. The existence of this new skilled group, the bureaucracy, in turn permitted the coordination of human activity on a scale which far surpassed that of the village community.

The emergence of this new class of public servants made it possible to alter the basic margins of human information networks. One of these limits, the territorial boundary or external margin, indicates the number of people who make up the communications network. Under the new system of written communications, centralized information storage replaced the decentralized storage of the oral system; the economies of scale to information processing therefore increased substantially. With the introduction of writing, it became possible for the external margin of the community to expand outward. New, larger political units – the temple-states – were formed.

The other margin of the state, the internal margin, separates individual from collective action, determining the share of the community's total resources at the disposition of the central authority. By permitting the construction and maintenance of extensive irrigation systems, the introduction of writing substantially increased the level of output available to feed the community's workers. The resulting surplus was in effect a rent to society resulting from the new information network. It could be taxed away and used to finance the construction of temples, sculpture, stores of food to be consumed in times of emergency, and the activities of the new class of scribes.

What remains to be seen is whether the evidence of a possible link between writing and the appearance of the first cities is a unique case or an example of a more general historical process. Do changes in territorial boundaries and the role of the state tend to occur at the same time? Are such changes linked to modifications in bureaucratic power structures? And are these modifications in turn associated with innovations that alter the capacity of communities to process information?

NOTES

1 William Kennett Loftus, *Travels and Researches in Chaldaea and Susiana* (Gregg International Publishers, 1971), pp. 72–3.
2 Ibid., p. 165.
3 Seton Lloyd, *Foundations in the Dust* (Thames and Hudson, 1980), pp. 131–3.
4 Adam Falkenstein, "The prehistory and protohistory of Western Asia," in *The Near East: The Early Civilizations*, eds J. Bottéro, E. Cassin, and J. Vercoutter (Weidenfeld and Nicolson, 1967), p. 21.
5 Shepard B. Clough, *The Rise and Fall of Civilization: An Inquiry into the Relationship between Economic Development and Civilization* (Columbia University Press, 1951), p. 33.
6 Sabatino Moscati, *The Face of the Ancient Orient* (Routledge and Kegan Paul, 1960), p. 20, n. 2.
7 McGuire Gibson, "By stage and cycle to Sumer," in *Biblioteca Mesopotamica*, vol. 4, *The Legacy of Sumer*, ed. Denise Schmandt-Besserat (Undena, 1976), p. 56.
8 Robert McC. Adams, *Heartland of Cities* (University of Chicago Press, 1981), pp. 58, 69.
9 Talcott Parsons, *Societies: Evolutionary and Comparative Perspectives* (Prentice-Hall, 1966), p. 62.
10 Ibid., p. 42.
11 Falkenstein, "The prehistory and protohistory of Western Asia," p. 25.
12 C. C. Lamberg-Karlovsky, "The economic world of Sumer," in *Biblioteca Mesopotamica*, vol. 4, *The Legacy of Sumer*, ed. Denise Schmandt-Besserat (Undena, 1976), p. 60, n. 4.
13 Falkenstein, "The prehistory and protohistory of Western Asia," p. 21.
14 Leonard Cottrell, *The Anvil of Civilization* (New American Library, 1957), p. 23.
15 A. Leo Oppenheim, *Ancient Mesopotamia: Portrait of a Dead Civilization* (University of Chicago Press, 1964), p. 84.
16 T. Jacobsen, quoted in Moscati, *The Face of the Ancient Orient*, p. 21.

17 Jacques Pirenne, *Civilisations antiques* (Albin Michel, Paris, 1951), p. 27.
18 Oppenheim, *Ancient Mesopotamia*, p. 84.
19 Ibid., p. 95.
20 Denise Schmandt-Besserat, "An archaic recording system and the origins of writing," *Syro-Mesopotamian Studies*, 1 (1977), p. 2.
21 Arnold Toynbee, *Mankind and Mother Earth: A Narrative History of the World* (Oxford University Press, 1976), p. 51.
22 Ignace J. Gelb, *A Study of Writing* (University of Chicago Press, 1963), p. 62.
23 Schmandt-Besserat, "An archaic recording system," p. 3.
24 Denise Schmandt-Besserat, "The origins of writing: an archaeologist's perspective," *Written Communication*, 3 (1986), pp. 36–7.
25 Gelb, *A Study of Writing*, pp. 63–4.
26 Ibid., p. 64.
27 Jack Goody and Ian Watt, "The consequences of literacy," in *Literacy in Traditional Societies*, ed. J. Goody (Cambridge University Press, 1968), p. 35.
28 Gelb, *A Study of Writing*, p. 66.
29 David Diringer, *Writing* (Praeger, 1962), p. 39.
30 Gelb, *A Study of Writing*, p. 215.
31 Ibid., p. 190, ff.
32 Falkenstein, "The prehistory and protohistory of Western Asia," p. 31.
33 Ibid., p. 3.
34 Ibid., pp. 39–40.
35 Max Weber, *The Theory of Social and Economic Organization* (The Free Press, 1964), pp. 330–2.
36 Marvin A. Powell, "Sumerian merchants and the problem of profit," *Iraq*, 23 (1977), p. 25.
37 A. Leo Oppenheim, "A bird's-eye view of Mesopotamian economic history," in *Trade and Market in the Early Empires*, eds K. Polanyi, C. M. Arensberg, and H. W. Pearson (The Free Press, 1957), p. 32.
38 See Robert McC. Adams, "Mesopotamian social evolution: old outlooks, new goals," in *On the Evolution of Complex Societies*, ed. Timothy Earle (Undena, 1984), p. 91.
39 Weber, *The Theory of Social and Economic Organization*, p. 332.
40 Jack Goody, *The Domestication of the Savage Mind* (Cambridge University Press, 1977), pp. 103–11.
41 Goody and Watt, "The consequences of literacy," pp. 39–41.
42 Falkenstein, "The prehistory and protohistory of Western Asia," pp. 45–6.
43 Lamberg-Karlovsky, "The economic world of Sumer," p. 63.
44 Ibid.
45 Moscati, *The Face of the Ancient Orient*, p. 31.
46 Adams, "Mesopotamian social evolution," p. 92.
47 Karl Polanyi, "Marketless trading in Hammurabi's time," in *Trade and Markets in the Early Empires*, eds K. Polanyi, C. M. Arensberg, and H. W. Pearson (The Free Press, 1957), p. 16.
48 See Adams, "Mesopotamian social evolution," p. 92.
49 Oppenheim, *Ancient Mesopotamia*, p. 84.
50 T. Jacobsen, quoted in Moscati, *The Face of the Ancient Orient*, p. 32.
51 Samuel Noah Kramer, *The Sumerians: Their History, Culture and Character* (University of Chicago Press, 1963), p. 76.
52 Parsons, *Societies*, p. 63.
53 Oppenheim, *Ancient Mesopotamia*, p. 95.
54 See Adams, *Heartland of Cities*, pp. 58, 69.

55 Ibid., p. 71.
56 Ibid., p. 85.
57 Falkenstein, "The prehistory and protohistory of Western Asia," p. 27.
58 Seton Lloyd, *The Archaeology of Mesopotamia* (Thames and Hudson, 1978), p. 50.
59 Ibid., p. 49.
60 Gibson, "By stage and cycle to Sumer."
61 Adams, *Heartland of Cities*, p. 71.
62 Idid., p. 85.
63 Robert L. Carneiro, "Theory of the origins of the state," *Science*, 169 (1970), pp. 733–8.
64 John Andrew Gallery, "Town planning and community structure," in *Biblioteca Mesopotamica*, no. 4, *The Legacy of Sumer*, ed. Denise Schmandt-Besserat (Undena, 1976), p. 73.
65 See, for example, William T. Sanders, "Pre-industrial demography and social evolution," in *On the Evolution of Complex Societies*, ed. Timothy Earle (Undena, 1984), p. 26.
66 Robert McC. Adams, *The Evolution of Urban Society* (Aldine, 1966), p. 126.
67 Ester Boserup, *Population and Technological Change: A Study of Long-Term Trends* (University of Chicago Press, 1981), p. 56, ff.; Reuven Brenner, *History – The Human Gamble* (University of Chicago Press, 1983), p. 67.
68 Lewis Mumford, *The City in History* (Harcourt, Brace and World, 1961), p. 97.
69 Arther Ferrill, *The Origins of War* (Thames and Hudson, 1985), p. 28.
70 Karl A. Wittfogel, *Oriental Despotism: A Comparative Study of Total Power* (Yale University Press, 1957).
71 Lamberg-Karlovsky, "The economic world of Sumer," p. 60, n. 4.
72 See, for example, V. Gordon Childe, "The urban revolution," *Town Planning Review*, 21 (1950), 3–17.
73 Gelb, *A Study of Writing*, p. 221.
74 Diringer, *Writing*, p. 13.
75 Parsons, *Societies*, p. 27.
76 William H. McNeill, *The Rise of the West: A History of the Human Community* (University of Chicago Press, 1963), p. 29.
77 Gibson, "By stage and cycle to Sumer," p. 51.
78 Adams, *Heartland of Cities*, p. 78.

2

The Age of Gilgamesh

Why did urban walls suddenly appear in Sumer after 2700 BC? Was there a new threat from nomadic tribesmen attracted by the accumulated wealth of the cities? Had the Sumerians themselves just learned how to build urban fortifications? Or had population growth led to increased conflict over access to scarce water supplies? None of these possible explanations resists close scrutiny. However, archaeological evidence indicates that at this time innovations in metallurgy permitted the development of new types of metal armor and weapons. These weapons appear to have increased the relative effectiveness of a large force over a smaller one and of trained soldiers over the civilian population. In the wars that followed, there occurred an extension of the territorial limit of the typical political unit. At the same time, there was a partial transfer of decision-making from the public bureaucracy to the individual and family. The walls of Sumer were a sign that a new age of competition between greatly enlarged and less centralized communications networks had begun.

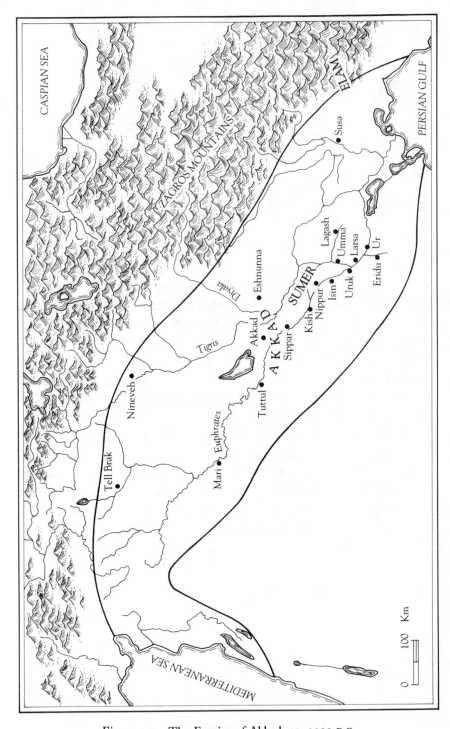

Figure 2.1   The Empire of Akkad, ca. 2300 B.C.
(*Source*: M. E. L. Mallowan, *Early Mesopotamia and Iran*, McGraw-Hill, New York, 1965, p. 130.)

Agga, King of Kish, was furious. For as long as could be remembered, his Semitic city in central Mesopotamia had been the region's dominant power. A few years previously, he had taken in the Sumerian outcast, Gilgamesh, and nursed him back to health. Impressed by the southerner's ability, Agga had placed Gilgamesh as his vassal ruler over the latter's native city of Uruk.[1] However, Gilgamesh was apparently too vain to support the idea that he owed his position to another. In an obvious provocation, he had bullied his fellow citizens into building a wall around their city. Trying to avoid war, Agga had sent an envoy to his rebellious vassal ordering him to submit. Now the northern king learned that Gilgamesh had addressed the younger men in Uruk's assembly and persuaded them to take up arms against Kish.[2]

Agga reacted rapidly and vigorously. Confident of his superior strength, he led his army down the Euphrates to Uruk. No sooner had the northern troops arrived on the plain before Uruk's gates, however, than they found themselves frustrated, unable to penetrate the city's stout brick ramparts. Agga had no choice but to order his army to besiege Uruk.

Meanwhile, behind the city's walls, Gilgamesh waited patiently, organizing his forces for resistance. Then at an opportune moment, he led his troops outside the ramparts to do battle. His daring counter-stroke caught the larger force of the northerners by surprise. Gilgamesh and his soldiers penetrated to the enemy's boat camp, where they managed to capture Agga. With his pride satisfied, Gilgamesh was now able to proclaim his loyalty to his lord and to the god of his city. "O Agga, this Uruk, the handiwork of the gods, the great wall, the wall founded by An, his exalted abode established by An, is entrusted to you, you are its king and defender, the bruiser of heads, the prince of the beloved An."[3] Although the previous order had been restored, it was evident that Uruk under Gilgamesh had become a power to be reckoned with on the Sumerian plain.[4]

This episode, taken from the epic poem of Gilgamesh, is one of the first recorded occurrences of war – organized violence between large groups of people. However, since even the most ancient versions of the story date from hundreds of years after the time at which these events supposedly occurred, the poem was long regarded as the product of the Sumerians' imagination. Then, in the 1920s, a research team of the German Oriental Society began the systematic excavation of Warka in Iraq, the site of ancient Uruk. They first dug a test pit through 20 m of stratified debris until they reached virgin soil. Since all that remained of once-vast structures was often only a thin layer of crumbling clay bricks, great care was required, each brick having to be separately articulated.[5] Collecting and classifying the remains from each layer, they were able to identify 18 different strata.

Over the following years, the German archaeologists extended their excavations throughout the Warka site. As they explored the circumference of the immense field of ruins, they discovered layers of a new type of brick. Instead of the traditional rectangular shape, each brick was flat on one side and rounded on the other; that is, plano-convex in form. These bricks were the remains of a wall 9 km long around the city. From the thickness of the structure, it was obvious that it had been designed for more than protection against floods. Here, in fact, was the first evidence of defensive walls in Sumer. From the other debris at the same level, it was possible to place their construction at about the twenty-seventh century BC.[6]

Were they the walls of Gilgamesh? A fragment of another ancient text mentions that a king of Uruk by the name of Gilgamesh built a shrine to the god Enlil in the holy city of Nippur to the north. However, since the person mentioned was the first of a list of rulers, it was thought that this was simply another element of the Gilgamesh legend. In the 1950s, however, the first lines of this text were identified from another document. They indicated that Gilgamesh was a younger contemporary of a king known to have lived in the twenty-seventh century.[7] In short, the legendary figure had actually existed, and much more recently than had hitherto been considered possible. Moreover, his dates, from the middle of the twenty-seventh century BC, correspond to the period of the construction of the wall at Uruk. Today, therefore, there is good reason to believe that the epic poem of Gilgamesh describes an actual series of events.[8] It is an indication that a new phase in human societies had begun and that there were leaders – and poets – who realized some of its implications.

OF WALLS AND WARFARE

Excavations in Palestine and Egypt have uncovered the remains of other strong urban fortifications dating from this same period, which is known as the Early Bronze Age.[9] The only other evidence of walled towns in the Fertile Crescent dates from some three thousand years earlier – about 5800 BC, at Jericho, on the west bank of the Jordan river (an even earlier set of walls at Jericho dates back to 7000 BC). However, this site is that of a small town and appears to be an exception, due perhaps to the extreme vulnerability of the location.[10] In contrast, the walls at Uruk are those of a large city and part of a widespread phenomenon. At another location outside the region, Catal Huyuk in Turkey, there were 5,000 to 6,000 people living in close proximity in the sixth millennium BC. However, this site was not that of a city with a complex physical and social structure. It was simply a large agricultural settlement in which one-room rectangular dwellings were built with adjoining walls so as to provide protection from raiders.[11]

The question that must be asked, therefore, is why urban walls suddenly appeared throughout the Middle East in the middle centuries of the third millennium BC. As the site at Jericho proves, it was not that communities had just learned how to construct fortifications; rather, the explanation must lie in their perception of a greater degree of external threat.

The most frequent explanation for the appearance of urban fortifications is an increase in the probability of attack from aggressive rival cities or from nomadic groups attracted by the wealth of their sedentary neighbors. The Israeli archaeologist Yigael Yadin wrote:

"There was a combination of compelling forces which led to the construction of powerful fortifications for the defense of cities at the beginning of this period. These were, in the main, the concentration of wealth in the cities, partly from agriculture and partly from commerce; expansionist aims of a well-organized people of one land and their encroachment upon spheres of influence of other kingdoms; and the presence of wandering tribes, large and strong, who drew their livelihood not only from their cattle but from predatory incursions into the cultivated fields of the settled population.[12]"

One of the most valuable documents for an understanding of this period in history is the Sumerian King List, several versions of which have been uncovered by archaeologists. The King List speaks of a Flood – a world deluge – occurring roughly a century before the construction of the walls at Uruk, i.e. during the twenty-eighth century BC. Flooding was a recurrent problem in Lower Mesopotamia, and there are clear strata of water-borne sand on the sites of Sumerian cities that date from this period.[13] However, the German archaeologist, Adam Falkenstein, suggested that the term flood may also have been used figuratively in this case to mean an influx of Akkadian Semites from the north-west. He argued that the picture of the Flood "perfectly portrays the event as it must have struck Sumerians who experienced it: an inundation of their country by outland immigrants."[14]

Whether or not one agrees with this interpretation of the term flood, one should note that there is strong evidence of Semitic influence in Sumer starting in this period. A new, more severe type of sculpture, frequently showing people with hands folded in position of worship, begins to appear in the north.[15] Uruk's rival in the legend of Gilgamesh is the northern Sumerian city of Kish:[16] most of the early rulers of this rival city in the King List have Semitic rather than Sumerian names.[17] One possible explanation of the fortifications at Uruk, therefore, is as a response to the threat from Semitic invaders coming from the north (see figure 2.1).

While the new fortifications were undoubtedly useful in defending the Sumerian cities against attacks from their neighbors or from nomadic tribes, Yadin's explanation is not entirely satisfactory. Aggressive neighbors and wandering nomads were certainly not a new phenomenon in the third millennium BC. After all, according to some scholars, the Sumerians themselves had occupied southern Mesopotamia by similar methods less than a thousand years earlier.[18] Yet, as far as is known, their infiltration had provoked no wave of defensive construction at that time. The reasons behind the appearance of walls must therefore be sought elsewhere.

An alternative to the aggressive-neighbor theory is that there occurred at about this time some innovation that changed the nature of armed conflict, increasing the potential gains from military conquest. What was the new element that might have upset the previous equilibrium in Sumer, built around the temple-state? The historian William H. McNeill argued that it was the invention of bronze that changed the nature of armed conflict. "In a limited sense," McNeill wrote, "the industrialization of war is almost as old as civilization, for the introduction of bronze metallurgy made specially skilled artisans indispensable for the manufacture of weapons and armor. Moreover, bronze was rare and expensive. Only a few privileged fighting men could possess a full panoply."[19]

McNeill extended his analysis from the impact of the introduction of bronze to the more general question of the effect of changes in military technology on the optimal size of the representative political unit. He suggested that "another feature of ancient empires deserves emphasis, to wit, the fact that there was an optimal size for such polities . . . the clutter of ancient dynastic and imperial history achieves a modicum of intelligibility when the rise and fall of empires is viewed within the framework of systematic changes in the military basis of political power."[20]

This notion of a causal link between military technology and the position of a political unit's external margin seems plausible. However, McNeill's discussion needs to be completed. In order to understand how technology determines political boundaries, it is necessary to take account of the hierarchical manner in which military forces are organized. The capacity to defend territory necessarily depends on the ability of each level of the military bureaucracy to command the obedience of the levels below it. Technology enters the discussion through its impact on this vertical power structure. An innovation that increases the degree of hierarchical control will permit an expansion of the territory that may be held, whereas one that weakens this structure will tend to lead to smaller political units.

Another element McNeill neglected is the extent of interaction between military technology and economic organization. He classed all societies prior to about 1000 AD as "command systems," based on the obedience of subordinate to superior. While McNeill recognized that armies and administrative bureaucracies are the "twin pillars" of a ruler's power, his analysis failed to take account of the mutual dependence of these two hierarchies.[21] Without a centralized fiscal administration to finance the equipment and wages of a class of professional soldiers, the ancient civilizations would soon have crumbled. What, then, determines the amount of taxes that may be collected?

The power of a state's ruling group will rarely be based on constraint alone. Rather, the community may be viewed as a communications network, from which all members derive benefits. To be sure, some degree of force is required to assure that those who benefit contribute to its maintenance. But if the contributions extracted are greater than the gains from community membership, the information network will eventually be abandoned. There is evidence from Mesopotamia that there were substantial variations in the degree of state control in ancient times.[22] It is worthwhile to ask whether these variations were related in any way to changes in military technology.

MILITARY CONQUEST AND CONTROL

Prior to the third millennium BC, an invading force attempting to conquer an enemy's territory and extract a regular flow of income from it suffered from severe handicaps. Not the least were the difficulties of conquest. To seize the territory of an enemy equipped with the same technology, an invading army must be assured of numerical superiority. The essential question then becomes the ratio of losses on the two sides when combat is engaged. If the larger force may be expected to lose on average as many men as the smaller, then one would say that there are no military economies of scale. In this case, the attacking army cannot engage in many battles on enemy territory without finding itself decimated. After a few engagements, it will find itself outnumbered on the battlefield and its forward movement brought to a halt. However, if the large force suffers on average substantially fewer casualties than any smaller force that opposes it, one would say that there exist considerable military scale economies. Then a large army may engage in a series of battles against smaller groups on enemy territory while keeping the bulk of its numbers intact. It may be seen that the extent to which hostile territory may be conquered will be determined by the degree of such military scale economies.

If the campaign happens to be successful, another problem will arise: that of territorial control. When the main invading force departs, it must leave behind a sufficient number of able-bodied soldiers to staff a garrison capable of controlling the conquered territory. Such an outpost would have to be sufficiently well-equipped to overcome light local resistance and to delay any more determined attack until a response could be organized. Under these circumstances, it is no longer economies of scale that are critical, since the garrison will by definition be outnumbered. What matters now is the effect of training and equipment, since the local population will generally be untrained and unequipped. The greater the advantage of disciplined soldiers over the general population, the lower will be the costs of territorial control.

Some idea of the types of weapons available for such a challenge may be gathered from the monuments of Egypt in the early third millennium BC. As Yadin observed, Egypt lagged behind other regions in the Middle East in the adoption of new methods of warfare.[23] It therefore provides an indication of how battles may have been fought in late Neolithic (New Stone Age) times. The main Egyptian weapons, well into the third millennium, were the heavy stone mace and the single-arc stave bow with flint arrowheads.[24] Furthermore, as late as the end of the third millennium BC, Egyptian soldiers appear to have fought frequently without protective armor or shields of any kind.[25]

This evidence indicates that prior to the application of metallurgy to arms production, the available weapons had limited destructive power. A large invading force would consequently be unlikely to inflict much more permanent damage on smaller groups of defenders than it received itself. Furthermore, existing military technology provided trained troops with little advantage over untrained opponents who were equipped with even the most primitive of arms. As a result, permanent occupation of hostile terrain would prove extremely costly. When control of territory changed hands, therefore, it was more likely to follow gradual infiltration and settlement by nomadic tribes and their flocks than outright conquest by military force. War as later generations would come to know it – invasion of a hostile territory by large numbers of trained soldiers – was simply not feasible.

Developments in Egypt over the course of the fourth millennium, prior to the formation of the First Dynasty around 2900 BC, indicate the difficulty of permanent conquest of distant territory. Geographical factors in Egypt strongly favored the formation of a single political unit. Its natural frontiers – the Mediterranean and Red seas to the north and east and the Sahara Desert to the west – offered exceptional protection against outside attack. Its only land link with other areas of advanced culture – the 140 km wide Isthmus of Suez – could be defended with a modest force.[26] Furthermore, internally, Egypt's geography greatly limited the potential for the recurrent conflicts over rights to water that characterized Mesopotamian history. The Nile itself offered excellent year-round transportation to all habitable regions. The Nile floods were sufficiently great and regular to render irrigation unnecessary, except for increasing the area of the naturally flooded basins.[27] Moreover, the linear structure of the Nile drainage system with its single water course meant that what occurred in one flood basin could not deprive other basins downstream of access to the river.[28] The one area in which claims to water or land might conflict was the delta. In the final battles before unification, this region seems to have been conquered by a possibly less-divided south.

Despite these natural factors favoring Egyptian unification, it was not until the last years of the fourth millennium BC that Upper and Lower Egypt were finally brought together. Three different kings of the First Dynasty asserted claims to have achieved political union. First Scorpion, then Narmer, and finally Aha claimed victory for the south over opponents in the north. One possible explanation for these conflicting claims is that for the technological reasons explained above, the initial attempts at unification proved to be temporary and had to be repeated.[29]

By the time the north and south had finally been brought under control from a single point, military technology was evolving rapidly throughout the Middle East. Metallurgy had been developed to a point at which it threatened to upset the existing balance of power. Indeed, the introduction of the first metal weapons, such as the copper cutting axe, into Egypt may have played some part in the victories of the kings of the First Dynasty. A copper axe-head has been found dating from the middle predynastic period; that is, prior to Egyptian unification.[30] However, the copper cutting axe was not in general use as a weapon until the third millennium BC.[31] At the very least, access to the new weapons must have made it easier for following rulers to maintain the new unified political structure. To appreciate the full impact of the new metallurgical technology, however, it is necessary to return to Mesopotamia, where the application of these techniques to military uses was to transform the nature of armed conflict.

The Discovery of Bronze

How had these metal weapons come to be developed? In central and southern Iraq, the evidence of metal-working dates back to at least the early sixth millennium BC.[32] Since the metals most commonly used – copper and lead – are not found in this region, they had to be imported. Their most likely sources were to the north-west in Turkey or the north-east in Iran.[33] Initially, the lumps of smelted metal would be worked by hammering. At some point in the fourth millennium, however, it was discovered that one could shape copper by pouring it into open molds.[34] Subsequent hammering not only would thin the metal and shape it further but also would have the effect of hardening it. By the beginning of the third millennium, Sumerian smiths were familiar with many of the basic techniques of metal-casting and working, including the use of two-part molds to cast three-dimensional objects.[35]

One final discovery (probably made in Syria or Iran) greatly increased the usefulness of these techniques in the manufacture of armaments. Copper by itself is not only soft but also difficult to cast, because the absorption of gases causes it to become porous. In the late fourth millennium it was found that the addition of a small amount of tin (about 4 percent of the total) to molten copper not only hardened the metal but also made it easier to cast.[36] The resulting alloy was known as bronze.

Because of the relative scarcity of tin in the Middle East, the new alloy was expensive and its diffusion slow. There is no trace of tin in the graves at Ur dating from the early third millennium BC.[37] However, once significant quantities of the metal had been discovered and trade routes developed, the technology spread quickly. Graves at Ur corresponding to the middle of the third millennium BC show a wide range of metals, including tin-bronze.[38]

The Line of Heavy Infantry

One indication of how the new metallurgical skills were applied to military ends is to be found in the victory monuments of the Sumerian rulers. The Standard of Ur (figure 2.2), dating from around 2500 BC, provides one of the first indications that the specialization which had developed in civilian life was beginning to be applied to the military. It depicts three classes of soldiers. In the middle row are heavy infantrymen shown advancing in battle formation with leveled spears.[39] The type of spear they hold is made from a thin, leaf-shaped metal blade tied to a long wooden shaft.[40] On their heads they wear a protective helmet made of either copper or bronze.[41] Their calf-length capes, studded with circular pieces of metal, are an early form of protective armor.[42]

Here, then, one sees the first signs of military training and specialized equipment. A line of these heavy infantrymen would certainly prove formidable against untrained club-wielding opponents. Accordingly, when used by garrison troops, the new technology would sharply reduce the cost of territorial control. Moreover, against a group of trained and equipped but less numerous opponents, the new technology would also prove effective. The larger group could by weight of numbers either break through the opposing army's line or envelop its unprotected wings. In either case, the larger force would maintain its unity, with each soldier protecting his neighbors, while at the same time destroying that of its enemy. Broken up into individuals fighting against a solid wall of shields, the smaller force would then be crushed.

In the upper row of the Standard appears a second class of soldiers – guardsmen wearing the same helmet but with upright spears. In their hands, they carry a secondary weapon, a light axe. This axe, with its

Figure 2.2   The Standard of Ur.

socketed head attached to a curved wooden handle, was one of the finest achievements of Sumerian technology. Its pointed blade was designed to pierce the metal helmets of the enemy.[43] Elite troops such as those pictured here might be used at a key moment in the battle to break through the enemy's line. Or they might be kept in reserve to strengthen a weak spot in one's own line that showed signs of giving way.

An attack by these spearmen in formation, accompanied by their king and his guard, would certainly be formidable; however, in the lower row appears another remarkable contribution of the Sumerians to military technology. The infantry advance would be preceded by an attack of four-wheeled chariots, designed to strike disarray into the line of the opposing troops. Pulled by four wild asses, each chariot had a team consisting of a driver and a spearman equipped with a quiverful of javelins. Other smaller two-wheeled chariots carrying a single soldier were probably used for communications on the battlefield.[44] The impact of this vehicle has been described as "revolutionary."[45] For the first time an element of mobility greater than that of marching soldiers had been added to military techniques. Although the chariot itself had few metal parts, its manufacture must have required considerable skill and the use of a wide range of metal tools.

Yet it is not so much the chariot itself as the hierarchical structure implicit in the Ur mosaic that marks the real revolution in warfare. The formation and protection of the wall of infantrymen required careful preparation and coordination of several different types of troops. Each of the specialized groups of soldiers would have had its own commander, who would expect unquestioning obedience from the troops serving under him. In addition to this officer class, the degree of cooperation demonstrated by the individual soldiers advancing in formation suggests that there must have been the equivalent of a non-commissioned officer to supervise the necessary prolonged sessions of drilling. At the top of this pyramid stands the king, with the elite guards at his disposal to assure that his commands are respected. It is the greater degree of access to the scarce metal, bronze, that appears to differentiate each level of the hierarchy from those below it.

The creation of this hierarchical structure within the military appears to have had its counterpart within the society at large, according to archaeological evidence from the excavations of Sumerian graves. Although sites from the beginning of the third millennium show few metal weapons, those dating from around 2500 BC are sharply differentiated by the presence of bronze armaments. Graves of poor citizens have few weapons, while graves of the more wealthy frequently have spears, battle-axes, and daggers. Social status, it would seem, had become strongly correlated with one's access to metal weapons.[46]

That the new military technology had a sharp impact on social structure is not surprising. Together, the chariots, the drilled and armored infantrymen, and the axe-wielding elite troops constituted a formidable new weapon system. Offering a significant advantage to trained and equipped soldiers over the general population, and increasing in effectiveness the greater the assembled force, the new technology overcame the principal limitations of Neolithic weapons. The most compelling explanation for the appearance of city walls throughout Sumer in this period is the heightened threat of attack and conquest that this new bronze-based weapon system posed. The simultaneous restructuring of social relationships appears to have had the same cause.

About 2460 BC, shortly after the events commemorated in the Standard of Ur, Eanatum, the king of the Sumerian city of Lagash, had a monument built to honor his victory over the neighboring city of Umma.[47] The "Stele of the Vultures" (figure 2.3) shows a somewhat different and more advanced kind of military formation. Instead of the line of caped soldiers with short

Figure 2.3   The Stele of the Vultures.

spears in loose array, one finds a corps of heavy infantry in shoulder-to-shoulder formation. They carry long spears and hold full-length rectangular metal-studded shields. This wall of shields bristling with spear tips marks the first appearance of the phalanx in military history.

There is one final important innovation in military technology that was introduced into Mesopotamia in the third millennium BC. The traditional stave bow made only of wood was not powerful enough to penetrate armor and accordingly was not used in Sumerian warfare. However, it was discovered that if several materials of varying elasticity – wood, animal horn, and sinew – were glued together, the increased tension permitted an arrow to be shot at much greater speed. Light in weight and, when equipped with metal-tipped arrows, able to penetrate armor, the composite bow had a maximum range of 300–400 metres.[48] However, considerable strength and training were required to use it effectively. Naramsin (ca. 2280–2244 BC), the Akkadian king shown using it in figure 2.4, must himself have been a skilled archer.

The requirements for successful conquest and permanent occupation of hostile territory were finally assembled: the technology of war had matured. The phalanx of heavy infantry with spear and shield, accompanied by light infantry with composite bows, offered a powerful instrument for attacking and destroying the forces of a less numerous enemy field army. Although there is no evidence that the Sumerians possessed siege equipment, the Akkadians' victories over the cities of Sumer show that they must also have been masters of the art of overcoming static defenses.[49] Once an enemy territory had been conquered, a small number of highly trained troops, fully equipped with metal arms and armor, could hold it against a much larger number of untrained opponents who did not have access to the new weapons.

FROM CITY-STATE TO EMPIRE

The first urban walls are an indication that the existing distribution of the population of Mesopotamia into autonomous towns and cities had been disturbed. Neolithic weapons had conferred only a slight potential advantage to a larger force over a smaller one or to trained soldiers over untrained adversaries. Since the number of subjects who could be conquered and permanently controlled by a given military force had therefore been small, warfare in the sense of armed attack with a view to permanent conquest was not feasible – at least in the absence of settlement. With the application of metallurgy to arms production, however, there emerged a new weapon system that greatly increased the number of subjects who could be controlled by a given number of trained warriors. It became feasible to form hierarchically structured military bureaucracies – that is, armies. The result was to greatly extend the territory that could be controlled from a single point.

How did the introduction of these weapons affect the territorial boundary or *external margin* of the typical state in Sumer? Archaeologists have been able to detect evidence of a decline in Sumerian civilization dating from the early centuries of the third millennium. There was a noticeable deterioration in traditional artistic forms, such as the engravings on cylinder seals. At the same time, the rounded, naturalistic forms observable in earlier Sumerian sculpture gave way to a new more severe, angular style.[50] Since

Figure 2.4   The Stele of Naramsin.

the new style appeared first in the north and then spread to the south, the most likely explanation is that it spread with the influx from the north of the Semitic people known as the Akkadians.

It is clear that around 2800 BC, Sumerian civilization was under severe external pressure coming from the north. This infiltration, however, was unlike any previous encroachment of nomads on the lands of sedentary farmers. The introduction of metal weapons with their greater killing power meant that the outcome of a single battle might give one side absolute dominance over its opponent. Something of this sort seems to have occurred in central Mesopotamia, as Semitic invaders armed with metal weapons threatened the prosperous Sumerian cities.

The response of the Sumerian temple-states seems to have been a regrouping for strategic purposes. In each region, one city achieved a sort of local pre-eminence over the surrounding towns and villages. Gradually the smaller temple-states gave way to larger territorial units.[51] By the middle of the third millennium Sumer was divided into a dozen or so contiguous territorial states.[52] Faced with an enemy equipped for conquest, the Sumerian cities were obliged to divert efforts from cultural and economic activities into preparations for defense. Thus it was that the Akkadians knew the southern king Gilgamesh of Uruk as a tyrant who forced his subjects into work gangs to build a wall around his city.[53]

The next four centuries were marked by frequent wars among the cities of Sumer and their neighbors. The conflict between Kish and Uruk broadened into a three-way struggle among these two cities and Ur for leadership in Sumer.[54] Additional external pressure was added from another area of civilization known as Elam in what is now western Iran. At one point in the twenty-seventh century, the Elamite kingdom of Alan was able to dominate its Sumerian neighbors. Following the restoration of the kingship to Kish, it was snatched by a second Elamite kingdom, before returning to Uruk.

As the city-states grew in population and wealth, conflicts among them became more frequent and bitter. A recurring problem was access to water, whose scarcity became increasingly a constraint on further expansion of production and population. In Egypt, the Nile flowed powerfully to the coast, its current little affected by whatever irrigation was necessary to supplement the regular flooding of its narrow valley. However, the Tigris and Euphrates were slowly flowing rivers with irregular flooding. Not only was irrigation essential to maintain regular production, but also the radial structure of the canal system meant that increased water diversion by one area significantly reduced the water available to neighboring communities farther downstream.[55]

Toynbee argued that these spillover effects, by which one group's production is affected negatively by the output of neighboring groups, explain the drive toward political unification in Mesopotamia. "In the lower basin of the Tigris and Euphrates," he wrote:

the completed network of waterways, natural and artificial, was indivisible; and, so long as this network was not controlled by a single authority possessing the power to regulate and distribute the waters that were the means of life, the management of these waters could not be either efficient or peaceful. Inevitably it was a perpetual *casus belli* between local sovereign states, for these would be bound to compete and conflict with each other in striving each to win the maximum amount of water-control for itself.[56]

This irrigation theory for the formation of larger states is very appealing; yet having something to gain collectively by cooperating does not necessarily mean that people will in fact choose to do so. As individuals, they may benefit more by not cooperating. If unification were potentially so advantageous, why was the leader of one state not able to impose himself upon a submissive and contented population earlier in the third millennium? The historical evidence indicates that it was only gradually, and coincidentally with the development of the new military techniques described above, that unified control of the whole of Sumer became possible. By the middle of the millennium, a series of Sumerian kings managed to achieve local dominance in Sumer and even to extend their influence to the north and the east. In the twenty-sixth century BC, Lugalannemundu of the city of Adab established his claim as "king of the four quarters (of the universe)." His influence apparently extended through the entire Fertile Crescent from western Iran to what is now Lebanon. The growing power of the Akkadians is reflected in the Semitic names of most of the *ensi*s or governors of the Sumerian cities who served under him.[57]

In the following century, Eanatum, the king of the city of Lagash in the south-east of Sumer, also succeeded in asserting his suzerainty over the other cities. Some support for Toynbee's irrigation argument is provided by the apparent motive for his first battle – a border dispute with neighboring Umma. One of the victor's first acts was to dig a new canal to mark the boundary between the two states.[58] It was in memory of this victory that his followers erected the Stele of the Vultures described above. However, as in the case of Lugalannemundu, the domain carved out did not last much longer than the life of the king himself.

By now, a weapon system for successful wars of conquest had been assembled: the torch of imperial power could begin to blaze into action. In the middle of the twenty-fourth century, an ambitious leader of Semitic descent, Lugalzagesi, came to power in Umma. One of his first achievements was to defeat Lagash and to destroy its holy places. After a successful military career that saw him conquering all of the cities of Sumer, he asserted for the first time the concept of a state beyond the city-state. Following his victory over Uruk, Lugalzagesi assumed the title "King of the Land of Sumer." Despite his assertions, however, like his predecessors, he made no real attempt to create a centralized government in Sumer.[59]

Within two decades of his first victories, around 2340 BC, Lugalzagesi was himself overthrown and brought in a neck stock to the holy city of Nippur to be exhibited in humiliation before the passers-by. His conqueror was a Semitic Akkadian who had been an official of the king of Kish when Lugalzagesi had deposed the latter in his rise to power.[60] The new king, Sargon the Great, went on to defeat Ur, Lagash, and Umma in a brilliant campaign that made him master of Sumer. He established his capital at a previously unmentioned site in the Semitic north, which he called Agade and was known as Akkad in the Bible. Further expeditions brought northern Mesopotamia under his control and extended Akkadian influence to the Mediterranean in the west and into Elam in the east.[61]

Although Sargon's seizure of power may recall that of some of the Sumerian rulers who preceded him, in fact his reign marked a sharp break with the traditions of earlier centuries. Previously it had been the custom of the dominant city to leave the other centers in Sumer intact and under the control of local leaders or *ensis*. The subordinate cities would probably be called upon to supply tribute and to furnish manpower for the *lugal*'s (king's) campaigns. Those cities which suffered defeat might also find their borders adjusted in their disfavor, as had occurred to Umma at the hands of Eanatum. However, if one may judge by the strength of the reaction it provoked, Lugalzagesi's destruction of the temples of Lagash seems to have been an exception to the usual treatment of a conquered rival. A Lagashite scribe wrote after the catastrophic events that "Because the Ummaite destroyed the bricks of Lagash, he committed a sin against the god Ningirsu; he (Ningirsu) will cut off the hands lifted against him."[62]

After capturing Lugalzagesi's capital, Uruk, and Umma, the city in which the latter had begun his rise to power, Sargon took the extraordinary step of destroying the walls of these cities.[63] To leave their inhabitants thus defenseless he must have been extremely confident in his own ability to overcome any external attack. This decision, along with the speed of his victories over any opposing force in the region, suggests the possession of a weapon system superior to that of any potential rival. Further steps taken by Sargon suggest a degree of confidence never before evident. Although the conquered cities retained their own nominal rulers, in fact it was Akkadian officials appointed by Sargon who held the posts of power in each city.[64] Under the new administrative system, officials often used the Akkadian language rather than Sumerian.[65] Finally, Sargon's capital was outside Sumer in Semitic Akkad. In effect, his kingdom was the first empire comprised of distinct ethnic units to be conquered by force and administered through a centralized authority.[66]

While Sargon was undoubtedly a brilliant military leader with a gift for organization, his successes reflect more than the personal characteristics of one man. His empire continued to thrive under his sons who succeeded him, reaching its peak under his grandson Naramsin. It was not until around 2159 BC, some 200 years after its founding, that the remains of the Akkadian empire finally succumbed to the invading Gutians, powerful invaders from the upper Tigris to the north.[67] In short, as the Sumerians themselves recognized, Sargon was something more than just one in a line of "big men."[68] The available evidence indicates that he and his successors had access to a military technology superior to that of their Sumerian predecessors. Not only were the Akkadians easily able to defeat any field army that could be organized against them by the Sumerian cities or their Semitic neighbors, but also they could hold conquered territory by force long after its initial capture. At Tell Brak in north-western Iraq, Naramsin constructed a hectare-sized garrison to control access to the key trade routes from Syria.[69] Such an effort would have been worthwhile only if the Akkadian force that manned this garrison were sufficiently powerful to overcome any local resistance and to hold out against an external invasion until relief could be organized.

The Limits to Conquest

The most likely explanation for the successes of the Sargonids was their access to and mastery of a new weapon system. As Yadin has suggested, it may have been the addition of the compound bow, with its ability to kill silently at a great distance, that gave them their military advantage.[70] When added to the existing panoply of weapons developed by Mesopotamian metallurgy, this deadly instrument further increased the economies of scale of the infantry army. Because the bow could be used by soldiers behind the front lines, the power of an army increased more than proportionally to the number of men it exposed. Thus a larger force would have a higher ratio of destructive power to exposed warriors than a smaller one. In this way, an able commander such as Sargon could organize a large field army that was all but invincible to any series of smaller forces that tried to stop its forward motion.

Evidently there was a territorial limit beyond which these techniques could no longer be effective, for Sargon wielded little real power outside of Mesopotamia. McNeill suggested that one of the determinants of the geographical limit of a political unit is the speed at which troops can move.

He argued that if the king wished to spend at least half of the year in his capital, an outward march of more than 90 days might threaten his hold on power.[71] The degree of mobility of military units was evidently a factor determining the limits of conquest.

The information presented in this study suggests, however, that the question of military control is somewhat more complex than this simple example implies. One additional element is the degree of shared interest among the people to be governed. In Egypt, a kingdom with 90-day-march frontiers was possible at the beginning of the third millennium, yet in Mesopotamia, it was not until over 600 years later that an empire of the size mentioned by McNeill was feasible. As argued earlier, there was very little incentive for one section of the Nile basin to break away from a central government. In Sumer, however, conflict over water rights meant that there was always an incentive for an upstream city to assert its independence of any larger grouping and appropriate water from its downstream neighbors.

Another consideration is the risk of outside attack. In Egypt, because of geographical factors, the probability of foreign invasion was very slight. A regime could consequently devote less of the society's income to internal security, leaving more for consumption and for the production of public works. In the more exposed setting of Sumer, however, a prudent ruler always had to divert considerable resources to defense against outside aggression, as the fortress at Tell-Brak indicates. The burden of such expenditures would necessarily weaken his internal support. In addition, the existence of foreign enemies provided a potential ally for any discontented subjects.

An additional determinant of the optimal external margin is the degree of battlefield economies of scale to military technology. What is at issue in the concept of scale economies is the expected cost of an enemy casualty for two forces of unequal size. This amount could be measured in terms of the outlay for wages, equipment, and supplies. If the cost of a casualty is lower for an army of 2,000 soldiers than for an army of 1,000 soldiers when the two groups engage in combat, then one would say that scale economies exist. A larger force could defeat a series of smaller bodies of troops, inflicting greater losses than it itself received.

The application of bronze to the technology of war permitted the development of a whole series of new weapons and accessories – the bronze-tipped spear, the sword, the battle-axe, the metal-reinforced shield, the helmet, and body armor. Together, these armaments made possible a new military formation, the line of heavy infantry. By enveloping or penetrating the enemy line without losing its own cohesion, a large army adequately equipped and trained could impose disproportionately greater losses on a smaller army than those it suffered itself. It was this ability of a large force of heavy infantry to give more than it received that constituted the essential contribution of bronze to the art of war.

With the development of the lightweight composite bow, ancient armies acquired a second type of formation. The line of disciplined light infantry armed with the new bow added an element of flexibility to the battlefield commander. Protected by their own heavy infantry, these troops could use their missile weapons to soften and disrupt the enemy's line prior to shock combat. Requiring skilled craftsmanship for its manufacture and strength and long practice for effective use, the composite bow gave the Akkadian troops a great advantage over their enemies. The Stele of Naramsin (figure 2.4) portrays Sargon's grandson using this weapon to rout hostile soldiers in the mountains bordering Akkad.

For a given degree of shared interest among ruled and rulers and openness to outside attack of the area being considered, economies of scale determine the labor input (the number of soldier-days per month) required to control a subject population of a given size. But what determines the total size of the subject population? If additional territory is conquered, can it not supply the manpower and the resources necessary to control it? Implicit in McNeill's 90-day-march argument is the idea that the ruler must be informed about what is occurring in his territory in order to control it effectively, and that distance constitutes a barrier to information flow. As an empire grows, scale economies are increasingly offset by distance. At some point, the ruler is no longer able to assure that his troops make the minimum effort required to control the territory from which they have been recruited. At this point, the empire ceases to expand.

If this argument is correct, the external margin of a political unit is determined by the interplay between two offsetting forces – scale economies on the one hand and the loss of control that results from distance on the other. The effect of metal weapons was to tip the balance in favor of scale economies, enabling a ruler such as Sargon to more easily overcome the loss of control that occurred as the distance from the capital to the borders increased.

PRIVATE PROPERTY AND PALACE RULE

At the same time that territorial boundaries were shifting outward in Mesopotamia, there is evidence that the *internal margin* between public and private activity was also changing. In their excavations of the ancient cities of Eridu and Kish, archaeologists have found the remains of large buildings that do not have the ground plan of temples. These structures date from the twenty-sixth and twenty-seventh centuries BC; in other words, coincident with or slightly later than the period of the wall at Uruk. From their layout, these new buildings can only be palaces – residences of secular rulers who have established a center of power distinct from the temple.

In addition to the appearance of palaces, there is other evidence to suggest that the power structure in Sumerian city-states was being transformed during this period. The earlier hierarchical organization corresponding to the mature temple-state is described in the epic tales from Uruk. The ruler of the city, the *en* (lord), lives in a part of the temple. He receives a foreign royal messenger in the temple courtyard.[72] However, it is clear from the pictures on cylinder seals that the same person also serves as high priest.[73] Not only does he lead the city's militia in battle and manage the irrigation system, but also he oversees the celebration of the cult of the temple's god.

The first written mention of a change in this traditional structure occurs in early texts from Ur. These writings speak of a *hai-kal* (big house or palace) in which the *lugal* (big man) or *ensi* (governor) resides.[74] These latter two positions represent the top rungs in a new political hierarchy distinct from the temple bureaucracy. The *lugal* is the king – a ruler of one city who asserts his pre-eminence over the leaders of other cities. This term, first applied to the rulers of Kish, appears at about the same time as the first urban walls, around 2700 BC. The *ensi* or city ruler is someone of lower standing – a prince or vassal who commands a more limited territory.[75]

The centuries between the first Akkadian encroachments, around 2800 BC and the final fall of Sumer to Sargon the Great, around 2340, were a period of great tension between the temple and the palace. As the threat of outside attack intensified, it became increasingly necessary to concentrate power in the hands of a single individual who had proven military skills. During the wars that characterized this period, the military leader would be forced to levy heavy taxes on the citizens. However, another source of revenue – and cause of conflict – was the sale of lands confiscated from the temples.[76] Some evidence of the intensity of this internal struggle may be inferred from documents left by the reformist ruler Urukagina who governed Lagash just before its conquest by Lugalzagesi in the twenty-fourth century BC. The documents record that Urukagina restored to the city's god, Ningirsu, lands that had been misappropriated by previous rulers and their families.[77]

During this conflict between two alternative power centers – temple and palace – the dominance of the priesthood in the exercise of power seems to have been broken. However, the result was not simply a transfer of the temple's authority to the secular administration. Rather, the scope for private activity seems to have increased, the palace officials ruling over the broad confines of the territorial state being unable to control activity as tightly as the priests had done in the narrower area of the temple-state. One sign of a reduction in public power is the appearance of land-sale contracts. Initially, in the period before 2600, such contracts are found almost exclusively in areas of Akkadian settlement. However, a century later, the archives of the central Sumerian city of Shuruppak record the transfer of land to private individuals in payment for services to the state. Other documents record sales of land between individuals.[78]

Another indication of a decline in the power of public authorities, whether religious or secular, is the first mention of bureaucratic corruption. In Lagash, in the period prior to Urukagina, officials had apparently used their positions to exact excessive payments for public services. Sales of property or cattle on unfavorable terms had been forced upon the weaker members of society. Problems such as these are a sign of a breakdown in the capacity of the state to control the behavior of its representatives. The new ruler found it necessary to reduce and fix the levels of fees for official services. In addition, he promised to protect the rights of widows and orphans.[79]

Several decades ago there was a debate among scholars who studied Sumer over the importance of the temple in the Sumerian city-state. The traditional opinion had been that the greater part of the lands belonged to the temple and were administered by a theocracy. However, subsequent computations by the Russian archaeologist Diakanoff indicated that temple holdings in the city of Lagash in the period after 2500 BC amounted to only about 10–20 percent of the total.[80]

The image of Sumerian society in the twenty-fourth century is therefore quite different from that of the temple-states five centuries earlier. In the earlier temple-centered societies, there had been only a limited place for market exchange. However, Kramer has suggested that in the later Sumerian city-states the town market played an important role. Here artisans and craftsmen sold their wares. Although some transactions were in kind, standardized weights of silver were also used as a medium of exchange.[81]

The extension of secular power received a further boost when Sargon the Great set up an administrative system at Akkad to rule over his conquests. Even though the captured cities retained their individual identities, Sargon made sure that it was his agents who exercised effective power over his subjects: he boasted of feeding 5,400 men at his table every day.[82]

It is not clear exactly how the Akkadian military and civilian bureaucracies were financed. Once the empire stopped growing, the flow of tribute from captured enemies would gradually cease. Revenues from royal properties and taxes on private land do not seem to have been sufficient to maintain the massive administrative structure. Manishtushu, Sargon's son, was forced to dip into the store of silver that he and his predecessor had received as tribute from captured enemies. He used these funds to buy land from private owners which he then granted to royal servants, including his own nephews and the sons of former rulers.[83] An additional source of revenue may have been profits from a state monopoly on foreign trade in certain key goods, such as wood, stones, and metals. Sargon lists among his conquests "The Cedar Forest" and "The Silver Mountain." However, the only way in which he could assure Mesopotamia of a permanent supply of wood and metals was through voluntary exchange. Accordingly Akkad became an entrepôt for Mesopotamian trade with distant lands in the Persian Gulf and the Indian Ocean along with other remote lands on the Mediterranean Sea.[84]

Together, the evidence of extensive private landholdings along with bustling foreign trade suggests a further shift in the line dividing private and public activity. In pre-Sargonid Sumer, a wide range of activities had consisted of internal transactions among the dependents of the temple or palace. A complex system of equivalences or accounting prices had been developed by the officials of the royal or divine household to determine how goods would be distributed.[85] These transactions were now increasingly relegated to the more impersonal mechanism of the market, at prices set by forces of supply and demand.

The Effect of Distance on Public Consent

These indications of a decrease in the central authority's control over the activities of the community suggest a relationship between space and the degree of consent for intervention on the part of the lawmaker's subjects. There are several factors that will tend to reduce the average acceptance of government action as the size of a state increases. One such factor is the extent to which the state's residents share common interests. The farther people live from one another, the more costly it is for them to interact. As a result, cultural diversity tends to increase with distance: as one proceeds away from a given location, one encounters ever-greater cultural differences with respect to one's starting point. Accordingly, the larger the area a leader attempts to control, the more diverse the interests of his subjects will tend to be and the less confident each will be that the ruler will act in his favor. Sargon's empire included more than a dozen cities, each jealous of its rights. Moreover, these cities were divided into two traditionally antagonistic regions, Summer and Akkad, between which there were strong cultural differences.

Another consideration is the cost of communication between the citizens and the lawmaker. Since the cost of sending messages between citizens and the central authority will tend to rise as the former's distance from the decision-making center increases, collective action will become increasingly inefficient as the size of the state grows. With an empire many times larger than the greatest of the Sumerian territorial states, the Akkadian bureaucracy could no longer hope to intervene effectively in the detailed day-to-day life of the empire's subjects.

In short, the state may be seen as a communications network whose benefits to additional members will tend to diminish as its borders expand. Because of the increasing diversity of the population and the greater cost of transmitting messages to outlying regions, the average consent for public intervention will decrease with distance from the capital. Consequently, the extension of the state's territorial boundaries signaled by the victories of soldier-kings such as Gilgamesh led to a diminished role for hierarchy and an enhanced place for the market in the allocation of society's resources.

FRONTIER GAMES

Why did defensive walls suddenly appear at Uruk and other cities in Sumer after 2700 BC? Since such fortifications were costly to build, to man and to maintain, their presence suggests an increase in the probability of external attack. However, the usual answer that these walls were due to the threat of aggression from expansionist neighbors or raiding nomads is unsatisfactory. There is no reason to believe that such potential opponents suddenly became more bellicose than in the past.

The hypothesis explored in this chapter is that a series of innovations in military technology in the third millennium BC increased the economies of scale in the application of force. These scale economies permitted the formation of a pyramid of military power based upon differentiated access to bronze weapons and tools, with one man commanding the obedience of a large group of specialized fighting men. The latter were in turn able to impose themselves on a much larger unequipped and untrained subject population. The result was an extension of the territory that could be controlled militarily from a single point under a given informational technology.

Prior to the development of metal weapons, armed conflict seems to have been limited to border raids or to gradual infiltration by nomadic groups. Evidence from Egypt indicates that the first successful seizure of control of an extended territory appears to coincide with the introduction of simple copper weapons (around 3000 BC). In Sumer, where the obstacles to political union were considerably greater, a more sophisticated technology was required to conquer and control a territory of equivalent size. It was not until Sargon the Great (2340 BC), with the development of a complete metal-based weapon system, that effective dominance of the Mesopotamian plain became possible.

Parallel to these shifts in territorial boundaries, there occurred other changes in the structure of Mesopotamian society. Faced with Akkadian encroachment, the temple communities of Sumer clustered together to form territorial states. Of necessity, power was transferred to those with military skills. Shortly after the appearance of city walls, therefore, comes evidence of palaces – the strong places of secular rulers. In the process of the struggle for internal control between palace and temple, the virtual power monopoly of the public bureaucracy was broken. As a result, the opportunity for private initiative increased. Private landholdings and market activity made their first appearance in historical records. Individual initiative subsequently received an additional boost under the Sargonid dynasty where, increasingly, private property and voluntary trade replaced collective property and bureaucratic fiat.

One way to interpret the historical developments described here is as a confirmation of McNeill's thesis that the boundaries of political units depend on military technology. However, these events also fit into a more general approach that views the community as an information network. To explain social change, this approach focuses on innovations that alter either the way information is processed or the way in which the network's territorial monopoly is defended. In the case of Sumer in the third millennium BC, the techniques for casting copper alloys permitted the development of a new armament system that replaced the stone and flint weapons of the Neolithic period.

The key to understanding the formation of the first empires is the concept of scale economies in the application of force. Prior to the development of metal weapons, the expected cost of a casualty inflicted by a large occupying force on a smaller group of rebels was high. Consequently, the cost of conquering and controlling a subject population of more than 40,000 or 50,000 people appears to have been prohibitive. With bronze weapons, a larger force in formation as a line of heavy infantry could generally defeat a smaller one while suffering fewer casualties than it itself inflicted. The metal-based technology also gave an increased advantage to trained and equipped soldiers over the general population, an essential requirement for the success of garrison troops used to keep conquered territory under control.

Changes in organizational scale economies brought about transformations in hierarchical structures. The increased destructive power of bronze weapons conferred an advantage to those with access to the new technology and with the inherent skills and acquired training to use them effectively. As a result, there emerged a new military bureaucracy – the army – based on differentiated access to bronze-based arms. The previous simple military structure of leader and followers was replaced by a multi-layered organization in which each echelon used the threat of force to command the obedience of those below it. At the bottom was the bulk of the civilian population, untrained and unarmed. The new techniques greatly increased a ruler's power to conquer and control territory from a distance.

Modifications in the structure of administrative power led in turn to shifts in the external and internal margins of the typical political unit. Within the closed linear system of the Nile river valley, the very simplest application of the new techniques permitted the unification of Upper and Lower Egypt under the kings of the First Dynasty. In the more open and conflictual setting of the Tigris and Euphrates valleys, unification was not achieved until much later, when the development of a complete metal-based weapon system greatly increased the advantages of a large force over a smaller force.

At the same time as these changes in the community's external margin, there occurred shifts in the internal margin between individual and collective action. The social control that the civilian bureaucracy was able to maintain in the Sumerian temple-states broke down as larger territorial units were formed. Public property and bureaucratic distribution systems were replaced in part by private property and use of markets. Under the Semitic Akkadians, the internal structure of Mesopotamian society evolved still further. Since the total territory of Sargon's empire was too vast to be administered effectively by a centralized bureaucracy, market rule was allowed to supplement hierarchical command. Internally, private activity was increasingly allowed to coexist with public intervention.

Gilgamesh takes his place in history as among the first of a new type of political leader. Combining military skill and administrative talent, he and his successors would use the new metal-based weapons to push their states' borders far beyond the land that could be viewed from the roofs of their home temples. Within the new empires, the rewards to individual initiative would increase to an extent that worshipers in the first Sumerian temple-states could not have imagined. At the same time, the disparities between ruler and ruled would widen, creating a spectrum of social gradings ranging from slave to emperor. The age of war had begun.

NOTES

1 Thorkild Jacobsen, *Toward the Image of Tammuz and Other Essays on Mesopotamian History and Culture*, ed. William L. Moran (Harvard University Press, 1970), p. 381, n. 55.
2 Elizabeth Lansing, *The Sumerians: Inventors and Builders* (McGraw-Hill, 1971), p. 161.
3 Jacobsen, *Toward the Image of Tammuz*, p. 381, n. 55.

4 Dietz Otto Edzard, "The Early Dynastic period," in *The Near East: The Early Civilizations,* eds J. Bottéro, E. Cassin, and J. Vercoutter (Weidenfeld and Nicolson, 1967), p. 65.

5 Seton Lloyd, *The Archaeology of Mesopotamia* (Thames and Hudson, 1978), p. 49.

6 Edzard, "The Early Dynastic period," pp. 61, 65.

7 Samuel Noah Kramer, *The Sumerians: Their History, Culture and Character* (University of Chicago Press, 1963), pp. 46–50.

8 Lloyd, *The Archaeology of Mesopotamia,* p. 92.

9 Yigael Yadin, *The Art of Warfare in Biblical Lands in the Light of Archaeological Study* (McGraw-Hill, 1963), p. 53.

10 Ibid., pp. 33–4.

11 Arther Ferrill, *The Origins of War* (Thames and Hudson, 1985), p. 30.

12 Yadin, *The Art of Warfare in Biblical Lands,* pp. 50–1.

13 Lloyd, *The Archaeology of Mesopotamia,* p. 92.

14 Adam Falkenstein, "The prehistory and protohistory of Western Asia," in *The Near East: The Early Civilizations,* eds J. Bottéro, E. Cassin, and J. Vercoutter (Weidenfeld and Nicolson, 1967), p. 51.

15 Edzard, "The Early Dynastic period," p. 60.

16 Ibid., p. 64–5.

17 Ibid., p. 58.

18 Kramer, *The Sumerians,* p. 42.

19 William H. McNeill, *The Pursuit of Power: Technology, Armed Force and Society since* AD 1000 (University of Chicago Press, 1982), p. 1.

20 Ibid., pp. 8–9.

21 Ibid., p. 7.

22 Robert McC. Adams, "Mesopotamian social evolution: old outlooks, new goals," in *On the Evolution of Complex Societies,* ed. Timothy Earle (Undena, 1984), p. 90.

23 Yadin, *The Art of Warfare in Biblical Lands,* p. 43.

24 John Ruffle, *The Egyptians: An Introduction to Egyptian Archaeology* (Cornell University Press, 1977), p. 122.

25 Richard Humble, *Warfare in the Ancient World* (Cassell, 1980), pp. 36–7.

26 Ibid., p. 37.

27 Karl W. Butzer, *Early Hydraulic Civilization in Egypt: A Study in Cultural Ecology* (University of Chicago Press, 1976), p. 106.

28 Ibid., p. 109.

29 Ruffle, *The Egyptians,* p. 24.

30 A. Lucas and J. R. Harris, *Ancient Egyptian Materials and Industries* (Edward Arnold, 1962), p. 213.

31 Yadin, *The Art of Warfare in Biblical Lands,* p. 43.

32 P. R. S. Moorey, "The archaeological evidence for metallurgy and related technologies in Mesopotamia, c. 5500–2100 BC," *Iraq,* 44 (1982), p. 17.

33 Ibid., p. 14.

34 Lucas and Harris, *Ancient Egyptian Materials,* p. 212–13.

35 Moorey, "The archaeological evidence for metallurgy," p. 21.

36 Lucas and Harris, *Ancient Egyptian Materials,* p. 217.

37 Moorey, "The archaeological evidence for metallurgy," p. 23.

38 Ibid., p. 29.

39 Humble, *Warfare in the Ancient World,* p. 16.

40 Yadin, *The Art of Warfare in Biblical Lands,* p. 45.

41 C. J. Gadd, "The cities of Babylonia," in *The Cambridge Ancient History,* 3rd edn, vol. I, part 2, *Early History of the Middle East,* eds I. E. S. Edwards, C. J. Gadd, and N. G. L. Hammond (Cambridge University Press, 1971), p. 123.

The Age of Gilgamesh   75

42 Yadin, *The Art of Warfare in Biblical Lands*, p. 49.
43 Ibid., p. 41.
44 Ibid., p. 38.
45 Ibid., p. 37.
46 Trevor Watkins, "Sumerian weapons, warfare and warriors," *Sumer*, 39 (1983), pp. 101–2.
47 Humble, *Warfare in the Ancient World*, p. 17.
48 Field Marshall Viscount Montgomery of Alamein, *A History of Warfare* (Collins, 1968), p. 36.
49 Humble, *Warfare in the Ancient World*, p. 21.
50 Edzard, "The Early Dynastic period," pp. 60–1.
51 A. Leo Oppenheim, "A bird's-eye view of Mesopotamian economic history," in *Trade and Market in the Early Empires*, eds K. Polanyi, C. Arensberg, and H. Pearson (The Free Press, 1957), p. 33.
52 Kramer, *The Sumerians*, p. 73.
53 Edzard, "The Early Dynastic period," p. 65.
54 Kramer, *The Sumerians*, p. 50.
55 Butzer, *Early Hydraulic Civilization in Egypt*, p. 109.
56 Arnold Toynbee, *Mankind and Mother Earth: A Narrative History of the World* (Oxford University Press, 1976), p. 66.
57 Kramer, *The Sumerians*, p. 51.
58 Ibid., p. 54.
59 Mogens Trolle Larsen, "The tradition of empire in Mesopotamia," in *Mesopotamia*, vol. 7, *Power and Propaganda: A Symposium on Ancient Empires*, ed. M. T. Larsen (Akademisk Forlag, Copenhagen, 1979), p. 77.
60 Jean Bottéro, "The first Semitic empire," in *The Near East: The Early Civilizations*, eds J. Bottéro, E. Cassin, and J. Vercoutter (Weidenfeld and Nicolson, 1967), p. 104.
61 Kramer, *The Sumerians*, pp. 60–1.
62 Ibid., p. 58.
63 Ibid., p. 60.
64 Bottéro, "The first Semitic empire," p. 111–12.
65 Larsen, "The tradition of empire in Mesopotamia," p. 78.
66 Humble, *Warfare in the Ancient World*, p. 20,
67 Bottéro, "The first Semitic empire," p. 119.
68 Aage Westenholz, "The Old Akkadian Empire in contemporary opinion," in *Mesopotamia*, vol. 7, *Power and Propaganda: A Symposium on Ancient Empires*, ed. M. T. Larsen (Akademisk Forlag, Copenhagen, 1979), p. 110.
69 Jean Bottéro, "The first Semitic empire," p. 112.
70 Yadin, *The Art of Warfare in Biblical Lands*, p. 47.
71 McNeill, *The Pursuit of Power*, p. 8.
72 Edzard, "The Early Dynastic period," pp. 73–4.
73 Falkenstein, "The prehistory and protohistory of Western Asia," p. 45.
74 Edzard, "The Early Dynastic period," p. 73.
75 Ibid., p. 71.
76 Kramer, *The Sumerians*, p. 80.
77 Edzard, "The Early Dynastic period," p. 82.
78 Ibid., p. 75. See also Carolyn Webber and Aaron Wildavsky, *A History of Taxation and Expenditure in the Western World* (Simon and Schuster, 1986), pp. 47–8.
79 Edzard, "The Early Dynastic period," p. 82.
80 Kramer, *The Sumerians*, pp. 75–6.
81 Ibid., p. 74.

82 Bottéro, "The first Semitic empire," p. 113.
83 Ibid., p. 114.
84 Ibid., p. 110.
85 Oppenheim, "A bird's-eye view of Mesopotamian economic history," p. 32.

3

The Shattered Mirror

*Why did the Roman Empire fall? To date, over 400 different answers
have been given to this question, none of them entirely satisfactory.
Economic explanations fail to account for the continued survival of the
Eastern Empire. The military approach, focusing on barbarian pressure
or on the erroneous decisions of individual leaders, cannot explain why
no state of comparable size has ever been established on Rome's territory.
Yet the empire's collapse had both military and economic components
that must be explained. The answer offered here is that a change in
military technology reduced the advantage of a large force over a smaller
one. Seized upon by both foreign invaders and internal challengers, the
new technology of cavalry warfare raised the cost of territorial control.
Only a much smaller political unit could obtain the consent for and
effectively administer the required increase in state intervention.*

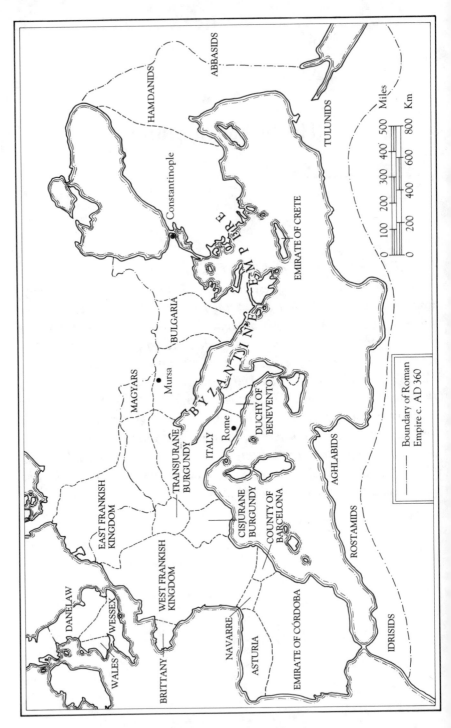

Figure 3.1 The Roman Empire, ca. AD 360 and its successor states ca. AD 900.
(Source: R. R. Sellman, *An Outline Atlas of World History,* St. Martin's Press, New York, 1970, pp. 19, 25)

On the plain before Mursa (the present-day Croatian city of Osijek in northern Yugoslavia), Constantius II addressed his soldiers. After encouraging them with an eloquent speech, he turned the command over to his generals and retired into a church some distance away to pray. His 40,000 men had spent the morning anxiously waiting for the fighting to begin. The army's right flank was anchored on the River Drave which at this point, just before it flowed into the Danube, was 8 km wide with its adjacent marshes. The left flank extended across the plain, far beyond the right wing of the opposing forces.

In the center of Constantius' line were legions of heavily armored infantrymen dressed in close order, the traditional strength of the Roman military. Flanking them were two new types of cavalry units: on the inner flank was the glistening steel of the cataphracts, fully armored lancers mounted on heavy horses that were also protected by armor; beyond these were auxiliary companies of mounted oriental archers. Constantius had added these new cavalry bodies to his army in imitation of the Persian forces he had been fighting virtually continuously for the past 14 years. To the rear was the traditional Roman light cavalry armed with javelin and sword.

Constantius was the son of the great Roman emperor, Constantine, founder of Constantinople. On his father's death in AD 337, he had inherited the Roman territories in the east, while the western provinces were divided between his two brothers. By the year AD 351, however, he was the only one of the three to have survived. Shortly after their father's death, one of his brothers had been killed while fighting the other for control of Italy. Then only a year before, in 350, the second brother had been murdered on the orders of a German-born general, Magnentius, who had been proclaimed emperor by the soldiers of Gaul. Constantius had hastily arranged a temporary truce in the border wars with Persia in order to bring his army west to deal with the usurper.

On the other side of the plain from Constantius on this morning of September 28, AD 351, stood 50,000 of the best troops the Western Empire could assemble. Although Magnentius' army included some cavalry units, it was predominantly an infantry force. The crack Gallic legions of the West had been reinforced by large numbers of German tribesmen. During most of the summer, the two armies had engaged in preliminary maneuvers, with the veteran Magnentius having the upper hand. Now the decisive encounter was about to begin. For each commander, it was a case of double or nothing: victory meant sole rule over the whole of the empire, while defeat meant loss of the half-empire already held and probable death.

As the battle got under way, the Western center advanced, cutting into the Eastern line. However, with legion fighting legion using the best of Roman military techniques, the Western advance was painfully slow and the losses to each side frightful. Meanwhile, the Eastern generals had ordered their left cavalry wing to advance in an oblique line. It then wheeled right and charged the exposed flank of the Western line. The right wing of the Western army crumbled under this unexpected pressure. Masses of Germans with only their shields to protect them from the deadly arrows fled into the Drave. However, the legions from Gaul held. It took alternating attacks by the Eastern cataphracts and horse archers before the Western center was slowly eroded. Once the legions gave way, the Eastern light cavalry, sword in hand, rode into the breaks in the lines to complete the destruction. Still Magnentius refused to yield. It was only after his camp was finally captured that he fled for safety toward the Alps and Italy.[1]

The battle of Mursa was a victory for Constantius. Although it took a further two years to hunt down Magnentius, the Empire was temporarily reunited. Indeed, Rome's borders in 353 were very similar to those it had known under Claudius some three centuries earlier. However, unity came at a high price: casualties at Mursa on both sides were extremely heavy. Gibbon placed the combined losses at 54,000, including 30,000 to Constantius.[2] A more moderate recent estimate cuts these figures in half.[3] Whatever the exact number of casualties, Rome had lost, irreplaceably, many thousands of its best legionary troops. Its long borders on the Rhine, the Danube, and in the east now lay exposed at a time when loyalty of the legions to a central command had been seriously weakened. Over the following decades, this mirror of an earlier period of stability would be shattered by a series of internal conflicts and external defeats.

By the time of Mursa, something had gone wrong in the military system that had permitted small numbers of troops to control large stretches of territory. To understand what had come apart, it is necessary to go back to examine the basis of Rome's success.

THE ROMAN STATE AT THE HEIGHT OF ITS POWER

The Roman Information Network

Roman society, like the civilizations that preceded it, was based on a combination of consent and constraint. Why would an individual consent to membership of the empire rather than attempt to flee beyond its borders or seek to overthrow it? Society has value to the individual primarily as a means of obtaining, storing, and transmitting information. In the case of the Sumerians, the development of logo-syllabic writing had permitted the storage of greatly increased quantities of data. Rather than do without the benefits that this information made possible – for example, the maintenance of extensive irrigation networks – the individual or family had consented to sacrifice a part of its time or income to the community. Taxation of this sort was thus a form of subscription fee to the urban communications network. The benefits of logo-syllabic writing were so obvious to the Akkadians and the Babylonians who succeeded the Sumerians that they adopted its main principles with little change.

One of the principal difficulties of the logo-syllabic system was the high cost of mastering the hundreds of word symbols retained from the pre-writing era. During the first half of the second millennium BC, the Semitic peoples of Palestine and Syria developed a streamlined form of writing that dropped the word signs, retaining only the compact set of syllabic notations. However, the resulting syllabary of some 30 symbols used by the Hebrews, Phoenicians, and other Semitic groups gave no indication of the vowel component of the syllable. The reader therefore had to infer the pronunciation of the vowel from the context in which the syllable appeared.

The first to discover a systematic means of indicating vowels were the Greeks. Early in the first millennium BC, they began adding a vowel indicator to each syllable. For example, instead of writing *t* for the syllable *ti*, they would add the second sign *y* to make *ty*. It soon became clear, however, that the symbol *t* now stood not for the whole syllable but only for the consonant, *t*. The result was the first true alphabet. In its standardized Ionic form, 24 written symbols represented the individual sounds (phonemes) of the spoken language. Originally, the Greeks wrote from right to left as the Semitic peoples had done. Then the practice of changing direction on alternate lines, like an ox drawing a plow, arose. Finally, by 500 BC, the custom of writing from left to right had become generalized in Greece. In Italy, the Greek alphabet was adopted in modified form by the Etruscans, who controlled the area around Florence. It was from the Etruscans that the Romans in turn borrowed most of the written symbols for their own alphabet. In its classical form, the Latin alphabet comprised 23 letters (J, V, and W were added subsequently).

The Graeco-Roman alphabet, with its limited number of symbols and its capacity to represent most spoken sounds, was much easier to learn than the cumbersome cuneiform script of the Sumerians. As a result, it became possible for a larger percentage of the population to learn to read and to write. Diffusion of information by means of writing was therefore less expensive for the Romans than it had been for the Sumerians and Akkadians. However, only a minority of the adult population of the empire could be considered literate. Moreover, the means of storage, through hand-written records, was essentially unchanged, as was the high cost of reproduction. The information system of the Roman Empire of Hadrian in the second century AD was therefore in many respects similar to that of the Akkadian and Sumerian Empire of Sargon the Great some 2,500 years earlier.

The Instruments of Conquest and Control

While consent is necessary for the cohesion of a community, it is not sufficient: constraint is also required. In terms of the means by which it constrained its citizens, the Roman Empire of the second century was a direct descendant of that of Sargon the Great over 2,000 years earlier. Each was a multi-ethnic state covering an extended territory. Tribute from the subject population financed an army large enough to put down any local resistance and defend against foreign invasion. The principal difference was in scale: a series of refinements in military techniques subsequent to Sargon enabled the Romans to control a territory and population many times greater than those of the Empire of Akkad.

Yet despite the evolution in military technology over the preceding two millennia, the basis of a ruler's power remained essentially unchanged. In the armies of the Sumerian cities, the basic element had been the line of heavy infantry in close formation. The soldiers had been armed with bronze-studded armor and bronze-tipped spears. During the first millennium BC, iron replaced bronze as the principal metal used to make weapons and armor. Iron's greater strength and lower cost permitted the addition of the sword to the standard equipment of the infantryman. However, more than 2,500 years after the victory of King Eanatum of Lagash, depicted in the Stele of the Vultures, the basic principles of warfare remained the same: an army used the cutting edge of a line of infantrymen with shock weapons to eat into its opponent's forces, the shield of each soldier protecting the flanks of his companions.

To be sure, the foot soldier was not the only element on the battlefield. The slow, clumsy chariots drawn by wild asses, introduced by the Sumerians to add mobility to their armies, had long disappeared. At first they had been replaced by lighter, faster chariots drawn by horses. By the eighth century BC, however, such vehicles no longer provided the main element of mobility. The Assyrian armies were making systematic use of cavalry – soldiers mounted on horseback – to harass enemy infantry and to pursue broken armies.[4] The use of mounted soldiers subsequently declined, after the Greeks discovered that disciplined heavy infantry presenting a wall of shields and swords could break up a cavalry charge.[5] Greek armies and early Roman armies used only small equestrian contingents. However, the Macedonians introduced heavy cavalry troops equipped with armor and spear, finding that they could be used effectively in shock combat against light and medium infantry.[6]

The Roman army of the first century AD represented the synthesis of this long line of development. The standard unit was the legion, a self-contained fighting force of about 6,000 men made up almost entirely of infantry.[7] Roughly half of this number were heavy infantry, each equipped with a large, oval shield, the *gladium* or short sword, and the *pilum* or heavy throwing spear, 3 m long. However, the legion also contained a small contingent of heavy infantry armed with the *hasta*, the traditional long thrusting spear, similar to that used by the Sumerians. In addition, the legion included light infantry armed with the sword, a small shield, and the *hasta velitaris*, a short, light javelin.[8] Since the relatively few *pila* and javelins were thrown before contact was made, it was the sword that constituted the principal offensive weapon.

To complement the solid but slow-moving line of legionary troops, the Romans relied on cavalry provided by their allies. In addition to its own small corps of 120 cavalry soldiers, each legion in the second century AD was accompanied by approximately the same number of auxiliary troops, of whom roughly one-third comprised horsemen.[9] The equestrian units were used for scouting and pursuit of fleeing soldiers. However, the mounted lancers were also effective as a shock element against light cavalry armed with bow and arrow and against undisciplined infantry.[10]

Despite the inclusion of these cavalry units, however, the Roman army of the early Christian era was basically an infantry force. It comprised some 150,000 to 175,000 legionary troops and about as many auxiliaries.[11] Of the total, only one soldier in six was mounted.

The External and Internal Margins of the Roman State

This force defended a territory whose boundaries stretched over three continents. The Roman Empire reached its greatest territorial limits under Trajan (reigned AD 98–117). At that time in Europe, in addition to Italy, Rome ruled over England, France, Belgium, the Iberian peninsula, Switzerland, south-west Germany, and all of the territory south of the Danube. To the north of the Danube, the Empire included the province of Dacia in present-day Romania. In Africa, Rome held all of the Mediterranean coast and Egypt. In Asia, it controlled a territory stretching from the Bosporus to the upper Tigris and Euphrates rivers and down into Palestine.

To protect the internal integrity of this vast territory, the Romans used a system of military leverage. The greater part of the strength of the Roman army was stationed near its northern and eastern borders. Of a total of 25 legions in AD 23, 16 were based along the Rhine, the Danube, and in

Syria. Seven of the remaining nine were in Spain, North Africa, and Egypt. A final two legions may have constituted a strategic reserve. They were stationed in Dalmatia, in north-eastern Yugoslavia, from where they could be called upon to defend Italy or be dispatched elsewhere as required. However, only about 10 percent of this total force was devoted to static defense. It was essentially a mobile field army distributed primarily in those sectors where the threats to security were greatest.[12]

The presence of the legions near the borders enabled Rome to keep pressure on client states and tribes outside the borders. These client states in turn served as a buffer around the empire, protecting its territory from attack by all but the most determined large groups of external invaders or from small bands of raiders. During the first half of the second century AD, under Hadrian, the imperial administration moved to close off the latter threat by instituting a preclusive system of defense around the empire's perimeter. A series of forts along the borders enabled the Roman army to move out to intercept attacking forces before they crossed into Roman territory.[13]

The efficiency of this defensive system was such that it made relatively modest demands on the society's resources. The backbone of Rome's economy was its agriculture and the vast majority of its inhabitants were peasants. Accordingly, it is not surprising that the main source of state revenues was a tax imposed on the rural sector. In the Republic of the first century BC, the tax rate in many of the provinces was the *decumae*, levied at one-tenth of total production.[14] As the burdens of administration were not significantly higher in the first century AD than they had been a hundred years earlier, an average tax rate of about 10 percent of production is a reasonable estimate. Such a rate, leaving by far the greater part of income in private hands, implied a relatively modest role for the state in the allocation of society's resources. The state's internal margin between private and public activity was therefore highly favorable to the private sector.

These, then, were the frontiers of the Roman state at the time of its greatest power. The Roman Empire was an extended political unit whose government intervened relatively little in the day-to-day functioning of its economy. Based on the informational scale economies of written records and the equally important military scale economies of heavy-infantry combat, it was the most efficient exchange network that the Western world had yet seen.

MILITARY PROBLEMS OF THE LATER ROMAN EMPIRE

Beginning in the last half of the second century AD, during the reign of Marcus Aurelius (161–180), the military system used by the Romans to defend their empire came under increasing pressure. In part, the problem was external. A serious threat came from the ruling Parthian dynasty in Iran. After a half-century of peace, they suddenly invaded Syria with their cavalry-based army in 162. Beginning in 166, the middle Danube frontier was penetrated by the Germanic Marcomanni and Quadi, whose tactics made use of mixed cavalry and infantry units.[15] Their raids, which penetrated into northern Italy, were thrown back only after bitter fighting. In the following decade, the lower Danube came under fierce attack from the Sarmatians, horsemen from central Asia.

However, the problem was also partly internal. The Roman response to the threats was weakened by the most serious internal divisions since the last days of the Republic. In 193, civil war broke out following the assassination of Marcus Aurelius' unpopular son, Commodus. It was only after four years of fighting, during which Roman legion was pitched against Roman legion, that Septimius Severus came out on top.

These three themes – conflict with Persia, incursions along the Rhine and Danube, and civil war – recurred with increased intensity over the following century and a half, particularly during a period of near-collapse from 235 to 268. Beginning in 213, a new German confederation, the Alemanni, who were known to the Romans as good horse soldiers, raided across the upper Rhine and Danube. According to the fourth-century Roman historian, Aurelius Victor, the Alemanni were "a numerous people who [fought] wonderfully on horseback."[16] In 259–60, they penetrated as far as southern France and Spain, as well as into northern Italy. Another serious threat came from the East German Goths, horsemen from the steppes between the Dnieper and the Don, who in 214 began to raid Roman territory south of the lower Danube.[17] Finally, the Sassanids, who had overthrown the Parthian dynasty in Iran, decided to profit from Rome's troubles in Europe. In 241, they invaded Roman Mesopotamia and Syria. With an improved administration and siege capacity and the traditionally strong Persian cavalry, the new regime represented a much more dangerous threat than its predecessor.

Internally, for Rome, this was a period of great political instability and frequent civil war between rival aspirants to the throne. During the 50 years from 235 to 284, there were 26 emperors of whom 25 were murdered.[18]

The Roman Response

Rome eventually survived these difficulties. Indeed, the external borders of the middle of the fourth century were very similar to those at the death of Claudius some 300 years earlier (the most important difference was the addition of Britain in the first century). In fact, however, a number of profound changes had occurred. Most obvious, perhaps, was an increase in the total size of the army. From 300,000 at the death of Augustus, it had grown to 400,000 under Septimius Severus (193–211) and to 500,000 under Diocletian (284–305).[19] In addition to this increased labor, the army fought with a much greater stock of capital for defensive purposes. The major cities were now walled. Moreover, the empire was surrounded by a powerful network of fortifications laid out in depth.[20]

Within the army, the proportion of mounted troops was raised, with an increasing fraction of equestrian units consisting of heavy cavalry. Large contingents of auxiliary light cavalry armed with missile weapons had first been introduced into the Roman army by Marius in 105 BC.[21] Heavy cavalry with spears had been used under Trajan (98–117), with armored heavy cavalry appearing under Hadrian (117–138).[22] In the second half of the second century, mounted auxiliaries of all types represented roughly one-fifth of the total number of troops; that is, 80,000 mounted soldiers of all types out of a total of 400,000.[23] By the time of Constantine, this percentage had increased even further. Cavalry made up one-quarter of the average Roman army, with the proportion much higher in the eastern regions that faced the Persians and Arabians. Moreover, instead of being assigned a secondary status behind the infantry legions, cavalry became the elite division of the army, the legions having been stripped in size from around 5,000 to 1,000 men each.[24]

Other changes suggest that military practice was evolving to adapt to new conditions. In order to reduce its vulnerability to heavy cavalry, infantry was forced to adopt tighter, more phalangeal formations.[25] In these denser groupings, relying increasingly on flat barbarian-style shields for protection, Roman soldiers gradually abandoned body armor.[26] Combined, these measures had the unfortunate consequence of leaving foot soldiers more vulnerable to missile weapons, particularly bows and arrows, whose use sharply increased. The result was inevitably an increase in the number of casualties and hence in the cost of waging war. Vegetius, the late fourth or fifth-century Roman military historian, lamented, "our soldiers fought the Goths without any protection for head and chest and were often beaten by archers."[27]

In short, the Julio-Claudian defense system based on concentrated shock warfare with disciplined infantry had been radically altered. Each of these modifications – the growth in the size of the army, the increasing use of cavalry, the construction of static defenses, the use of missile weapons, and the reduction in protective armor – raised the cost of military control of a given territory. It would appear that something had occurred that undermined the effectiveness of the infantry-based military techniques that had enabled Rome to dominate the Mediterranean world.

CHANGES IN THE INTERNAL AND EXTERNAL MARGINS

The changes in military techniques during the late Roman Empire were accompanied by shifts in the state's internal and external margins. Changes in the degree of state intervention came first, as the empire attempted to maintain its existing borders. Inheritance taxes levied on Roman citizens were an important source of revenue. In 212, to pay for the increased size of the army, Severus' son, Caracalla, extended Roman citizenship to all the inhabitants of the provinces, thereby making them eligible for inheritance taxes. Another revenue source suited to the crisis years of the middle and late third century was currency debasement. Frequent recourse to this temporary expedient reduced the value of the denarius to 10.5 percent of its previous value by the end of that century.[28]

It might be thought that the most effective means of maximizing tax revenues from the vast territories administered by Rome would be to auction off the right to collect taxes in each province to the highest bidder. Tax farming of this sort was practiced by the Roman Republic.[29] However, as Rome's empire grew, there proved no effective means to prevent distant tax farmers from collecting more than the rates stipulated by law, thereby weakening the long-run fiscal base. As a result, early in the Principate, tax farming in the imperial provinces was replaced by the state fiscal bureaucracy.[30]

The bulk of Rome's revenues came from levies on agriculture: over 90 percent of tax receipts came from a combined land and poll tax assessed on agricultural property and on the rural population.[31] By the end of the third century AD, because of inflation, the proceeds from those levies that were assessed in monetary terms were no longer sufficient to pay for the greatly increased military presence along the borders. Accordingly, Diocletian introduced a ruthless system of taxes in kind whose aim was to assure that his troops were adequately provisioned.[32] However, even these measures were not sufficient to attract the necessary manpower. He therefore resorted to annual conscription, compelling landholders to provide men from their estates. His eventual successor, Constantine, took the further step of requiring the sons of veterans to serve in the army.[33]

By 360 under Constantius II, the victor at Mursa, taxes had been raised even further. According to Aurelius Victor, those levied by Diocletian now appeared *"modestia tolerabilis"* compared with the *"pernicies"* required to support the current imperial administration.[34] Writing in 364, Themistius declared that the rate of taxation had approximately doubled in the previous 40 years. However, even the new rates proved insufficient. The next century saw the introduction of a sales tax.[35] The oldest surviving imperial fiscal records date from the reign of the eastern emperor Justinian (reigned 527–565). They show tax rates on agricultural land belonging to the church amounting to over one-quarter of the gross yield. In the same period, taxes on land in private hands amounted to almost one-third of the yield. Thus the privileged categories of landowners paid over twice as much as provincials in the first century BC and ordinary landholders some three times as much.[36]

Inevitably, under the new military conditions it was necessary to accept changes in the empire's territorial boundaries. During the period of relative peace of the first and second centuries, Rome had added Dacia (Romania) and the critical Rhine–Danube triangle, the *agri decumates*, in south-western Germany to its territory. In the third century, however, barbarian pressure forced the abandonment of these lands and withdrawal to the Rhine–Danube frontier. For long periods in this century, particularly during the reign of Gallienus (253–68), large sections of the empire were virtually independent. During the interval from 259 to 274, Postumus established a provincial empire in Gaul, Britain, and Spain. Similarly, from 259 to 271, a considerable area in the eastern Mediterranean, including Egypt, fell into the hands of the Roman-Arab Odenathus and his wife Zenobia. It was only under Aurelian (270–275) that Roman control was re-established in these key provinces.

By 292 Diocletian realized that under existing conditions, the empire was too vast to be administered from a central point. Accordingly, he divided it into four regions: he himself controlled Thrace, Egypt, and Asia; his associate or "Caesar," Galerius, administered the Danube provinces; his co-emperor or "Augustus," Maximian, controlled Italy and Africa; the other Caesar, Constantius, ruled over Postumus's former Gallic empire. At the same time, Diocletian greatly decentralized the civilian administration, setting up a separate bureaucratic structure within each of twelve dioceses into which he divided the empire.

There are, of course, many ways to slice a cake. Unfortunately, when the leaders of this tetrarchy resigned in 305, no one could agree on just how and among whom the empire should be divided. There followed almost two decades of civil war before the son of Constantius, Constantine, finally seized complete control of the entire empire. He in turn instituted a series of reforms that have come under intense criticism from Gibbon to the present.[37] The most important change was to strip the borders of their best troops to permit the formation of mobile cavalry-based field units (*comitatenses*) stationed centrally. Luttwak has argued that the result was a deepening of the defense-in-depth strategy initiated by his predecessors.[38] Henceforth, it would be much less probable that invaders would be stopped outside or at the borders. The idea was essentially to delay any major incursion by use of the border troops (*limitanei*) until the field army could be brought into play. Since the bulk of any fighting would occur on Roman territory, however, this strategy in effect implied a shrinking of the *effective* frontiers of the empire to a dimension which could be controlled by mobile centrally located forces.

Subsequent events showed that even this strategy was overly ambitious. Upon Constantine's death, the empire was divided into Eastern and Western sections. It was seldom to be controlled by a single person again, the division becoming permanent in 395. In 476 the Western Empire was extinguished, its former territory being divided among the four main Germanic groups, the Franks, Visigoths, Ostrogoths, and Vandals. Although the regions held by the latter two peoples were later recovered temporarily by the Eastern Empire, Rome never regained its former boundaries. Finally, in the ninth and tenth centuries, the Mediterranean world broke up into hundreds of small states (see figure 3.1).

In the other three centers of civilization on the Eurasian land mass, similar internal and external pressures against the centralization of power were felt during this period. In the Middle East, the Persian Empire was badly shaken by nomad invasions, civil war, and conflict with a temporarily reinvigorated Eastern Roman Empire during the fifth and sixth centuries. By 650 it had fallen prey to the Arab followers of Mohammed. Although the latter subsequently expanded their territory into a band that stretched from Spain to Pakistan, their initial political unity was soon broken. Between 850 and 1500, the Middle East and North Africa were divided into numerous small and medium states. Similarly, in India, the Gupta Empire was overthrown by the White Huns in 480. It would take a further millennium before the greater part of the subcontinent could again be governed by a single administration – under the Mogul dynasty in the sixteenth century. Finally, in China, the Han Empire collapsed at the beginning of the third century. There followed four centuries of internal strife and external attacks before the empire was reunited under the Sui dynasty around 600. Over the following millennium, there were alternating periods of centralized rule and imperial decline (the latter occurring in the tenth, fourteenth, and sixteenth centuries). It was not until the mid-seventeenth century, under the Manchu Ch'ing dynasty, that the dual threats of nomad invasion and feudal breakup were finally dispelled.

It should be noted that the Mongol rulers of the thirteenth century briefly controlled a larger area than any land empire before or since. Because their victories were based on disciplined heavy and light cavalry, their success would seem to contradict the thesis that there was a trend to smaller states over the millenium from AD 400 to 1400.[39] However, since the Mongol Empire developed no mechanism to assure its own survival, it cannot be considered a viable state in the same sense as the Roman, Han, and Sassanid empires. Based on pillage and conquest, the Mongol Empire was inherently unstable: once it ceased to expand, its rapid breakup and collapse were inevitable.

MILITARY AND ECONOMIC EXPLANATIONS OF ROME'S FAILURE

The changes in territorial boundaries that accompanied the fall of Roman civilization in Western Europe between the second and ninth centuries AD have long been a favorite subject of discussion. The German historian, Alexander Demandt has compiled a list of over 400 explanations for the fall of Rome.[40] Most of these hypotheses, however, fall into one or the other of two categories.

According to one approach, the reasons for the decline of Roman influence and the subsequent rise of feudalism in Western Europe were military, the principal factors being increased external pressure and the flawed defensive strategy chosen by the region's military leaders. Among modern historians, A. H. M. Jones and Arther Ferrill placed the crucial events at the time of the barbarian invasions in the late fourth and fifth centuries. Ferrill, following Edward N. Luttwak, argued that earlier decisions by Constantine – the barbarization of the army and the creation of a central reserve – weakened the capacity of the Empire to respond to this threat. For Heinrich Brunner and subsequent scholars of the rise of feudalism, however, the crucial change occurred in the eighth century, when Charles Martel reorganized the Frankish kingdom along feudal lines in response to Arab attacks from Spain.

One difficulty with the external-pressure argument is that many of the principal battles of the critical fourth century were not between Romans and barbarians but between Romans and other Romans and their allies. Casualty figures for ancient battles are notoriously inaccurate. However, according to one recent estimate, in the First Battle of Adrianople between Constantine and Licinius in 323, there were more than 20,000 casualties.[41] The battle of Mursa in 351 between Magnentius and Constantius left some 27,000 casualties.[42] Finally, at the Second Battle of Aquileia (Battle of the Frigidus) in 394 between Eugenius and Theodosius, a large percentage of the more than 200,000 troops involved perished in two days of fighting.[43] Similarly, in the eighth century, the leaders of the Franks spent at least as much time fighting among themselves or against other Christians as they did fighting Moslems. In the words of White, "Martel turned his attention to Islam only after he had consolidated his realm."[44] As for flaws in Rome's defensive strategy, Benjamin Isaac has recently argued that the Roman army in the east was never conceived as a defensive force but was intended rather as an instrument for conquest and for the control of captured territory[45]. If it ultimately failed in this role, the explanation would appear to have more to do with increases in the cost of conquest and control of territory than with strategic errors.

An alternative approach argues that the causes of the change were what might be termed economic; namely, increased bureaucracy, higher taxes, class conflict and a decline in agriculture, trade, and industry. Rostovtzeff, Bernardi and others have dated Rome's decline in the fourth and fifth centuries and explained it by internal economic collapse.[46] Their versions are quite consistent with Olson's thesis that over time the formation of interest groups within a society gradually reduces economic efficiency.[47] Pirenne and Friedman, however, place the transition in the eighth and ninth centuries, arguing that the principal factor was a decline in trade resulting from the Arab conquests.[48]

If the problem was economic, however, it must be explained why the Eastern Roman Empire survived the barbarian invasions and, although reduced in scale, the rise of Islam. More generally, any attempt to explain the reduction in the size of political units between the first and the ninth centuries must deal with an obvious fact: no European state with anything approaching the frontiers of the Roman Empire has ever been re-established since, except for brief intervals, despite the decline in barbarian and Moslem attacks and the revival of the European economy from the near autarky of the Dark Ages.

The Technological Factor

Ultimately, the search for a coherent explanation for the observed contraction of territorial boundaries and decrease in market activity accompanying the decline of Roman civilization hinges on the discovery of a factor that is irreversible. Disruptions to trade or the formation of interest groups within a given social structure are unacceptable because they too are likely to be temporary. Similar problems apply to other possible explanations for the fall of Rome. For example, McNeill suggested that an important factor in the decline of Roman civilization was a series of outbreaks of infectious diseases that killed large numbers of adults in the densely populated cities of the Mediterranean world but had little effect on the scattered nomadic peoples of central Asia.[49] Another possible theory is that climatic variation in the homelands of nomadic peoples set off great migrations that exerted unbearable pressure on imperial borders. These explanations are not satisfactory since their effects would tend to disappear within a few generations.

In a penetrating essay, White suggested a possible candidate for such a factor; namely, the introduction of the stirrup into warfare.[50] He argued that in permitting horse, rider, and lance to be joined into a single fighting instrument, the stirrup made possible a new type of warfare based on mounted shock combat. In the near-barter economy of the eighth-century Frankish kingdom, the only means of financing such expenditure was to endow an equestrian elite with land and the rights to its income.

One troublesome fact for White's argument of the impact of the stirrup is that the metal stirrup was apparently known in Eastern Europe many centuries before the events he describes. White himself noted that miniature iron stirrups have been found in the Soviet Union dating from the first century AD.[51] Millar asserted that the Sarmatians had introduced the use of the stirrup by the second century BC.[52] Even if one accepts that the stirrup had a great impact when introduced into Western Europe in the eighth century, there remains the question of continuity. Was it this single development that terminated Roman civilization in the West? Or was the transition to feudalism merely the final step in a process that had begun much earlier? There also remains the relation between military and economic events. Was the decline in the market economy in the West a necessary condition for the rise of feudal political institutions, as White implies? Or was it itself a result of technological change?

Since White was concerned with the emergence of feudalism, he did not analyze in detail the implications of earlier developments in mounted combat. However, the impact of innovations in cavalry warfare on the Roman Empire dates back to at least 53 BC. In that year the Parthians annihilated a Roman legionary army under the triumvir Crassus at Carrhae in Syria. Their tactic was to attack the legions with heavy cavalry to stop their forward motion and force them into tight formation. Immobile and closely grouped, the Roman foot soldiers then made easy targets for Persian mounted archers. What was new in this battle was the introduction of chain armor for both the horse and rider by the Parthians. The new armored heavy cavalry performed a dual role, keeping the enemy infantry in check while at the same time protecting the Persian light cavalry from Roman attack.[53]

The heavy horses that made the new type of warfare possible had been developed several centuries earlier in eastern Iran. They were strong enough to carry armored riders and their weapons along with additional armor to protect the animals themselves from enemy missiles.[54] Not only were the horse and rider better protected, but also they made up a greater mass for shock combat with infantry. A further and equally important improvement occurred in the first century AD when the saddle began to be introduced into Roman territory to replace the horse-blanket or saddle-cushion.[55] The result was a more stable platform for bowmen or lancers. Combined, then, these two innovations greatly strengthened the position of cavalry relative to its traditional competitor, infantry.

The first to exploit if not to invent these techniques were the Sarmatians, an Indo-European people from central Asia who gave Marcus Aurelius considerable trouble at the beginning of Rome's grave border problems in the late second century. They used a combination of light cavalry, armed with bows, and heavy armored cavalry equipped with lances and long swords.[56] By the beginning of the first century AD, the various Sarmatian tribes controlled an extensive territory extending from the Caspian Sea in the East to the Danube in the West. For the following four centuries, they were to constitute arguably Rome's most consistently threatening enemy apart from the Persians, particularly on the Danube frontier. Both the Romans and the Germans recruited Sarmatian horsemen for their forces from an early date, and improvements to the Germanic cavalry were inspired in part at least by the Sarmatian example.[57]

Germanic Cavalry

There is some disagreement over the extent to which the German tribes such as the Goths and Alemanni used cavalry before the fifth century. According to one source, only the Franks were primarily foot soldiers, the other German tribes mixing cavalry with infantry.[58] However, others have argued that the Germans fought primarily on foot.[59] One of the key studies of this question is an essay by E. A. Thompson. Although Thompson recognized that the Germans did have good cavalry, he suggested that because of the cost of maintaining horses, it was probably limited to the nobility.[60] The archaeological evidence from Germany and Scandinavia supports this position.[61]

Nevertheless, the fact remains that by 378, in the initial phase of the Second Battle of Adrianople, the Ostrogoth cavalry was able to annihilate a force of 10,000 to 20,000 Roman cavalry.[62] An interpretation consistent with the available evidence is that from Caesar's time the Germanic cavalry had been good but limited in numbers. In the forces of the Marcomannic chief, Maroboduus, in the early first century, roughly one soldier in 20 was a horseman.[63] Over the first two centuries AD, the Germanic tribes in the north-east, such as the Goths and Vandals, who came into direct contact with steppe nomads from Asia, gradually improved their cavalry and increased its relative importance.[64] At Adrianople perhaps half of the total Gothic force was made up of Ostrogoth and allied horsemen. The other half, predominantly Visigoths, was made up of infantrymen.[65] Further westward diffusion of the use of cavalry as the dominant arm was, however, very slow – perhaps because of lack of adequate pasture for large numbers of horses.[66]

Military Scale Economies

What connection could there be between improvements to cavalry combat and the inward shift of territorial boundaries? Many have tried to explain why the observed shift in military techniques toward cavalry at the expense of infantry might have been unfavorable to Rome. The German historian, Franz Altheim, argued that since the barbarians were better horsemen than the Mediterranean peoples, it was inevitable that they should eventually capture the throne.[67] But if so, why were the Roman boundaries never restored under barbarian rulers? For Andreski, centralization of power will follow improvements in the art of attack.[68] Thus Rome's expansion in the Mediterranean area was due to its mastery of the art of siegecraft.[69] Decentralization occurs when defense becomes the stronger aspect of warfare. Because the barbarians were never able to develop skills of siege warfare, their kingdoms were smaller than the empire of their predecessors.[70] But if the offense–defense theory is correct, cavalry with its greater mobility should favor the offense and therefore centralization. Precisely the opposite seems to have been the case during the Roman Empire.

A possible link between cavalry and Rome's fall is to be found in the concept of military scale economies. Bean argued that because centralized training was less important for cavalry than for infantry, a greater emphasis on equestrian units permitted decentralization.[71] However, the key lies not in training economies but in the relation between the size of a military force and its destructive power, as measured by the ratio of casualties suffered by the two sides when a small force comes up against a larger one. In the case of infantry, from the Spartans onward it had been realized that there was safety in numbers, that a wall of shields could not be broken easily by opposing troops or light cavalry. As Luttwak observed, from the time of Sparta onwards, cavalry had been obsolete against disciplined foot soldiers.[72] However, the soft underbelly of such a force – its flanks and rear – were vulnerable. Accordingly, the objective of classical infantry battles was to attain local numerical superiority by flanking, enveloping, or penetrating an enemy's line.

Although casualty data for ancient battles are invariably open to question, there is considerable evidence that if one infantry army could disrupt its opponent's shield wall, the losses it inflicted were far greater than those it suffered itself. For example, Carthaginian casualties at Zama in 202 BC may have been more than ten times those of Rome. At Pharsalus in 48 BC, Pompey's losses may have outnumbered those of Caesar by more than seven to one.[73]

In short, there were great economies of scale in the use of disciplined infantry. It was these scale economies which in AD 23 enabled a relatively small force of 150,000 Romans and roughly the same number of auxiliaries to control and protect a population of 50 million in an empire which stretched from the English Channel to the Nile.[74] As perfected by the post-Flavian emperors in the late first and early second centuries AD, the Roman military constituted what Luttwak has called a preclusive defense system, designed to suppress any potential threat outside of the borders before it could spill over into imperial territory. Although the legions included small equestrian units (reintroduced under Augustus), the Romans relied on the auxiliary forces for the bulk of their cavalry support.[75]

One might have expected increased use of cavalry to lower the cost of controlling territory by permitting more rapid movements of centrally based forces. However, this off-battlefield effect seems to have been more than offset by reduced scale economies on the battlefield. Cavalry fighting tended to be much more individualistic than infantry combat. Although efforts were made to impose organization and discipline on equestrian units, cavalry combat was essentially one man on a horse against another man on a horse replicated many times. It therefore offered few occasions for economies of scale. This conclusion is supported by estimates showing roughly equal casualties to both sides in battles of the fourth century AD, after the proportion of mounted troops to foot soldiers had been considerably increased. In the battles between Constantine and Licinius in AD 323, each side suffered very heavy losses. Similarly, at Mursa in AD 351, Constantius and Magnentius may *each* have lost 25 to 30 percent of his soldiers.[76] In addition, increased use of cavalry appears to have enhanced the possibility for a beaten army having suffered heavy losses to escape, with the remains of its force intact and available to fight again at a later date. Compare, for example, the decisive civil war battles of the first century BC with the three battles just mentioned and with the civil war of AD 314. In the latter cases, the defeated commander managed to retreat in sufficient strength to represent a continued threat.

Military theorists have long noted the slightness of the gains to the coordination of cavalry combat and the effectiveness of mounted troops against infantry only as long as the numbers fighting remained small. The Byzantine emperor, Leo VI the Wise, writing in the ninth century, advised the commanders of his well-drilled cavalry based armies to avoid shock combat with the undisciplined Frank and Lombard horsemen. "So formidable is the charge of the Frankish chivalry with their broadsword, lance and shield," he wrote, "that it is best to avoid pitched battle with them."[77] Clausewitz recommended that cavalry be used alone against infantry only when the latter was dispersed. "Useful as cavalry may be against single bodies of broken demoralized troops, still when opposed to the bulk of the beaten Army it becomes again only the auxiliary arm."[78]

As a result, any change that favored cavalry relative to infantry may be seen to have reduced the economies of scale in applying military force. Here then was the threat posed by the introduction of the saddle and the heavy horse.

TECHNOLOGY AND THE FALL OF ROME

It is time to draw the threads of the discussion together. The Roman Empire constituted the largest and most efficiently administered information network that the western world had known. Why did it come apart? The beginning of Rome's decline can be dated from the latter half of the second century AD. From the outset, this decline was characterized by a reduced capacity to defend the empire's borders against external threats, by frequent civil wars, by increases in taxes, and by reductions in the territory which the Romans attempted to control from a central point. These changes coincided with the introduction of a number of innovations in cavalry warfare that led to lower economies of scale in the application of military force.

The resulting increase in the cost of controlling territory meant that a higher level of taxes was required to permit control of a political unit of a given size. However, the necessary rise in state intervention was not possible in a state the size of the Roman empire of the early second century AD. The consent for greater intervention and the effective coordination of dispersed public employees were only possible in a more homogeneous state with shorter lines of communication. To reach a new political equilibrium consistent with the higher levels of taxation required to finance the new military technology, there had to be a decline in the size of the typical political unit.

It may be concluded that the period of Roman history from the late second to the early fourth centuries AD is an example of the effect of a change in military technology on the ability of the state to defend its territory. Viewed from this perspective, the collapse of Roman power in the West in the fifth century appears to represent simply a set of points on a trajectory that began much earlier and would continue on for several more centuries. The subsequent transition to feudalism following the introduction of the stirrup in the eighth century, as analyzed by White, represented a continuation of this trend toward smaller states with higher tax levels.

The victory of Constantius II at Mursa in AD 351 thus provides a potential key to understanding the decline in Roman civilization in Western Europe between the second and the ninth centuries AD. It also helps to explain the accompanying rise in levels of taxation. Despite the hundreds of books and articles that have been written on this subject, there is still no convincing explanation for Rome's failure. Military interpretations of these developments are unable to demonstrate why the collapse was accompanied by civil conflict that was at least as costly as external invasion. Economic explanations are incapable of accounting for the continued survival of the Eastern Roman Empire after the fall of Rome itself.

The defeat of the crack western infantry legions at Mursa suggests that a consistent explanation for these events lies in the gradual adoption of a new military technology. These innovations destroyed the returns to scale in the application of military force upon which Rome's pyramid of power was based. The introduction of the first two components of this new technology, the saddle and the heavy horse, in the first century AD, was followed by the contraction in effective external boundaries of the Roman Empire and a rise in taxation. As White argued, the third component, the stirrup, appears to have precipitated the final eclipse of Roman civilization in the Frankish Kingdom and the rise of feudal institutions.

In short, Rome's decline from the latter half of the second century onward appears to have occurred for both military and economic reasons. The boundaries of the mid-second century AD could be maintained only by resort to a level of taxation which, because of its crippling effects on economic incentives, could not be sustained. Or to express the same idea differently, with the existing inflow of public revenues, the empire was vulnerable to attack, both from hostile external enemies and from its own generals. Each could offer better protection than the imperial administration for the same level of taxation but within a narrower set of borders. The precipitating factor in this decline seems to have been a series of innovations in cavalry warfare that reduced the economies of scale in applying military force.

NOTES

1 See Edward Gibbon, *The History of the Decline and Fall of the Roman Empire* (Peter Fenelon Collier, New York, 1899), vol. II, pp. 123–6; Richard Humble, *Warfare in the Ancient World* (Cassell, 1980), p. 238; David Eggenberger, *An Encyclopedia of Battles*, 2nd edn (Dover, 1985), p. 290.
2 Gibbon, *The Decline and Fall of the Roman Empire*, p. 125, n. 79.
3 Eggenberger, *An Encyclopedia of Battles*, p. 290.
4 Humble, *Warfare in the Ancient World*, pp. 30–1.
5 Edward N. Luttwak, *The Grand Strategy of the Roman Empire from the First Century AD to the Third* (Johns Hopkins, 1976), p. 43.
6 Humble, *Warfare in the Ancient World*, p. 171.
7 Luttwak, *The Grand Strategy of the Roman Empire*, p. 16.
8 Ibid., p. 40.
9 Ibid., pp. 14–15.

10 Ibid., p. 43.
11 Ibid., p. 16.
12 Ibid., p. 18.
13 Ibid., p. 74.
14 A. H. M. Jones, *The Roman Economy* (Blackwell, 1974), p. 83.
15 R. Ernest Dupuy and Trevor N. Dupuy, *The Encyclopedia of Military History from* 3500 BC *to the Present,* 2nd edn (Harper and Row, 1986), p. 134.
16 E. A. Thompson, "Early Germanic warfare," *Past and Present,* 14 (1958), p. 6.
17 Dupuy and Dupuy, *The Encyclopedia of Military History,* p. 138.
18 Crane Brinton, John B. Christopher, Robert Lee Wolff, and Robin W. Winks, *A History of Civilization,* 6th edn, vol. I (Prentice-Hall, 1984), p. 83.
19 Dupuy and Dupuy, *The Encyclopedia of Military History,* pp. 147–8.
20 Luttwak, *The Grand Strategy of the Roman Empire,* p. 176.
21 Dupuy and Dupuy, *The Encyclopedia of Military History,* p. 98.
22 Luttwak, *The Grand Strategy of the Roman Empire,* p. 186.
23 Ibid., p. 71.
24 Arther Ferrill, *The Fall of the Roman Empire* (Thames and Hudson, 1986), p. 49.
25 Dupuy and Dupuy, *The Encyclopedia of Military History,* p. 150.
26 Ferrill, *The Fall of the Roman Empire,* pp. 50, 145.
27 Ibid., p. 129.
28 Jones, *The Roman Economy,* p. 168.
29 See Margaret Levi, *Of Rule and Revenue* (University of California Press, 1988).
30 Carolyn Webber and Aaron Wildavsky, *A History of Taxation and Expenditure in the Western World* (Simon and Schuster, 1986), pp. 113–19.
31 Jones, *The Roman Economy,* p. 83.
32 Luttwak, *The Grand Strategy of the Roman Empire,* p. 177.
33 Ferrill, *The Fall of the Roman Empire,* p. 43.
34 Jones, *The Roman Economy,* p. 83.
35 Ibid., p. 82.
36 Ibid., p. 83.
37 Ferrill, *The Fall of the Roman Empire,* pp. 15, 43–50.
38 Luttwak, *The Grand Strategy of the Roman Empire,* pp. 127–190.
39 I am indebted to Gordon Tullock for this observation.
40 Alexander Demandt, *Der Fall Roms* (C. H. Beck, Munich, 1984), p. 11.
41 Eggenberger, *An Encyclopedia of Battles,* p. 4.
42 Ibid., p. 290.
43 Ferrill, *The Fall of the Roman Empire,* pp. 71–5.
44 Lynn White, Jr, *Medieval Technology and Social Change* (Oxford University Press, 1964), p. 11.
45 Benjamin Isaac, *The Limits of Empire: The Roman Army in the East* (Clarendon, 1990).
46 See Michael I. Rostovtzeff, *The Social and Economic History of the Roman Empire* 2nd edn, 2 vols, (Oxford University Press, 1957); Aurelio Bernardi, "The economic problems of the Roman Empire at the time of its decline," in *The Economic Decline of Empires,* ed. Carlo M. Cipolla (Methuen, 1970), pp. 16–83.
47 Mancur Olson, *The Rise and Decline of Nations* (Yale University Press, 1982).
48 See Henri Pirenne, *Medieval Cities: Their Origins and the Revival of Trade* (Princeton University Press, 1925); David Friedman, "A theory of the size and shape of nations," *Journal of Political Economy,* 85 (1977), pp. 59–78.
49 William H. McNeill, *Plagues and Peoples* (University of Chicago Press, 1976).
50 White, *Medieval Technology,* pp. 1–38.
51 Ibid., p. 16, n. 6.

52 Fergus Millar, *The Roman Empire and its Neighbours*, 2nd edn (Holmes and Meier, 1981), p. 284.

53 Luttwak, *The Grand Strategy of the Roman Empire*, pp. 43–4.

54 William H. McNeill, *The Rise of the West: A History of the Human Community* (University of Chicago Press, 1963), pp. 321–2.

55 White, *Medieval Technology*, p. 7.

56 Millar, *The Roman Empire and its Neighbours*, pp. 284–5.

57 Ibid., pp. 285, 299, and 314.

58 Dupuy and Dupuy, *The Encyclopedia of Military History*, pp. 134–6.

59 Luttwak, *The Grand Strategy of the Roman Empire*, p. 71; and Ferrill, *The Fall of the Roman Empire*, p. 144.

60 Thompson, "Early Germanic warfare," p. 5.

61 Malcolm Todd, *The Northern Barbarians* (Hutchinson, 1975).

62 Dupuy and Dupuy, *The Encyclopedia of Military History*, p. 157.

63 Todd, *The Northern Barbarians*, p. 174.

64 See E. Darko, "Influences touraniennes sur l'évolution de l'art militaire des Grecs, Romains et Byzantins," *Byzantion* 12 (1937), p. 142; Millar, *The Roman Empire and its Neighbours*, pp. 314–15.

65 Dupuy and Dupuy, *The Encyclopedia of Military History*, p. 157.

66 See Ferrill, *The Fall of the Roman Empire*, p. 142.

67 Franz Altheim, *Le déclin du monde antique: Examen des causes de la décadence* (Payot, 1953), pp. 13–14.

68 Stanislav Andreski, *Military Organization and Society* (University of California Press, 1968), p. 75.

69 Ibid., p. 77.

70 Ibid., p. 75.

71 Richard Bean, "War and the birth of the nation state," *Journal of Economic History*, 33 (1973), p. 208.

72 Luttwak, *The Grand Strategy of the Roman Empire*, p. 43.

73 Dupuy and Dupuy, *The Encyclopedia of Military History*, pp. 71, 110.

74 Ferrill, *The Fall of the Roman Empire*, p. 26.

75 Luttwak, *The Grand Strategy of the Roman Empire*, p. 43.

76 Dupuy and Dupuy, *The Encyclopedia of Military History*, pp. 152–3.

77 Quoted in Ibid., p. 219.

78 Carl von Clausewitz, *On War*, tr. J. J. Graham (Routledge and Kegan Paul, 1956), vol. 1, p. 294.

4

Hexagon Dynamics

Over the course of the fifteenth century, the boundaries of the territory controlled by the French monarchy were pushed outward into the hexagonal shape of present-day France. Previous studies have explained the extension of royal power in France and other Western European countries during this period as a consequence of either the professionalization of military combat or the commercialization of economic activity. However, neither approach is able to account for the sudden turnaround in the fortunes of Charles VII during the decade from 1435 to 1445. Trade flows during this period were at their lowest point in centuries, while the professional army had not yet been introduced. The key factor in the formation of the French hexagon appears to have been an innovation in artillery techniques that increased military scale economies. However, the introduction of this new technology was accompanied by a reduction in state economic intervention rather than the increase suggested in other studies.

Figure 4.1   Boundaries of the French state in 1435 and 1491.
(*Source: The New Cambridge Modern History Atlas*, 1979, p. 107.)

During the winter of 1438, packs of wolves roamed the suburbs of Paris. Driven desperate by the exceptional cold, they would occasionally penetrate into the city. There they would kill and eat any children they came upon before being driven off. Meanwhile, the population of the city was slowly starving. An attack of smallpox struck, killing thousands of people already weakened by malnutrition.[1]

Much of the city's food supply was usually shipped up the River Seine from the north-west or down its tributary, the Marne, from the north-east. However, the "goddams," as the French called the occupying English troops, controlled strong-points on each river, depriving Paris of its most important sources of provisions. Despite the campaigns of the following spring and summer, little relief came to the beleaguered city.

One of the English-held strong-points was the town of Meaux, on the Marne river some 30 km to the north-east of Paris. The town itself, on the right bank of the river, was fortified. A bridge linked it to a powerful fortress on the left bank built on a point of land formed by a bend in the river. In the spring of 1439, the French king, Charles VII, ordered the commander of his forces, Richemont, to attempt to retake Meaux. During a three-week siege, in July and August of that year, the French built seven forts around the town. Under the command of Gaspard Bureau, they also set up several batteries of cannon. The effectiveness of the French artillery was decisive: after three weeks of shelling, the royal forces stormed the ramparts and took the town by assault.

At this point, an English army arrived from Normandy to relieve the troops in the fortress. The besiegers were now in turn besieged. The English forces managed to recapture two of Meaux's supporting forts and resupply their garrison in the fortress across the river. However, lacking adequate heavy artillery, they proved unable to break through the town's hastily repaired defenses. After a few weeks, the English commander gave the order to retreat and the foreign troops returned to Normandy. Isolated, the English garrison in the fortress on the left bank then had little choice but to surrender.[2] In two short months, the stranglehold on Paris had been broken.

The operation at Meaux was small compared to the great battles of ancient times: fewer than 7,000 men took part on the French side.[3] Although it relieved the pressure on Paris, it still left Normandy, Guienne in the south-west, and parts of the Ile-de-France to the north and west of Paris in English hands. Nevertheless, this victory marked a turning point in the fortunes of Charles VII and, more generally, in the efforts of West European kings to control the vast territories over which they were the nominal rulers.

THE SIZE AND SHAPE OF THE MEDIEVAL STATE

How are the territorial boundaries between states determined? In the simplest terms, one may see political borders as the outcome of two opposing forces. Economies of scale in the application of military force tend to push the boundaries of the typical state outward, while the loss of control and decline in popular support that tend to occur as distance from the administrative center increases limit such expansion.[4] If population and resources were distributed uniformly, the ideal shape of a political unit might therefore appear to be a circle with radius equal to the distance at which scale economies are exactly offset by rising costs of control. Anyone who has played with a compass and paper will realize, however, that the problem of using non-overlapping circles of identical radius as the basis of political boundaries is that they leave unoccupied spaces between the borders of adjacent "states."

As the German economist August Lösch observed, the regular shape that is closest to the circle but which, when replicated, allows an entire surface to be covered is the hexagon.[5] (G. William Skinner has used such a structure of hexagonal regions to analyze the commercial and administrative systems of imperial China.[6]) It is interesting to note that French people today often refer to their country as *l'Hexagone*. As figure 4.1 indicates, the English Channel, the Atlantic, the Pyrénées, the Mediterranean, the Alps, and the Ardennes give France its characteristic six-sided shape. These borders have changed very little from the days of Charles VIII in the late fifteenth century.

However, fewer than a hundred years earlier, in 1400, the boundaries of the French state were very different. Part of Guienne in the south-west was a fief of the crown of England, while Brittany, Burgundy, and Provence were ruled as independent fiefs. In the other fiefs outside the royal domain, the king's right to tax was sharply circumscribed by feudal privilege. Even in the royal domain itself, the king's power to tax was incomplete, since control of many of the largest fiefs had been delegated to royal offspring in the previous century. Following the English victory at Agincourt in 1415, the upper half of this territory was in effect amputated, as most of the country north of the Loire was occupied by foreign troops with the support of their Burgundian allies.

Nor was France an exception. During the Middle Ages, the boundaries of the German Empire, England, and Spain were also far from the hexagonal form that Lösch's theory would seem to imply. A question which must be asked, therefore, is why in the medieval period state boundaries apparently differed so greatly from the compact shape suggested by *a priori* reasoning. Another question is what happened in the course of the fifteenth century to lead to the formation of the centralized monarchies of England, Spain, and France, along with coalescence at the regional level within many of the parts of the German Empire.

One way to define a state is as a territory within which a dominant group holds a recognized right to use force to raise revenues. In other words, a state is an area within which there exists a monopoly to tax, supported by a parallel monopoly to use force. As Joseph Strayer has observed, the essential structures of the modern European state, particularly the legal and fiscal systems, had their origins in institutions created in the twelfth and thirteenth centuries.[7] Nevertheless, prior to 1400 in France, the strength of these institutions was generally weak outside of the royal domain. At the beginning of the fifteenth century, in France as in other parts of Western Europe, the primary taxing power was in the hands of the feudal nobility. In Burgundy, for example, it was the duke who received the *taille* and other feudal dues. The king, as the largest landholder in France, received the traditional income from the royal domain. Although the strong kings of the thirteenth century had succeeded in extending their domain to cover about half of the kingdom, it had since been reduced by a series of territorial grants or appanages to royal heirs. In addition to traditionally autonomous fiefs such as Brittany, Provence, Burgundy, and Armagnac, the fiefs of Alençon, Maine, Anjou, Berry, Bourbonnais, Auvergne, La Marche, and Angouleme were all held as appanages.

Over the course of the fourteenth century, it had been recognized that the French kings had the right to levy several new royal taxes over the entire kingdom. These levies included the *gabelle* or salt tax, excise taxes, and the royal *taille*. Yet toward the end of that century, the revenue from these new imposts amounted to only 10–30 percent of the net receipts of the royal treasury.[8] To a great extent, therefore, the king still lived "*du sien*"; that is, on his own feudal income from the royal domain.

Like most of the duchies and counties outside the royal domain, Burgundy was itself geographically concentrated; indeed, France in 1400 could be considered as essentially an unstable alliance among a small number of relatively autonomous compact feudal states. In 1410, following the assassination of a royal uncle by followers of the Duke of Burgundy, the alliance came unstuck and a civil war broke out between two factions, the Armagnacs and the Bourguignons. It was the decision of the latter faction to appeal to England for help that led to a renewal of the Hundred Years War. This conflict, which had begun in 1337 because of a dynastic dispute between the crowns of France and England, had been in a dormant state for several decades.

By the end of the fifteenth century, the situation of France had changed dramatically: the power to tax was firmly in the hands of the king and his advisers. In the intervening period, the borders of the typical fiscal unit had expanded outward: the French kings controlled most of the territory covered by metropolitan France today. As yet, however, the communications network was weak. There were two principal Romance language groups in France, the *langue d'oïl* in the north and the *langue d'oc* in the south, so named for their respective words for "yes." In Brittany, the population spoke Breton, a Celtic dialect. The population of the state was still divided into linguistic regions speaking more than a dozen different dialects and sharing no common tongue. Nevertheless, the modern French state had been created; within its boundaries, the French nation would subsequently emerge.

The transfer of fiscal power from the French nobility to their king has been described as "one of the decisive steps in the history of Western civilization."[9] However, there is considerable disagreement as to why this development occurred. Moreover, a change of this magnitude was bound to affect all aspects of economic activity. Yet there has been little attention paid to what earlier chapters have referred to as a society's *internal margin*; that is, the boundary between private and collective decision-making. Was the centralization of fiscal power accompanied by a rise in the total tax burden or by a greater recourse to individual initiative?

The "Professionalization" Thesis

The outward shift in the boundaries of the typical state in the late Middle Ages has not gone unnoticed by historians. Various explanations have been advanced for the rise of the extended monarchy in France. One approach, the "professionalization" thesis, has attributed the change to the appearance of professional infantry armies equipped with new types of artillery weapons. One factor was an improvement in the strength of infantry relative to cavalry. According to the economic historian, Richard Bean, "The burghers of Flanders at Courtrai (1302 AD) and the Scots at Bannockburn (1314 AD) showed that under favorable circumstances the pike-phalanx could be invulnerable to the cavalry charge." A further development occurred when the English "combined dismounted men-at-arms with masses of archers armed with the longbow . . . to beat the feudal cavalry of France at Crécy (1346 AD)."[10]

Although Bean did not explain why foot soldiers should suddenly become more effective, a number of possible reasons have been suggested. In part, the change may have been due to new weapons such as the crossbow and the English longbow that were able to fire with sufficient force to penetrate armor. Similarly, the halberd – a pike with an axe at the end – enabled infantrymen to confront horsemen on more equal terms. In part, it may have been improved training and battlefield tactics that permitted foot soldiers to fight together more effectively.[11]

The problem with the argument that the emergence of centralized governments was due to the increasing effectiveness of infantry is that it is contradicted by the facts. The fourteenth and early fifteenth centuries actually saw a *decline* in the relative importance of infantry. As the French historian Philippe Contamine pointed out, whereas in the early fourteenth century, foot soldiers made up an important part of armies in Europe, from the mid-fourteenth to the mid-fifteenth centuries they were increasingly replaced by archers who, if they fought on foot, generally travelled on horseback.[12] The defeat of the French knights at Courtrai was exceptional, due in large part to the marshy terrain on which the battle was fought. Two years later, at Mons-en-Pévèle the knights were able to defeat the Flemish pikemen.[13] At Crécy, the English archers and men-at-arms were all horsemen.[14] The stunning victories of the mobile English cavalry armies forced other European powers to follow suit.

Another explanation that has been advanced for the emergence of the nation state in fifteenth-century France is the creation of the first standing army in Europe since Roman times, under a royal ordinance issued in 1445.[15] Douglass North and Robert Thomas argued that by forming a permanent military body, Charles VII was able to appropriate for the monarchy the sole legitimate right to use force: "Charles instituted a set of military reforms which, by establishing a permanent organization of twenty regular companies of heavy cavalry, created a professional army, the main advantage of which was that it did away with the need to rely entirely upon un-trustworthy mercenaries."[16]

In evaluating this position, one should note that the concept of professional soldiers at the command of the sovereign was not new to mid-fifteenth-century France. The method of indenture, by which the king's vassals provided him with standing contingents of troops in return for payment, had been introduced by the Plantagenets in England in the previous century.[17] It was this system that had enabled Edward III and later English sovereigns to embark upon a series of extended campaigns on French soil – the Hundred Years War. Even in the French army, by the 1430s the majority of the king's troops were professional soldiers.[18] What was new in 1445 was not that there were career soldiers stationed full-time on French soil. Rather it was the method of financing them. Instead of letting them live off the land for much of the year, the ordinance stipulated that they be paid from tax revenues. To be able to apply the ordinance, the king necessarily had to have the financial means to back up his decree. Thus a tax-financed army may be seen as more a result of than a precondition for the seizure of absolute fiscal power.

A final military factor that has been offered to explain the expansion of the monarch's power in fifteenth-century France is the improvement of artillery techniques. As Bean pointed out, "Nominal feudal superiors and foreign invaders faced the same handicaps: Very often it simply cost more to conquer a region than the region was worth. . . . In the middle of the fifteenth century, the cannon drastically altered the balance between offense and defense."[19]

While it is conceivable that artillery gave the attacking force an advantage – at least until fortifications were modified to take account of the destructiveness of the new weapons – it is not obvious that such a change should necessarily favor the centralization of power. Why could the nobility not use cannon to batter down the walls of the king's garrisons? For example, Germany was in the lead in the development of late medieval armaments, including artillery.[20] Yet during the fifteenth century, the period of most rapid development of artillery techniques, the power of the emperor actually declined. The increasingly independent German towns, along with strong national leaders in Bohemia and Hungary were able to successfully challenge the imperial authority.[21] What must be demonstrated is why the new technology should have favored the French monarchs while at the same time serving to erode the power of the German emperor.

Even if one admits that the successful use of artillery was perhaps the key factor in the rise of absolutism in France under the Valois monarchs, there is a question of the timing of the innovation. McNeill suggested that the key period was between 1465 and 1477, when an arms race between France and Burgundy led to rapid developments in artillery techniques.[22] For other observers, the crucial period was the late 1440s, when the French developed the artillery force that enabled them to drive the English out of Normandy in little more than a year.[23] The difficulty with these relatively late dates is that they leave no convincing explanation for the consolidation of the royal tax power in France, which occurred a decade earlier.

The "Commercialization" Thesis

There is another explanation that has been offered for the extension of the monarch's power in fifteenth-century France. According to what might be called the "commercialization" thesis, this change was due to the increasing commercialization of economic activity that occurred in the late Middle Ages. In the words of Fernand Braudel, "The new [French] state . . . was borne along on the economic upsurge which favored its growth."[24] Similarly, David Friedman argued that feudalism declined because with the exogenous rise in inter-regional trade that occurred in this period, the medieval state was no longer the appropriate taxing authority: "For the collection of taxes on trade there exist economies of scale up to . . . the width of a network of parallel trade routes."[25] In other words, owing to the considerable increase in trade flows, the extended monarchy had become the optimally sized political unit for purposes of taxation.

Developments in France in the fifteenth century appear to support this position. Trade had been sharply reduced by a half-century of near anarchy and warfare. The key event, it has been argued, occurred in 1439 when the representatives of the towns, who dominated the French parliament, granted a taxation monopoly to the king. The *Ordonnance* of 1439 removed the nobility's right to tax: "*aucune creue par dessus la taille du roy*" – no surtax could be levied by the feudal lords.[26] In the words of North and Thomas, Charles VII's "control over taxing power had actually become complete after 1439. The Estates General had surrendered control over taxing power in the process of providing Charles VII with the finances to maintain an army that would defend the borders and eliminate the marauders from within."[27]

In examining this thesis, one should note that the taxing powers granted to the king in 1439 were not intended to be permanent. As Martin Wolfe pointed out, preparations were made for a subsequent sitting of the Estates General the following year.[28] Moreover, one might ask, even if the enhanced royal fiscal powers were intended to be only temporary, why did the commercial interests believe that the king could enforce such a monopoly? Although Charles VII had been able to levy the royal sales tax, the *aides*, for three years, he had experienced only moderate success in imposing his authority over his barons and other, irregular taxing authorities. During the recent fighting at Meaux, for example, the Duke of Bourbon had neglected to aid the royal forces.[29] Over the previous years, Charles VII had been powerless to prevent his own mercenary troops from pillaging the center and south of France between campaigns.[30]

The next part of the usual analysis of French public finances in this period is that the Valois kings subsequently used their new fiscal powers to extract large increases in taxes from the population. North and Thomas state, "the result of the virtual elimination of close rivals to the state from within and the intensification of competition with rivals from without was a dramatic increase in taxes under Louis XI (approximately a fourfold increase during his reign)."[31]

In assessing changes in the burden of taxes, however, a time series of nominal royal tax receipts is not the best measure. During the period from 1440 to 1500, France was recovering from the effects of a prolonged war that had devastated large parts of the country north of the Loire river. With growing income, tax revenues could be expected to rise. The number of taxpayers also rose during this period, both by natural increase and because of the addition of new territory, such as Burgundy. Another consideration is that the last half of the fifteenth century was a period of persistent though moderate inflation, as measured in terms of food prices.[32] Moreover, one should not overlook the sharp decrease in the burden of *non-royal* taxes in the form of feudal *taille* and the levies of plundering mercenary troops subsequent to 1440.

A final element in the accepted assessment of the changes in France's internal margin concerns the effect of government intervention on the private sector. It has been suggested that the French crown was less favorable to individual initiative than the English parliamentary government and that this orientation began in the fifteenth century. In the words of North and Thomas once again, "the fiscal policy of the French Crown, whether intentionally or not, did almost everything conceivable to thwart the spread of an extensive market and thereby surrendered the gains that lay therein."[33]

With regard to the effects of government intervention on the French economy, one should be careful to distinguish the fifteenth century from the period that followed. While per-capita income in France may have changed very little between 1500 and 1789, there is no evidence that such was the case during the latter half of the fifteenth century. Introducing a recent collection of papers on this period, Philippe Contamine suggested that the years from 1490 to 1500 may constitute the economic and social "apogee" of pre-revolutionary France.[34] Although the economy continued to be separated into largely self-sufficient regions, the most important reason for the low volume of internal trade was the high cost of transport, rather than government policy. The internal tolls that were levied should be viewed as a means of financing the maintenance and protection of the transport system. Otherwise, internal trade was essentially free.[35]

It may be concluded that there are several weaknesses in current analyses of political and economic developments in fifteenth-century France – at least those appearing in the English language. Studies of changes in territorial boundaries have emphasized the effects of improved infantry when in fact infantry was in decline until well beyond the middle of the century. The constitution of a professional army paid from public revenues was more a result of the centralization of power than a contributing factor. And no compelling argument has been advanced as to why improvements in artillery should have favored the French monarch while at the same time serving to weaken the German emperor.

As for the internal margin, the causes and effects of the transfer of the power to tax from the nobility to the French crown also bear re-examination. On balance, the representatives of the taxpayers seem not to have opposed the change. While there was an increase in the revenues of the crown in current prices, it is not evident that total taxes as a share of income rose in consequence. Finally, it is difficult to reconcile the image of the crown as the major obstacle to the development of markets with the current assessment of the late fifteenth century as the high point of the French economy prior to the Revolution.

The Margins of the French State in 1435

There is general agreement among historians that many of the key developments in the emergence of a strong monarchy in France occurred over the decade from 1435 to 1445. To assess the events of this crucial period, one should consider the initial situation in 1435 at the signature of the Treaty of Arras between the French King, Charles VII, and the Duke of Burgundy, Philip the Good, who had formerly been allied to the English. In that year, both the territorial boundaries and the limits to the king's taxing power – the external and internal margins of the state – were the subjects of bitter disputes.

In the north, France's territorial frontiers lay well within its traditional borders. Although the inspiration of Joan of Arc had momentarily stimulated the French troops, the war with England had subsequently settled into a stalemate. The Duke of Burgundy, Philip the Good, had withdrawn his support of the English and his opposition to the government of Charles VII, but Paris and much of the surrounding Ile-de-France, along with Normandy, were still in English hands. In addition, England maintained its traditional hold over Western Guienne and Gascony in the south-west. The independent fiefs of Brittany and Burgundy were essentially neutral. Only the Loire valley, parts of Champagne, and the south and east of France were firmly under the king's control.

As for the internal margin between private and public activity, the French King, had two main sources of revenues: receipts from the royal domain and general taxes. As seigneur of his own feudal estates, he received a category of revenues which were called *domaines* or *ordinaires*.[36] These included a share of the crops grown on the royal domain, and the *champart*, fees for manorial functions such as milling, baking, and pressing wine which the seigneur monopolized. In addition, serfs were required to pay the lord various types of dues: the *chevage*, a poll tax, *formariage*, when they married outside the lord's domain, and *mainmorte* if a serf died without a son as heir. To make up the difference between their expenditures and the revenues from all of these sources, the feudal lords could also levy a lump-sum tax. Since this sum then had to be allocated by the towns and villages into the portion or *taille* that each household had to pay, this tax was known as the *taille*.

Potentially one of the most important non-monetary powers of the king as feudal lord was his right to call upon his vassals (the *ban*) and his vassals' vassals (the *arrière-ban*), along with their tenants, for military service. While this method was satisfactory for short periods of service, it was less suited to prolonged campaigns, since it meant sacrificing the productive activities of the manor. Moreover, at battles from Crécy to Agincourt, the undisciplined French feudal levies had proven themselves unequal to smaller bodies of professional soldiers. The king was therefore forced to rely increasingly on mercenary troops.

The total monetary yield of the king's various feudal revenue sources apart from the *taille* was small. For example, in 1460, the last year of the reign of Charles VII, they amounted to only 50,000 livres, or 3 percent of the total receipts of the royal treasury.[37] To pursue the war against the English effectively, therefore, Charles and his ministers were forced to levy additional general taxes of the type used periodically by French kings since the previous century. The bulk of these extra revenues came from a general direct tax or *taille*. In addition, from 1428 on, the king received large sums in the form of indirect levies on commerce known as *aides*, as well as smaller sums from the salt tax, the *gabelle*. Given the situation of the economy, Charles was remarkably successful in raising funds. In total, the king was voted more than a million livres a year during the 1420s and slightly more in the 1430s.[38] Although the sums actually received often differed from the amounts voted, the crown generally had sufficient funds to pay its soldiers during the campaign season.

With the Burgundians neutralized and a sufficient source of revenues to continue the war, the French would probably eventually have been able to regain most of the territories held by the English, as they had done in the previous century under Charles V. On the basis of past experience, the crisis over, one might then have expected the feudal nobility to demand that the king live on the resources of the royal domain – *vivre du sien*. France would then have resumed its existence as a rough alliance of relatively autonomous feudal baronies. However, this was not what happened.

DEVELOPMENTS IN METALLURGY AND ARMS

To understand the shock that was about to transform the French state, it is necessary to backtrack at this point to examine the technology of arms production. Iron had been used for weapons since the second millennium BC. It was obtained by the heating of iron ore with charcoal in a brick furnace until a spongy mass of molten metal and semi-liquid slag was obtained. Although this sponge iron contained too many impurities to be used directly, it was found that the slag could be removed if the metal were hammered while hot. Since the resulting product, wrought iron, had a very low carbon content, it was too soft for most military purposes.

However, it was discovered that when iron was heated in charcoal, the outer surface of the iron absorbed enough carbon to greatly increase its strength. It could then be shaped by hammering into armor, swords and other products.

Unfortunately, the iron produced in this way had too high a melting point to be cast into molds in the way bronze was used. Before iron could be used in casting, some way had to be found to lower its melting point. During the high Middle Ages, metal workers learned how to harness water power to work bellows that blew air over the charcoal, thereby enabling smelting furnaces to be greatly enlarged and to be operated at higher temperatures. In the fourteenth century, it was discovered that in addition to the usual bloom of sponge iron, the new furnaces produced a liquid metallic substance which came to be known as pig iron.[39] Further experimentation showed that if the iron were kept in contact with the charcoal for long periods of time – up to two weeks – larger quantities of this new substance could be obtained. Its high carbon content – between 2 and 4.5 percent – lowered its melting point, enabling it to be reheated easily and cast into molds.

This product, cast iron, was one of the great innovations of the Middle Ages. Its principal advantage was its low cost; however, it was a brittle metal and could not be worked further once it had been cast. For products requiring a greater ratio of strength to weight or more precise finishing after casting, the preferred metal in the late Middle Ages was copper. By the middle of the fifteenth century, 10 percent tin was added to the copper to yield an even stronger alloy – bronze.[40]

Before these metals could be used for artillery, some way had to be found to cast large objects. Here again, considerable progress was made in the fourteenth and early fifteenth centuries – particularly in the casting of church bells. The most difficult part of the process was to prepare the mold.[41] First a full-sized model of the object to be made was prepared, usually of wood. The mock-up was then covered with specially-prepared clay and reinforcing materials and baked. When the wooden model was withdrawn, the baked clay that remained formed the exterior part of the mold. A clay core strengthened by an iron bar was then prepared. Once the mold had been set into the ground and the core set carefully in the middle, liquid bronze was poured into the space between the two components and allowed to cool. The mold and core were then broken up, with the casting left to be finished and polished.[42]

Early Artillery

Mechanical missile-throwing siege weapons had been developed in antiquity. As late as the last half of the fourteenth century, crossbow-like ballista and catapults were still an important part of the arsenals of many towns and rulers. In 1388, for example, the Flemish town of Lille had 11 ballista, large devices in the shape of a crossbow for projecting large stones or metal quarrels. Because of their slow rate of fire and short range, however, these instruments were used infrequently.[43] The introduction of gunpowder into Europe in the thirteenth century set in motion numerous attempts to find alternative methods of propelling objects by means of the energy released by expanding gases. These efforts soon resulted in the production of the first artillery weapons. The first illustration of an artillery weapon appears in an English manuscript by Walter de Milemete, written in 1326. The first written mention of cannon is in a Florentine document of the same year.[44]

Since most of the artillery pieces produced over the next century were similar in their structure and operation, it is worthwhile to examine them in some detail. Most large guns were made from wrought iron and consisted of two pieces, the barrel and the firing chamber. The steps in their manufacture, as described by O. F. G. Hogg, are as follows:

Wrought-iron rods were lashed round the circumference of a mandril [a metal bar serving as a core] over which was passed a series of wrought-iron hoops at white heat. These, on cooling, shrank on to the rods, compressing them firmly together. . . . The chamber portion, in the form of a jug with a short, slender neck, was then forged from the solid, the tapered end being fashioned to fit the breech. This double operation was necessary as the craftsmen of the day found it impossible to produce a barrel without a mandril, consequently it had to remain open at both ends.[45]

In the early fourteenth century, artillery weapons fell into two types. The massive stubby short-range guns, known as bombards, fired heavy projectiles and were usually loaded from the muzzle.[46] Although the rear or chamber end was sometimes welded to the barrel, in the largest pieces it was detachable for transport.[47] One of the largest of these guns, "Dulle Griet," was over 5 m long and weighed 16,400 kg.[48] The other type, narrower, longer-range cannon, were usually breech-loaders. Some of these weapons, called *veuglaires*, had two or three removable firing chambers which screwed onto the barrel.[49] The earliest artillery pieces often fired metal arrows (quarrels) of the type used by crossbows and ballista. However, by the end of the fourteenth century, the standard projectile was a stone ball cut to fit the dimensions of the particular weapon from which it was fired.[50] The guns were fired by ignition of an early form of gunpowder known as serpentine, made by combining saltpeter, charcoal, and sulfur.

In terms of destructive power, the wrought-iron artillery of the early fifteenth century represented a considerable advance over the mechanical missile weapons which it replaced. However, it was subject to a number of serious shortcomings. The imperfect fit of the chamber to the barrel led to what is known as obturation, the escape of gas from the rear of the gun. Since the stone balls that the guns shot were cut by hand, there was invariably a gap between the wall of the barrel and the ball which let some of the propellant escape. Moreover, because of the hydroscopic nature of saltpeter, it tended to absorb moisture. Accordingly, the gunpowder tended to burn unevenly and was often too damp to be fired.[51] Owing to the weakness of their wrought-iron construction, the guns themselves were unable to withstand very high levels of pressure. Consequently, the weight of gunpowder relative to that of the ball remained low – in the range of 10–30 percent for bombards.[52]

As a result of these problems, the maximum range of wrought-iron artillery with stone projectiles was relatively short – about 100 m in the case of the bombards.[53] Although the breech-loaders had a longer range, they had their own drawback: since the weapons had to be cooled after each firing, often for several hours, their rate of fire was low.[54] Another problem was that because the circumstances of each firing varied considerably, the weapons were highly inaccurate. Moreover, even when the shot hit the target, the effect was not always that desired, since the stone balls often broke apart on impact. Finally, given the condition of the roads of the time, overland transport of the heaviest pieces was a major problem. In 1409, a bombard weighing 3,500 kg, pulled by 32 oxen and 31 horses along with 25 drivers, took eight days to cover 32 km.[55] Water transport was usually more rapid, although not without problems. In 1410, a weapon of the same size made a 60 km trip along the Saone river in Franche-Comté in three days, but only at the cost of demolishing the sluice-gates.[56]

The application of artillery was confined entirely to siege operations. Interestingly enough, the first bombards were not used against fortifications; rather they were fired over the walls with the intention of destroying property and killing personnel within the defenses.[57] In the field, wrought-iron weapons were too difficult to transport, too slow in firing, and had too short a range to be of much practical value.[58] The wagon forts of John Ziska during the wars of the followers of John Huss in Bohemia against the Papacy and Empire (1419–1436) were perhaps an exception to this general rule. The Hussites placed bombards between the wagons of their *wagenburg* (wagon fortress) to cut down attacking soldiers.[59]

Innovations in Artillery in the Fifteenth Century

In the second quarter of the fifteenth century, the two parallel series of developments in metal refining and casting described above intersected, providing a means of overcoming some of these difficulties. One of these innovations was the substitution of cast iron cannon balls for stone balls.

Since iron was denser than stone and less liable to shatter, the new munitions greatly increased the destructive power of artillery. Because the metal balls were cast from molds instead of being cut by hand, they were more regular in form and uniform in size. It was therefore possible to have a limited number of types of weapons of standardized calibers, all guns of the same caliber sharing the same ammunition. One of the first records of the use of iron cannon balls is in 1431, by the Duke of Burgundy.[60]

A second key innovation was the substitution of cast-metal artillery weapons for wrought iron, as techniques for casting large pieces improved. Since the new guns were usually cast in a single piece and were loaded from the muzzle, the problem of obturation was to a great extent solved. Moreover, because cast metals was much stronger than welded pieces of wrought iron, it was possible to make lighter weapons capable of withstanding higher internal pressures. Records of French bronze cannon of the early sixteenth century indicate that the powder charge was 67–87 percent of the weight of the ball, an increase of two or three times over wrought-iron weapons.[61]

The French Artillery Corps

In some ways, the men who manufactured and operated the new artillery pieces may be considered to be simply the descendants of the craftsmen who had built the siege engines of the Assyrians and Romans. In other ways, however, they represented something that was new in military administration: a class of technicians specialized in the art of war. A successful artillery captain in the fifteenth century had to master skills that were unknown to his counterpart in classical times. Since the distinction between gun-founders and gunners was not always very sharp, many were former bell-makers, skilled in casting bronze. In addition, since early artillerymen made their own gunpowder from the raw ingredients, they had to have an elementary knowledge of chemistry.[62]

As artillery pieces and munitions became standardized, it was necessary to measure and to quantify: the artillery captain must also be an applied mathematician. Moreover, the nature of the artillery commander's responsibilities assured a constant feedback between the effectiveness of the weapons – their range, accuracy, and destructive power – and the methods used to build and operate them. This development marked the beginning of the modern profession of engineer. Nor was such improvement limited to one's own discoveries. An artillery commander who failed to keep up with developments available to potential enemies might soon find himself outclassed in the field. Anxious not to fall behind what was happening in other jurisdictions, a sovereign would therefore often hire experts who had served other rulers to update the information of his own gunners. In 1380, the master of bombards of the Duke of Brabant travelled to the city of Trèves to confer with the cannoneer of Strasbourg concerning *"eim neue kunst"* – a new development – in artillery techniques.[63] The notions of innovation and diffusion of technology were familiar to the artillerymen of the late Middle Ages.

During the first half of the fifteenth century, the techniques for casting bronze and iron spread quickly throughout Western Europe, as skilled workers carried their knowledge from one employer to another.[64] In no area was diffusion faster than in military applications – at least north of the Alps. At the siege of Sancenay in 1431, only 24 balls, all of stone, had been fired. However, at the siege of Dinant in 1466, 502 cast-iron balls of 18–40 cm were fired along with 1200 smaller balls for serpentine – newer wrought-iron weapons designed to fire metal projectiles.[65]

However, it was the French who were among the first to seize upon the possible advantages of combining these two innovations – cast-iron shot and cast-metal artillery pieces. The key individuals were the brothers Jean and Gaspard Bureau, who took effective control of the French artillery corps in 1437.[66] One of their first innovations was to wrap stone projectiles in rings of iron to increase their destructive power against masonry walls[67].

It was the Bureau brothers who emphasized the introduction of cast-metal artillery weapons and projectiles. Initially, only the smallest weapons were made of cast metal, but eventually the process was extended to all models.[68] Although the largest cannon – enormous bombards – were usually cast as a single piece, the smaller weapons continued to have a removable breech.[69] At first, the new pieces were made of cast iron, but as the royal finances improved during the 1440s, copper and bronze were increasingly substituted.[70] The Bureau brothers also took the lead in introducing cast-iron projectiles in place of stone cannon balls. The new projectiles had a range of 1 km – ten times that of the old bombards. Because of the greater density and velocity of the iron balls, the calibre of artillery pieces could be reduced, with the result that the weapons became much more mobile.[71] It now became feasible to use artillery on the battlefield.

The outcome of these efforts was an artillery force unmatched in mobility and destructive power. In the words of a contemporary, Jacques du Clerq, the Bureau brothers were founders, engineers, and captains who succeeded in giving Charles VII:

le plus grand nombre de grosses bombardes, gros canons, veuglaires, serpentines, crapeaulx d'eaulx, colleuvrines et ribaudigues que n'estoit lors mesmoire d'homme avoir veu a roy chrestien (the greatest number of large bombards, cannon, *veuglaires*, culverins and other artillery pieces that has been seen in human memory in the possession of a Christian king).[72]

The total number of trained individuals involved was not large. Little is known about the size of the artillery corps of Charles VII; however, documents have survived from the reign of his son, Louis XI. In 1469, a year of peace, the master of artillery Gaspard Bureau commanded a force of 45 men. They included a guard, a wagon-master, two wheelwrights, and 40 cannoneers; in addition, there was another artillery team of ten men in Normandy.[73] In time of war, these skilled artillerymen would be reinforced by hundreds of additional men and animals for transporting the artillery pieces.

This small force had an impact disproportionate to its size. One artillery piece alone could do little damage to a castle wall during the few weeks for which it was feasible to maintain a siege. However, when a sufficient number of the new weapons were trained on a small number of points in a masonry wall and armed with iron-reinforced or cast-iron cannon balls, they could reduce any medieval fortress in short order. An Italian observer in the 1480s wrote that by firing day and night, a French artillery team with 30 or 40 pieces could quickly breech a wall over 2 m thick.[74] Provided that a ruler was wealthy enough to finance the number of cannon required for an effective siege, the cost of controlling territory fell sharply. The development of more effective artillery weapons and projectiles in the 1430s and 1440s therefore brought about a leap in the economies of scale of military force and a fall in the cost of controlling territory.

An effective siege train was beyond the means of the lord of a small county. However, it was financially feasible for a ruler of a medium power such as the king of France or the duke of Burgundy, who controlled large territories along France's northern and eastern borders. In an area larger or more populous than the kingdom of France, however, there appear to have been no significant further scale economies in artillery. Thus the German emperor seems to have had no advantage over a well-organized vassal state such as Bohemia. In attempting to maintain control of his vast territory, the emperor would be forced to divide his artillery corps into several optimally sized bands of roughly the same size as that of his regional rivals. Since each of the large states within the empire was rich enough to afford its own full corps of artillery, the additional resources of the emperor would confer no military advantage.

THE TURNING POINT FOR FRANCE

France had reached a decisive turning point. Under the Treaty of Arras of 1435, Burgundy had withdrawn from the conflict between the French and English monarchies. Nevertheless, the challenge facing Charles VII was considerable. The English forces were more numerous, better equipped, and better organized.[75] They held the largest city, Paris, and the surrounding region, along with the rich territories of Normandy and Guienne (see figure 4.1). It is true that in the year after the Treaty of Arras, Charles managed to retake Paris, but this success was due more to an uprising by the local inhabitants against the English occupying troops than to any superiority of French arms. In early 1437, a new offensive by the English enabled them to capture Pontoise and several other towns in the Paris region. Subsequent enemy raids on French supply columns attempting to bring food to the beleaguered city left it in desperate straits.[76]

Then, slowly, the tide began to turn in favor of the French. The town of Montereau on the Seine to the south-east of Paris was taken after a brief siege and fierce fighting in the fall of 1437, the king himself taking part in the final attack. It was Jean Bureau who commanded the French artillery during this siege.[77] In the following year, however, events showed the weakness of cavalry unsupported by artillery. French troops reached the walls of Bordeaux in the south-west but were unable to take the city for lack of siege equipment. Meanwhile, systematic efforts to release the English grip on Paris continued. It was in the late summer of 1439 that the strongpoint of Meaux to the north-east of Paris was taken from the English.

The Praguerie

The events of 1437–39 showed the emerging superiority of French artillery over its English counterpart. It quickly became evident to many in the king's entourage that guns which could be used effectively against the English could easily be turned against internal opponents. It is no coincidence that in the fall of 1439, following the French victory at Meaux, Charles VII and his advisers decided that their power was strong enough to issue a tough decree, approved by the Estates-General at Orléans. The *Ordonnance* of November 1439 stripped the feudal nobles of their most important powers. It proclaimed an end to private armies, giving the king a monopoly to the legal use of force in France. It also deprived the nobles of the right to impose a *taille* on their own free peasants.[78]

It is one thing to issue a decree; it is another thing altogether to enforce it. The feudal response came the following spring. Under the leadership of the dukes of Bourbon, Brittany, and Alençon, a group of nobles attempted to intimidate the king into resigning and yielding power to a regency that would rule in the name of the Dauphin, the future Louis XI. In memory of the bloody Hussite revolts recently concluded in Bohemia, the insurrection was known as the *Praguerie*. Charles reacted quickly.

Accompanied by his military commander, Richemont, he led an army to attack the rebels' headquarters at Niort, in western France, south of the Loire. When the Dauphin and the dukes retreated into Auvergne in the center of France, the king's forces doggedly pursued them. In a few short weeks, the royal artillery enabled Richemont to seize 30 fortresses from the rebels, whose alliance quickly came apart.[79] Although Charles pardoned all those who had taken part in the plot, he made sure to retain the essential military and fiscal powers stated in the *Ordonnance* of 1439.

It took time, however, for the nobles to absorb all the implications of the failure of the *Praguerie*. In 1443, the Count of Armagnac used his private army to occupy the neighboring county of Comminges on the Spanish border. In response, the king sent the Dauphin with a royal army to reassert the authority of the crown. Once again, it was a one-sided match. The royal artillery quickly reduced the fortresses of Armagnac. The Count was captured and thrown into prison.

The Expulsion of the English

With unprecedented control over his own barons, Charles could turn to the problem of the English occupation. In 1441, the French retook Pontoise, the town north-west of Paris that controlled access to the lower Seine valley and the port of Rouen. This success, along with other victories of the preceding months, gave the royal forces complete control of the vital Ile-de-France territory surrounding Paris. If efforts had then been concentrated on regaining Normandy, where French supply lines were short and the population hostile to the occupying English, the king could probably have succeeded in steadily retaking the greater part of occupied France.

Instead, in 1442, Charles attempted to capture distant Guienne in the south-east. The inhabitants of this rich wine-growing region had been loyal subjects of the English crown for three centuries; moreover, they depended on markets in England and the Low Countries for an important part of their sales. Although the French artillery had been strong enough to cope with discontented barons, it was not yet sufficiently powerful to rout quickly professional soldiers entrenched in a well-fortified site. The fortress at La Réole on the Garonne river south-east of Bordeaux held out for 57 days, fatally delaying the advance of the royal troops. When winter arrived, Bordeaux was still in English hands, and the king's army was forced to retreat.

By this point, both the English and the French were exhausted from 30 years of continuous warfare. In 1444, a truce was signed for a period of 22 months. It was subsequently renewed several times until the summer of 1449. During this interim period, the French succeeded in forming a standing army composed of cavalry and new units of unmounted archers. The king also took advantage of the lull in the fighting to reinforce his artillery, both quantitatively and qualitatively.

The improvements to French artillery during this period were numerous. A Genoese expert, Louis Giribault, hired by the Bureau brothers, developed a mobile gun carriage to replace the heavy four-wheeled wagons used until that time. Another expert from Germany introduced *"certaines choses subtiles"* – subtleties whose exact nature is unclear – concerning artillery to his French counterparts.[80] Perhaps the subtleties included improvements to gunpowder, since the close-to-optimal ratio of six parts of saltpeter to one part each of carbon and sulfur began to be used in this period. Although most of the new weapons were lighter guns that fired metal shot, ways were also found to rejuvenate the older stone-shooting bombards. It was found that if a flatter trajectory were used, these heavy cannon could be used more effectively against walls and gates.[81]

By July of 1449, the French were confident of their military superiority. Using enemy violations of the truce as a justification, Charles VII broke off negotiations with the English ambassadors. Immediately, the armies of the king and his Breton allies invaded Normandy. Outnumbered, the English commanders chose to refuse battle and withdraw into fortified sites. Their intended strategy was to exhaust the French forces in a series of lengthy sieges. Instead, however, the French artillery quickly took one town after another. Even the castle of France's second city, the port of Rouen, was forced to capitulate after a siege which lasted only ten days. By early November, most of Normandy was in French or Breton hands.

The English were not about to give up a territory they had held for 30 years without a fight. In March of the following year, an English cavalry army under Thomas Kyriel landed at Cherbourg, intent upon retaking the towns captured by the French. On April 25, his army met that of the Count of Clermont at Formigny, near Bayeux in lower Normandy, and dug into a defensive position to await the expected French cavalry attack. Instead, the French brought up their light artillery pieces, loaded them with small metal balls, and began to fire into the English lines from beyond longbow range. The English had little choice but to abandon their prepared positions and attempt to capture the French guns. They had almost succeeded in this objective when French reinforcements under Richemont arrived and turned a close fight into a rout.

The battle of Formigny was the decisive event in the Normandy campaign. By August, French artillery had driven the remaining English garrisons from their fortifications. In one year and six days, Charles VII had recaptured the 60 towns that Henry V had taken four and a half years to conquer a generation earlier.[82]

In the spring of 1451, it was the turn of Guienne to face the improved French artillery. In a few weeks the French army managed to retake the main towns in the Dordogne and Garonne valleys and had arrived before the walls of Bordeaux. After negotiating favorable fiscal treatment, the city's leaders opened their gates to the king's army. By the end of August, Bayonne in the south had also fallen. However, over the next year, the new French administration in Guienne imposed heavy taxes, despite the promises made earlier by the king's representatives. The region hastily sent a delegation of nobles to London. In October, a new English force under Talbot arrived by sea. It quickly retook Bordeaux and many towns in the surrounding region.

In the following year, the French began an attempt to recover the territory lost. By July of 1453, the royal forces had retaken a number of the towns held by the English and were besieging Castillon, a strong point on the Dordogne river, east of Bordeaux. When they learned of the approach of an English relief force under Talbot, the besieging troops hastily built a fortified camp with palisade and ditches. The French gunners then trained their weapons on the area in front of the palisade, where they expected the enemy to attack, and waited. Once the battle was joined, the French released their horses, tricking the English into thinking they were fleeing. When the English cavalry then attacked what it thought was only a rear guard left within the palisade, it was met by a withering fire from the French artillery. At the same moment, the English force was attacked on the flanks by hidden Breton troops and in the center by the French from the fortifications.[83] It was another total victory for the king's forces and one that permanently sealed the fate of Guienne.

As the French historian Ferdinand Lot observed, Formigny and Castillon receive only slight mention in most history books (especially those in the English language) compared with Crécy and Agincourt.[84] However, in many ways they were more important. They were the first field battles in history in which artillery played a major role. The combination of foot soldiers and cavalry, supported by artillery, that the French used at Formigny and Castillon was to become the general standard for field armies over the next four centuries. In addition, these battles played an important part in giving England and France the frontiers that they have today.

Charles VII died in 1461, after a reign of almost 40 years. However, his son, Louis XI, and his grandson, Charles VIII, who succeeded him in turn realized the importance to their power of having a strong artillery force. By the 1490s, the French artillery was the best in the world.[85] It is no coincidence that the French monarchy was also the most powerful in Europe. With the incorporation of Burgundy, Provence, and Brittany into the kingdom in the intervening decades, France had acquired external frontiers very similar to those of today. From Paris, the king controlled most of the territory within which the French nation would emerge.

THE ROYAL FISCAL MACHINE

During the period from 1440 to 1453, backed by the powerful royal artillery, Charles VII was able to silence most of the competing fiscal authorities on French territory. How was the new royal fiscal monopoly to be applied? One of the lasting contributions of his reign to France was the completion of a permanent fiscal bureaucracy to administer the new tax monopoly. Although many of the components of this fiscal administration had been introduced under his predecessors, it was during the last decades of his reign that the structure became permanent.

In the case of the most important tax, the *taille*, one component of this bureaucracy, the *élus* and *asséeurs*, had the task of assessing the amounts levied by parish and individual respectively. These officials, who acted at the local level, were unpaid representatives elected by their communities.[86] A second group, the *trésoriers, receveurs*, and *collecteurs*, backed up by royal constables, was concerned with tax collection. Finally, a third body, the *Chambre des généraux conseillers sur le fait de la justice des aides*, dealt with appeals from those who felt they had been unjustly assessed or with penalties for those who failed to comply. In the case of the indirect taxes or *aides*, rates were set by the king and collection in each locality was farmed out to the highest bidder at an annual auction.[87]

Did overall tax levels rise or fall? According to one interpretation of the rise of the French monarchy, the creation of this bureaucracy was accompanied by a rise in the share of total income captured by the state. It is suggested that these acquired powers enabled the kings to finance a professional army that was first used to drive out the English and was subsequently employed to extract large increases in taxes from the French people. State intervention in the economy, it is argued, then inhibited the development of the network of contractual relationships necessary for economic progress.

Both the French military victories over the English and the French kings' success in expanding the area under their control within France appear to reflect less the political astuteness of the sovereign and his advisers than the impact of new artillery technology. What, though, should one make of the argument that the new royal tax powers stifled economic development in France? For this view to be correct, it must be shown not only that the relative tax burden increased over the latter part of the fifteenth century, but also that economic growth was less in this period than might have been expected under a more decentralized regime.

The Evolution of the Relative Tax Burden

Those who argue that the seizure of absolute tax powers by the French kings resulted in an increase in taxation usually compare the level of the royal revenues at the end of the reign of Charles VII in 1460 with those in the final years of the rule of his successor, Louis XI, in the early 1480s.[88] There are several objections to this comparison. Whereas the earlier year was a time of peace, the latter years of the reign of Louis XI were a period of war. The king was fighting the German Emperor's son, Maximilian of Hapsburg, over the Burgundian estates in Flanders. In addition, the events of the year 1460 occurred two decades *after* Charles VII's denial of his nobles' right to tax their free peasants. A valid comparison of relative tax burdens should therefore compare two periods of peace or two periods of war, one before 1440 and the other after this year.

The last year of peace before the second phase of the Hundred Years War was 1413. It may be seen from table 4.1 that the royal revenues in that year amounted to roughly 0.235 *livres tournois* (l.t.) per capita at 1490 prices. A comparable year of peace after the fiscal reforms was 1490, the final year of the regency of Anne and Pierre de Beaujeu, during the minority of Charles VIII. The royal revenues in that year amounted to 0.25 l.t. at current prices. These figures imply a slight increase in real taxes per capita over the intervening decades.

There are, however, reasons to believe that these data may exaggerate the actual change in the tax burden of the typical French citizen. The figures for 1413 exclude the tallages paid by French free peasants to feudal lords other than the king. Since each feudal noble had his own private army and since armed conflict between them (for example, the dispute between the Armagnac and Bourgignon factions) was frequent, total taxes paid were considerably greater than those taxes paid to the king alone. By 1490, as a result of the *Ordonnance* of 1439, these feudal taxes had been virtually eliminated. Another consideration is that in 1413, France had still not recovered from the destructive effects of the first phase of its war with England. As a result, the country's per-capita income was undoubtedly lower than in 1490, almost 40 years after the final battles of that war. Although the data to make these two adjustments are not available, it is very likely that the result would show a decline in total taxes as a fraction of income between 1413 and 1490.

The fiscal reforms of the fifteenth century also affected tax receipts in times of war. The figure of 1 million l.t.for the 1420s represents the second

Table 4.1   Annual revenues of the French crown (in *livres tournois*)

	Period before 1440	Period after 1440
Period of peace		
Year	1413	1490
Revenues in current prices[a]	1.2	3.5
Price index (1490 = 1.0)	0.51	1.00
Revenues in constant prices[a]	2.4	3.5
Population[a]	10.0	14.0
Real per capita revenues	0.235	0.25
Period of war		
Year	1420s	early 1480s
Revenues in current prices[a]	1.0	5.0
Price index (1490 = 1.0)	0.61	1.06
Revenues in constant prices[a]	1.64	4.7
Population[a]	5.0[b]	13.0
Real per capita revenues	0.33	0.36

[a] Millions.
[b] Assumes that areas controlled by Charles VII in 1426 represented half of French population.
Sources: Revenue from E. B. Fryde and M. M. Fryde, "Public credit with special reference to north-western Europe," in *The Cambridge Economic History of Europe, Economic Organization and Policies in the Middle Ages*, eds M. M. Postan, E. E. Rich, and E. Miller, Cambridge, 1971, p. 482; *Vol. III*, R. Bean, "War and the birth of the nation state," *Journal of Economic History*, 33 (1973), p. 215; Wolfe, *The Fiscal System of Renaissance France*, Yale University Press, New Haven, 1972, p. 27; Charles Petit-Dutaillis, *Charles VII, Louis XI et les premières années de Charles VIII (1422–1492)*, Paris, 1981, p. 436. General commodity price index from A. P. Usher, "The general course of wheat prices in France: 1350–1788," *Review of Economics and Statistics*, 12 (1930), pp. 162–7. Population from R. Bean, "War and the birth of the nation state," *Journal of Economic History*, 33 (1973), p. 215.

phase of the Hundred Years War, while the corresponding amount for the early 1480s, 5 million l.t., indicates the situation in the final years of Louis XI's war against Maximilian and the Flemish. As table 4.1 shows, there was once again a slight rise in the crown's real receipts per capita, which increased from 0.33 to 0.36 l.t. at constant prices of 1490.

Once more, however, these data require some qualification. In addition to the omission of feudal *tailles* and the rise in real income per capita once the Hundred Years War was over, the data suffer from another weakness – the omission of the levies of plundering soldiers. Because of these problems, it is very unlikely that the period following the reforms saw a rise in total taxes as a fraction of income. Nor could the overall tax level be considered excessive relative to income. At the end of the regime, royal taxes represented approximately 2.3 to 3.5 percent of GNP.[89]

The Flayers

A serious shortcoming of the royal fiscal receipts as a measure of the tax burden in the first part of the reign of Charles VII is that they exclude the informal system of taxation used by leaders of the late Middle Ages to finance their wars. The greater part of the French forces by the latter years of the Hundred Years War consisted of companies of mercenaries whose first loyalty was to their captains, most of whom were members of the minor nobility.[90] Under the best of circumstances, these soldiers were paid from royal revenues for a campaign of six months of the year and even then only during periods in which there was actual combat.[91]

At other times, since the mercenaries usually had no other source of income, and since there was no legal military force to oppose them, they lived off the land. As a result of the treatment they often inflicted on peasants who fell into their hands – skinning them alive to force them to reveal where they kept their money – they became known as *Ecorcheurs* or Flayers. Between 1422 and 1445 they turned much of the countryside of northern France into a wasteland. During lulls in the fighting, they wandered in companies throughout France, leaving a swath of destruction behind them.

What was the difference between the royal army and the companies of *Ecorcheurs?* In the 1420s and 1430s, the two forces were in many ways virtually indistinguishable.[92] When there were battles to be fought, the mercenaries were paid by the king to kill Englishmen; when the fighting lapsed, the same men were paid by the peasants and towns and even by the king himself not to kill Frenchmen. In 1438, Charles VII levied a special tax in the Languedoc region to buy off the mercenaries of Villandrando.[93] The itinerary of one of the most famous *Ecorcheur* captains, Jean de Blanchfort, indicates that from the end of 1437 to the fall of 1438 he travelled in a broad arc from the North Sea into Flanders, circled through Champagne and Burgundy, reaching the Languedoc region in the south of France in September 1438. He then moved north-east into the German Emperor's territory in Alsace. By August 1439, de Blanchfort had returned to France to take part in the siege of Meaux, after which he retired to raid the English-occupied territory of Normandy.[94]

The French had been aware of the disadvantages of using mercenary troops since the depredations of the *Grandes Compagnies* under Charles V in the previous century. These soldiers were bands of mercenaries who fought against the English during the reigns of Jean II and Charles V. When the Treaty of Brétigny temporarily interrupted the fighting in 1360, the soldiers proceeded to pillage large areas of France. Before 1440, to the extent that the *Ecorcheurs* raided the lands of neighboring states or vassals rather than the royal domain, the king could tolerate this system, since it enabled him to maintain a permanent body of soldiers without overly straining the royal budget. Once Charles VII had seized absolute tax powers throughout France, however, a *livre* of income collected by the Flayers represented considerably more than a *livre* lost to the more efficient royal tax collectors. Moreover, while they were fulfilling their fiscal role, mercenary troops were not available for military service. Even worse, if they felt they were not being paid sufficiently by one side in a conflict, they could easily change employers.

The question was not whether enough taxes could be raised to finance a permanent military force. Rather it was whether a ruler could control companies of soldiers away from battle sites where, since they were concentrated, they could be supervised fairly closely. After all, it might be argued, why use public revenues to pay soldiers who, once dispersed over the countryside, were free to pillage as they pleased anyway? In 1439, for example, no sooner had Toulouse paid a bribe of 2,000 *écus* to the *routier* Rodrigue de Villandrando than he took his soldiers into the neighboring region around the town of Mende and extracted a further payment.[95] The hiring of one group of mercenaries to discipline another, as had been done in Auvergne the previous year was no solution.[96] If the first band could not be controlled, how could one hope to command the second?

By the early 1440s, this situation was beginning to change. In 1441, Charles VII attempted an experiment. He led his army to arrest two of his former captains who had supported his enemies. Both expeditions ended in the capture and execution of the dissident leaders and their principal lieutenants. The successful conclusion of this exercise coincided with the growing strength of the one unit which distinguished the king's power from that of an *Ecorcheur* captain; namely, artillery. As noted earlier, improved cannon and projectiles had been the key factor in the victories of Charles VII over the English at Meaux in 1439 and over his vassals in the *Praguerie* of 1440. It would appear that in this period, improvements to artillery substantially lowered the cost of taking any strong-point occupied by disloyal or disobedient troops. As a result, the king was able to increase dramatically his power over his own army.

The Permanent Military Bureaucracy Reappears

A bureaucracy, as defined by Max Weber, is a continuous organization of appointed officials who act within a specific sphere of competence according to a set of rules.[97] By this definition, the French army of the 1430s was not a bureaucracy. Its units were hired on an *ad hoc* basis for limited periods of time. Moreover, its behavior on and especially off the field of battle frequently escaped the control of the king, and often spilled over from the military into the fiscal sphere. This situation was about to change.

With the French monarch's new ability to discipline geographically dispersed troops, it now became feasible in Western Europe for the first time in a thousand years to separate the roles of tax collector and soldier. The formation of permanent companies of soldiers financed 12 months a year from royal revenues had actually been part of the *Ordonnance* of 1439, but in the turmoil created by the *Praguerie* had never been applied. When the fighting against the English ceased temporarily at the truce of Tours in 1444, however, an opportunity arose to make use of the king's new power.

As a temporary expedient, Charles VII attempted to allow the disadvantages of the mercenary system to be borne by his eastern neighbors. He charged his son with escorting an army of idle *Ecorcheurs* onto the lands of the Duke of Burgundy and the German Emperor. Not surprisingly, the neighboring rulers protested against the damage done to their countrysides by the mercenaries, adding their voices to the numerous complaints from within France.

A new decree, the *Ordonnance* of 1445, called for the hiring of units of heavy cavalry that became known as *Compagnies d'ordonnance.* Each company was to be composed of 100 spears or *lances fournies*. A lance in turn was made up of six mounted men – an armored man-at-arms, two archers, two pages and a *coutillier*, a soldier armed with a dagger.[98] When the army was at full strength, prior to the reconquest of Normandy, there was a total of 1,800 lances of heavy cavalry, or about 10,800 men.[99] In practice, the bulk of the new units comprised simply those companies of former *Ecorcheurs* that Charles VII and his advisers felt would be most effective. These units were then used to purge the country of all mercenaries not chosen by the king. In addition to these units of campaign troops, there was a second category of soldiers hired for garrison duty. These *mortes-payes*, so-called because they were paid for duty at a certain spot and did not participate in campaigns, were initially mounted. However, the use of cavalry for these posts was gradually cut back after the end of the war against England.[100]

The units created by the 1445 decree were all permanent troops who served both in peace and in war. However, a further decree in 1448 called for the formation of units of reserve troops of bowmen who were called *franc-archers* since they were exempt from the tallage. These men were to be recruited at the parish level, one for every 80 households.[101] Following the death of Charles V in the previous century, the army that he had formed had been disbanded.[102] However, when the Hundred Years War was concluded in 1453, there was no cry for the dismissal of the units created by the decrees of 1445 and 1448.[103] Even at the death of Charles VII in 1461, it was accepted that the *Compagnies d'ordonnance*, the *mortes-*

payes, and the *francs-archers* would continue to serve at the expense of the royal treasury.[104]

The fiscal and military functions of the medieval soldier had been successfully transferred to two specialized bureaucracies. Henceforth, the collection of taxes would be reserved for assessors and collectors who acted in the name of the king and whose power was enforced by royal constables.[105] At the same time, the legitimate use of military force would be limited to a full-time body of soldiers who owed their appointments to their sovereign rather than to their company commanders.

The Apogee of the French Economy

Even if one admits that there is little evidence of a sharp increase in the tax burden of French citizens subsequent to the reforms of the 1430s, it is still nevertheless possible that the centralization of government administration created distortions that impeded economic growth. What evidence is there then that the French economy was less prosperous during the following decades than it might have been under a more decentralized or more liberal administration?

An important factor in determining the degree of prosperity of a country is the extent of its foreign trade. Exchange with other countries allows an economy to import products that would be costly to produce at home in return for exporting other goods that it can produce cheaply. The structure of France's foreign trade in the pre-industrial period was already well-established by the fifteenth century. The country exported wine, wheat and cloth; in exchange, it imported iron and non-ferrous metals. This trade had been badly disrupted by the war with England and by renewed tensions in the 1470's. However, after the treaty of Picquigny of 1475 between Louis XI and Edward IV, those sectors dependent on export markets experienced growth and prosperity during most of the last quarter of the fifteenth century.[106]

With the eviction of the English and the suppression of most of the pillaging by mercenary soldiers, internal trade in France also rebounded. However, well into the nineteenth century, the country would continue to be handicapped by the high cost of internal transport. Where navigable rivers were not available, land transport had to be used – at a cost six to seven times greater than that of water transport.[107]

The Valois kings, aware that their tax revenues depended on the health of the economy, undertook numerous steps to facilitate economic recovery. Bridges were rebuilt and roads restored. In addition, those taxes that had the greatest impact on economic activity were removed. In 1444, to encourage river transport, tolls were abolished on the Seine and its tributaries.[108] Certain of the most prominent fairs were exempted from indirect taxes. The fairs at Lyons were allowed to escape the royal edict that only French currency be used for transactions. The effects of the more prosperous times appear to have been felt by all social classes. Real wages increased, both in the countryside and in the towns. At the same time, landowners experienced a substantial improvement in their revenues.[109]

Although French historians agree that there was economic growth during the last half of the fifteenth century, they are divided as to its nature. A Malthusian school under Emmanuel Le Roy Ladurie and Michel Morineau has asserted that in the countryside there was simply a recovery to the per-capita income levels that France had experienced in the early fourteenth century, prior to the ravages of the Black Death and the Hundred Years War. In the absence of technical progress in agriculture, Le Roy Ladurie argued, Malthusian demographic pressure then held family incomes at the subsistence level until the nineteenth century.[110]

Another hypothesis, proposed by Fernand Braudel, is closer to the ideas of Adam Smith than to those of Malthus. After 1450, Braudel argued, there was an expansion of trade, an increasingly efficient division of labor, especially in the towns, and greater use of capitalism. Conscious of the differences between the France of 1500 and that of earlier centuries, Braudel suggested that during this period there was a second take-off into modern economic growth which complemented that of the high Middle Ages.[111]

At issue is whether this economic expansion was followed by decline or simply by stagnation at constant per-capita income levels during the six-teenth century. The weight of recent research seems to indicate that the growth that did occur in the decades prior to 1500 did not involve any important change in production techniques.[112] However, subsequent to the turn of the century, there seems to have been a deterioration in real income levels.[113] In short, per-capita income in France appears to have peaked in the last decades of the fifteenth century at levels that were not to be exceeded until the nineteenth century. This evidence indicates that the end of the fifteenth century did not see the economic stagnation that North and Thomas argue resulted from the tax reforms of Charles VII. If there was a slowing down of economic growth in France compared with England, it appears to have begun only in the sixteenth century. If so, then, the relative decline of the French economy in the modern period must be attributed to some cause other than the centralization of fiscal powers.

An alternative interpretation of the events of the fifteenth century is that the substitution of the more distant royal tax authority for the regional feudal lord led to a fall in total effective tax rates. Collusion between the royal constables and powerful local families, which would have the effect of lowering the effective taxes of the latter, appears to have been a constant problem. In the sixteenth century, constables were forbidden to hold office in the same district for more than a year at a time.[114] In addition, as seen in the suppression of tolls on the Seine and the fiscal concessions to the fairs, the remaining levies were reallocated in a way that offered less distortion of economic activity. The result was an increase in prosperity which enabled France not only to recover from the cataclysms of the fourteenth and early fifteenth centuries, but also to attain levels of well-being that were not to be matched until the Industrial Revolution.

THE SHELL OF THE NATION STATE

A state may be thought of as a communications network backed by a territorial monopoly over the use of force. The earlier feudal duchies and counties of Europe corresponded roughly to the areas in which people spoke a mutually understandable regional dialect. In northern and central France, for example, there were more than a dozen different regional idioms. However, because of earlier patterns of migration and conquest, the regions of Europe were in their turn grouped into larger families of related dialects, the English, French, Spanish, Italian, Portuguese, German language groupings.

Artillery permitted the extension of state boundaries beyond the dialect. In some cases, the new boundaries corresponded closely to those of a family of related dialects. This was the case in France, England, Spain, and Portugal, where internal geographical barriers to troop movements were moderate and oceans and mountains offered protection from external attack. One central government was able to control all those speaking related dialects, as well as important minority linguistic groups. The new political units were in effect the shells of nation states. All that was required was a means of linking the dialects for a more powerful communications network to emerge.

In other cases, largely because of geography, the artillery boundaries were smaller than those of the family of dialects. Nations would not form here until a more powerful military technology appeared. The German-speaking people were spread over a considerably more extended territory within which there were substantial barriers to internal movement. More-over, particularly in the north and in the Danube valley, the empire was vulnerable to attack from external groups. Similarly, the Italian-speaking people were distributed over a peninsula along and across which internal transport was difficult. Although there was a tendency for larger regional groupings to form within each of these linguistic areas in the late Middle

Ages (for example, the Swabian League in Germany, and Florence and its protected states in Italy), effective national unification was not to be possible until the nineteenth century.

In a final set of cases, in eastern and south-eastern Europe, the equilibrium state boundaries were larger than those of cultural groups. Nation states could emerge here only if the gunpowder empires of the Russians, Turks, and Hapsburgs were broken apart. To do so would require communications technologies that would not be available until the twentieth century.

The dominance of European history over the following four centuries by a small number of Western European countries therefore appears to be due to a technological coincidence: that the scale economies to effective artillery peaked at the size of territory occupied by families of related dialects. In the Netherlands, England, Spain, France, and Portugal, the introduction of effective artillery had created the shells for powerful new communications networks, within which the first nation states would subsequently emerge.

Arms and the Monarchy

What occurred in fifteenth-century France to permit the area in which the king had a fiscal monopoly to expand to the compact form predicted by simple spatial models of resource allocation? According to one current of recent research, the professionalization thesis, the explanation is military. Improvements to the bow and crossbow, along with new weapons such as the pike and halberd, increased the effectiveness of foot soldiers relative to horsemen. The king was therefore able to build up a disciplined professional infantry-based army capable of defeating the heavy feudal cavalry. The problem with this argument is that during the century from 1350 to 1450 there was actually a decline in the use of infantry in France. First the English invaders and subsequently the French defenders themselves switched from the ineffective combination of feudal foot soldiers and armored knights to highly mobile professional all-cavalry armies consisting of two mounted archers for every man-at-arms.

Observers of this period have also pointed to the increasing effectiveness of artillery. It is suggested that improvements to these weapons enabled national rulers to knock down the castle walls of rebellious nobles. Some suggest that the change occurred in the late 1440s, others a decade or two later. But what was the crucial improvement and when did it occur? And why should better artillery favor the king rather than the lord of a smaller territory? How can one explain that the might of the German Emperor was in decline at the same time that the power of the French monarch was on the rise?

Another approach, the commercialization thesis, emphasizes economic changes that required a modification in the tax system. It is argued that with the rise of inter-regional trade, the feudal state was no longer the optimally sized taxing authority. Because of the destructive effects on trade of the absence of a single central fiscal authority, the representatives of the French towns decided in 1439 to grant a tax monopoly to the king. According to this version, the French monarchs then used this authority to build up a permanent army financed by the receipts generated by a fiscal bureaucracy. With this army to enforce its monopoly to tax, the monarchy was able to consolidate its power within the territorial limits of the French linguistic group. Furthermore, it has been suggested that the distortions created by royal interventions resulted in a slowing of economic growth in France relative to England where the king's fiscal power was limited by parliament.

However, this theory too has a number of shortcomings. Why should the representatives of the towns have believed that the French king could actually enforce a monopoly over taxation in 1439 when he had been unable to do so previously? Subsequent to 1440, royal tax receipts as a share of income seem not to have risen markedly. Moreover, the period following the consolidation of the royal fiscal powers witnessed a prolonged economic expansion, with per-capita income in France reaching levels that were not to be seen again until the nineteenth century.

Although existing theories of the rise of the extended monarchy in France leave a number of questions unanswered, they nevertheless focus attention on the most important elements of a possible answer. A professional army, artillery, and absolute tax powers all play a part in the story, but not necessarily the roles that historians have assigned to them. The crucial events seem to have been the introduction of iron-reinforced and cast-iron shot along with cast-metal muzzle-loading cannon. By increasing the range, precision, rate of fire, and destructive power of artillery, these innovations greatly facilitated the task of those who were besieging a strong-point. They enabled the attacker to concentrate a volley of highly destructive projectiles at a single point on a wall or gate, from a range sufficiently distant to be safe from defending archery.

This small unit of martial power was inserted near the top of the military hierarchy, responsible directly to the king. Since it was too expensive for a lesser noble or military captain to form his own optimally sized artillery unit, the innovations greatly increased the ability of the sovereign to control his own army. In 1438, the French king had been forced to subsidize his mercenary captains to prevent them from pillaging. In 1441, however, he was sufficiently strong to send his army to arrest and execute two of his own mercenary captains who had been collaborating with his enemies.

One effect of the introduction of improved artillery was to enable the king to extend the *external margin* of the territory he controlled. The artillery corps was turned against his own rebelling nobles during the *Praguerie* of 1440. It was also used to great effect against the English invaders. From 1437 to 1442 the improved ordnance enabled Charles VII to retake the towns in the Ile-de-France, freeing Paris from the stranglehold of enemy occupation. Subsequently, at Formigny in 1450 and at Castillon three years later, the French artillery played an important role in the victories that drove the English from French soil. By the time of the majority of Charles VII's grandson, Charles VIII, in 1491, the artillery corps had helped push the territorial boundaries of the state outward until they corresponded to the approximate limits occupied by the French-speaking people.

In France, the improvements in artillery also had important implications for the *internal margin* between private and public activity. In extending his political boundaries, Charles VII eliminated virtually all competing taxing authorities, beginning with the nobles in 1440, and ending with the pillaging *Ecorcheurs* in 1445. In the process, the distance of the typical taxpayer from those who taxed him increased. The result appears to have been what models of bureaucratic behavior predict. When allowance is made for the differences in spending between periods of peace and those of war, total taxes as a share of income seem to have decreased between the first and the last halves of the fifteenth centuries. It is no coincidence that as the century closed, France experienced a period of expanding trade and relative prosperity that was not to be equaled until the beginning of the Industrial Revolution in the nineteenth century.

That large states appeared first in the western part of Europe was primarily due to geography. Along the western periphery of the continent, in Portugal, Spain, France, and England, low internal troop movement costs and substantial geographic barriers to outside attack enabled a single effective artillery unit to dominate the space occupied by a group of related dialects. In other parts of Europe, where barriers to external attack were slight or internal mobility difficult, unification into larger political entities was incompatible with fifteenth-century military and informational technology.

NOTES

1 Charles Petit-Dutaillis, *Charles VII, Louis XI et les premières années de Charles VIII* (1422–1492) (Tallandier, 1981), p. 102.

2 Philippe Contamine, *Guerre, état et société à la fin du moyen âge. Etude sur les armées des rois de France*, 1337–1494 (Mouton, 1972), p. 263.
3 Ibid.
4 Ulrich Blum and Leonard Dudley, "A spatial approach to structural change: the making of the French hexagon," *Journal of Economic History*, 49 (1989), pp. 662–5. See also Arnold M. Faden, *Economics of Time and Space* (Iowa State University Press, 1977), pp. 554–5.
5 August Lösch, *The Economics of Location* (Yale University Press, 1954).
6 G. William Skinner, "The Structure of Chinese History," *Journal of Asian Studies*, 44 (1985), pp. 271–92.
7 Joseph R. Strayer, *On the Medieval Origins of the Modern State* (Princeton University Press, 1970).
8 Martin Wolfe, *The Fiscal System of Renaissance France* (Yale University Press, 1972), p. 20.
9 Ibid., p. 25.
10 Richard Bean, "War and the birth of the nation state," *Journal of Economic History*, 33 (1973), p. 206.
11 R. Ernest Dupuy and Trevor N. Dupuy, *The Encyclopedia of Military History from 3500 BC to the Present*, 2nd rev. edn (Harper and Row, 1986), pp. 279, 331–2.
12 Philippe Contamine, *War in the Middle Ages* (Blackwell, 1984), p. 132.
13 Dupuy and Dupuy, *The Encyclopedia of Military History*, p. 369.
14 Ibid., p. 335.
15 Ibid., p. 425.
16 Douglass C. North and Robert Paul Thomas, *The Rise of the Western World: A New Economic History* (Cambridge University Press, 1973), p. 121.
17 Dupuy and Dupuy, *The Encyclopedia of Military History*, p. 335.
18 Contamine, *Guerre, état et société*, p. 265.
19 Bean, "War and the birth of the nation state," p. 207.
20 Claude Gaier, *L'industrie et le commerce des armes dans les anciennes principantés belges du XIIIme, à la fin du XVme siècle* (Les belles lettres, 1973), p. 314.
21 Dupuy and Dupuy, *The Encyclopedia of Military History*, p. 427.
22 William H. McNeill, *The Pursuit of Power: Technology, Armed Force and Society since AD 1000* (University of Chicago Press, 1982), p. 87.
23 See Maurice Daumas, *Histoire générale des techniques*, vol. II, *Les premières étapes du machinisme* (Presses universitaires de France, 1965), p. 88; Bean, "War and the birth of the nation state," p. 207.
24 Fernand Braudel, *Civilization and Capitalism 15th–18th Century*, vol. 2, *The Wheels of Commerce* (Harper and Row, l982), p. 515.
25 David Friedman, "A theory of the size and shape of nations," *Journal of Political Economy*, 85 (1977), p. 61.
26 Petit-Dutaillis, *Charles VII*, p. 279.
27 North and Thomas, *The Rise of the Western World*, p. 121.
28 Wolfe, *The Fiscal System of Renaissance France*, p. 34.
29 Jean Favier, *La guerre de cent ans* (Fayard, Paris, 1980), p. 557.
30 Ibid., pp. 567–9.
31 North and Thomas, *The Rise of the Western World*, p. 122.
32 A. P. Usher, "The general course of wheat prices in France: 1350–1788," *Review of Economics and Statistics*, 12 (1930), pp. 163–4.
33 North and Thomas, *The Rise of the Western World*, p. 122.
34 Philippe Contamine, "La France à la fin du XVe siècle: pour un état des questions,"

in *La France à la fin du XVe siècle*, eds B. Chevalier and P. Contamine (Centre national de recherche scientifique, Paris, 1985), p. 3.

35 Henri Dubois, "Le commerce de la France au temps de Louis XI: expansion ou défensive?" in *La France à la fin du XVe siècle*, eds B. Chevalier and P. Contamine (Centre national de recherche scientifique, Paris, 1985), pp. 17–18.

36 Wolfe, *The Fiscal System of Renaissance France*, p. 5.

37 Petit-Dutaillis, *Charles VII*, p. 278–9.

38 Wolfe, *The Fiscal System of Renaissance France*, p. 27.

39 Gaier, *L'industrie et le commerce des armes*, pp. 189–90.

40 H. Dubled, "L'artillerie royale française à l'époque de Charles VII et au début du règne de Louis XI (1437–1469): les frères Bureau," *Sciences et techniques de l'armement*, 50 (1976), p. 568.

41 Daumas, *Histoire générale des techniques*, p. 60.

42 O. F. G. Hogg, *Artillery: Its Origin, Heyday and Decline* (Hurst, London, 1970), p. 36.

43 Gaier, *L'industrie et le commerce des armes*, p. 91.

44 Hogg, *Artillery*, pp. 32, 34.

45 Ibid., p. 35.

46 J. R. Partington, *A History of Greek Fire and Gunpowder* (Heffer, 1960), p. 110.

47 See Hogg, *Artillery*, p. 36; Daumas, *Histoire générale des techniques*, p. 90.

48 Gaier, *L'industrie et le commerce des armes*, p. 273.

49 Partington, *A History of Greek Fire and Gunpowder*, p. 115.

50 Contamine, *War in the Middle Ages*, p. 145.

51 Hogg, *Artillery*, p. 127.

52 Contamine, *War in the Middle Ages*, p. 146.

53 Pierre-Roger Gaussin, *Louis XI: Un roi entre deux mondes* (Nizet, Paris, 1976), p. 191.

54 Carlo M. Cipolla, *Guns, Sails and Empires* (Pantheon, 1965), p. 24.

55 Gaier, *L'industrie et le commerce des armes*, p. 355.

56 Ibid., p. 353.

57 Daumas, *Histoire générale des techniques*, p. 92.

58 Contamine, *War in the Middle Ages*, p. 200.

59 Dupuy and Dupuy, *The Encyclopedia of Military History*, pp. 404, 432.

60 Partington, *A History of Greek Fire and Gunpowder*, p. 117.

61 Contamine, *War in the Middle Ages*, p. 147.

62 Ibid., p. 297.

63 Gaier, *L'industrie et le commerce des armes*, p. 235.

64 Ibid., p. 270.

65 Gaier, *L'industrie et le commerce des armes*, p. 95.

66 Contamine, *Guerre, état et société*, p. 238.

67 Dubled, "L'artillerie royale française," p. 579.

68 Ibid., p. 567.

69 Ibid., pp. 572–3.

70 Ibid., pp. 567–8.

71 Ibid., pp. 579.

72 Petit-Dutaillis, *Charles VII*, pp. 113–14.

73 Contamine, *Guerre, état et société*, p. 297–8.

74 Contamine, *War in the Middle Ages*, p. 201.

75 Contamine, *Guerre, état et société*, p. 272.

76 Favier, *La guerre de cent ans*, pp. 546–7.

77 Contamine, *Guerre, état et société*, p. 238.

78 Wolfe, *The Fiscal System of Renaissance France*, pp. 33–4.

79 Favier, *La guerre de cent ans*, p. 554.

80 Petit-Dutaillis, *Charles VII*, p. 114.
81 Favier, *La guerre de cent ans*, p. 592.
82 Daumas, *Histoire générale des techniques*, p. 88; Dupuy and Dupuy, *The Encyclopedia of Military History*, p. 412.
83 Favier, *La guerre de cent ans*, p. 611.
84 Ferdinand Lot, *L'art militaire et les armées au moyen âge en Europe et dans le proche orient*, vol. 2 (Payot, Paris, 1946), p. 86.
85 Contamine, *War in the Middle Ages*, pp. 148–9.
86 Wolfe, *The Fiscal System of Renaissance France*, p. 307.
87 Ibid., p. 321.
88 See, for example, North and Thomas, *The Rise of the Western World*, p. 122; Bean, "War and the birth of the nation state," p. 217.
89 Dubois, "Le commerce de la France," p. 19.
90 Contamine, *Guerre, état et société*, p. 268.
91 Favier, *La guerre de cent ans*, p. 566.
92 Ibid.
93 Ibid., p. 568.
94 Contamine, *Guerre, état et société*, p. 266.
95 Favier, *La guerre de cent ans*, p. 568.
96 Ibid.
97 Max Weber, *The Theory of Social and Economic Organization* (The Free Press, 1964), pp. 330–2.
98 Contamine, *Guerre, état et société*, p. 278.
99 Ibid., p. 282.
100 Ibid., p. 291.
101 Ibid., p. 304.
102 Contamine, *War in the Middle Ages*, p. 168.
103 Contamine, *Guerre, état et société*, p. 283.
104 Contamine, *War in the Middle Ages*, p. 170.
105 Wolfe, *The Fiscal System of Renaissance France*, p. 309.
106 Dubois, "Le commerce de la France," p. 21.
107 Ibid., p. 17.
108 Favier, *La guerre de cent ans*, p. 583.
109 Contamine, "La France à la fin du XVe siècle," pp. 3, 4.
110 Emmanuel Le Roy Ladurie, "Les masses profondes: la paysannerie," in *Paysannerie et croissance*, by Emmanuel Le Roy Ladurie and M. Morineau, vol. 1, part 2 of *Histoire économique et sociale de la France*, eds Fernand Braudel and E. Labrousse (Presses universitaires de France, 1977), p. 647.
111 Fernand Braudel, "Profits et bilan de plus d'un demi-millénaire," in *Histoire économique et sociale de la France*, vol. 4, part 3, eds Fernand Braudel and E. Labrousse (Presses universitaires de France, 1977), p. 1689.
112 Contamine, "La France à la fin du XVe siècle," p. 9.
113 Ibid., pp. 3–4.
114 Wolfe, *The Fiscal System of Renaissance France*, p. 309.

5

The Eclipse of the Caravans

When did the modern period in history begin? Some have suggested that it was with the voyages of discovery, while others have favored the outset of the British industrial and urban revolutions. However, in neither case were there basic changes in social structure with respect to preceding periods. Here it is argued that the application of typography to standardized versions of spoken languages permitted a fundamental restructuring of European society. The transformation was first apparent in the United Provinces of the Netherlands in the late sixteenth century. During a three-decade burst of innovation, the Dutch introduced the multinational corporation, the stock exchange, efficient financial markets, the modern army, the federal state, and a decentralized bureaucracy capable of levying tax rates comparable to those of the present day. These developments suggest the emergence of a new type of political unit – the nation state – based on generalized literacy in the vernacular. The decline of the spice caravans from the Persian Gulf to the Mediterranean was but one of the world-wide consequences of this transformation.

Groningen

N O R T H   S E A

Zuider Zee

AMSTERDAM

Leiden

The Hague

Utrecht

ROTTERDAM

Brill

Breda

ANTWERP

Bruges

GHENT

BRUSSELS

FLEMISH

WALLOON

LIÈGE

LILLE

Tournai

Arras

Cambrai

Scheldt

Meuse

Rhine

Mosel

Luxemburg

Figure 5.1   The formation of the United Provinces, 1565–1607.
(*Source: The New Cambridge Modern History Atlas,* 1979, p. 151.)

Hormuz is a small island at the mouth of the Persian Gulf. As it receives no rainfall, it is uninhabited today. But in the late fifteenth century it was the site of a prosperous town and a powerful Portuguese fortress whose food and water were all brought in by sea. The island was a trans-shipment point for pepper and other spices carried by armed merchantmen from the East Indies. From Hormuz, the spices were generally shipped in smaller boats to Basra, in Ottoman territory (present-day Iraq) at the head of the Persian Gulf, where they were loaded on barges to be transported up to Baghdad on the Tigris river. After a short journey by camel over to the Euphrates river, the goods then continued by barge to Birecik in the southeast corner of present-day Turkey. A final voyage by camel brought the spices to Aleppo in Syria, where traders from Europe were waiting to carry them further westward.[1]

Since ancient times, the people of Europe and North Africa had obtained oriental spices in this way from caravans traveling overland from the Persian Gulf and the Red Sea to the eastern Mediterranean. Throughout the sixteenth century, despite Portuguese trading voyages around the Cape of Good Hope, this overland commerce continued to flourish.[2] However, during the first decades of the seventeenth century, the spice caravans suddenly stopped. They were never resumed. In this same period, the eastern Mediterranean actually began to import spices from Western Europe.[3] In 1622, with insufficient resources to keep its fortress in repair and control the surrounding sea lanes, Hormuz fell to a combined British and Persian attack. The town and fortress were subsequently destroyed.

Twenty years before the fall of Hormuz, in 1602, the people of the United Provinces – the new Protestant republic in the northern Netherlands – had been offered an unusual opportunity. In that year, with strong government encouragement, the separate Dutch companies that had been trading with the orient over the previous few years were merged. The new *Verenigde Oostindische Compagnie,* or Dutch East India Company, was granted a ten-year monopoly over Dutch trade in the Indian Ocean and the Pacific. The Company's charter stipulated that all citizens of the United Provinces had the right to participate "for as little or as much as they pleased" in the initial public offering.[4] Within a month, the enormous sum of over six million florins had been raised.[5] By 1605 the new company had begun a series of territorial conquests that was to give it a monopoly over trade with Indonesia. At the height of its power, in 1675, it would have some 30 ships plying the routes to the Indies.[6]

Did the eclipse of the caravans create a windfall opportunity for profitable ocean trade between the orient and Europe that the Dutch traders were quick to exploit? Or was it the rise of new commercial organizations that somehow led to the decline of more traditional trading institutions?

THE BEGINNING OF THE MODERN AGE

The explanation for the decline of the caravans is important because it helps determine when the modern period in history began. Among historians, there are several different opinions on this issue. In what is perhaps the majority view, many have argued that there was some sort of discontinuity around the year 1500. According to this position, the voyages of discovery of the late fifteenth and early sixteenth centuries marked a break between the pre-modern period of limited contact between the world's major civilizations and the more recent period of Western dominance. For example, Immanuel Wallerstein asserts that in the sixteenth century the mode of production in Europe was transformed from feudalism to capitalism on a world scale.[7] William McNeill also picks 1500 as the beginning of the period of world dominance by European societies.[8]

Although it is clear that world trade routes shifted in the years following the great discoveries, it is less evident that the structure of the society and economy of Europe underwent any fundamental change as a result. The new monarchies of Charles V, Francis I, and Henry VIII in 1545 were essentially similar to the extended territorial state put together almost a hundred years earlier by Charles VII of France with the help of his artillery corps. Moreover, the economic and social structure of sixteenth-century Europe, with entrepôt trading cities serving an agricultural hinterland, continued a pattern that had existed in antiquity and reappeared in the twelfth and thirteenth centuries. Venice and Genoa were in essence the heirs of Athens and Carthage.

Another date frequently mentioned as the boundary between the pre-modern and modern periods is the beginning of the Industrial Revolution, around 1750. For Carlo Cipolla, there were two major breaks in human social development. The first occurred around the eighth millennium BC when humans began to plant seeds and consequently changed from a migratory to a sedentary way of life. The second took place in the mid-eighteenth century, when large numbers of people first began to work in mechanized factories. He suggested that "continuity is broken between the cave-man and the builders of the Pyramids, just as all continuity is broken between the ploughman and the modern operator of a power station."[9]

But what was really new in eighteenth-century industrialization? The application of inanimate power to machines had been practiced for centuries: wind and water mills had been in use for industrial processes since the high Middle Ages. Even the move from the countryside to the towns and cities in Europe was not new to the Industrial Revolution. Already, by the early sixteenth century, the majority of the population of Holland was urbanized.[10]

Between these two dates of 1500 and 1750, there occurred a century of upheaval and convulsion lasting from about 1550 until 1650. Charles Wilson, who studied this period in detail, pointed out that by its end Europe had become more tolerant of diversity than it had been a century earlier. Wilson focused on the experience of the Dutch Republic which was formed during this century, arguing that it constituted something that was new in European history. It was the first large state run by commoners rather than by an aristocracy. In addition it introduced the first economy in which exchange by means of the market became the dominant mechanism for allocating resources.[11]

What was there about this particular interval that might distinguish it from earlier periods of history? The notion of a discontinuity between the pre-modern and modern periods suggests a remarkable change in the way people lived, worked, and interacted socially and politically. However, Europe had experienced turmoil and upheaval in previous centuries. And the Venetian Republic had originally been governed by a council elected by the bourgeoisie. Moreover, Venice, Florence, and other Italian cities had developed capitalism to a highly refined state in the late Middle Ages.

Within the century singled out by Wilson, the events of three critical decades – the years from 1590 to 1620 – deserve closer examination. During the first half of the sixteenth century, Antwerp had been the center of commercial credit for Europe. Short-term interest rates in this city had varied from 20 percent in 1510 to 10–14 percent in the decade from 1550 to 1560.[12] Even when adjusted for the inflation of this period, the implicit real interest rate (defined as the nominal interest rate less the expected rate of inflation) was extremely high by present-day standards. A little over a half century later, however, rates in Amsterdam had reached real levels comparable to those of the recent postwar period. In the 1620s, the Dutch East India Company was paying the Amsterdam Exchange Bank 5 percent interest for commercial credit.[13]

The usual method for engaging in long-distance trade in pre-modern Europe was the partnership. Those who advanced funds or entrepreneurial ability to a trading venture agreed to share in its profits in proportion to their contributions. However, once the venture was completed, the partnership was usually wound up. As a result, there was little incentive to engage in fixed investments for long-term returns. Then, the Dutch East India Company was founded with a monopoly on trade between the Netherlands and Asia. Instead of winding up the company once its first given set of activities had been completed, the owners developed the practice of leaving their capital in the firm. The Company differed from earlier firms with a permanent capital base – such as the English East India Company, founded two years earlier in 1600 – in shipping the goods it traded directly to the markets where they could command the highest price, without necessarily passing through the home country. To preserve the liquidity of shareholders, a secondary market quickly developed in which owners of shares could transfer their holdings to other investors.[14] Here then was the first multinational corporation and the first true stock exchange.

Since the appearance of the first historical records, humans had been led by small numbers of individuals who exerted control through highly centralized bureaucracies. Yet once the class of wealthy merchants or regents who led the municipal governments of the Netherlands had cast off the yoke of Spanish rule, they were extremely reluctant to grant power to a single individual. Instead, this geographically dispersed patriciate insisted on governing their new state themselves, collectively, on the basis of consensus. The result was the first true federal state. (The Swiss Confederation, which dates back to 1291, was at this time still an alliance of independent cantons: it was not until 1647, for example, that Switzerland formed a federal army.) Although decision-making was often long and arduous, the procedure not only managed to keep the United Provinces together, but also provided the basis for the first world-wide trading empire.

A final example from this key period concerns the way in which foot soldiers in European armies went into battle. Before the seventeenth century, they usually did so at their own pace, responding to the orders issued by their commanders in confused and unpredictable fashion. In the final decade of the sixteenth century, however, Maurice of Nassau, the Dutch stadholder, developed a method of training soldiers to march in regularized fashion in small units, keeping in step with one another. By repeated drill, infantrymen could be taught to respond automatically to complicated commands. The result was the birth of the modern foot soldier and a great increase in the effectiveness of infantry.[15]

All of these developments – the fall of interest rates to modern levels, the creation of efficient methods for raising risk capital for foreign ventures, the first federal state and the first rigorously drilled army – were crammed into a few decades after 1590. In each case the United Provinces was at the forefront of new developments. The question which therefore arises is whether there is any deeper significance to this cluster of events, both in time and in space. Was this grouping merely coincidental, or had something occurred to change the nature of European society?

The External Margin of the New Monarchies

By the middle of the sixteenth century, the states of Western Europe had reached a position of uneasy equilibrium. For the preceding half-century, with their power over their own nobility consolidated, the new monarchical states had been attempting to expand outward. In areas in the Americas,

Africa, and Asia that had not yet mastered gunpowder technology, two of these powers, Spain and Portugal, had been able to carve out vast empires. Similarly, in central Europe, within the German Empire, the Hapsburgs continued to increase the territory under their control, incorporating Bohemia and a strip of western Hungary into their domains.

In Western Europe, however, despite frequent clashes in disputed territories, the areas that the new monarchies controlled virtually ceased to grow. In Italy, the Netherlands, and western Germany, France's efforts to expand were blocked, due in large part to opposition from Spain. However, France itself was quite strong enough to prevent England or Spain from seizing any of its territory. As a result, the political boundaries of Western Europe were beginning to become stabilized in their present-day positions.

It is interesting to compare these political boundaries with the cultural frontiers that circumscribed groups of related dialects. In the case of France and England, the two sets of borders roughly coincided. Nationalism could develop without major changes in political boundaries. In the case of Italy and Germany, however, state borders were much narrower than the cultural frontiers. The growth of national identities would require the unification of numerous small states. Finally, in the Hapsburg domains, including the Netherlands, the political boundaries lay outside the cultural boundaries. Here national aspirations could be fulfilled only by obtaining independence from foreign domination.

Within these territorial boundaries, as Edward Fox observed, there was a considerable gap between the trading cities with access to water transport and the more autonomous hinterland dependent on land transport.[16] Yet while shipment by road was too expensive to permit the trade of heavy commodities such as grain over long distances, it was nevertheless perfectly adequate for the movement of cannon and troops. As a result, the new gunpowder-based armies were quite strong enough to keep the commercial cities under the monarch's control.

The fate of the cities of the Netherlands illustrates the extent of the monarch's power and the stability of the new equilibrium. In 1477, the heiress to the Burgundy estates had married Maximilian of Austria. As a result, the Netherlands had come under the control of the Austrian Hapsburgs. Maximilian had then married his son Philip to Joanna of Castile, the heiress to the throne of Spain. The oldest son of this couple, Charles V, therefore inherited an immense territory. By 1550, the Hapsburg Empire over which he reigned included Spain, southern Italy and Sicily, Austria, and Bohemia as well as the Netherlands. In 1540 the city of Ghent in Flanders revolted against what it considered an excessive level of taxes levied by its Hapsburg overlord. However, the rebellion was easily crushed and the city's privileges were transferred to its rival, Antwerp.

The Internal Margin of the New Monarchies

Although the area under the monarch's direct control had increased following the military innovations of the fifteenth century, the overall role of the state in society had generally diminished. The complex reciprocal sets of rights and obligations that bound the medieval peasants and their lords had in many places – particularly in the towns and the surrounding regions – been replaced by an exchange of monetary tax payments for a limited range of public services. The primary concern of the monarchical bureaucracies was to protect and increase the physical assets under their control. Accordingly, the state's intervention was limited in large part to defense against foreign attack and to the protection of property rights.

In contrast to twentieth-century practice, the state devoted a relatively small part of its resources to maintaining the community's accepted rules of behavior; that is, what Douglass North defined as a society's ideology.[17] In practice, since most people acquired language and other forms of knowledge outside of formal institutions, most elements of ideology were not easily controlled. As a result, the cultural role of the state itself was to a great extent limited to the protection of the Catholic Church. In practice, this duty meant the imprisonment or execution of heretics or other deviants condemned by the Church's own bureaucracy.

Although the ideological role of the pre-modern state may have been relatively modest, that of the Catholic Church was virtually all-encompassing. During the Middle Ages, the Church's virtual monopoly of a limited store of manuscripts had been the basis for a network of written and oral communications made up of three distinct levels. At the top were the Pope and the Church government or *curia* who determined the types of information that the network could transmit. At a somewhat lower level were the monasteries, seminaries and, later, universities, that stored this information and transmitted it to a literate elite taught to read and write. Although communication at this level was originally entirely in Latin, by the last centuries of the Middle Ages, written forms of the spoken or vernacular languages were being used increasingly, particularly for correspondence within the lay community. At the third and lowest level of the medieval information network were the thousands of individual churches and priests. They constituted the basis for oral reproduction of information in the vernacular, enabling the elite to control the illiterate majority of the population.

Why not permit other beliefs? The Church may be seen as the principal organization by which European society accumulated and transmitted information; that is, it was the dominant institution in Europe's information system. In return, the Church was able to extract a great flow of tithes, and bequests as well as income from its own extensive landholdings. It also received revenues from the sale of indulgences – payments in return for the pardon of earthly and purgatorial punishment for sin (it was not until 1562 at the Council of Trent that the sale of indulgences was forbidden). To permit other beliefs would therefore have led to a reduction in the considerable rents that this system generated.

Because the Church itself controlled medieval society's principal information network, an effective challenge to its dominance was in any case extremely difficult. The Inquisition, which had been established in the thirteenth century, had been successful in suppressing the various heretical movements that arose. Since threats to ideology were relatively few and quite localized, most of the states' military resources could be devoted to the protection of physical assets. In any case, the international mobility of artisans and merchants across political frontiers limited the share of the society's total income that could be channeled into the tax system. By the end of the fifteenth century, the public sector in the more advanced areas of Western Europe consisted of a relatively modest state–Church apparatus whose principal roles were the protection of physical assets and the maintenance of the three-tiered information network. Although the written symbols and military hardware had changed, late medieval European society was based on essentially the same religious and secular institutions that had been developed some four thousand years earlier by the Sumerians.

Even in the private sector (the part of the society's resources not controlled by the state or Church bureaucracies), a Sumerian from the middle centuries of the third millennium BC would probably have had no difficulty in adapting to European practices of this period. It is true that in the thirteenth and fourteenth centuries AD, the cities of northern Italy had introduced a number of innovations, particularly in the sphere of banking: cheques, holding companies and double-entry book-keeping were all invented in Florence.[18] However, the major concern of the new capitalist class continued to be the movement of relatively small quantities of goods with a high value per unit of weight, such as spices and textiles, from places where they were inexpensive to other places where they were more costly. By the mid-sixteenth century, the institutions used to conduct this type of exchange had become standardized and stabilized.

Although the Italian city-states remained prosperous after 1500, they were no longer at the center of European trade and finance. Following the voyages of discovery, trade routes had shifted from the Mediterranean to the Atlantic. Antwerp in the north had become the focal point for European commerce. The city's business sector offered a remarkable synthesis of Italian developments. However, it contributed little that was new. In the words of Fernand Braudel, "Antwerp did not set out to capture the world – on the contrary, a world thrown off balance by the great discoveries, and tilting toward the Atlantic, clung to Antwerp, *faute de mieux.*"[19]

As for the lands immediately to the north of Antwerp, they were considerably less wealthy than the southern Netherlands.[20] In 1514, Amsterdam had a population of 13,500; by the mid-sixteenth century, it had grown to a town of 30,000.[21] In contrast, Antwerp in the same period had a population of about 100,000.[22] However, the northern Netherlands had several geographic advantages which would prove crucial in the century that lay ahead. Their position on the North Sea coast at the mouth of the Rhine and Meuse rivers would allow them to control traffic from the Baltic to southern Europe and from the Atlantic into central Germany. In addition, the canals that the Dutch built to link their many rivers and lakes gave them an unexcelled system of internal transport. Finally, the great rivers and the marshy terrain offered the northern Netherlands considerable protection from attack by land, except in winter months.

THE COMMUNICATIONS BOTTLENECK

The underlying stability in social, economic, and political structures of early sixteenth-century Europe may be explained in part by the existing communications technology. As of the first decades of the sixteenth century there was no way of reaching the majority of a society's members with an identical storable message. The consequences were evident in every field of human endeavor. Potential leaders of dissident political or religious movements were unable to communicate quickly with those whose support would be necessary for their success. Military commanders could not be sure that their orders would be carried out in uniform fashion by dispersed bodies of troops. Information of possible arbitrage gains from commercial activities circulated very slowly and was likely to be obsolete before it could be acted upon.

Part of the difficulty was that until the middle of the fifteenth century, European society had known no means of reproducing and storing information accurately in large quantities. Messages could be reproduced in non-oral form only by hand, one laborious copy at a time. Because of the high cost of written information, only a small amount of it was produced, and it circulated among a limited subset of the total population. Moreover, because of copying errors, a given text tended to diverge increasingly from its original version with each successive reproduction.

Even if written information had been less expensive to reproduce, however, its circulation would not have had a great impact. As late as the early sixteenth century, the number of people capable of sending and receiving information in non-oral form was quite limited. Moreover, the bulk of existing manuscripts were written in Latin, which by the end of the Middle Ages was a second language for all who used it.

It is extremely difficult for anyone raised in a print culture to imagine what it was like to live in a society dependent upon manuscripts in a foreign language for its accumulated store of information. Even if one were among the fortunate few who knew how to read, the information to which one had access remained exceedingly limited. A well-stocked library might contain 80 manuscripts. Moreover, because of the inevitable mistakes made in copying, each of these manuscripts was in fact a unique document. Thus the page illuminated by one's candle had its own individual identity, whose relation with the rest of great dark mass of accumulated knowledge would always remain uncertain.

In the late Middle Ages, a fall in the cost of the medium for storing information served to focus attention of the cost of copying. Manuscripts were originally written on parchment, a product made from the skins of calves or sheep.[23] Because of the limited supply of such animals, this material was very costly. Accordingly, the introduction of paper, made from more plentiful linen rags, in the twelfth century, and its subsequent widespread diffusion led to an important reduction in the cost of writing material. By the early fifteenth century, the principal bottleneck to information reproduction was the high cost of the labor necessary for copying.

The Invention of Printing

The idea of a mechanical means of reproducing symbols drawn or written by the human hand is very old. The cylinder seals used by the Sumerians to identify the sender of an object or message were one of the earliest applications of the concept. However, it was not until the late fourteenth century that Europeans began to apply this technique to an entire body of text. Under one technique, known as xylography, the reverse of an original image or set of characters was carved into wood. this method dramatically reduced the cost of the second and further copies. However, the great expense of the first copy meant that this method could compete with the manuscript only for illustration. In a related technique known as metallography, metal dies were used to punch a series of characters into a soft substance such as clay or lead. Lead poured on this surface and left to harden could then be used to print multiple copies. Since the plates of fixed type could be used for only one document, however, this method was also extremely expensive.

To lower the cost of the first copy of a text, some way had to be found to permit reuse of the characters. The idea of breaking a written message into its component symbols and carving each of these symbols individually so that they could be reused was being systematically applied in China and Korea by the fourteenth century. However, while movable wooden type was adequate for large Chinese characters, it proved unsatisfactory for texts written in the Western alphabet. Not only was it extremely difficult to carve uniform characters of the small size used in European texts, but also the resulting type proved too delicate for repeated use. Experiments with movable wooden characters were carried out at Haarlem by a Dutchman named Laurens Janszoon Coster in the years around 1430.[24] (According to a Dutch legend of the sixteenth century, it was actually Coster who invented movable metal type.)[25]

The invention of the printing press or, more accurately, typography in Europe is generally credited to Johann Gensfleisch zur Laden, known as Gutenberg. Born in Mainz in central Germany, in the last years of the fourteenth century, Gutenberg was trained as a goldsmith. His invention was actually a synthesis of two instruments that were well known in medieval Europe. One was the punch that goldsmiths used for striking inscriptions into metal. As explained by S. H. Steinberg, the key was to find a way to reproduce this punch cheaply.

A single letter, engraved in relief and struck or sunk into a slab of brass, would provide the intaglio or "matrix" (female die) of that letter in reverse; from this matrix any number of mechanical replicas of that letter could be cast by pouring lead into it. The replica-letters, the types, had to be cast with a long enough shank to permit finger and thumb to grasp them securely while they were being fitted together into words and lines.[26]

The second component, and one that was unique to European typography, was the wine-press, which had been introduced into Germany by the Romans. Its great advantage for printing was that it permitted considerable pressure to be applied uniformly to a surface for a short period of time. Gutenberg's final contribution was the perfection of an ink that would adhere to metal type.

Although the first book produced with movable metal type was a Bible published in 1455 in Mainz, there are surviving samples from earlier products of the same technology; namely, indulgences and a calendar that may date from late 1447.[27] Actual reproduction costs by the new method fell to one three-hundredth of those of a manuscript.[28] By 1450, then, it had become technically and economically feasible in Europe to copy written documents accurately and cheaply on a large scale.

The Standardization of the Vernacular

Despite the remarkable reduction in the cost of reproducing information that printing made possible, for the first three-quarters of a century following its discovery, the new invention had little direct impact on the lives of most Europeans. The reason for this situation is that during its initial decades printing had only a modest impact on what was read and the number of people who read it. For the communications network to broaden, people had first to be able to understand easily what was written. However, the vast stock of existing manuscripts that were the principal source material for the first half-century of printing were almost entirely in Latin. As a result, three-quarters of all matter printed before 1500 was in Latin.[29]

As long as most printed information was in Latin, a language that the great majority of people could not speak, there was little incentive to learn to read. However, since the majority of the literate public could read Latin, there was little incentive to publish in the vernacular, especially since in each linguistic zone, the spoken language comprised numerous regional dialects, with no standardized written language or spelling. Accordingly, for a half-century, the printing had a limited impact on existing structures.

To escape from this stable low-literacy equilibrium, two conditions had to be satisfied. First, a significant amount of published material had to be available in standardized versions of the spoken languages. Second, the majority of the population had to be trained to decode messages printed in the vernacular. The translation of a significant number of works into the vernacular and the preparation of new books in the spoken languages took many decades. One of the problems was to determine conventions for writing in the vernacular. Here the printers and grammarians in Europe's major printing centers played an important role: in the first half of the sixteenth century, they were the leaders of a massive effort to standardize spelling rules.[30]

The turning point at which the majority of publishing occurred in languages other than Latin probably did not take place until late in the sixteenth century.[31] However, by 1515 the phenomenon had become sufficiently important for the papacy to order censorship to be applied to all works translated from Latin into the vernacular.[32] In 1539, Francis I made the dialect of the Parisian region the official language of France.[33] This switchover, as it occurred, assured the decline of Latin and the permanent survival of the particular versions of the vernacular that were spoken in the principal printing centers of Western Europe. It was in this manner, for example, that because of the importance of Antwerp as a printing center, the low-Frankish dialect spoken in Brabant developed into a separate language: Luther's original German texts would have been perfectly understandable to sixteenth-century Netherlanders.[34]

The Initial Spread of Literacy

Once books began to be available in standardized forms of the spoken languages, societies had to be willing to undergo the enormous cost of teaching large numbers of people to read and write; that is, to acquire literacy. Since teachers themselves had first to be trained and since outside the upper social classes it was mainly the children who had enough time free from production activities to master the new skill, the extension of the ability to read and write was bound to be gradual. Even in those regions where initial literacy was highest, had other factors not intervened, it would have taken many generations before the majority of the adult population of any European society could read and write.

It was in the trading cities of northern Italy, central Germany, and the southern Netherlands that initial literacy rates were probably the highest. The primary reason was economic: the ability to read, write, and perform simple arithmetic were essential in most commercial activities. Carlo Cipolla reported that in the year 1338, 40 percent of the school-age children in Florence attended classes.[35] However, literacy rates prior to the introduction of printing seem to have peaked at about this time – perhaps because of the effects of the Black Death of 1348. In the following century, two-thirds of the adult population of Venice were essentially illiterate.[36]

The new print technology should have had its greatest impact in the already literate societies of these commercial centers. Initially, indeed, the evidence of a flourishing printing industry in the principal towns of these regions suggests that they were able to maintain their lead in cultural development over the rest of Europe. Yet by the middle of the seventeenth century, the publishing industries in Venice, Antwerp, Munich, and Vienna no longer dominated the European book trade. Two hundred years later (the earliest date for which there are reliable literacy statistics), none of these regions was among the most literate areas of Europe.[37] What had happened in the intervening period?

THE REFORMATION AND LITERACY

It has been estimated that in the seventeenth century more books were published in the United Provinces of the Netherlands than in all other countries together.[38] That the commercial centers of the early sixteenth century lost their initial cultural advance to this former economic backwater of sand dunes and marshes may be explained in part by one of the initial uses to which the new print medium was applied. By the early sixteenth century, printing had rendered obsolete the upper level of the Catholic Church's information network, based on differentiated access to manuscripts. Any person able to read could now have access to more information than had been available in even the best monastic or university libraries a century earlier. Moreover, as the written forms of the vernacular became increasingly standardized, it became possible for anyone with access to a printing press to launch a competing ideology, confident of being able to reach rapidly all those able to read.

Although its information dominance had been eroded, the Church continued to monopolize the sale of its principal commodity, the assurance of salvation. Yet an increasing number of people were highly critical of the monopoly rents that the Church extracted for this service. The Christian population of Western Europe was subjected to an unprecedented level of demands for funds in the form of tithes, indulgences, benefices, and other payments. In 1517, Martin Luther, a German theologian at the university of Wittenberg in eastern Germany made public 95 theses in Latin criticizing various practices of the Church.

Luther's theses were abstract points intended for debate among theologians. A century earlier, the issue might have smoldered for years before breaking into flame. Even then, its effect would have been purely local, as in the case of the followers of John Huss whose revolt (1419–1436) had been confined to Bohemia. In actual fact, Luther's criticisms were given wide diffusion in an astonishingly short lapse of time. Within two months, they had been translated into the vernacular languages, printed and widely distributed throughout Europe.[39] The combination of the printing press and the increasing number of people who could be reached through the vernacular had generated an explosive new communications medium.[40]

In 1520, to attract support for his cause, Luther published two further documents, one in Latin, directed to theologians, and the other, in German, addressed to the German princes. Barely two years later, in the Knight's War, a group of minor nobles challenged the Church's temporal power in Germany. This was the first incident in a period of religious strife that was to last until the middle of the following century.

Protestantism and the Extension of Literacy

In his study, *The Protestant Ethic and the Spirit of Capitalism*, Max Weber argued that Calvinism taught spiritual values – in particular the concepts of predestination and the calling – that favored those qualities required for success in capitalistic endeavor.[41] However, it has since been shown that Calvinism was initially hostile to capitalistic practice; for example, bankers were not allowed to take communion in Holland in 1574.[42] In addition, it has been noted that the characteristic shared by the new capitalist class in European cities in the late sixteenth and early seventeenth centuries was not the Calvinistic faith but rather the status of immigrant.[43] Nevertheless, as Elizabeth Eisenstein pointed out, there is evidence to support the position that the Reformation did have a profound indirect impact on society through its effects on literacy levels – both in Protestant Europe and in the regions that retained their Catholic faith.[44]

As long as the mass of the people remained illiterate, the lower layer of the Church's information network, based on oral communication between the priest and the faithful, remained intact. It quickly became evident to Protestant leaders, therefore, that for their movement to gain wide appeal it would be necessary to attack this foundation of the Church's popular support. The method they chose was to short-circuit this system by means of direct communication between Protestant writers and the people, through the printed page.

The Protestants attacked the Catholic faith by proposing what was in effect a religious innovation – a means of obtaining the same product more efficiently, with a smaller amount of resources. The principal service offered by the Church, the assurance of salvation, could be obtained by means other than those prescribed by the Catholic religion. It was erroneous, they taught, to believe that the state of grace required for salvation could be attained through a decision by a member of the Church hierarchy. The Bible rather than the Pope was the ultimate authority for questions of faith, the individual rather than the institution the ultimate arbiter of spiritual values.

To reach the faithful with this new message, two steps were required. First, it was necessary to have material that the majority of people could read easily. Most of Luther's time during the decade from 1520 to 1530 was devoted to the translation of the Old and New Testaments into German and to the preparation of catechisms and other documents that formed the textual basis for this new religion. In the 1530s, when the French theologian John Calvin proposed an alternative approach to the interpretation of the Scriptures, he followed a similar route. Whereas Luther emphasized salvation by faith and grace, Calvin adhered to the doctrine of predestination whereby an individual's state of grace had already been determined. As the primary vehicle to attack the existing ideology, both reformers chose the new increasingly standardized forms of the spoken language. Indeed, Luther in German and Calvin in French were among the first great writers in their respective languages.

Once this initial publishing effort had been made, it was essential to increase the number of people able to read the new texts. Therefore, the Protestants favored literacy in the vernacular and placed few restrictions on the freedom of the publishing industry. Although Luther strongly believed that even the humblest members of society should be educated, he had to struggle against the absence of any tradition of popular education in most of Europe. As a result, it took several decades before elementary schools teaching reading and writing in German began to be set up.

Calvin, even more than Luther, insisted that everyone be able to interpret the Scriptures for himself. In the 1550s and 1560s, when Calvinist doctrines first began to spread widely in the Netherlands, the extension of literacy was carried on at an informal level. However, once an independent state had been created, the Dutch Calvinists insisted on government intervention in the educational system. The municipal administrations together with the Calvinist churches supervised the privately run elementary schools that most children attended from their seventh to twelfth years.[45] In addition, beginning with the Synod of the Hague in 1586, the Calvinists made provision for increasing the number of secondary or "Latin" schools established previously by the Catholic Church. Financed from publicly guaranteed revenue sources, these schools were the key to training the middle classes that were to run Dutch society.[46] From the first days of their republic, the Dutch also placed great emphasis on universities to educate the elite who would hold the highest offices in the state. The University of Leiden was founded in 1575 and the University of Franeker in 1585; others were established in the early seventeenth century.[47]

Bootstrap Promotion of a Communications Medium

Like previous heresies, Protestantism entailed the learning of doctrines different from those taught by the Church. Protestantism demanded that its adherents invest in the mastery of a set of beliefs and religious practices – an ideology – distinct from those of Catholics. In contrast to earlier groups of dissidents who were dependent largely on oral transmission, the new sects had the advantage of being able to give permanent form to their ideas through the print medium. Consequently, in addition to a first type of knowledge in the form of religious beliefs, the Protestant movements insisted on the acquisition of a second form of learning: the ability to read in the vernacular. However, someone who is able to read the Scriptures will also be able to understand a bill of lading or a political tract. In the longer run, therefore, it was this second type of human investment that was to have the most profound effects on European societies.

The permanence of Protestantism compared to earlier, largely orally transmitted heresies was therefore the result of two elements. One was the diffusion of a powerful new message – the notion that access to salvation could be obtained at a lower cost through the teachings of the Bible than through the Catholic mass. The second element was a revolutionary new communications medium – standardized vernacular languages in printed form. For the first time in history, it became feasible to reach the majority of a society's members with an identical message. In short, the new information technology pulled itself up by its own bootstraps, publicizing its own extension through its first important message.

Those who were converted to the new faith acquired not only a set of beliefs but also a whole new way of viewing the world. The Catholic Church had relied on a vertical information structure, in which the primary direction of information flow was from the top downward. The Protestant movements substituted a horizontal structure based on two-way communications in printed and written form between individuals and between congregations. Within a community of their co-religionists, Protestants were in an environment that enabled them to link up horizontally with others who looked on the world in similar fashion.

The Counter-Reformation and the Attack on Lay Literacy

The social stability of Europe prior to the sixteenth century had been based on a particular information technology; namely, hand-written communication among a literate elite in Latin or non-standardized forms of the vernacular, supplemented by oral reproduction for the masses of the people in their local dialects. Under this technology, it was virtually impossible for large numbers of people to share an identical storable message, whether a historical fact or a new decision or proposal. Because of the low productivity of this information system, the membership fees it could charge were modest. Taxes as a share of income were accordingly low.

In the first decades of the sixteenth century, there had appeared a competing technology – printed messages in the vernacular – that promised a great reduction in the cost of reaching large numbers of people with information in permanent form. The first important message for this medium was a criticism of the Catholic Church together with proposals for a new more efficient Christian religion based on general access to printed texts. Since the innovators themselves promoted the extension of the new medium, it appeared that Europe was about to undergo a gradual and generalized transformation. In the event, the transformation was to prove neither gradual nor generalized.

Initially, interest in reading religious literature in the vernacular was to be found throughout Western Europe.[48] However, this situation was not allowed to persist. It is in the nature of information networks that there are important scale economies to their use. Once Catholic Europe's infrastructure of church headquarters, and regional institutions of monasteries, universities, charities, and individual churches was in place, it cost very little to supply its services to additional members. As a result, the Church with its revenues from tithes, indulgences, benefices and dispensations, and other income generated large surpluses. However, these surpluses were dependent upon the maintenance of a monopoly position. Any loss of significant numbers of the faithful to competing networks would leave the Church with large overhead costs to be borne from substantially smaller revenues. Both the Church hierarchy and the monarchical administrations dependent on it were therefore willing to spend large amounts to defend this information monopoly.

As Harold Innis observed, innovations in communications technology invariably lead to realignments in the structures that control knowledge.[49] The great attractiveness of the religious innovation developed by Luther, Calvin, and other Protestant leaders was that it promised to provide essentially the same service offered by the Catholic Church, the assurance of salvation, but at a much lower cost. A literate population obtaining its religious doctrine primarily from the printed page could dispense with the top-heavy administrative structure required for oral diffusion of information. As a result, local economies would no longer be subject to a large outflow of funds to Church headquarters in Rome.

As the principal beneficiaries of the established ideology, the leaders of the Catholic Church and the monarchical states soon realized that they could not gain by a freer circulation of information. In any open competition with the Protestant sects, the Church was bound to lose large numbers of adherents. And once the infallibility of the Pope had been brought into question, it was a logical extension to raise doubts about the divine right of kings to govern. Therefore, the Church, supported by the secular administrations, decided to discourage the extension of literacy in the vernacular and placed tight controls on what could be printed.

At the Council of Trent in northern Italy, where representatives of the Catholic hierarchy met in three sessions between 1545 and 1563, it was decided to bar the sale of Bibles written in the vernacular. In addition, the Church placed many of the most popular works written in the spoken languages on its Index of forbidden books.[50] Like the Protestant sects, the Catholic Church instituted reforms to the educational system in countries which remained under its control. However, the emphasis was not on popular education but on the rigorous training of an elite to watch over the spiritual integrity of the faithful. The new Jesuit order, whose first college was set up in 1548, took the lead in laying out a disciplined program of study in grammar, rhetoric, philosophy, and theology. Latin continued to be the usual language of instruction. In effect, Catholic Europe was opting for a set of communications protocols that was incompatible with those of Protestantism.

As long as this congruence between religion and communications network lasted, the only practical solution was a physical separation into geographically distinct communities. Protestantism was able to take permanent root only on the developed periphery of the territories controlled by the German Empire and the centralized monarchical states. It was in northern Germany and the Netherlands, Switzerland, Scotland, Scandinavia, and south-western France that the Protestant movement was initially centered. Here, where distance served to weaken the power of the state and church bureaucracies, literacy in the vernacular made rapid progress. England was in an intermediate position, where a nationalized Church fought to maintain its dominance in the face of challenges from an increasing number of nonconformist sects.

As a result in part of this difference in institutional attitudes to reading in the vernacular, the traditional gap in literacy that favored southern Europe was eroded and eventually reversed. In Catholic France, of 76 departments for which data are available from 1686 to 1690, in none could a majority of those newly married sign their names. In 51 of these departments, fewer than one person in four was literate by this measure.[51] In contrast, in Calvinist Amsterdam in 1680, 57 percent of those who were married were able to sign their names.[52] In Paris, the ratio of teachers to population was actually higher in 1380, in the Middle Ages, than it was some 300 years later in 1672.[53] By the mid-nineteenth century, Europe was divided into two regions: the Catholic countries where in no case could more than 60 percent of the population read, and the Protestant areas where at least two out of three adults were literate.[54]

THE CHALLENGE TO MONARCHIC RULE

Religious differences complicated what was already an extremely difficult position for the ruler of the Hapsburg possessions. The dispersion and heterogeneity of his territories was such as to prevent him from intervening closely in local matters in each region. In 1548, Charles V issued an Imperial Declaration incorporating the Netherlands into a Burgundian circle that was virtually independent of the Holy Roman Empire and had considerable autonomy on internal matters. However, limited decentralization of this sort in the civilian sphere proved incompatible with centralized military control. In the face of simultaneous attacks from more efficient, territorially compact states, such as France and Saxony, along with continual pressure from the Ottomans, the extended Hapsburg realm proved increasingly ungovernable. Accordingly, when Charles abdicated in 1556, the Hapsburg possessions were split into two more manageable states. His brother Ferdinand was granted the German and central European territories, while his son Philip II took Spain, the Italian possessions and the Burgundian circle including the Netherlands.

A reduction in the territory administered by a ruler will generally permit him to increase his degree of control over the area that he continues to govern. In 1563, Philip attempted to reorganize the bishoprics of the Netherlands, making the bishops royal appointees responsible to his nominee for Archbishop of Mechlin. Viewing this proposal as a threat to the powers of their own Council of State, the executive body of the Netherlands, the nobles protested.

If this quarrel between king and nobility had been the only problem, the crisis could probably have been resolved by some moderate show of force on the part of the king. In the Netherlands of the 1560s, however, the political situation was complicated by the growing strength of the Protestant sects. Philip's attempts to extend his father's edicts against heresy aroused great resentment among Lutherans, Anabaptists, and Calvinists. Although Protestants were a minority of the total population they were supported by many moderate Catholics. In 1565 a league of minor nobles met to condemn the Inquisition. In April of the following year, several hundred nobles gathered in Brussels to present a petition to the king's regent. According to legend, one of the latter's advisers contemptuously referred to the nobles as "Gueux!" (beggars).

With the religious factor complicating the political dispute, events rapidly took an explosive turn. The nobles' cause was taken up by bands of workers, many of them unemployed, led by Calvinist preachers opposed to the Catholic Church. In August, the groups pillaged and desecrated dozens of churches, including the Antwerp cathedral. Philip replied to the iconoclasts by extending the full force of the Inquisition to the Netherlands, where previously its application had been sporadic. In August of the following year, royal authority was backed up by a force of 10,000 soldiers who arrived from Spain under the command of the Duke of Alba.

Alba attempted to apply to the Netherlands the authoritarian policies practiced by Spanish monarchs in their home peninsula. Within the following five years, there were 12,000 trials, 9,000 convictions and 1,000 executions. However, policies that might have worked in rural Spain were much less effective in the urbanized Netherlands, which had long been accustomed to a considerable degree of local autonomy. The brutal execution of two of the more moderate nobles who had taken part in the original protests sparked an outbreak of resistance that soon degenerated into full-scale civil war. At the head of the revolt was William of Orange, the stadholder or lieutenant governor of three northern provinces, where his family had extensive holdings. A German prince raised as a Catholic, he became a Lutheran in 1566; seven years later, he was to convert to Calvinism.

It was at this point that the key question involved in any occupation of marginal territory arose. Could the Netherlands be made to pay their way without unduly draining the resources of the Spanish crown? The States-General, a consultative body dominated by representatives of the Netherlands towns, strenuously objected to Alba's proposal for a permanent 1 percent property tax and 10 percent sales tax modeled on the Spanish *alcabala*. Instead, it approved a flat grant of four million florins. However, over the next four years, Alba managed to extract more than three times that amount from the Netherlands.[55] Unfortunately for Philip, the man he sent as Alba's successor in 1573 proved much less successful at raising tax revenues locally. In the words of Charles Wilson, "since the Netherlands would neither pay nor obey, it was the peasants of Castile who did."[56]

Philip's incapacity to make the Netherlands pay their way was to prove the primary obstacle to maintaining his hold on this territory. In 1575, Spanish troops, who had not received their wages for two years, mutinied. There followed a wave of pillage and murder known as the "Spanish Fury," culminating in the sack of Antwerp. In their rage, the rampaging soldiers massacred some eight thousand people. The immediate effect of this violence was to drive all of the Netherlands provinces into an anti-Spanish alliance known as the Pacification of Ghent, under William of Orange. The south was to remain Catholic, but Calvinist practices were to be permitted there; it was accepted that the Calvinists would dominate in the north.

The Geographical Factor

The traditional view holds that it was geography that permitted the northern provinces of the Netherlands to obtain their independence from Spain. The Meuse and Rhine rivers, it is argued, constituted a water barrier that protected the northern provinces from invasion by land.[57] Indeed, the first series of victories by the rebel forces was due to their command of the coast and rivers. The Sea Beggars, a group of privateers who had been commissioned by William of Orange, took their name from the original "beggars" of Brussels. By attacking Spanish shipping, they had made it extremely difficult for Philip to support his troops by sea. In 1572, in a surprise attack, they took the town of Brill on the south side of the Meuse estuary. Other victories soon followed, culminating in 1574 in the relief of the town of Leiden, which had been besieged by Spanish forces.

However, this geographical interpretation of events is not altogether satisfactory. The Spanish *tercios* who fought for Philip were the best troops in Europe of this period, the first army to master the use of infantry small arms.[58] Behind them, they had the wealth of the Spanish Empire. Once the Spanish might began to be applied intelligently, the results were striking. A victory for Philip's troops at Gembloux in 1578 sparked an outbreak of anti-Catholic violence in the north, leading in turn to a Catholic reaction in the south. With the revolting provinces increasingly divided by religion, the opportunity arose for Spain to regain the initiative. In 1578 Philip appointed as governor Alexander Farnese, an Italian noble who combined military skill with diplomacy. By the following year, Farnese had rallied the French-speaking southern provinces to the Spanish cause in the Union of Arras. Only four of the northern provinces could be convinced to sign the opposing Union of Utrecht of 1579 which was to be the basis of the Dutch state; however, three other northern provinces offered their rather tepid support.

To achieve his principal objective of retaking the rich Flemish-speaking provinces of the south, Farnese devised a strategy of political moderation and military rigor. The Inquisition was not allowed to return to the Netherlands. Instead, Calvinists in the south were offered the choice of converting to Catholicism or emigrating to the north. In those regions of the south that resisted Spanish authority, Farnese's soldiers raided virtually unchecked. This combination of the carrot and the stick proved remarkably successful. By 1584, when William of Orange was assassinated, the Flemish-speaking regions in the south had lost much of their resolve to fight. One after another, the towns of Flanders and Brabant surrendered, with Antwerp, the most important, opening its gates to the Spanish troops after a long siege in 1585.

Although the rivers offered the northern Netherlands some protection from invasion, they froze in the winter, and could therefore be crossed on foot for at least part of the year. In the late 1580s, as the troops of Farnese (named Duke of Parma in 1586) celebrated one victory after another, it appeared that gunpowder would win out over geography. There seemed to be no effective method to combat the great scale economies that military technology offered to the centralized monarchies of the sixteenth century. The northern Netherlands were threatened with the loss of their traditional autonomy.

The Information Factor

Nevertheless, by the late 1590s, the forces of the new Dutch state had captured large parts of the territory previously taken by Parma (see figure 5.1). The Spanish never again recovered the initiative. How can this turnaround be explained? More than any other factor, the Dutch success seems to have been due to the innovative way in which they applied the resources at their disposal. The Dutch developed new ways of using their limited manpower and natural resources in virtually all aspects of their society, including the military effort. To explain these innovations, it is necessary to examine the intellectual climate prevailing in the United Provinces in the final decade of the sixteenth century.

Initially, the Reformation had led to an increase in cultural diversity throughout the Netherlands, as Lutherans, Anabaptists, and Calvinists began to practice their religion where previously almost all of the population had been Catholic. As the war progressed, however, these people sorted themselves increasingly into two more homogeneous regional groups. In the southern Netherlands, where Parma's strategy allowed Spanish control to be maintained, virtually all Protestants and Jews who were unwilling to renounce their faith emigrated. As a result, the population of the south became almost entirely Catholic. In 1582, Antwerp had 83,700 inhabitants; by 1589, it had shrunk to a population of only 42,000.[59]

Most of those who left the Spanish provinces moved to the towns of the North. There they were joined by refugees from other parts of Europe, including Huguenots fleeing the religious wars in France. For the United Provinces, the result was the concentration in a small territory, mainly in the province of Holland, of many of the most highly educated people in Europe at that time. By virtue of their profession or their religion, the majority of the newcomers had mastered the new communications technology based on printed messages in the vernacular. They created a new print-based information network that was considerably more efficient than the transmission network of the church in pre-modern Europe, with its combination of written messages in Latin and oral messages in the vernacular.

One of the characteristics of a communications system is that the fixed costs of establishing it are usually very high. However, once this expense has been borne, it generally costs very little to send additional messages. As a result, a system established primarily for one type of information is often subsequently used for many other different types of messages. Although the Dutch network had been set up primarily for the transmission of religious messages, it was quickly put to other uses. One of these was military information.

In 1588 the 21-year-old son of William of Orange, Maurice of Nassau was appointed captain and admiral-general of the Union's forces. With a university training in mathematics and classics, Maurice was one of the first to make systematic use of the body of military techniques that had been accumulated since ancient times and was now beginning to be made available to the European public through the print medium. As William McNeill has pointed out, Maurice used as his main inspiration a study of tactics written by a Greek, Aelian, in the second century AD, at a time when the Roman Empire was at the height of its power. It had been translated into Latin and published for the first time in 1550. Among the Roman methods that Maurice reintroduced were the use of the spade for digging defensive works during the siege operations that played a major role in the Dutch strategy. He also reinstituted a hierarchical command structure and systematic drill, so that soldiers could be conditioned to obey commands automatically under battle conditions.[60]

The print medium not only supplied information input for Maurice's army; it also provided the means of diffusing information to officers and soldiers. Maurice broke down the movements involved in loading and firing a matchlock gun into 42 separate steps and trained his soldiers to execute these steps on command.[61] In 1607, a set of drawings and accompanying text that explained these positions to officers and their men was published in book form.[62]

Admittedly, one should not exaggerate the contribution of printing to the Dutch military effort. If Maurice had become aware of the value of the Aelian text, he was presumably wealthy enough to have purchased a hand-written copy of the manuscript. Nor should one forget the importance of the Dutch control of the sea in crippling the economy of the southern Netherlands and hampering Spanish efforts to supply their troops. In 1585, by blocking the Scheld estuary, the Dutch fleet succeeded in preventing access to the key southern port of Antwerp. Three years later, the destruction of the Spanish Armada by the English in 1588 left the Dutch in absolute control of the coastal waters of the Netherlands.

In 1589 Philip, confident of success in the Netherlands, made the mistake of recalling Parma to lead Spanish troops fighting on the Catholic side in the religious wars in France. There the great general died of wounds in 1592. Taking advantage of the weakened Spanish presence both at sea and on land, Maurice took the offensive. Systematically, he began the process of recapturing towns in the central Netherlands that had only recently been recovered by Philip's troops. Breda fell after a surprise attack in 1590 and other centers followed. Making use of rapid deployment of troops by water and land, backed up by a fine artillery unit, Maurice not only broke the Spanish threat but also managed to seize additional territory south of the rivers.

By 1597 the Dutch had consolidated their hold on the present-day Netherlands. For the next decade, most of the fighting took place in the southern county of Flanders. The advantage swayed back and forth as a function of the resources that Spain was able to devote to the war effort.

Finally in 1607, both sides realized that their ultimate objectives were unattainable. The Catholics of the Flemish-speaking regions of the south had no strong desire to find themselves under the control of the Calvinist north. At the same time, the Protestants of the north would never accept rule by Catholic Spain. In 1609, a truce was signed between the United Provinces and Spain for a period of 12 years. Although the fighting resumed at the end of this period, there were no further important territorial gains by either side. In the Treaty of Westphalia of 1648, which put an end to the Thirty Years' War, the Spanish recognized the United Provinces as an independent state.

THE INTERNAL MARGIN OF THE DUTCH STATE

Although Maurice of Nassau's tactical skills and organizational ability were of vital importance in determining the successful outcome of the war with Spain, there was another important factor that distinguished the Dutch from their opponents. From the 1590s onward, Maurice was able to equip, feed, and pay his soldiers, most of whom were foreign mercenaries, on a regular basis during a prolonged campaign.[63] This accomplishment may sound insignificant from today's standpoint, but for the sixteenth century it was a radical innovation.

What was the political structure that made this military success possible? The traditional position is that the Dutch state was an archaic set of institutions based on the medieval concept of municipal autonomy. The historian J. H. Huizinga argued that the Union of Utrecht was not the constitution of a state but rather an *ad hoc* military alliance.[64] Moreover, he contended that the Dutch success was made possible by keeping organization to a minimum.[65] Yet this lack of organization is belied by the extremely rapid growth rate of The Hague, the administrative capital for both the United Provinces and the province of Holland. From a town of a few thousand at the beginning of the Revolt, it grew to be the third largest city in the Republic by the middle of the eighteenth century.[66]

Others have argued that the United Provinces were not a territorial state in the way that England or France was; rather they were, like Venice and its *Terraferma*, another example of a medieval trading city and its hinterland. For Violet Barbour, Amsterdam in the seventeenth century marked the last time that "a veritable empire of trade and credit could be held by a city in her own right unsustained by the forces of a modern state."[67] In a similar fashion, Fernand Braudel wrote, "the interesting thing about [the Amsterdam] episode is that it lies between two successive phases of economic hegemony: on the one hand the age of the city, on the other hand that of the modern territorial state and the national economy, heralded by the rise of London with the backing of the entire English economy."[68]

In short, according to this view, the success of the Dutch in the seventeenth century represented the last curtain-call of an aging comedienne, the "old-style economy dependent on a city."[69] The difficulty with this position is that it fails to explain how a region with a population of fewer than two million people could manage successfully to combat the resources of the Spanish Empire, buoyed as it was by the wealth extracted from its American colonies. Elsewhere in Europe, trading cities such as Milan, Genoa, Florence, and even Venice were struggling to maintain their independence in the face of incursions by the centralized monarchical states. While these former urban powers were eclipsed, the Netherlands not only managed to free itself from Spanish dominance but also for the first three-quarters of the seventeenth century went on to become Europe's dominant economic power.

One factor in this success was that the Dutch were able to channel a greater percentage of their economy's resources into military and naval activities than any contemporary European state.[70] In 1601 the army under the stadholder numbered almost 20,000 men. This was the size of the military force that the much larger French state had used to drive the English from its soil at the end of the Hundred Years War. By 1648, at the conclusion of hostilities against Spain, the Dutch army had grown to 55,000, representing the equivalent of 3 percent of the total population.[71] In comparison, the French in this period were able to mobilize only 100,000 men – 0.5 percent of their population.[72]

How was the unprecedented level of taxes required to finance this effort possible? Part of the explanation lies in the reduced mobility of labor and owners of capital that followed the religious migrations and the emergence of standardized national languages in sixteenth-century Europe. When medieval rulers had raised taxes to levels that peasants found unacceptable, the latter simply moved to other jurisdictions. During the 1380s, for example, when the Duc de Berry attempted to tax the people of Languedoc heavily, thousands fled to neighboring Aragon.[73] Similarly, the organizers of medieval fairs took advantage of competition among states to obtain fiscal concessions for their activities. By the early seventeenth century, the degree of international mobility had fallen. For a Dutch-speaking artisan or merchant of any faith, emigration would result in a substantial fall in income, due to the loss of access to the unprecedented efficiency of the Dutch information network centered in Amsterdam. For a Dutch-speaking Calvinist, there was an additional loss: to leave the United Provinces was to experience a considerable reduction in the productivity of his investment in a linguistically specific religious doctrine. The Dutch state took advantage of this reduced mobility of labor and capital to raise tax levels.

The Transformation of Public Administration

Yet for the Dutch to succeed in maintaining their independence it was not sufficient for them simply to raise more tax revenues than their opponents. The survival of the new state also depended on an improved capacity to administer public funds effectively. Present-day Western analysts of political systems are accustomed to studying governments in what might be called functional terms. A distinction is usually established between those organisms that make decisions and those that carry them out. In the case of the making of decisions, it is customary to distinguish three separate bodies; namely, the executive, the legislature, and the judiciary. Perhaps because the executive and legislature are usually elected, attention tends to focus on their roles. As for the carrying out of policy, it is often assumed, whether explicitly or implicitly, that once made, these decisions are put into practice by the civil service or bureaucracy.

In fact, as has often been recognized, few if any states have ever actually been run along these lines. Since the stock of existing legislation invariably far outweighs the flow of new policies during a legislator's term of office, the decisions taken by bureaucrats in implementing existing policy are usually far more important than those taken by elected representatives in formulating legislative initiatives. Moreover, even on questions to which legislators are able to devote specific attention, bureaucratic autonomy may serve to distort the original intentions of the so-called "decision-making" bodies of government.[74]

An approach to government centered on bureaucratic behavior has several important advantages over one which assumes that public servants are passive implementers of decisions taken by the three functional branches of the state. It avoids the exclusion of actors who play a role in the allocation process and the informal channels by which many of them participate. Also, it focuses attention on the flow of information among participants. Finally, it admits that the allocation process is not simply a matter of a decision being taken by one body and dutifully applied by another; rather, at each level and among levels there are exchanges among the participants.

The sharp fall in the cost of reproducing storable information that occurred in the sixteenth century would transform bureaucratic structures. Since it now became possible to have many identical copies of the same written text, information storage could be decentralized. A more symmetrical distribution of data among bureaucratic layers and among regional subdivisions enabled more individuals to participate in decisions that would affect the whole of society. The greater access to information at all levels of the hierarchy also made it possible to develop more effective rewards and sanctions to encourage individuals to further the goals of the collectivity: the rule of law could replace royal prerogative.

Regent Government as a Bureaucracy

In theory, the United Provinces of the early seventeenth century were a federation of seven equal states. The central organ was the States-General, a legislative body composed of representatives of the provinces. Since decisions had to be unanimous and each province had a single vote, the constituent states each had a veto over decisions taken at the federal level. At the regional level, each of the seven provinces had its own assembly or States. In the case of the province of Holland, there were 19 members, one from each of the region's eighteen towns, and a representative of the nobility. The towns in turn were governed by municipal councils made up of burgomasters and aldermen. Each of these three layers of government – federal, provincial, and municipal – had its own area of jurisdiction and its own fiscal powers, although the two were not always balanced; in times of war, for example, the central government would often be short of funds. At each level there was also a judiciary and a civil service.

Although the Dutch retained institutions such as the town councils, the provincial States and the States-General from the pre-modern period, by 1620 the roles of these bodies had been transformed.[75] It is only by putting aside organization charts that one can begin to understand how the United Provinces were actually governed in the seventeenth century. Most aspects of economic and political life in the Netherlands were dominated by a bourgeoisie of roughly 10,000 people.[76] Within this group of merchants, bankers and professionals there was an inner core composed of several hundred of the wealthiest non-aristocratic families. Their members, known as the regents, monopolized the town councils and the provincial States in the two maritime provinces, Holland and Zeeland, as well as positions of authority within the civil administrations of these provinces. Elsewhere in the Dutch republic, the regents shared power with the nobility and landowning farmers. However, by virtue of the importance of their control of the two key states, they also dominated the federal States-General. Although an urban patriciate had existed in the Netherlands since the late Middle Ages, it was only during the Revolt against Spain that this caste was able to seize power.[77]

How might one categorize regent government? Although the heads of the aristocratic House of Orange supplied military leadership in times of war, the United Provinces were certainly not a centralized monarchy like the other major European governments. Since the majority of Dutch society was excluded from the decision-making process, the system might be called an oligarchy. However, the number of persons who participated in the governing bodies of the United Provinces was much greater than in previous oligarchic regimes. Moreover, power was geographically decentralized, the provincial veto over decisions taken at the federal level usually resulting in extensive consultation with the constituent governments and bargaining among their delegations.

Might the United Provinces of the early sixteenth century be considered a democracy with a limited franchise? Although a large number of people participated in decisions, not all of these participants were equal. The most important member of the regent class was undoubtedly the land's advocate (after 1618, the council pensionary) of the province of Holland. As the agenda setter and the first to vote in the Holland States, Johan van Oldenbarnevelt exercised great power during the period from 1585 until his execution after a dispute with the stadholder Maurice of Nassau in 1618. Unlike democratic governments, moreover, majority vote was not the usual decision procedure. The substantial powers reserved for the provinces and the municipalities meant that in practice decisions were often taken only after a consensus had been reached, rather than by majority vote.

In many ways, regent government had the characteristics of a bureaucracy. The members of the regent class were in effect appointed by those who already belonged to that class and usually had tenure for life. The stadholder chose the local magistrates from a double list presented to him from the town council.[78] As the example of the council pensionary indicates, there was a definite hierarchy of power. The representatives from Amsterdam, the most important commercial city, responsible for half of the tax revenues of the province of Holland, were able to dominate that province's assembly. Since Holland contributed 58 percent of the total federal budget, it in turn dominated the States-General.[79] In addition, a particular form of prior training was a prerequisite for membership in the regent elite. Members of the patriciate invariably obtained a secondary education at the Latin schools followed by a degree from one of the fine Dutch post-secondary institutions such as the University of Leiden.[80]

Yet if regent government was bureaucratic, it was clearly of a different sort from previous administrative hierarchies where officials were expected to unquestioningly execute orders transmitted from their superiors. Differences were apparent in the structure, in the efficiency, and in the scope of activity. Rather than a single bureaucracy, there was an interlocking structure of multiple regionally based governing groups. Instead of the high level of corruption that was tolerated elsewhere as an inevitable part of the cost of obtaining public goods, regent government was characterized by relative honesty, at least by the standards of the time.[81] Finally, rather than confine themselves to defense, justice, and the provision of public works as most previous regimes had done, the regents extended state intervention into the areas of education, health, and welfare. The provinces financed the secondary-level Latin schools. By 1625 a uniform curriculum had been established in Holland, whence it spread to the other provinces.[82] What little regulation there was of the privately run elementary schools was directed by the municipalities.[83] The towns also hired health inspectors and helped finance hospitals.[84] In times of famine, the municipalities distributed free food.

One measure of the efficiency of a government bureaucracy is the credit rating that it obtains on the market for its debt instruments. In the sixteenth century the governments of the monarchical states were faced with spending needs that greatly outran their administrative capacities and their tax revenues.[85] As a result, they were forced to make frequent use of short-term credit at rates of interest much higher than those paid by commercial borrowers. For these countries' creditors the results were not always favorable. First in 1557 and subsequently on five separate occasions during its 80 years of struggles with the Netherlands, the Spanish court was forced to declare bankruptcy.[86] In the United Provinces, the States-General and the provinces also used the credit markets. However, thanks to their sound financial administration they were able to finance most of their needs with long-term annuities at a low rate of interest.[87]

The Private Sector

The influence of the regents was not limited to the political sphere: it extended into all the major institutions on which Dutch economic success was built. Many historians have been reluctant to concede much credit to the Dutch as economic innovators. Their most important financial institutions, it has been pointed out, were copied from the Italians. The central clearing bank, marine insurance and double-entry book-keeping had all been invented in Italy.[88] By the eighteenth century, the Dutch were the most prosperous nation in Europe.[89] However, according to some assessments, their economic success was in large part the result of favorable external circumstances; for example, in the seventeenth century, the price of grain, which the Netherlands imported and traded, declined relative to prices of other products.[90] There were many clever Dutch inventors, such as Cornelis Drebbel, builder of the first navigable submarine; but most of their innovations were marginal improvements over existing designs. The *fluit* or flyboat, for example, was a seagoing barge that required fewer hands to operate than existing merchant vessels and proved well suited to carrying bulk cargoes over long distances.[91] The Dutch, it has been noted, were later to miss the first century of the Industrial Revolution.[92]

This reluctance to concede originality is perhaps the result of excessive concentration on the form of individual economic institutions rather than on the use to which they were put. One important difference between Italy and the Netherlands was the greatly enlarged scale on which the Italian innovations were applied.[93] Not only was the Dutch economy itself considerably larger than that of the Italian city-state, but also its influence extended around the world rather than only to the eastern end of the Mediterranean Sea as in the case of Venice. The extension of scale occurred not only in space but also in time. Instead of the quarterly trading and financial fairs of pre-modern Europe, the market was established on a year-round basis.[94] Another feature of the Dutch was their ability to integrate the achievements of earlier financial centers into a "balanced whole." The *Amsterdamsche Wisselbank* (Amsterdam Exchange Bank), founded in 1609, consolidated all clearing operations in the Republic's financial capital within a single institution using a stable money of account.[95]

The feature that most distinguished the Dutch economy from that of earlier states was the manner in which all sectors became linked into an integrated system based on the market mechanism. Agriculture grew increasingly specialized, concentrating on specialty products such as flax, hemp, and hops, along with cattle; grain, produced more cheaply abroad, was imported.[96] In the manufacturing sector, the medium-sized towns of Holland specialized in different stages in the process of transforming raw or semi-finished materials. Coarse linens from Germany were bleached and finished in Haarlem, while light-weight textiles, the "New Draperies," were produced in Leiden from English wool.[97]

North and Thomas have argued that the explanation for the Dutch success lies in decisions by the Dutch state to assure the protection of property rights. Since government revenues depended largely on indirect taxes such as sales and excise taxes, the state had an incentive to encourage transactions. The establishment of permanent markets such as the Amsterdam *Bourse* lowered the search costs of buyers and sellers. Here for the first time it became possible to trade shares in the permanent-capital companies that were to revolutionize the world economy. Another factor was a reduction in negotiating costs. Because of the large volume of trade, standardized trading practices sanctioned by the government developed. A final cost of doing business was the expense of enforcing contracts. To enable merchants to sue those who failed to respect the terms of their contracts, the government set up law courts near the marketplaces.[98]

While state support for property rights was clearly a necessary condition for economic success, it is difficult to believe that this was the main factor distinguishing the Netherlands economy from that of other states. One must ask why such enlightened policies were not practiced by all governments: surely any ruling group had an interest in promoting taxable transactions. Indeed, by the seventeenth century most Western European governments had created a body of laws and administrative procedures favorable to property rights. Yet during the first three-quarters of this century, it was Amsterdam rather than Madrid, Paris, or London that dominated the European economy.

The Information Economy

What was it that made the Dutch economy so special? A possible answer to this question lies once again in the concept of an information network. As the frontiers of the Dutch state were gradually established and its political structure determined, the interlaced print-based information structure that had made the military and political innovations possible could be turned increasingly to economic uses. The result for Dutch society was a deeper penetration of market institutions than had existed in previous communities. The examples of the Amsterdam Exchange Bank and the *Bourse* illustrate this point. The great popularity that these institutions enjoyed from the moment they were founded could be possible only in a literate society familiar with the notion that a written document could be just as valuable as gold or silver coins.

A further example of the extension of the Dutch information grid into the economic sphere is the *Verenigde Oostindische Compagnie,* the Dutch East India Company. Since the original constituent companies or *voorcompagnieën* had been ordinary trading partnerships formed for a single venture and wound up once the ships returned, they had experienced little incentive to engage in fixed investments. However, the Dutch quickly became aware that their superior military technology gave them a great potential advantage over both their trading partners and their European rivals, an advantage that could be exploited only by joint action. At the same time increased competition among the Dutch traders themselves had driven down the prices of the spices they were bringing into the European market. By the turn of the century, therefore, the Dutch had come to realize that there could be significant gains from establishment of permanent foreign bases and from the coordination of trading activities.

The key to success of the East India Company, as in many other areas of Dutch society, was an increase in productivity due to the integration of a pre-existing form into the new print-based information network. The notion of a company with a permanent capital base had been developed in Germany and by the mid-sixteenth century was being used to finance fixed investments in mining ventures.[99] Although the founders of the Company had not originally intended to form an entity with a permanent capital structure, they accepted leaving a stock of goods in the East Indies on the island of Java that could be sold or returned to Europe at short notice. From this practice, the company's managers developed a fund of capital circulating in Asia for the profit of its European shareholders.[100] They then overcame the potential threat to the investors' liquidity by developing a secondary market on which shares in the firm could be traded.[101]

As in other aspects of Dutch society, it was the regent class that dominated the East India Company. The directors of the six regional chambers into which the enterprise was divided were chosen by the provincial States from among the most important shareholders. They in turn chose an executive committee of 17 members known as the *Heeren XVII*. This decentralized administrative structure enabled the company to gather information on market conditions from all parts of the country. A second information sub-network was centered at Batavia (present-day Jakarta) on the island of Java. This port controlled the busy Sunda Strait, through which passed much of the traffic between the Indian and Pacific Oceans.[102] Whereas previous foreign trading firms had usually been formed for bilateral trade between their home country and a foreign region, the East India Company made a practice of directing its ships to markets where prices were highest, without necessarily passing by Amsterdam.[103]

Here then was the beginning of the multinational corporation, a permanent organization dedicated to the maximization of its shareholders' wealth even when to do so was not necessarily in the short-run interests of its home government.

THE UNITED PROVINCES AS NATION STATE

In fifteenth-century Western Europe, the expansion of the monarchs' power that followed the development of efficient artillery had permitted the *external margin* of the state to be pushed outward. By 1500, in England, France, Spain, and Portugal, the limits of the king's monopoly to tax coincided with the approximate borders of a major linguistic group. But could the people within the new borders be considered to form distinct nations?

In most definitions of the term nation, there is the idea of self-awareness.[104] It is not sufficient to share common cultural characteristics such as language, religion, or a common set of historical experiences. The "spark of consciousness" must also be present: the group must have expressed a desire to be self-governed.[105] Since the term nationalism itself does not appear until the end of the eighteenth century, one might well conclude that nations did not emerge before the French Revolution. However, among French writers the concept of "patrie" or political community appeared before the Revolution during the Enlightenment of the eighteenth century.[106] In England, the awareness of a collective political identity appears to have taken form in the decades of transition from absolutist to constitutional monarchy following the Glorious Revolution of 1688.[107]

Can the first moment of collective self-awareness be pushed further back in time? If, as some have argued, the ability to communicate with one's fellow citizens is a prerequisite for nationalism, a date prior to the mid-sixteenth century would appear difficult to justify. It was only in the first half of that century that standardized vernacular languages began to appear under the impact of the spread of printing.[108]

Why should there be a link between nationalism and literacy in the vernacular? The relationship may perhaps be explained most easily if one uses an alternative definition of nationalism; namely, the willingness to pay to be able to interact with those who share one's culture. When the gains from this type of interaction are weak, as in the case of illiterate agricultural societies, the amount people will consent to pay is low, and nationalist sentiment is weak. However, when literacy in the vernacular is widespread, it creates a stock of differentiated knowledge whose extension offers great advantages to each member of the network. Increased literacy broadens the scope for social interaction that crosses class and professional barriers.[109] The extension of the ability to read and write using a specific set of coded symbols therefore increases people's willingness to pay in order to be allowed to interact with those of the same culture.

If one applies this definition of nationalism to the United Provinces, the period following 1609 would appear to be critical. During the four decades that preceded the truce of that year, the primary motivation for resisting Spanish rule was undoubtedly religious.[110] The initial differences in interests between the citizens of the southern and northern Lowlands had nevertheless clearly widened as the revolt progressed. The brutal fashion in which the Spanish attempted to impose their authority shocked northerners of all religious persuasions. Printed descriptions of the massacres perpetrated by Spanish troops after the sieges of Naarden, Haarlem, and Antwerp were circulated widely in the north. Yet as long as there remained a majority of adult citizens who were unable to read and write in the Dutch vernacular, a separate national consciousness would be slow to emerge.

A half-century later, the situation had changed. With the extension of primary education and production for the market to the majority of the population, the northern Netherlanders had established a culture and economy that were distinct from that of the area in the south under Spanish rule. As an indication of the willingness of the Dutch to pay to protect their independence, one need only look at the size of the army and the unprecedented level of taxes that the Dutch were willing to bear in order to finance it. Comparing relative levels of taxation in England, France, and the Netherlands, Charles Wilson cites figures compiled by the seventeenth-century statistician, Gregory King. In 1695, by these estimates, taxes as a share of income in the United Provinces were 50 percent higher than in France and over twice as high as in England.[111]

By the mid-seventeenth century, the Dutch had formed a cohesive nation. Whether or not they were the first to have done so is a matter of definition. However, if one measures nationalism by the capacity of an extended group to channel a large amount of its income into collective activities, the United Provinces had certainly established a precedent that distinguished their state from earlier political bodies.

As the experience of the Netherlands demonstrates, the effect of the new communications medium on territorial boundaries depended on the cultural heterogeneity of the groups within the original political borders. Where these groups were too diverse to be spanned by the output from a single printing center, as in the case of the Hapsburg Empire of Charles V, the result was a reduction in the capacity of the fiscal bureaucracy to collect tax revenues. However, where regional cultural differences were sufficiently small to permit a single printing center to dominate, the new technology, by reducing the degree of labor mobility, permitted a remarkable increase in the share of income that could be captured by the state's fiscal bureaucracy.

The First Modern Society?

The concern of this chapter has been to explore the dividing line between the pre-modern and modern periods in history. One date often suggested, the year 1500, appears to be too early, while another, 1750, seems too late. Between these two extremes lies a remarkable period of roughly three decades when many of the institutions of modern society first emerged. In the short interval between 1590 and 1620, the multinational corporation, the stock exchange, efficient year-round financial intermediation, the federal state and a systematically drilled infantry army all made their first appearance. In each case, the Dutch Republic was the scene of the innovation. While these individual changes together are perhaps insufficient by themselves to justify the term modernity, they reflect an underlying transformation in Dutch society that marked a sharp and irrevocable break with the past.

Why did these changes occur? The essential stability of European society from the thirteenth century until the middle of the sixteenth century, despite wars, plagues, and famine, may be explained by the nature of the three-tiered communications system dominated by the Catholic Church. A small elite trained to read and write in Latin by Church institutions assured the maintenance and transmission of the existing stock of recorded information in manuscript form. This elite then communicated orally with the illiterate public in the vernacular dialects that had arisen in each region. By the fifteenth century, the Church's dominance was beginning to be challenged by a literate minority in the towns and courts able to write in the vernacular. However, the lack of standardized forms limited the diffusion of such messages. Under these conditions, the net accumulation of knowledge was halting and uncertain and social change painfully slow.

It was in this setting that the invention of printing appeared around 1450. For most of the following century, the social impact of the innovation was restricted by the small number of people able to read and write Latin. By the first decades of the sixteenth century, however, significant amounts of printed material began to appear in standardized versions of the vernacular languages. All that then remained was to increase the number of people able to interpret these printed messages.

One might have expected the new communications medium to spread gradually throughout European society over a number of generations as an increasing percentage of the population was taught to read and write. That this did not occur was due in large part to one of the first uses to which the new information system was put. Protestant reformers used printed messages as a means of challenging the Church's religious monopoly. The result was a sharp divergence in attitudes toward generalized literacy on the part of the new Protestant sects on the one hand and the Catholic Church on the other hand. In the northern part of Europe where Protestantism was able to establish itself, literacy was favored. However, in southern and central Europe, which remained under the control of the Church, literacy in the vernacular was sharply discouraged.

Beginning in 1568, in the Netherlands, an additional factor that accentuated the impact of this difference in political attitudes came into play. There occurred a revolt against Spanish rule which, largely for geographical reasons, was successful only in the northern provinces. Offered a chance to vote with their feet, most of the Protestants and Jews who emigrated from the Spanish-controlled southern territories settled in the north. By 1590, therefore, a 100 km square region with excellent internal transport centered in the province of Holland had become the home of the most highly educated population that the world had seen up to that time. The result was the creation in a short space of time of a network for circulating information written in the vernacular. Although this system was at first used mainly for religious and political messages, it was quickly put to other purposes.

The guardians and chief beneficiaries of the new network were several hundred of the wealthiest Dutch middle-class families, the regents. Domination by the regents and the 10,000 strong bourgeoisie that they headed extended into all aspects of Dutch society, from the States-General to the universities and the East India Company. Regent government had all of the characteristics of a bureaucratic regime; however, it was a bureaucracy unlike any the world had experienced previously. The reduced cost of reproducing information enabled a larger and more dispersed group of people to participate in decision-making than had been practical under the previous communications technology.

One of the most obvious effects of the new informational techniques was on territorial boundaries. States such as Charles V's Hapsburg Empire, made up of heterogeneous cultural groups, were to become increasingly unwieldy. Even in the smaller territory ruled by his son, King Philip II of Spain, it proved impossible to collect sufficient taxes to impose a single decision-making structure on groups with interests as diverse as the Spanish Catholics and the Dutch-speaking Lowland Protestants. Consequently, the United Provinces of the northern Netherlands managed to obtain their independence. However, once the highly educated Dutch had created their own information network, the resulting efficiency gains were so great that they were able to bear a load of taxes that astonished their European contemporaries. Not only were the Dutch able to humiliate mighty Spain, but also they succeeded in setting up an economic empire that stretched around the world.

If a nation may be defined in terms of an extended group's ability to make collective sacrifices for its own preservation, it may be suggested that the Dutch had succeeded in creating the first nation state. The modern era had begun.

NOTES

1 Niels Steensgaard, *The Asian Trade Revolution of the Seventeenth Century* (University of Chicago Press, 1973), p. 37.
2 T. Bentley Duncan, "Niels Steensgaard and the Europe–Asia trade of the early seventeenth century," *Journal of Modern History*, 47 (1975), p. 512.
3 Jan A. Van Houtte, *An Economic History of the Low Countries* 800–1800 (Weidenfeld and Nicolson, 1977), p. 197.
4 George Masselman, "Dutch colonial policy in the seventeenth century," *Journal of Economic History*, 21 (1961), p. 460.
5 Van Houtte, *An Economic History of the Low Countries*, p. 198.
6 Ibid., p. 200.
7 Immanuel Wallerstein, *The Modern World System II: Mercantilism and the Consolidation of the European World-Economy*, 1600–1750 (Academic Press, 1980), pp. 7–8.
8 William H. McNeill, *The Rise of the West: A History of the Human Community* (University of Chicago Press, 1963). pp. 569–74.
9 Carlo M. Cipolla, *The Economic History of World Population*, rev. ed. (Penguin, 1964), pp. 29–30.

10 Van Houtte, *An Economic History of the Low Countries*, p. 126.
11 Charles Wilson, *The Transformation of Europe, 1558–1648* (University of California Press, 1976), p. xi.
12 Jan A. Van Houtte and Leon Van Buyten, "The Low Countries," in *An Introduction to the Sources of European Economic History 1500–1800*, eds Charles Wilson and Geoffrey Parker (Cornell University Press, 1977), p. 101.
13 Herman Van der Wee, "Monetary, credit and banking systems," in *The Cambridge Economic History of Europe*, vol. 5, *The Economic Organisation of Early Modern Europe*, eds E. E. Rich and C. H. Wilson (Cambridge University Press, 1977), p. 357.
14 Violet Barbour, *Capitalism in Amsterdam in the Seventeenth Century* (Johns Hopkins, 1950), p. 77.
15 William H. McNeill, *The Pursuit of Power: Technology, Armed Force and Society since AD 1000* (University of Chicago Press, 1982), p. 129.
16 E. W. Fox, *History in Geographic Perspective: The Other France* (Norton, 1971), p. 55.
17 Douglass C. North, *Structure and Change in Economic History* (Norton, 1981), p. 49.
18 Fernand Braudel, *Civilization and Capitalism 15th–18th Century*, vol. 3, *The Perspective of the World* (Harper and Row, 1984), p. 128.
19 Ibid., p. 145.
20 Bernard Hendrik Slicher van Bath, "The economic situation in the Dutch Republic during the seventeenth century," in *Dutch Capitalism and World Capitalism*, ed. M. Aymard (Cambridge University Press, 1982), p. 28.
21 Van Houtte, *An Economic History of the Low Countries*, p. 125.
22 Braudel, *The Perspective of the World*, p. 152.
23 Harold A. Innis, *Empire and Communications* (Clarendon, 1950), p. 131.
24 Warren Chappell, *A Short History of the Printed Word* (Nonpareil Books, 1970), p. 5.
25 Pierce Butler, *The Origins of Printing in Europe* (University of Chicago Press, 1940), pp. 108–10.
26 S. H. Steinberg, *Five Hundred Years of Printing* (Penguin, 1955), p. 27.
27 Butler, *The Origins of Printing*, pp. 71–2.
28 Elizabeth L. Eisenstein, *The Printing Press as an Agent of Change* (Cambridge University Press, 1979), p. 46.
29 Steinberg, *Five Hundred Years of Printing*, p. 81.
30 Rudolf Hirsch, *Printing, Selling and Reading*, 2nd printing (Otto Harrassowitz, Wiesbaden, 1974), p. 135.
31 Ibid., p. 132.
32 Ibid., p. 90.
33 Daniel Boorstin, *The Discoverers* (Vintage, 1983), pp. 518–19.
34 Steinberg, *Five Hundred Years of Printing*, pp. 84–5.
35 Carlo M. Cipolla, *Literacy and Development in the West* (Penguin, 1969), p. 46.
36 Ibid., p. 58.
37 Ibid., pp. 113–14.
38 Eisenstein, *The Printing Press*, p. 645.
39 Ibid., p. 307.
40 Marshall McLuhan, *The Gutenberg Galaxy: The Making of Typographic Man* (University of Toronto Press, 1962), p. 235.
41 Max Weber, *The Protestant Ethic and the Spirit of Capitalism* (George Allen and Unwin, 1930).
42 Albert Hyma, "Calvinism and capitalism in the Netherlands, 1555–1700," in *Capitalism and the Reformation*, ed. M. J. Kitch (Longmans, 1967), p. 15.
43 H. R. Trevor-Roper, "Religion, the Reformation and social change," in *Capitalism and the Reformation*, ed. M. J. Kitch (Longmans, 1967), p. 34.

44 Eisenstein, *The Printing Press*, pp. 414–15.
45 Paul Zumthor, *La vie quotidienne en Hollande au temps de Rembrandt* (Hachette, Paris, 1959), p. 122.
46 Ibid., p. 130.
47 Ibid., p. 132.
48 Eisenstein, *The Printing Press*, p. 407.
49 Harold A. Innis, *The Bias of Communication* (University of Toronto Press, 1951), p. 4.
50 Eisenstein, *The Printing Press*, p. 415.
51 Cipolla, *Literacy and Development*, pp. 20–2.
52 Ibid., p. 54.
53 Ibid., p. 53.
54 Ibid., pp. 113–15.
55 Wilson, *The Transformation of Europe*, p. 153.
56 Ibid., p. 154.
57 Pieter Geyl, *The Netherlands in the Seventeenth Century*, part 1, 1609–1648 (Ernest Benn, 1961), p. 17.
58 R. Ernest Dupuy and Trevor N. Dupuy, *The Encyclopedia of Military History from 3500 BC to the Present*, 2nd edn (Harper and Row, 1986), p. 449.
59 Van Houtte, *An Economic History of the Low Countries*, p. 133.
60 McNeill, *The Pursuit of Power*, pp. 128–30.
61 Ibid., p. 129.
62 Ibid., p. 134.
63 Anthony Bailey, *The Low Countries* (American Heritage, 1972), p. 94.
64 J. H. Huizinga, *Dutch Civilization in the Seventeenth Century* (Collins, 1968), p. 28.
65 Ibid., p. 23.
66 Jan De Vries, *The Economy of Europe in an Age of Crisis* (Cambridge University Press, 1976), p. 151.
67 Barbour, *Capitalism in Amsterdam*, p. 13.
68 Braudel, *The Perspective of the World*, p. 175.
69 Fernand Braudel, quoted in Maurice Aymard, "Introduction," in *Dutch Capitalism and World Capitalism*, ed. M. Aymard (Cambridge University Press, 1982), p. 10.
70 J. H. Plumb, "Introduction," in *The Dutch Seaborne Empire 1600–1800*, by C. R. Boxer (Hutchinson, 1965), p. xxi.
71 E. H. Kossmann, "The Low Countries," in *The New Cambridge Modern History*, ed. J. P. Cooper, vol. 4 (Cambridge University Press), 1970, p. 383.
72 Richard Ehrenberg, *Capital and Finance in the Age of the Renaissance* (Jonathan Cape, 1928), p. 340.
73 Barbara W. Tuchman, *A Distant Mirror: The Calamitous 14th Century* (Ballantine, 1978), p. 458.
74 See Dennis C. Mueller, *Public Choice II* (Cambridge University Press, 1989), pp. 247–73.
75 Kossmann, "The Low Countries," p. 361.
76 C. R. Boxer, *The Dutch Seaborne Empire 1600–1800* (Hutchinson, 1965), p. 11.
77 D. J. Roorda, "The ruling classes in Holland in the seventeenth century," in *Britain and the Netherlands*, vol. 2, eds J. S. Bromley and E. H. Kossmann (J. B. Wolters, Groningen, 1964), p. 115.
78 Ibid.
79 Kossmann, "The Low Countries," pp. 362–3.
80 Zumthor, *La vie quotidienne en Hollande*, p. 132.
81 Bailey, *The Low Countries*, p. 123.
82 Zumthor, *La vie quotidienne en Hollande*, p. 130.

83 Ibid., p. 122.
84 Ibid., p. 170.
85 J. Hurstfield, "Social structure, office holding and politics, chiefly in Western Europe," in *The New Cambridge Modern History*, vol. 3, *The Counter-Reformation and Price Revolution*, ed. R. B. Wernham (Cambridge University Press, 1968), p. 139.
86 Ehrenberg, *Capital and Finance*, p. 334.
87 Ibid., p. 357.
88 Charles Wilson, *The Dutch Republic and the Civilization of the Seventeenth Century* (McGraw-Hill, 1968), p. 25.
89 Joel Mokyr, *Industrialization in the Low Countries, 1795–1850* (Yale University Press, 1976), p. 24.
90 Slicher van Bath, "The economic situation in the Dutch Republic," p. 32.
91 Wilson, *The Dutch Republic*, p. 24.
92 Mokyr, *Industrialization in the Low Countries*, p. 24.
93 Douglass C. North and Robert Paul Thomas, *The Rise of the Western World: A New Economic History* (Cambridge University Press, 1973), p. 135.
94 Ibid.
95 Van der Wee, "Monetary, credit and banking systems," p. 346.
96 Slicher van Bath, "The economic situation in the Dutch Republic," p. 30.
97 Wilson, *The Dutch Republic*, pp. 30–1.
98 North and Thomas, *The Rise of the Western World*, p. 136.
99 Barry Supple, "The nature of enterprise," in *The Cambridge Economic History of Europe*, vol. 5, *The Economic Organisation of Early Modern Europe*, eds E. E. Rich and C. H. Wilson (Cambridge University Press, 1977), p. 441.
100 Niels Steensgaard, "The Dutch East India Company as an institutional innovation," in *Dutch Capitalism and World Capitalism*, ed. M. Aymard (Cambridge University Press, 1982), pp. 238–9.
101 Ehrenberg, *Capital and Finance*, pp. 357–8.
102 Steensgaard, "The Dutch East India Company," p. 238.
103 Ibid.
104 See Hugh Seton-Watson, *Nations and States* (Methuen, 1977), p. 1; and John Edwards, *Language, Society and Identity* (Blackwell, 1985), p. 13.
105 Ibid.
106 William F. Church, "France," in *National Consciousness, History and Political Culture in Early-Modern Europe*, ed. Orest Ranum (Johns Hopkins, 1975), p. 65.
107 John Pocock, "England," in *National Consciousness, History and Political Culture in Early-Modern Europe*, ed. Orest Ranum (Johns Hopkins, 1975), p. 117.
108 McLuhan, *The Gutenberg Galaxy*, pp. 235–6.
109 Eisenstein, *The Printing Press*, p. 422.
110 Kossmann, "The Low Countries," p. 359.
111 Charles Wilson, *Economic History and the Historian* (Weidenfeld and Nicolson, 1969), p. 120.

6

Sonderweg or Railway

Did the German-speaking people follow a special path or Sonderweg *different from that taken by other European nations? Or was it their geography that forced them into the tough-guy role? Neither approach adequately explains the timing and vigor of German expansionism. Here it is argued that the introduction of the railroad and telegraph in the second quarter of the nineteenth century permitted the coordination of larger numbers of soldiers than had previously been possible. In Germany, the impact of these innovations was greater than elsewhere because of the population's density and degree of literacy. Mastery of the new technology by the Prussian General Staff reduced the cost of controlling territory of a given size, permitting the creation of a German nation state. It was the consequent excess of potential public resources over the amount required for territorial control that constituted the unique feature of Germany over the following three-quarters of a century.*

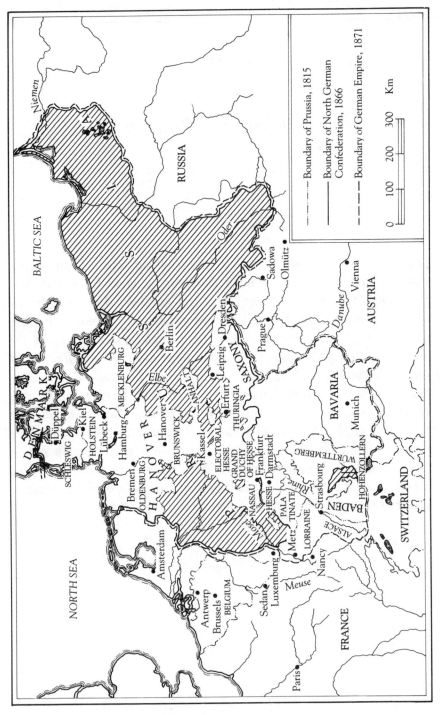

Figure 6.1   The unification of Germany, 1815–71.
(*Source: The Times Atlas of World History,* 1984, p. 216.)

The invitation to become a director of the new railway linking Berlin and Hamburg came as a surprise to Moltke. For four of the five years previous to 1841, he had been outside Germany as an adviser to the army of the Ottoman Empire. Yet the project seemed guaranteed to be a success, promising a great saving in time for travel between the two major north German cities. The new line would also make it easier for Moltke himself to visit the home of his fiancee at Itzehoe in Danish-ruled Holstein. As a result of his mission to Turkey, he had 10,000 talers to his credit. Boldly, he decided to invest these funds in stock in the *Berlin-Hamburger Eisenbahn.*[1]

Helmut von Moltke, 40, was a major on the Prussian army's General Staff. A Dane by birth, he had undoubtedly been chosen for the board of directors in order to facilitate negotiations with Denmark for a right of way across Danish territory. Yet once committed to the railway's success, he threw himself into the details of the undertaking with great energy. He studied the plans for the right of way, visited the site of the Berlin terminal, and gathered information from the engineers and surveyors. He also took part in the negotiations with Denmark.

The more Moltke studied the project, the more he became convinced that its implications for his own profession were profound. In a series of memoranda that formed the basis for newspaper articles, he exposed his ideas. The lines connecting the main cities were precisely those that would be needed to transport troops and cannon in times of war. All that was required was to take special precautions to assure the defense of the frontier lines in case of conflict. However, the private sector could not be counted upon to build the secondary lines necessary for integrating the main arteries. The construction of a true network of railroads could only be assured with state intervention. Such a network would be able to unite Germany and, beyond, the whole of Europe.[2]

Although his own duties on the General Staff compelled him to resign his position with the railroad in 1844, the experience made a lasting impression on him. The directorship of Moltke was only the beginning of a special relationship between the railways and the armed forces of Prussia.[3]

THE EMERGENCE OF A SUPERPOWER

In the decades immediately following the Napoleonic Wars, Prussia was one of Europe's staunchest bulwarks of the political status quo. Under its king, Frederick William III, it was both quick to stifle internal dissent and firm in its support of the international boundaries laid down by the Congress of Vienna. Prussia was but one, albeit the largest, of some 40 independent political units into which the German-speaking areas of Europe were divided (see figure 6.1). (Although the total population of the Austrian Empire was over twice that of Prussia, its German-speaking population was only one-third as large.) At the time of Frederick William III's death in 1840, the year before Moltke's railroad appointment, these German states seemed an unlikely cause for concern in political capitals elsewhere in Europe. It appeared that they shared little other than a fear of their restless western neighbor, France.

Yet barely 30 years later, a superpower unifying the majority of Germans had been formed around the Prussian nucleus left by Frederick William III. France, Europe's dominant military power over the previous 400 years, was prostrate after her defeat at the hands of this "upstart nation." For three-quarters of a century after 1871, world attention was to be focused on the latest and most threatening of nation states. What had happened to permit the German people to distinguish themselves so suddenly from their European neighbors?

Over the past century, people have repeatedly asked whether there were particular factors that have led the Germans along a *Sonderweg*, a special road that differed from that traveled by other nations. Prior to the Second World War, the *Sonderweg* issue was of interest mainly to German nationalists. As David Blackbourn and Geoff Eley have pointed out, pre-war generations of German historians tended to argue that their country was indeed different. Invariably, they attributed a positive value to its distinctive characteristics.[4] However, in the aftermath of the National Socialist experiment, both German researchers and their foreign colleagues began to hunt for more sinister traits in the nation's historical record, flaws that might explain how it was that German aggressiveness could have been implicated in the outbreak of two world-scale wars in three decades.

One current of recent study has focused on German social history in the nineteenth century. Ralf Dahrendorf argued that because of the manner in which capitalism developed in Germany – in the form of large-scale production units – the country lacked an authentic bourgeois revolution.[5] Instead of a transfer of power from the landowners to a numerous middle class, there occurred Bismarck's famous "marriage of iron and rye": a small number of industrial capitalists joined forces with Junker landholders to keep power out of the reach of the maturing labor movement.[6] As a result, the feudal nobility remained a powerful force in German politics until the end of the Second World War.

Another avenue of research has emphasized the authoritarian nature of German society and the weakness of the democratic institutions that it developed in the nineteenth century. By trial and error over long periods, England and France were able to evolve means of constraining the application of executive power. In Germany, in contrast, the National Liberals of the 1860s and their successors, divided among themselves, proved incapable of using their numerical strength to institute adequate constitutional controls on the exercise of authority.[7]

However, as David Calleo pointed out, it is by no means evident that a more democratic regime in Germany would have behaved in a less expansionist manner.[8] The Weimar constitution was certainly more "liberal" than that of 1871; yet it proved no more capable than its predecessor of containing the German collective desire for self-affirmation. Nevertheless, as Calleo has demonstrated, there is little evidence that Germans have been more aggressive or brutal than many other cultural groups.[9] There are few nations that do not have the remains of incidents of brutality buried at different levels in the mounds of their collective histories.

Calleo has suggested that what was unique about Germany from the mid-nineteenth century onward was that its geographical position in central Europe meant that it could expand only by upsetting the entire continental balance of power. It therefore posed a threat to political and social stability unmatched by any other European state. Sound though this argument may appear at first glance, it is somewhat less convincing under more prolonged scrutiny. The expansion of any of the nation states on the European continent would have had immediate repercussions for all other powers.

What must be explained is not why German expansionism proved to be destabilizing but rather why it expressed itself with such extraordinary vigor and persistence. How in so short a time could a state that had been the bulwark of conservatism have become the principal threat to European stability? To come to grips with this question, it is necessary to have some understanding of the German people and their geography.

The German People and their Geography

Until the forced movements of population that followed the Second World War, the German-speaking people occupied a vast crescent in central Europe that stretched from the Baltic coast in the north-east to the Rhine in the west and around into the Danube valley in the south-east. Penetrating into this crescent from the east was the Bohemian salient, occupied by Slavic-speaking groups. Within the crescent, it was the Rhine valley and the southern rim of the north German plain that were the most heavily populated. Most Germans were clustered in a tight inner arc beginning in Dresden, running west to Hanover and then down the Rhine valley. There were few natural barriers to outside attack or influence. In particular, the north German plain lay open to invasion from east or west.

If geography favored outside contact, it tended to hamper internal communications far more than in France, England, or the Netherlands. The relatively short stretch of sea coast on the North and Baltic seas was interrupted by the Jutland Peninsula. Although several large rivers penetrated from the north into the center of this region, travel from east to west was extremely difficult. Moreover, chains of old mountains served to cut southern Bavaria and Austria off from northern Germany. Since roads were poor and the rivers were blocked by ice for several months of the year, mobility between regions in Germany was limited. For example, the philosopher Kant (1724–1804) never left his home province of East Prussia, while Goethe (1749–1832) never visited Vienna or most of the large German cities.[10]

In the first quarter of the nineteenth century, three Germans out of four still lived in the countryside.[11] However, Germany had a long urban tradition. From the Middle Ages, the German towns had been important centers of culture and trade. A greater proportion of the German population was literate than that of any other large national group: in 1850, adult illiteracy in Prussia was 20 percent, as opposed to 30–33 percent in England, 40–45 percent in France, and 75–80 percent in Italy.[12]

The External Margin

In terms of the territorial boundaries or external margins of their political units, the German-speaking people stood apart from most of the rest of Western Europe. Elsewhere, with the exception of Italy, the introduction of effective artillery several centuries earlier had permitted the rise of powerful states spanning adjacent regions that spoke related dialects. Yet until the beginning of the nineteenth century, Germany had been divided into a patchwork of several hundred sovereign political units under the nominal leadership of the Emperor. It was Napoleon who had destroyed the Holy Roman Empire and forced most of the smallest states into larger groupings. In 1815, the European powers meeting at the Congress of Vienna had decided in effect to ratify this consolidation. Nevertheless, in the post-Napoleonic period, there were still 40 different political units in which German was the dominant language.

Why had a single state linking all of the German-speaking people not been formed? It is true that since the fifteenth century, the Austrian Empire had risen in the south and the Prussian Kingdom in the north. Intermediate states such as Bavaria and Saxony had also grown in territory. However, no single dominant German state had emerged: Prussia, the state with the most Germans, accounted for only 40 percent of the total German-speaking population. There are several factors that may explain the political division of Germany in the early nineteenth century. One reason is that apart from the Russians, the German-speaking people were more numerous than those of other west European linguistic groups. Moreover, the area over which they were spread was less compact and had greater internal barriers to military domination than the territories controlled by the Dutch, English, French, and Russian states. Prior to the nineteenth century, the cost of defending the Danube valley, the Rhine valley, and the Baltic coast from a hypothetical pan-German state centered in western Saxony, would have been prohibitive.

Most importantly, the transformation and inter-regional exchange of goods played a much more important role in the economy of Germany than was the case in Europe's other two most populous nations, Russia or France. As a result, there was considerably less consent for intervention by a remote authority. For centuries, the cities of the Rhine and its tributaries had successfully resisted the attempts of their powerful neighbors to include this region within their boundaries. Under the existing military technology, therefore, it had proved impossible for one state to span the territory occupied by the German-speaking people.

Of the 40 German states in 1840, all but Switzerland belonged to the *Bund*, a loose confederation set up by the Congress of Vienna. Among the *Bund* members, there were considerable differences both in religion and in attachment to non-German populations. Austria and Bavaria were predominantly Catholic, but Bavaria had a substantial Protestant minority. In the other German territories, Protestants were in the majority, but many states, including Prussia, had important Catholic minorities.

The influence of neighboring cultural groups was perhaps strongest in Austria, where the Hapsburg emperor ruled over a large population of Slavs, Hungarians, and Italians. In northern Germany, British influence was important: it was not until 1837 that the crowns of England and Hanover had been separated. Attachment to France was strong in the Rhine valley, particularly in the territories on the left bank that had been incorporated into the French state from the revolutionary period until 1815. In that year, the northern Rhineland along with adjacent Westphalia had been granted to Prussia in compensation for her territorial concessions to Russia in the east.

Formally, the German Confederation was constituted as a federal league of states (*Staatenbund*) with its capital at Frankfurt. In practice, however, each member retained almost all of the powers of a sovereign state. Under the federal constitution there were only two important limits to the sovereignty of the constituent political units. Members of the Confederation could not make war on other members. And they agreed to form a permanent military alliance against any attack on a member state from outside the *Bund*.[13]

The Federal Diet was not an elected body, but rather an assembly of persons appointed by the constituent governments. A total of 70 votes was divided among the member states, with four votes each going to Austria, Prussia, and the other four kingdoms (Bavaria, Württemberg, Saxony, and Hanover). Since a two-thirds majority was required for any decision, the six large states had an effective veto over legislation. In practice, the Confederation was dominated by its two largest members, Austria and Prussia, the latter usually being content to follow the former's lead in shoring up continental conservatism.

The Internal Margin

The division of the German-speaking people into dozens of different states contrasted sharply with the situation of most other European language groups. However, the limit to the role of the public sector (the *internal margin*) within most of these political units was similar to that it filled elsewhere on the Continent. With the exception of the constraints imposed by membership in the *Bund*, all German states managed their own military, economic, and political affairs. Most of them had their own armies, their own corps of ambassadors and fiscal administrations, and even their own currencies.

Throughout Europe, the seventeenth and eighteenth centuries had been a period of heightened intervention of the state in the economy. This intervention was most evident in the area of taxation. England and France had each developed a distinctive national identity, as standardized printed languages spread within boundaries that had been established previously by the gunpowder-fired expansion of a dominant region at the expense of its neighbors. In the Netherlands, this expansion entailed the breaking of links with a distant state of a different language and religion. In essence, each of these nations consisted of an information network. Within the networks, labor mobility was enhanced but between them it fell sharply. Taking advantage of this immobility, the fiscal bureaucracies had been able to extract an unprecedented share of their societies' total income.

Germany had, of course, been subjected to the same technological influences as the rest of Western Europe. As the home of Gutenberg, the inventor of the printing press, and Luther, the first person to use it effectively as a means of communication in the vernacular, it had been deeply perturbed by the print revolution. The Thirty Years War (1618–48), which had pitted the German Protestant states and their allies against the Catholic Hapsburgs, had been fought largely because of conflicting visions about how the new information technology should be applied in the sphere of religion.

One reason that a national political unit had not formed was that the Germans were strongly attached to their individual states. As the historian Frederick Hertz explained, the primary identification of most Germans was with the political unit in which they lived: they considered themselves Prussians, Austrians, Bavarians, and so on first, and Germans second.[14] Yet loyalties to these individual states were not strong enough to deter emigration. In the second quarter of the nineteenth century, large numbers of Germans, mostly from the agricultural areas, left their homeland to settle in North America, South America, and Russia.[15]

Data to permit estimation of the tax share of income in the German states in the years immediately following the Napoleonic Wars are not available. However, tax rates in Germany were undoubtedly high by peacetime standards, as they were in other parts of Europe. Incomes had not recovered to the levels of the previous century. At the same time, considerable public outlays were necessary for interest on the public debt and for projects that had been delayed during the years of conflict.

With the exception of England, European states also intervened actively in industrial development. In most parts of Germany there was also general agreement over the need for the state to play an active role in developing the economy.[16] The mercantilist model developed elsewhere on the Continent had been reproduced most faithfully in Prussia. Since four out of ten Germans lived in this kingdom, its influence over the rest of Germany was not unimportant. In the first decades of the nineteenth century, a substantial part of the non-agricultural sector of the Prussian economy was state-owned. Civil servants ran the coal mines in the Saar along with others in Silesia and Westphalia. The Prussian state also owned iron, lead, silver, and zinc mines and held a near-monopoly over salt production. Frederick II (the Great) had established a number of royal ironworks to support his military activities, and other furnaces had been built under his successors. It was also under Frederick the Great that the *Seehandlung* (Overseas Trading Corporation) had been established to direct trade in the Kingdom's eastern provinces through Prussian ports. In 1820 this corporation was reorganized to provide credit to a wide range of state economic activities. By the 1840s, it operated textile mills, metal and engineering plants, and chemical and paper works, in addition to a fleet of vessels.[17]

Like Prussia, the other large German states had active policies to stimulate industrialization. Bavaria operated coal and iron mines, saltworks and a porcelain factory. Public enterprise exploited a third of the extensive Bavarian forests, and the state controlled a major bank. Hanover, too, had nationalized saltworks. Even in liberal Saxony, a cannon factory and a porcelain factory were state-owned.

The Civil Bureaucracy

A state's internal margin marks the limit to the power of its civil bureaucracy. If Germans consented to a considerable degree of government intervention, it was because they expected a high level of performance from their public employees. Dedicated civil servants, it was felt, were better able to manage industrial firms in the public interest than profit-seeking entrepreneurs.[18]

The same attitude carried over into the political sphere. Decision-making in most of the German states was highly centralized. In the state with the greatest number of German-speaking citizens, Prussia, there was no representative institution of any kind at the national level, although provincial estates dominated by large landholders had been set up in 1823. It was only in the four southern states (Württemberg, Bavaria, Baden, and Hesse-Darmstadt) that the power of the prince was subject to approval by an elected legislature.[19] In all parts of Germany, freedom of the press was tightly restricted under legislation that the Austrian minister Metternich had persuaded the Confederation to approve in 1819.[20] In 1832, the Federal Diet enacted articles submitted by Metternich which reaffirmed that all political power resided with the princes and that the latter could not be constrained by the decisions of representative assemblies.[21] When German liberals looked for a model to be used as a starting point for reforms in their own country, they turned to France, where a constitutional monarchy had been established after the July Revolution of 1830.[22]

Unlike many other parts of Europe, the public bureaucracies in Germany seem to have been run with considerable efficiency. In this respect, Prussia offered a model for the other German states. Under Frederick II (the Great) following the Seven Years War (1756–63), Prussia had developed a professional bureaucracy of *königliche Bediente* (royal servants) who gradually substituted codified public law for the traditional law of earlier periods. In 1770, a century before England, Prussia had established compulsory entrance examinations and a civil service commission for its public service.[23]

In short, the civil bureaucracies of the German states were generally highly centralized and efficiently run. The administrative structure for governing a large political unit had been developed. But would military technology allow a single state to control the extended and densely populated territory that the German people occupied?

The Military Bureaucracy

Although the military administrations of the Confederation's members were as efficient as their civilian counterparts, there were strong technological constraints blocking the creation of a single German state by military means. In the early decades of the nineteenth century, European soldiers and their provisions moved over land much as they had done in antiquity; that is, either by foot or pulled or carried by animals. Compared with present-day techniques, non-mechanized transport suffered from several major disadvantages. One was speed. It often took months to mobilize a force and assemble it near the territorial borders where it could be put to use. Another difficulty was the effect of prolonged marches on the physical condition of troops. By the time they had reached the site of battle, they were often exhausted and unable to fight effectively.

A further problem was that of supply. The high cost of transporting provisions by road had limited eighteenth-century armies to under 100,000 men. Through imaginative use of pillage, French armies in the revolutionary and Napoleonic periods had managed to exceed this limit. Nevertheless, the results had not always been favorable: supply problems had been the principal cause of the disaster that befell Napoleon's armies of half a million men in the Russian campaign of 1812.[24]

Since communications were also limited to the speed of a horse, it was in any case difficult to coordinate an army much larger than 100,000 men. Even a force of this size could be effectively controlled only if it was in its commander's field of vision. In battle, Napoleon's tactics were often to concentrate great masses of troops for an overwhelming thrust at a weak point in the enemy's line. Such tactics required precise execution of orders on the part of subordinate officers.[25] The commander must therefore be able to observe developments and to redirect his troops in response to the flow of fighting. The example of Napoleon seemed to confirm that the most efficient fighting unit was the largest number of soldiers whose activities on the field of battle could be coordinated by a single individual.

Although these problems of transport and communications were common to all European powers, it was perhaps in Prussia that their impact was felt most severely. Ever since 1618, when the territory of East Prussia had come into the hands of the Elector of Brandenburg, Prussia's military leaders had been faced with a strategic dilemma. The state had no natural borders yet lay exposed to attack on three sides by more powerful enemies – Austria, Russia, and France. After 1815, Prussia's defense was complicated by its division into two large non-contiguous units separated by territories belonging to Hanover and Brunswick. Moreover, since Russia had absorbed what remained of Poland and Prussia itself had been awarded the Rhineland, there were no longer buffer states isolating the Kingdom's territory from France and Russia.

Prussia's critical strategic problems had preoccupied Christian von Massenbach, a colonel in the Prussian Quartermaster-General's Staff that was responsible for administering the army's camps and fortresses. In 1802 he had suggested the creation of a permanent military planning section. This unit, which was to become the General Staff, would function even in peacetime and would draw up contingency plans to meet any kind of military eventuality. Separate plans would be drawn up for each of the three probable theaters of war.[26] The Prussian General Staff was finally set up in 1813 under Scharnhorst. It was his successor, Gneisenau, who as Chief of Staff to Blücher rallied the Prussian troops after their defeat by Napoleon at Ligny in 1815. His efforts therefore made possible the Prussians' arrival at the critical moment at Waterloo two days later, just in time to destroy the French right wing.[27]

After 1815, while armies elsewhere in Europe settled into a somnolent peacetime routine, the Prussian General Staff continued to devote itself to assuring the state's military security. Its thinking was based on the concept of "internal lines": Prussia would keep its forces concentrated and develop improved internal communications in order to be able to meet simultaneous threats coming from several quarters.[28] In 1818, Prussia imposed three years of compulsory service on all males at the age of 20.[29]

During this period, European armies were all attempting to absorb the lessons to be learned from the Napoleonic Wars. One of the most astute observers was Carl von Clausewitz, a Prussian officer who had served on the General Staff during the last campaigns against Napoleon and in 1818 had become head of the Prussian War Academy. From his own experience, he realized that war was no longer the hobby of monarchs but had become an instrument in the arsenal of entire peoples. As such, he explained in *Vom Kriege*, it necessarily became subordinate to politics: "war is a continuation of State policy by other means."[30] Furthermore, with all of the resources of a society now capable of being mobilized, war required a total effort for which preparations must be made in time of peace.[31]

At the level of military strategy, Clausewitz rejected the search for general principles that had fascinated previous generations of military theorists. Nevertheless, one important conclusion stood out in wars over the previous century. With all major powers using essentially the same military technology, victory required numerical superiority.[32] How could a country such as Prussia, with less than half the population of any of its three potential enemies, hope to achieve numerical superiority in battle? Here was the dilemma facing the Prussian General Staff: their state was large enough to constitute a potential irritant to its larger neighbors, but too small to compete against them successfully under existing military technology.

If this analysis is correct, the factor limiting the size of political units in Germany in the first decades of the nineteenth century was the existing military technology; in particular, the problem was the time and expense required to move soldiers and their equipment over long distances.

Roads and Canals

In other parts of Western Europe, the cost of overland transport had fallen and its speed had increased during the eighteenth century. In 1764, a

French engineer, Pierre Marie Jérôme Trésaguet had developed a technique for building all-weather roads of broken stone that was graded in size.[33] In the second half of the eighteenth century, the French and English used this and similar methods to construct the first networks of high-quality roads in Western Europe since the days of the Roman Empire.

In Germany, it was not until after 1815 that the individual states began to systematically improve the condition of their road and water transport. Between 1816 and 1845, the Prussian government's road network jumped from under 4,000 km to over 13,000 km.[34] Despite these improvements, however, the cost of overland transport remained high. The freight charges to carry coal 30 km by road could triple the original price of the coal.[35] During the 1830s, the German states also made considerable efforts to improve their canals and river waterways. In Prussia, average annual new investment in waterways was twice as high in this period as it was in the preceding decade.[36] Yet it was not until the end of the nineteenth century that this network was to be completed.

The Zollverein

The improvements in road and water transport in Germany during the decades that followed the Napoleonic Wars reduced the cost of sending civil servants, soldiers, and messages from an administrative center to a distant border. It therefore became less expensive to enforce a uniform set of fiscal regulations on a territory of a given size and population. As a result, the optimal scale of a state increased. It became advantageous for a large state such as Prussia to offer concessions to smaller ones in order to entice them into its political and economic orbit.

Beginning in 1819, Prussia offered to collect customs duties for its small neighbors (the enclaves), provided that they let Prussian goods enter duty-free and accept the Kingdom's low external tariff schedule. Revenue was divided on the basis of population. Between 1828 and 1834, Prussia maneuvered most of the states in central and southern Germany, with the notable exception of Austria, into accepting this formula, creating the *Deutscher Zollverein* (German Customs Union). By 1840, 21 of the 39 members of the Confederation had joined the *Zollverein*, forming a potential internal market of over 25 million people – roughly the same population as the United Kingdom. However, in terms of effective economic integration, the German states lagged far behind Britain. Except for Saxony, where deposits of iron ore and coal favored early industrialization, the German economy was dominated by the production of agricultural products for local consumption and export.[37]

The *Zollverein* treaty that came into force in 1834 provided for a general congress to be held every two years to discuss changes in tariffs. Any modification in tariff rates required unanimous approval. Although there had been considerable resistance to the tightening of economic ties with Prussia, the more reluctant participants in the customs union soon realized that their revenues from duties were higher than they had been previously.[38] The principal weakness of the *Zollverein* in 1840 was that it had no direct access to the North Sea: all goods had to pass through Belgium, the Netherlands, or non-member north German states.

Fiscal Policy

When the fiscal boundaries of the state are extended to include a larger territory, the distance of the typical citizen from the center of power increases. In addition, the diversity of the interests encompassed by the fiscal borders increases. Each citizen consequently feels less confident that public funds will be used in ways compatible with his own interests. Because of this decline in consent for taxation, one would expect average tax rates to fall as fiscal borders are extended. This is indeed what appears to have occurred: between 1815 and the 1840s, tax levels fell in most of the German states.

In 1815, Prussia experienced a substantial increase in population when the western provinces of the North Rhineland and Westphalia were added to its territory. In 1818, the state adopted the Maassen tariff which suppressed all internal duties and taxed goods entering the country at rates much lower than those prevailing elsewhere in Europe. Raw materials were admitted duty-free, manufactured goods generally paid a tariff of 10 percent, while wines and colonial products were taxed at 20–30 percent in order to raise revenue.[39] An English survey in 1833 found that taxes per head were three times as high in England as in Prussia. Admittedly, however, English wages were also considerably higher.[40]

Tax rates also declined in the other German states. In part, low taxation was a consequence of the *Zollverein*, since the majority of members had been obliged to reduce their tariff rates in order to bring them into line with those of Prussia. Yet relative levels of other forms of taxation also fell. Saxony in the early 1840s was able to rebate part of its revenues from direct taxation. In Bavaria, total receipts from direct taxes actually fell between 1819 and 1845.[41]

Members of the customs union were pressured to adopt the Prussian system of excise taxes to replace levies on trade.[42] In general, the fiscal systems of most German states remained highly dependent on indirect taxes.[43] Such taxation was inherently regressive, capturing a higher proportion of income from the low and middle income groups than from the upper income groups. When entrepreneurial incomes began to rise as industrialization proceeded, state revenues would fail to increase proportionately.

LIBERALISM AND NATIONALISM

The reasons that led Germans to reduce their consent for previous levels of taxation carried over to their attitudes toward other aspects of state intervention. With the widening of state borders, there came increasing demands to reduce the arbitrary power of the central authorities in the individual states. By 1840, there was a strong liberal movement in Germany supported by an active press. The following decade saw a great increase in the number of German daily newspapers, many identifying with the interests of a particular political grouping. The founding of the *Rheinische Zeitung* in Cologne in 1842–3 and the *Deutsche Zeitung* in Baden in 1847 was followed by a great expansion of the political press in 1848.

Frederick William IV, who succeeded his father to the Prussian throne in 1840, aroused the hopes of German liberals by relaxing press censorship. In 1847 he issued a royal patent which allowed the eight provincial estates of Prussia to meet together in Berlin as the lower chamber of a United Diet. The new assembly would have the right to approve new taxation and government borrowing. However, when the monarch refused to agree to a more liberal constitution, the estates withheld approval of a state loan to finance railroad construction. Enraged, the king ordered the Diet to be dissolved.[44]

The year 1848 was a time of revolution across Europe. At issue was the extent of participation in political decisions. In February, the French monarch Louis-Philippe was forced to abdicate and the Second Republic was proclaimed. Two months later in Berlin, popular pressure forced Frederick William IV to agree to elections for a national assembly to draw up a constitution for Prussia. However, in November 1848, when this body proposed to abolish titles of nobility, the King ordered it to leave Berlin. He then issued his own constitution without approval by the assembly and proceeded to dissolve the latter.

Despite the adhesion of a majority of the German population to the *Zollverein* by the 1840s, most of those in the smaller states mistrusted Prussia.[45] Nevertheless, the absence of a central government in Germany left the minor states without an adequate defense against the aspirations of their powerful French neighbor. In this way, nationalism of the Germans may be seen to have arisen primarily as a defensive mechanism, a desire to protect the conditions they already enjoyed. The first direct evidence of increased nationalism came in the summer of 1840, when France mobilized its army in preparation for the reconquest of the Rhineland. These territories, which now belonged to Prussia and Bavaria, had been an integral part of France from 1792 to 1814. In contrast to the preceding quarter-century of Austrian leadership, it was Prussia under her new King Frederick William IV that persuaded a reluctant Austria to sign a *Punktation* calling upon France to disarm.[46] As a result of this war scare on the Rhine, German nationalists began to look increasingly to Prussia for direction.

The revolutionary spirit in Germany in 1848 was not limited to Prussia. Delegates from several German states meeting at a conference held in Heidelberg in March decided that there should be direct elections with universal suffrage to form a national parliament to sit in the federal capital of Frankfurt. When the federal Diet approved this resolution, summer elections were held in each German state. The members of the new Frankfurt parliament favored a constitutional monarchy grouping all those who spoke German. However, when they proposed the crown of this *Grossdeutschland* (Big Germany) to the Austrian Emperor, he declined, objecting to the exclusion of his non-German territories from the proposed union. In the spring of 1849, after approving a draft constitution, the Frankfurt parliament fell back on a second-best choice, proposing the monarchy of *Kleindeutschland* (Little Germany) excluding Austria to the Prussian King, Frederick William IV. The latter, averse to letting his legitimacy depend upon an elected body, also refused the proposed crown. Thus the parliament was left with no base of power. It was subsequently dissolved, and in 1851 the *Bund* was revived.

The Prussian king's rejection of the *kleindeutsch* solution offered by the Frankfurt parliament did not stop him from initiating his own variant of the plan. In the spring and summer of 1849, taking advantage of the Austrian regime's difficulties in putting down a revolt in Hungary, Prussia organized a weak union of 17 German states whose capital was to be at Erfurt in Prussian Saxony. Once its Hungarian difficulties had been solved, however, Austria quickly intervened to block the Prussian initiative. The conflict between the two German powers flared into the open in October 1850 when they found themselves on opposite sides of a dispute over the right of the ruler of a small German state, Hesse-Kassel, to collect taxes. The elector of Hesse-Kassel, which lay between the Prussian provinces of the Rhineland and Brandenburg, had fled to Frankfurt to seek help from the Austrian-dominated federal Diet. An Austrian army supplemented by contingents from Bavaria marched north. After a last-minute mobilization designed to prevent Austria from occupying this key territory, Prussia backed down. In the Olmütz *Punktation*, Prussia agreed to the dismantlement of the Erfurt Union and the restoration of the *Bund*.

By 1851 it appeared, at least on the surface, that the German princes had successfully weathered the revolutionary storm of 1848. Prussia's new constitution imposed nominal constraints on the royal bureaucracy's power, but political institutions elsewhere in Germany were little changed from a decade earlier. However, the introduction of new techniques was radically altering the lives of large numbers of Germans. It would not be long before the twin forces of liberalism and nationalism would regroup for another, more successful attack on existing structures.

THE RAILWAY

By the 1850s, despite the establishment of the *Zollverein*, the movement toward larger political units seemed stalled in Germany. Any further expansion of Prussia's influence would bring that state into conflict with Austria. In the end, it was technological progress that was to break the deadlock. Although improvements to roads and water routes had reduced freight and travel costs, the limitations of transport by animal or human power were evident to many observers. In fact, a potential means of overcoming them had actually been available for almost a century. The first operational steam engine had been built by Newcomen in 1705 and improved by Watt in the years after 1765. Yet in the first years of the Napoleonic era, land transport was still non-mechanized.

Why did it take so long to find an effective means of harnessing steam for transportation? The steam engines of the eighteenth century were low-pressure machines in which the temperature of the water vapor was only slightly above 100° C. Although they were adequate for pumping or turning machinery, they were too weak and too heavy to move their own weight. It was not until around 1798 that a Welshman, Richard Trevithick, completed an engine which heated steam to high pressure and did away with the heavy condenser developed by Watt.[47] By 1804, Trevithick had devised a means of connecting this power to wheels running on a smooth track. His device was able to pull 10 tons of iron and 70 men at a speed of 8 km an hour. Ugly though this contraption was, its impact was to be revolutionary. Humans had finally found a way to move over land by a means other than their own power or that of animals.

Over the next two decades, the steam locomotive was gradually improved. It was not until 1825, however, that George Stephenson opened the world's first commercial railway between the coal field of Darlington in western England and the river port of Stockton. The first train on this line hauled 600 passengers at 20 km an hour. The commercial success of the railroad was demonstrated decisively three years later when Stephenson and his son Robert completed a line between Manchester and Liverpool built according to the principle of keeping grades as low as possible. In the following year the Stephensons' *Rocket* won a contest by pulling 30 passengers at from 40 to 50 km an hour over this line.

Among those who followed with great interest the success of the railroad in England was a German economist and nationalist, Friedrich List. Noting that Germany lacked England's advantage of a complete canal system and extensive coastal shipping, List argued that the railroad was more important for Germany than for England. In a brochure published in 1833, he proposed the outlines of a national railway system for Germany.[48]

It was not long before the initial pieces of List's network began to be built. The first German railroad, a 7 km passenger line between Nürnberg and neighboring Fürth was completed in 1835. However, the first important line was a 115 km railroad between Dresden and Leipzig completed in 1839.[49] During the 1840s, construction began in earnest. On the north German plain, where there were fewer geographical obstacles to railroad development than in Britain, construction costs were low. In part for this reason, railroad building in Prussia was left primarily in the hands of the private sector; however, the state provided guarantees to the dividends of private investors. In southern Germany, where geography was less favorable, the state governments played an active part in railroad development.[50]

By 1850 there were 5,874 km of railroads in Germany, compared with 10,653 km in Britain.[51] The impact on haulage fees was dramatic: on the new lines, freight rates fell by 80–85 percent compared to road transport.[52] As the main centers such as Berlin, Cologne, and Munich became connected together, the individual lines began to form a network, just as List had foreseen. With each key junction that was added, the efficiency of the whole system jumped in discontinuous fashion.[53] By 1860, the main links in the network had been completed.

The Telegraph

The value of information often depends on the speed at which it may be transmitted. News of a scarcity of goods in one region, for example, is of value in another region if it can be acted upon before it is obsolete. By reducing the cost of overland transport, the railroad made it possible for more information to circulate over a greater radius. However, the relative speed at which information moved had actually decreased. By the mid-1830s, with the development of trains able to keep pace with the fastest horses, bulky commodities such as coal and wheat could be moved at virtually the same speed as messages. The result was a communications bottleneck, the flow of information no longer being able to flow fast enough to permit effective control of the rapidly increasing volume and greater speed of trade in goods.

In 1794, Claude Chappe developed an ocular telegraph consisting of a chain of towers at the top of each of which was a three-piece wooden signaling device. Using a telescope, the operator of one tower would observe the signal at an adjacent tower and then relay the message to the next tower down the line. Expensive to operate and effective only in the daytime in clear weather, the Chappe telegraph saw limited application.[54] However, the idea of relaying coded information rapidly was there: all that was required was a means of reducing the cost and increasing the effectiveness of transmission.

In 1800, at the beginning of the new century, Alessandro Volta discovered how to create an electric current artificially by means of an electric battery. How might this new energy source be used? About 1825, an English physicist, William Sturgeon, showed how this current could be used to create an electromagnet. All that remained was to develop a practical means of varying the current in such a magnet from a distant point in systematic fashion so that messages could be transmitted. By the early 1830s, dozens of people were working on this problem.[55]

In 1837, two attempts to send messages by electric current were successful. William Cooke and Charles Wheatstone in England transmitted a communication over a 2 km line from London to Camden Town. In the same year, Samuel Morse of the United States transmitted a message along a wire over a distance of 500 m.[56] Within ten years of these inventions, networks of telegraph lines linking the principal centers had been built in each of these countries.

On the Continent, among those most interested in the new device was a young artillery officer in the Prussian army, Werner Siemens. He introduced several improvements to the device developed by Wheatstone. In 1847 and 1848, he supervised the construction of government lines linking Berlin with other parts of Germany. Realizing the potential of this new communications system, he resigned his commission in 1849 to found a firm that manufactured telegraph equipment.

The Effect on the Cost of Territorial Control

By the revolutionary year, 1848, it was clear to many military officers that the introduction of the railroad had implications for their profession. The new form of transport could move troops at 15 times their marching speed.[57] In addition, it could make it possible to ship sufficient supplies and reinforcements to keep soldiers in the field for an extended period. What was not clear, however, was the circumstances under which it would be practical to rely on rail transport. In Britain and France, the railroad attracted initial interest as a means of rushing troops from distant barracks in order to put down urban riots.[58] During the revolution of 1848, three Prussian battalions were transported by rail in this way to put down an uprising in Dresden in neighboring Saxony.[59]

Many military observers felt that railway tracks and bridges were too vulnerable to destruction to be relied on heavily in time of war. Nevertheless, when Prussia attempted its last-minute troop build-up during the Olmütz crisis of November 1850, it had little choice but to use its rail system. Unfortunately, the army's conception of mobilization by rail had not evolved much beyond the idea of loading soldiers onto trains at one point and unloading them at another. The result was chaos: "men, animals, and supplies piled up at loading centers and shuttled aimlessly from station to station on trains whose destination was a mystery."[60]

A change in the top personnel of the Prussian army would be necessary before the implications of the Olmütz humiliation could be fully absorbed. During the six years that had passed since his resignation from the board of directors of the Berlin–Hamburg Railway, Moltke had continued to study the potential effects of the new technology on military strategy. The chaotic Prussian troop build-up of 1850 during the Olmütz crisis confirmed his opinion that transport and communications could not be improvised in the final weeks before a conflict. For a small country such as Prussia facing the possibility of war on several fronts against three more powerful neighbors, time was the essential factor in determining whether or not a military effort would be successful. Only meticulous prior planning could allow Prussia the time needed to defeat one of its potential enemies before the others' resources could be fully mobilized. For this reason, he felt, the mobility provided by an integrated rail system would prove more important than fortifications.[61]

In 1857, Moltke was named head of the Prussian General Staff. Responsible for long-term planning and for the training of officers, this body had little direct power over the actual operation of the army, either in peacetime or in war. It had no authority to issue orders to commanders in the field. Under the pre-railway military technology, it was a useful but not essential component of the Prussian army and one that had no direct counterpart elsewhere. It was Moltke who was to introduce the series of organizational changes that transformed this body into what has been described as "perhaps the greatest military innovation of the nineteenth century."[62]

Soon after his appointment, Moltke began attempts to convince the War Ministry, responsible for the day-to-day operation of the armed forces, and the Commerce Ministry, in charge of the railways, of the necessity of peacetime coordination to prepare for war.[63] The logic of Moltke's arguments was demonstrated with force in 1859 when Napoleon III intervened in northern Italy in support of Piedmont against Austria. Mobilizing its forces by rail for the first time in the history of war, France was able to dispatch an army to the Italian theater in 11 days rather than the two months it would have taken to march that distance.[64] Despite prior mobilization by Austria, French, and Piedmont forces succeeded in carrying the day in battles at Magenta and Solferino.

France's victory altered the balance of power in Europe, revealing to all that this nation with its battle-hardened army and aggressive leader was the force to be reckoned with. Suddenly the German Confederation realized the extent of its exposure, should the French attack the southern states from across the upper Rhine. If successful, a French initiative would separate Austria and Prussia and threaten the latter's hold on its Rhineland province.

In Prussia, the Prince Regent, who was crowned as William I on his brother's death in 1861, resolved to strengthen his country's military position. He and his new war minister, Albrecht von Roon, supported a series of reforms proposed by Moltke. A joint commission was established with Austria, Bavaria, and Hanover to assure that Germany's railroads could be used as a unified network in case of war.[65] The General Staff was reorganized into three geographically specialized sections. A separate railway department was created, responsible for coordinating timetables with the Ministry of Commerce.[66] Each infantry battalion near a rail terminal was ordered to detach two noncommissioned officers for railway responsibilities. All contingency plans were to be accompanied by a set of railroad timetables.[67]

The railroad made it feasible to throw unprecedented numbers of soldiers into a battle. However, the increase in numbers meant that it would no longer be physically possible for a single commander to observe the entire field of battle, issuing commands in response to what he saw. In place of his own visual information the military leader would have to rely on written messages. Accordingly, the telegraph which permitted virtually instant transmission of information assumed a crucial importance. Moltke, like his French counterparts, organized mobile telegraph trains to assure communications between headquarters and the battlefield.

Yet the information that could flow over a telegraph line was a tiny fraction of what the eye could capture. Accordingly, a commander could not hope to issue detailed orders as Napoleon had done. Moltke therefore adopted the practice of giving his field officers general directives outlining their objectives, leaving them to fill in the details. With greater delegation of responsibility, it became essential that all ranks of the officer corps share a common training and experience. The Prussian *Kriegsakademie* offered a level of military training that was unexcelled in Europe prior to 1871. This formal instruction was supplemented by extensive field experience. Moltke

insisted that the General Staff officers be rotated between general headquarters and the field armies.[68]

The new command system was put to the test during extensive rail
transport exercises held by the German armies in the area of Hamburg
and Lübeck in 1862. In the following year, these maneuvers were to provide
the basis for military strategy in the first of three wars in which the frontiers
of the German states would be redrawn.

Expansion of the Zollverein

The introduction of the railroad and telegraph in the nineteenth century
affected social organization in virtually every corner of the world. However,
nowhere was the impact greater than in Germany. By 1850, with the
exception of East Prussia, there were rail lines running out of every major
German city. Over the next two decades, these individual lines were rapidly
linked into an efficient network. Once mastered by the military, the new
technology would permit Prussia to overturn the table set up in 1814 and
1815 at the Congress of Vienna.

Initially, however, Prussian efforts to form tighter links among the German states were limited to the political level. The Kingdom's first attempt
to form a more tightly knit federation, the Erfurt Union, had been abandoned under pressure from Austria in the Olmütz *Punktation* of 1850.
Nevertheless, realizing that the power to tax is the power to govern, Prussian leaders continued their attempts to extend the boundaries of the
Zollverein. A crucial step came in 1851, when the kingdom of Hanover
with its access to the North Sea was persuaded to join. When neighboring
Oldenburg too agreed to Prussia's terms in the following year, the German
customs union formed an unbroken block from the Baltic to the Rhine,
from the North Sea to the Alps. In 1853, the advantageous conditions
conceded to Hanover were extended to the other *Zollverein* members and
the treaties were renewed for a further 12 years. By the 1860s, the abolition
of feudal obligations on peasants, along with the removal of restrictions on
entry into trades, had led to the creation of a national labor market. German
workers could move from one state to another with a minimum of
interference.[69]

Although economic frontiers were being pushed outward, there was a
limit to what could be controlled from a single point. As far as Prussian
officials in the 1850s and 1860s were concerned, Austria lay beyond that
limit. They preferred a *kleindeutsch* union that Prussia could dominate to a
larger *grossdeutsch* federation in which power would have to be shared. In
1853, Prussia refused to consider Austrian membership in the *Zollverein*.

However, she agreed to the signing of a preferential trade agreement by which Austria and the customs union lowered tariff barriers on products crossing their mutual border.[70] Again in 1860 Austria applied for entry into the *Zollverein* but was rebuffed by Prussia.[71] Relations between the two dominant German states became even more strained in 1862 when France and Prussia signed a commercial treaty granting each other most-favored-nation status. Since the preferential duties between Austria and Prussia violated this clause, the Austrian treaty could not be renewed. Finally, in 1863, Austria proposed to transform all of Germany including Austria into a federal state.[72] When Prussia categorically rejected this initiative, it became increasingly probable that the frontiers of the German states would be determined by an extension of policy into the military sphere.

TOWARD UNIFICATION

The Prussian Constitutional Crisis

Although the railroad and telegraph lowered the cost of territorial control, the two major German states were not the only potential beneficiaries of these new technologies. After France's victory over Austria at Solferino in 1859, it was she who loomed as the major threat to the autonomy of the smaller German states. Indeed, political developments in Germany during the 1860s may be interpreted in large part as a reaction to the presence of an aggressive Napoleon III with his battle-tested troops on the western border of the *Bund*.[73]

In Prussia, William the Prince Regent and his war minister introduced an army reform bill into the lower house of the parliament in 1860. Under the proposed legislation, the standing army would be doubled in size and the *Landwehr*, the militia, greatly reduced in numbers and autonomy. Compulsory military service was to be for three years, with a further five years in the reserves and 11 years in the militia.[74] This enhanced military profile would be financed directly out of the Prussian taxpayer's pocket: the army would now absorb 25 percent of government revenues.[75]

At issue was not just the amount to be spent, but also the number of people who would participate in the spending decision. The Prussian constitution that had been proclaimed by royal decree in 1848 and revised in 1850 provided for a parliament or *Landtag* consisting of two chambers. The upper chamber was composed in part of representatives of the landed estates and towns and in part of people appointed by the king. The lower chamber was made up of representatives elected by all taxpayers. However, since the electorate was divided into three classes based on the amount of taxes paid, the votes of the wealthy were weighted much more heavily than those of people with lower incomes. The constitution stipulated further that the army was to be placed directly under the orders of the king. However, at the same time it specified that government expenditures had to be approved by the lower house. It was this ambiguity that was to give rise to a major constitutional crisis.

In March of 1862, the newly elected *Landtag*, dominated by liberals, demanded the itemization of the government budget, thereby implicitly rejecting the King's right to additional spending for the army reforms without its prior approval. William I, who had been crowned the previous year, thereupon dissolved the parliament and ordered that new elections be held. By the end of the summer a compromise seemed to have been worked out under which the newly elected legislature would approve the military spending proposals, provided that the king reduced the length of service in the standing army from three to two years. However, William I balked at any measure implying limits to his military authority.

It was a career diplomat from a Junker background, Otto von Bismarck, who found a way around the impasse. Recalled from his post of ambassador to the French Emperor in September of 1862, he was appointed Minister President and foreign affairs minister. Sensing that public support for the liberals in the legislature was less than unanimous, Bismarck argued that there was a gap in the Prussian constitution in that it provided for no solution if the king and the parliament should fail to agree about spending proposals. Under these conditions, according to Bismarck, the king had no choice but to continue spending money until an agreement could be reached. In May of 1863, he adjourned the *Landtag* without its having approved the budget. Nevertheless, the government continued to function by decree and, most importantly, Prussians continued to pay their taxes without protest.

After new elections, yet another *Landtag* met in November of 1863 and once again took up the question of the government's military spending estimates. By this time, however, the external setting had changed. Denmark had moved to put down a revolt of the German-speaking population of the duchies of Schleswig and Holstein. To refuse approval of the credits needed for mobilization would threaten the efforts to defend the rights of fellow Germans.

In fact, the constitutional crisis was not finally resolved until three years later, following Prussia's war with Austria. The Prussian *Landtag* passed an indemnity bill submitted by Bismarck under which the government admitted that tax revenues had been spent illegally for the previous four years in return for the *ex post* approval of these expenditures.

The Danish War

When war came, it was not with France but with the small kingdom of Denmark. Surprisingly, the two major German states found themselves – temporarily, at least – as allies. At issue was the frontier between two linguistic networks. The Duchy of Holstein was German-speaking while neighboring Schleswig to the north had a mixed German and Danish population. Although the nominal sovereign of both duchies was the King of Denmark, Holstein was a member of the German *Bund*. In 1848, the Danish ruler's attempt to integrate Schleswig into his kingdom had provoked a revolt of his German-speaking subjects, who had obtained military support from Prussia. It was only after pressure from Britain and Russia that Prussia had reluctantly withdrawn her troops. Denmark in turn had promised to respect the autonomy of the two duchies.

Now, in March 1863, under pressure from its own nationalists, the government of Denmark issued a new constitution, and the Danish sovereign threatened to integrate Schleswig into the Kingdom. Germans nationalists both inside the duchies and elsewhere in Germany were enraged. When in November the Danish king died with no male descendant, the duchies revolted, proclaiming their independence under the German prince, Duke Frederick of Augustenburg. Danish forces quickly took control of the disputed territory. However, in December, they were forced to withdraw from Holstein when the German Diet sent Saxon and Hanoverian troops to assert its authority over one of its constituents.

What was to be done about Schleswig, which remained firmly in Danish hands? In January of 1864, Prussia and Austria signed a *Punktation* under which they agreed to deal jointly with the two duchies, neither taking action without the other's consent. They then gave Denmark 48 hours to withdraw its constitution. When Denmark rejected this ultimatum, Austrian and Prussian troops crossed the Eider river into Schleswig.

Militarily, the Danish campaign was noteworthy for several reasons. In terms of logistics, it demonstrated the effectiveness of the meticulous preparations carried out by the German armies and perfected in the rail exercises of 1862. It took only three days to transport a brigade of 6,000 troops from Saxony to camps near the Holstein border. Once Prussia and Austria had entered the fighting, a mixed commission was established at Altona, on the Elbe near Hamburg, to coordinate rail transport over the single-tracked line into the duchies.[76] Ironically, Moltke and the General Staff were kept out of the initial phase of the campaign. It was only when the field commander's chief of staff had to be replaced that Moltke was given a line position.[77]

The main episode in the war was the Prussian storming of the Danish fortress of Düppel on the east coast of Schleswig. The Danish army was equipped with new muzzle-loading cap and ball rifles that combined a long range and great accuracy. Observing the heavy losses suffered by the attacking Prussian troops, Moltke realized that wars would no longer be won by frontal attacks on defended positions. However, the implications of this conclusion were not limited to tactics. The lesson for strategy was that an army must try to turn the enemy's flanks. Ideally, the result should be the *Kesselschlacht* – an encirclement of the enemy's forces and their annihilation. However, for such a result to be possible, it was essential to have superiority of numbers.[78]

By July, Denmark had been defeated. Under the Treaty of Vienna of October 1864, joint administration of the duchies was ceded to Austria and Prussia. In August of the following year at Bad Gastein, after failing to agree on how the conquered territories should be governed, the two victorious powers divided the spoils. Austria was to have the administration of Holstein, while that of Schleswig was awarded to Prussia.[79]

The Austro-Prussian War Mobilization

The Danish War had demonstrated the military scale economies offered by the railroad and the telegraph. The previous limits to the number of troops that could be supplied and coordinated in a single campaign had been shattered. By threatening a small state with disproportionate losses, a large power could blackmail it into submission. It became increasingly obvious that the small German states would be drawn into the whirlpool of one of their larger neighbors. The only question to be decided was which state it would be, the principal candidates being Austria, France, and Prussia.

Austria was more than ever determined to assure that it was she who came out on top in the struggle that lay ahead. In order to gain the support of the third Germany, the smaller members of the *Bund*, she decided to support the claim of Duke Frederick to both of the duchies. As expected, this policy met with a vigorous protest from her nominal ally, Prussia. Austria responded in March by building up her military forces in Bohemia. In April, Bismarck arranged a secret treaty between Italy and Prussia giving Italy an option on Austrian-held Venetia if she assisted Prussia in a campaign against Austria within the next three months.[80] Finally, at the end of April, alarmed at Italian troop movements, Austria proceeded to full-scale mobilization on her northern and southern borders. As the last days of the month slipped by, Moltke insisted repeatedly that he be allowed to begin Prussia's mobilization, but the king stubbornly refused.[81]

Why was the moment of mobilization so important? As Clausewitz had recognized, superiority of numbers was the most important factor in determining the outcome of a battle. In recent decades, technological developments had made numerical superiority even more imperative. Düppel had demonstrated that the increased firepower of rifled smallarms made frontal attack suicidal. However, the alternative of flanking and encirclement was possible only if one had greater numbers than the enemy. How could Prussia with less than a third the combined population of Austria and the small German states hope to achieve numerical superiority? It was only by mobilizing first and attacking her potential enemies' forces separately before they could be concentrated that she could hope to win.

Austria, however, was also faced with a dilemma. Although she had greater potential manpower than Prussia, there was only one railroad leading north into Bohemia where her forces could be launched. In contrast, Prussia had five rail lines leading to jumping-off points on her borders with Saxony and the Austrian Empire. To be able to cope with Prussia's greater mobility, Austria had to begin her build-up first.[82] It was here that Clausewitz's dictum that war was only a continuation of policy by other means came into play. As events in Schleswig–Holstein in 1848 had shown, it was not enough to gain victory on the battlefield. To avoid losing one's gains at the conference table under pressure from a hostile coalition, it was essential to appear as the defending side in a conflict. Austrian mobilization, dictated by its inferior transport system, provided Bismarck with the *casus belli* for which he had been waiting.[83]

On May 3, 1866 King William was finally persuaded to order a limited mobilization of the Prussian army.[84] It is interesting to note that under the tightly synchronized plans of the Prussian General Staff, this order was virtually equivalent to a declaration of war. During the ten days that it took to mobilize a division, it was essential to simultaneously prepare its transport. Therefore, mobilization and transport orders must be issued at the same time. Once the massive war machine had begun to roll, it could not be stopped without creating chaos and leaving the state vulnerable to attack. In essence, mobilization meant deployment.

A month after the king's decision, the concentration of Prussia's forces within striking distance of the borders of Saxony and Bohemia–Moravia had been completed. Of course there were still minor problems: for example, units on the Silesian front were receiving stale bread baked many days before in their home districts on the Rhine. However, appropriate corrective measures were quickly taken; in the case mentioned, the establishment of bakeries close to the front solved the problem.[85]

On June 1, the technical justification for a declaration of war occurred. Austria violated the terms of its 1864 alliance with Prussia by submitting the Schleswig–Holstein question to the federal Diet. Two weeks later, Prussia withdrew from the Confederation and ordered Saxony, Hesse-

Kassel, and Hanover to demobilize. When they refused, Prussia invaded them on June 16, 1866.[86] Elsewhere in Europe, the war was expected to be of long duration, with Austria and its allies having the edge.[87]

The Battle of Sadowa

Classical military doctrine suggested that Prussia, with its inferior numbers but compact territory (provided that the links with its Rhine province could be maintained), should remain on the defensive. Concentrating its troops on *interior* lines, it could repel any attack from the geographically dispersed Austrian and allied forces. Instead, Moltke spread the bulk of his soldiers along a 400 km arc on Prussia's borders with Saxony and Bohemia.[88] The Prussian forces of over 200,000 men were divided into three armies. In this way, any Austrian push north from its single Bohemian railhead could be turned and outflanked. What Moltke had prepared was a radically unorthodox concentration along *exterior* lines.

The danger of this policy was that it exposed the individual Prussian armies to attack from a single unified Austrian force before they could be brought together. To prevent this from occurring, Moltke relied on a field telegraph system that kept him in contact with his army commanders and allowed him to coordinate their movements. To do so, however, he must be able to assert his authority. During the Danish War, the General Staff's campaign role had been passive: Moltke had participated as chief of staff to the field commander. On June 2, 1866 the Chief of the General Staff was for the first time given power to issue orders, subject only to keeping the War Minister informed.[89]

Where Prussia strategy was based on a complex balance of time, space, and movement, Austria selected a static, defensive strategy. The Austrian commander Benedek and his chief of staff, recognizing their logistic handicap of a single railroad, decided to concentrate their forces in a strong position near Königgrätz (the German name for the Czechoslovakian city of Hradec Kralove). They were confident that their strength was sufficient to repel any Prussian attack.

During the initial week of the war, the Prussian Elbe Army in the west overran Saxony, managing to seize its well-developed rail network virtually intact.[90] In the center, the First Army plunged south through Bohemia to link up with the Elbe Army south of the Iser river. Meanwhile, far to the east, the Second Army advanced slowly southward and westward against strong Austrian resistance. The first battle between Prussians and Austrians, at Podol on the Iser on June 26, was a Prussian victory. Over the next week it was followed by other Prussian gains, as the three armies converged according to Moltke's plans.

Pushed hard by the Prussian attack, the Austrians and their Saxon allies fell back to their prepared defensive position between Sadowa and Königgrätz. There in the morning of July 3, the Elbe Army and the First Army made contact with Austrian units, signaling the commencement of a major battle. With a combined force of 220,000 men, the Prussians had a slight advantage in numbers. By midday, after hours of bitter fighting, the outcome was uncertain, as the Austrians desperately counter-attacked the Prussian center in the Swiepwald wood. Meanwhile, the Prussian Second Army to the east had been held up and had not yet entered the fighting. Finally, however, in the early afternoon, the delayed force smashed into the Austrian right on the heights of the village of Chlum, causing the Austrians to break and flee.

The result was a one-sided victory, with Austria suffering some 25,000 casualties and 20,000 prisoners, compared to Prussian losses of under 10,000 men.[91] Meanwhile, the armies of Austria's German allies were being picked off one by one by Prussian divisions left behind. Seven weeks after the war began, Prussian troops were outside Vienna and resistance elsewhere in Germany had been crushed.

The North German Federation

The Danish War had resulted in a modest change in Germany's borders, as Schleswig–Holstein had passed from Danish to Austro-Prussian administration. However, the Austro-Prussian War produced a major restructuring of political boundaries in which the essential features of the German national state as it was to exist until the 1930s were created. Under the Treaty of Prague, Austria ceded to Prussia the right to reorganize political boundaries north of the Main river, excluding Saxony. Prussia proceeded to unite its two blocks of territory by annexing the states of Hanover, Hesse-Kassel, Nassau, and Frankfurt. In addition, it now acquired unquestioned jurisdiction over Schleswig and Holstein.

The other states in Prussia's zone of influence were not absorbed directly but were incorporated into a new political grouping, the North German Confederation, that replaced the *Bund.* Since Austria and the south German states were excluded from this new federation, it was dominated by its major shareholder, Prussia, which accounted for over 80 percent of its total population.[92] Under the federal constitution which came into force in April 1867, the Diet was replaced by a federal council, the *Bundesrat,* to which each state nominated representatives. By retaining the votes of the states she had annexed, Prussia assured for herself a veto over legislation requiring a two-thirds majority.

In addition, to this upper house, there was a second chamber, the

Reichstag, that was elected by universal suffrage. Prussian ministers headed the new federal bureaucracy, but only one of these, the Chancellor, was empowered to appear before the lower house. Moreover, this body did not have the power either to appoint or to dismiss him. The budget had to be approved by the *Reichstag,* but for the first four years of the federation, the military budget did not have to be submitted to this body.[93]

Although the states below the Main river in south Germany (Württemberg, Bavaria, Baden, and Hesse-Darmstadt) were nominally outside Prussia's zone of influence, they were in fact members of the new federation in all but name. They continued as members of a new *Zollverein,* which now included the duchies of Schleswig, Holstein, and Mecklenburg. As before, this body was governed by a customs council. However, it now had its own customs parliament made up of members of the *Reichstag* and elected representatives of the south German states.[94] Whereas each member of the old *Zollverein* had held a veto, now a simple majority was sufficient to carry a proposal.[95] In 1866 and 1867, Bismarck signed military alliances with the four southern states obliging them to put their armies under Prussia's control in case of foreign attack.[96]

The Ems Telegram

Contemporary explanations for Prussia's success against Austria placed great weight on the Prussian Dreyse breech-loading needle-gun. An important factor, it was argued, was its rate of fire of five rounds per minute, three times the speed of the muzzle-loading Minié cap and ball rifles used by most other European armies.[97] In fact, the evidence on this question was mixed. When properly used by disciplined soldiers, as by the Saxons at Gitschin on June 29, 1866, the superior range and accuracy of the Minié enabled it to hold its own against the breech-loader.[98] At any rate, opting for better weapons rather than more men, the French generals had decided to re-equip their relatively small professional army with the Chassepot, an improved version of the Prussian breech-loader.

The French commanders had failed to learn the principal lesson of the two recent wars fought by Prussia. Since frontal attacks were prohibitively costly with the firepower of the new small arms, only a strategy of maneuver and encirclement could hope to succeed. Yet such a strategy required a decisive superiority in numbers of men to be effective against armies equipped with the same quality of weapons. In France, universal conscription on Prussian lines had been proposed in 1868 but had barely got under way by 1870.[99] Thus as tensions built up in the early summer of that year, France's *armée de métier* of 350,000 troops faced a combined German force of 500,000 men in the process of being expanded even further.[100]

The immediate cause of conflict was a dispute over whether a Hohenzollern cousin of the Prussian king could accede to the throne of Spain. After French protests, King William agreed to the withdrawal of the German prince. However, on July 13, 1870 the French ambassador in Berlin made the mistake of interrupting the sovereign's afternoon walk at his Ems residence to press for assurance that the candidacy would not be renewed. The king, who had promised the ambassador an audience after his walk, replied stiffly but without hostility. However, when telegraphed reports of this incident, the Ems Telegram, reached the press, it was interpreted as an insult by both nations.[101] Napoleon III decided that his nation's honor was at stake and on July 15 declared war on the North German Confederation. France's action automatically set off the Confederation's alliances with the south German states, who immediately began to mobilize.

The Franco-Prussian War

Within two weeks, Germany had assembled three armies totalling almost 400,000 men on the west bank of the Rhine. The First and Second Armies were positioned near Saarbrücken, poised to strike to the west of the Vosges. The Third Army was farther east near Landau, ready to penetrate into French territory to the east of the Vosges. The German strategy was to attack and defeat the smaller French forces quickly before they could be reinforced.

As the initial fighting broke out on August 2, the French hastily regrouped their 224,000 men on the eastern border into two armies. The army of Lorraine under Marshal Achille Bazaine was concentrated near Metz, west of the Vosges, along the northeastern border. The smaller Army of Alsace under Patrice MacMahon, stationed to the north of Strasbourg, defended the east side of the Vosges. Confident of their invincibility, the French naively planned to crush the German armies and march, "On to Berlin!"

Two key battles occurred on August 6, Bazaine's three corps were sufficiently spread out that they could not mutually assist one another. One of these corps managed to hold the heights of Spichern for a day against a more numerous German force until threatened with envelopment. Failing to receive reinforcements, it was compelled to withdraw toward Metz. However, a rapid advance of the German Second Army enabled it to sweep east and south of Bazaine's forces. By August 18, the Germans had sealed the French Army of Lorraine into a perimeter around Metz. Meanwhile, farther east, at Wörth in northern Alsace, the German Third Army used its greatly superior numbers to envelope MacMahon's small French force.

After suffering heavy losses, MacMahon retreated toward Châlons, leaving the Vosges barrier open to the Germans.

Napoleon III now intervened personally in an attempt to avert disaster. He joined MacMahon's reinforced army as it moved out of Châlons to relieve Bazaine. MacMahon chose a northerly route, moving toward the Belgian border. Reacting quickly, Moltke detached part of the Second Army from the besieging force at Metz to head off MacMahon from the east. At the same time, the German Third Army, which had now penetrated deep into France, pursued the French north. By August 31, MacMahon was himself encircled at the town of Sedan. The following day, caught in the murderous artillery fire of the besieging Germans, the French marshal and his emperor surrendered their remaining forces. In the Battle of Sedan, the French had lost an army of 100,000, with 17,000 casualties. In contrast, the Germans had lost only 9,000 soldiers. On October 27, Bazaine's army of 170,000 at Metz also capitulated.[102]

By December Moltke had a million German soldiers occupying northern France.[103] Although pockets of French troops continued to resist until February of 1871, the outcome of the war was now inevitable. On January 22, the French provisional government under Léon Gambetta requested an armistice. By the Treaty of Frankfurt of May 1871, France ceded Alsace and northwestern Lorraine to Germany and agreed to pay a large indemnity.

An even more important change in German frontiers had occurred in January, when Prussia and the four states south of the Rhine reached agreement for the entry of the latter into the North German Confederation. On January 18, the Second German Reich was proclaimed, with the Prussian king as German Emperor. Under the bilateral treaties signed the preceding November, each of the new states could retain its own post and telegraph service, railways, and excise taxes. Bavaria even retained the right to administer its own armed forces.[104] In all important respects, however, the new Empire retained the structure Bismarck had drawn up for the North German Confederation.

THE GERMAN NATION STATE

A Hiatus in State Intervention

The widening of political borders due to the introduction of a military innovation permitting greater scale economies may be expected to result in a reduction of tax rates. To assure the consent of distant citizens brought within its new borders, an expanding state will tend to reduce the extent to which it intervenes in economic activity and lower its average tax rates. Did this occur in Germany?

During the eighteenth century and the first decades of the nineteenth century, the German states – particularly Prussia – had intervened heavily in their economies. In the First World War and the interwar period of the present century, public direction, as measured by the state's share of total spending, was also important.[105] Between these two periods, however, lies an interval in the third quarter of the nineteenth century when the state to a considerable extent withdrew from direct participation in the German economy.[106]

Government ownership of industrial enterprises had been important in Prussia since the eighteenth century. During the 1840s, however, industrialists and merchants began to question the effectiveness of state management of industry. In 1848, the activities of the state holding company, the *Seehandlung*, were cut back. By 1854, most of its factories and ships had been sold to private interests. The 1850s and 1860s were the periods of most rapid industrialization in Germany. Its production of woolen textiles doubled and its consumption of raw cotton tripled. In this industrial growth, the state played a negligible role.

Another measure of public intervention is in the construction of railroads. During the 1850s, the Prussian state played a major role in financing railways. Only 611 km of line were laid by private firms, while 2,249 km were built under state authority. In the early 1860s, however, liberals in the lower house of the Prussian legislature defeated the government's railway legislation. If one includes the Hanover rail system, taken over by Prussia in 1866, 2,856 km of line were built by private interests during this decade compared with 2,375 km by the state.[107]

Taxes are yet another indicator of state intervention. Prior to the twentieth century, tariffs accounted for a major part of the revenues of most governments. By 1871, when the *Zollverein* was absorbed into the German Reich, tariffs had been eliminated on most raw materials, manufactured goods and agricultural products. Although revenue duties continued to be imposed on coffee and tobacco, Germany was one of a bloc of countries practicing a policy close to free trade. It is true that cane-sugar continued to pay an import duty; however, because of the rapid growth of domestic beet production, by the late 1870s the revenue impact of this tariff was minimal.[108]

National accounts data are not available for the German states for the period prior to unification. However, some idea of the relative size of the public sector may be gained from data for the first year after unification. In 1872, public spending in Germany represented only 7.5 percent of GNP, compared to 9 percent in the non-interventionist United Kingdom in the same period (1870).[109]

A Disequilibrium Solution

During the 1860s Prussia had shown an exceptional capacity to channel her production into military activities. However, in 1872, the German defense budget absorbed a modest 1.8 percent of GNP.[110] Nevertheless, the threat from this new European superpower remained. The amount it could mobilize for military purposes greatly exceeded that required to defend its own territory. Moreover, unlike France and Great Britain, Germany had no world-wide empire to claim its military resources. The German territorial boundaries of 1871 thus represented a disequilibrium solution.

Where could further German expansion occur? Calleo has argued that there was a lack of space for "German vitality" to be worked out.[111] However, when one examines the map of Europe in 1871, this conclusion is far from self-evident. To the west and north, additional territory could be gained only at a prohibitive cost. But to the south and east, an obvious zone of expansion was the German-speaking regions of Austria and Bohemia. A further possible area of influence lay in the Balkans, where the power of the Ottoman Empire was steadily decaying. Not surprisingly, therefore, in 1879, Germany signed a bilateral alliance with the Austro-Hungarian Empire. (In 1867, following the Austrian defeat at Sadowa, the Hungarians had asserted their right to local autonomy under their own king. Under the constitution of the new Dual Monarchy, the Hungarians controlled the Slavic peoples living within the boundaries of the ancient Hungarian kingdom.) This accord was incorporated into the constitutions of both empires.[112]

Inevitably, south-eastward penetration of German influence would lead to conflict with Russia. However, there was arguably room in Europe for two major powers to expand to the limits of their capacity to control territory. The danger of Germany did not lie in its expansive foreign policy: all major European states behaved in similar fashion. The threat lay rather in the extent of the potential surplus available for military purposes. The introduction of the railroad and telegraph technologies in Germany unleashed an unprecedented capacity to allocate resources efficiently. Europe would not find stability until these resources were either fully committed to territorial control or destroyed.

Yet the effort by Germany to expand need not have precipitated *two* world wars in the space of a few decades. If Europe had been left to work out its own destiny, a restructuring of boundaries consistent with stability would probably have occurred as a result of the First World War. That the settlement of 1919 was no closer to an equilibrium than that of 1871 was not due to lack of effort on the part of Germany. Rather, the persistence of disequilibrium resulted directly from further technological advances that brought Europe within the reach of another expanding power – the United States.

What if anything, then, was special about German sociopolitical development in the nineteenth and twentieth centuries? According to one body of research, Germany's political institutions lagged behind its economic and military capacity. However, there is little reason to believe that a more representative system of government would have led to an outcome that was substantially different. One of the sources of strength of the nation's leaders was that their actions received strong support from a majority of their citizens. Another line of reasoning suggests that it was Germany's geographical position in the center of Europe that led to difficulties. According to this argument, any attempt by Germany to push out its borders would threaten the interests of other major powers. However, there was arguably room in central and south-eastern Europe for both Russia and Germany to expand.

The evidence suggests that if there was anything special about Germany, it began in the middle decades of the nineteenth century. The virtually simultaneous introduction of the railroad and telegraph had a greater impact on Germany than on other European societies. Because of the overall size and density of the German population and the low costs of railroad construction over much of the country, it could be linked by rail and telegraph at relatively low expense. Yet because the same lines that transported passengers and freight could be used for soldiers and cannons, the military implications of the new developments were equally as important as their economic impact.

Prior to the railroad, supply problems had prevented a large military force from remaining for very long in hostile territory. As a result, there was a limit to the pressure that a large state could exert upon a small neighbor. With the introduction of the railroad and telegraph, however, this supply constraint was no longer binding. Provided that rail and wire connections with the home state could be maintained, an army of a million men – twice the size of the force that came to grief on Napoleon's Russian campaign – could now be supplied beyond its home border. The Prussian army, directed by its General Staff, was the first army in Europe to master the coordination of mass troop movements by rail.

The most obvious effect of the technologies was on the *external margin* of the German states. Improvement in road and water transport in the 1820s and 1830s had been an important factor leading to the formation in

1834 of a Prussian-led customs union, the *Zollverein*. In the years between 1836 and 1852, this union was expanded to include all but a handful of the 39 German states other than Austria. Then in the context of three wars between 1864 and 1870 Prussia pushed out her borders to annex the rest of Germany along with Schleswig–Holstein and Alsace–Lorraine within a new federal state, the Second *Reich*.

However, the improvements in transport and communications also affected the *internal margin* separating public from private activity. By the 1840s, relative tax levels had already fallen from the period immediately following the Napoleonic Wars; however, the state still continued to intervene in industrial development, particularly in Prussia. Over the following two decades, the state in Germany all but withdrew from active industrial promotion. Owing to rapid growth and the establishment of virtually free trade, the public share of total spending fell to quite moderate levels.

Even after these changes in territorial boundaries and tax levels, however, Germany still had resources to burn. For nearly three-quarters of a century, German political leaders had at their disposal a great surplus of resources beyond what was necessary to control their territory militarily. This surplus made it possible to introduce the world's first program of social insurance in the 1880s. Eventually, however, it was highly probable that circumstances would occur under which it would be considered acceptable to devote these extra resources to an attempt to push the territorial boundaries of the German state outward.

NOTES

1 Franz Herre, *Moltke, der Mann und sein Jahrhundert* (Deutsche Verlag-Anstalt, Stuttgart, 1984), p. 104.
2 Ibid., p. 105.
3 Dennis E. Showalter, *Railroads and Rifles* (Archon, Hamden, Conn., 1976), pp. 29–31.
4 David Blackbourn and Geoff Eley, *The Peculiarities of German History* (Oxford University Press, 1984), p. 3.
5 Ralf Dahrendorf, *Society and Democracy in Germany* (Doubleday, 1967), p. 35.
6 Blackbourn and Eley, *The Peculiarities of German History*, p. 7.
7 Ibid., p. 18.
8 David Calleo, *The German Problem Reconsidered* (Cambridge University Press, 1978), p. 208.
9 Ibid., p. 206.
10 Frederick Hertz, *The German Public Mind in the Nineteenth Century* (Rowman and Littlefield, Totowa, NJ, 1975), p. 165.
11 William Carr, *A History of Germany 1815–1945* (Edward Arnold, 1969), p. 6.
12 Carlo M. Cipolla, *Literacy and Development in the West* (Penguin, 1969), p. 115.
13 Agatha Ramm, *Germany 1789–1919* (Methuen, 1967), p. 141.
14 Hertz, *The German Public Mind*, p. 227.
15 Ibid., p. 167.

16 W. O. Henderson, *The Rise of German Industrial Power* (Temple Smith, 1975), p. 71.
17 Ibid., pp. 72–4.
18 Ibid., p. 71–2.
19 Carr, *A History of Germany*, p. 15.
20 Ibid., p. 18.
21 Ramm, *Germany 1789–1919*, p. 162–3.
22 Carr, *A History of Germany*, p. 28.
23 Hans Rosenberg, *Bureaucracy, Aristocracy and Autocracy: The Prussian Experience 1660–1815* (Harvard University Press, 1958), p. 178.
24 Michael Howard, *War in European History* (Oxford University Press, 1976), p. 85.
25 Walter Goerlitz, *History of the German General Staff* (Westview Press, Boulder, 1985), p. 75.
26 Ibid., p. 20.
27 Ibid., p. 46.
28 Ibid., p. 54.
29 Larry H. Addington, *The Patterns of War since the Eighteenth Century* (Indiana University Press, 1984), p. 48.
30 Carl von Clausewitz, *On War*, tr. J. J. Graham. (Routledge and Kegan Paul, 1956), vol. 1, p. xxiii.
31 See Hew Strachan, *European Armies and the Conduct of War* (George Allen and Unwin, 1983), pp. 90–8, and Addington, *The Patterns of War*, pp. 41–3.
32 Clausewitz, *On War*, vol. 1, p. 193.
33 Richard S. Kirby, Sidney Withington, Arthur B. Darling, and Frederick G. Kilgour, *Engineering in History* (McGraw-Hill, 1956), pp. 200–1.
34 R. H. Tilly, "Capital formation in Germany in the nineteenth century," in *The Cambridge Economic History of Europe*, vol. 7, *The Industrial Economies: Capital Labour and Enterprise*, eds P. Mathias and M. M. Postan (Cambridge University Press, 1978), p. 411.
35 Martin Kitchen, *The Political Economy of Germany 1815–1914* (Croom Helm, 1978), p. 47.
36 Tilly, "Capital formation in Germany," p. 413.
37 Dudley Dillard, *Economic Development of the North Atlantic Community* (Prentice-Hall, 1967), p. 305–6.
38 Henderson, *The Rise of German Industrial Power*, pp. 37–8.
39 Ibid., p. 33.
40 Hertz, *The German Public Mind*, p. 170.
41 Ibid., p. 171.
42 W. R. Lee, "Tax structure and economic growth in Germany (1750–1850)," *Journal of European Economic History*, 4 (1975), p. 156.
43 Ibid., pp. 154.
44 Carr, *A History of Germany*, p. 37.
45 Ibid., p. 27.
46 Ramm, *Germany 1789–1919*, p. 168.
47 Kirby et al., *Engineering in History*, p. 175.
48 Henderson, *The Rise of German Industrial Power*, p. 45.
49 Ibid., p. 47.
50 Kitchen, *The Political Economy of Germany*, p. 50.
51 Ibid., p. 51.
52 Clive Trebilcock, *The Industrialization of the Continental Powers 1780–1914* (Longman, 1981), p. 56.
53 David S. Landes, *The Unbound Prometheus* (Cambridge University Press, 1969), p. 153.
54 Kirby et al., *Engineering in History*, p. 336–7.

55 Ibid., p. 337–8.
56 Ibid., pp. 338–9.
57 Addington, *The Patterns of War*, p. 44.
58 Howard, *War in European History*, p. 97.
59 Showalter, *Railroads and Rifles*, p. 36.
60 Ibid., p. 37.
61 Goerlitz, *History of the German General Staff*, p. 76.
62 Howard, *War in European History*, p. 100.
63 Showalter, *Railroads and Rifles*, pp. 39–40.
64 Howard, *War in European History*, p. 97.
65 Showalter, *Railroads and Rifles*, p. 44.
66 Goerlitz, *History of the German General Staff*, p. 77.
67 Addington, *The Patterns of War*, p. 49.
68 Ibid., p. 47.
69 Henderson, *The Rise of German Industrial Power*, p. 112.
70 Ibid., p. 105.
71 Ibid., p. 149.
72 Ramm, *Germany 1789–1919*, p. 290.
73 Thomas Nipperdey, *Deutsche Geschichte 1800–1866* (Beck, Munich, 1983), p. 768.
74 Ramm, *Germany 1789–1919*, p. 281.
75 Goerlitz, *History of the German General Staff*, p. 77.
76 Showalter, *Railroads and Rifles*, p. 50.
77 Goerlitz, *History of the German General Staff*, p. 84.
78 Addington, *The Patterns of War*, p. 49.
79 Carr, *A History of Germany*, p. 111.
80 Ramm, *Germany 1789–1919*, p. 297.
81 Showalter, *Railroads and Rifles*, p. 57.
82 Ibid., p. 224.
83 Ibid.
84 Ibid., p. 60.
85 Ibid., pp. 70–1.
86 Carr, *A History of Germany*, p. 114.
87 Showalter, *Railroads and Rifles*, p. 213.
88 Ibid., p. 58.
89 Goerlitz, *History of the German General Staff*, p. 86.
90 Showalter, *Railroads and Rifles*, p. 68.
91 R. Ernest Dupuy and Trevor N. Dupuy, *The Encyclopedia of Military History from 3500 BC to the Present*, 2nd edn (Harper and Row, 1986), p. 831.
92 Antje Kraus, *Quellen zur Bevölkerungs-, Sozial- und Wirtschaftsstatistik Deutschlands 1815–1875*, Band I (Harald Boldt Verlag, Boppard am Rhein, 1980), pp. 34, 40, 58, 64, 226, 330.
93 Walter M. Simon, *Germany in the Age of Bismarck* (George Allen and Unwin, 1968), p. 34.
94 Ramm, *Germany 1789–1919*, p. 308.
95 Henderson, *The Rise of German Industrial Power*, p. 157.
96 Ramm, *Germany 1789–1919*, p. 313.
97 Showalter, *Railroads and Rifles*, p. 94.
98 Ibid., p. 129.
99 Addington, *The Patterns of War*, p. 87.
100 Ibid., p. 88.
101 Ramm, *Germany 1789–1919*, p. 311.

102 Dupuy and Dupuy, *The Encyclopedia of Military History*, pp. 832–6.
103 Addington, *The Patterns of War*, p. 90.
104 Ramm, *Germany 1789–1919*, p. 316.
105 Suphan Andic and Jindrich Veverka, "The growth of government expenditures in Germany since unification," *Finanzarchiv*, 23 (1964), p. 243.
106 See Trebilcock, *The Industrialization of the Continental Powers*, pp. 74–8.
107 Kitchen, *The Political Economy of Germany*, p. 98.
108 J. A. Perkins, "Fiscal policy and economic development in XIXth century Germany," *Journal of European Economic History*, 13 (1984), p. 326.
109 Trebilcock, *The Industrialization of the Continental Powers*, p. 87.
110 Andic and Veverka, "The growth of government expenditures," pp. 241, 269.
111 Calleo, *The German Problem Reconsidered*, p. 206.
112 Ibid., p. 17.

7

The Petrograd Paradox

It is paradoxical that the diffusion of techniques for mass communication in the early twentieth century should have had its greatest impact in Russia, the most backward region of Europe. In other studies, the success of the Bolsheviks has been explained by the occurrence of a power vacuum in 1917 or by the leadership characteristics of Lenin. However, Lenin was only a journalist, with little administrative experience, and his group was but one of several that were competing for power in Petrograd (now Leningrad) at that time. The explanation, it is argued here, is a combination of internal innovation and external pressure. Lenin was the first to link the new communications vehicles – the high-speed press and mechanical typesetter, the typewriter, and the telephone – to an exclusionist ideology; that is, to a set of beliefs implying that any power center other than his own was necessarily opposed to the interests of the majority. He also found a means of substituting abundant labor for scarce information, using a political party as a duplicate supervisory hierarchy. The resulting unprecedented degree of public control over individual behavior permitted an underdeveloped state with limited internal communications to capture the resources needed to protect itself from more advanced predators.

Figure 7.1   The consolidation of Bolshevik Russia, 1918–21.
(*Source: The Times Atlas of World History,* 1984, p. 259.)

It was 11 o'clock on a spring evening when the train with its brightly lit coaches pulled into the Finland Station in the Russian capital of Petrograd (the city's name was changed to Leningrad in 1924). The platform was crowded with members of different revolutionary groups who had been joined by large numbers of workers, soldiers, and sailors. When Lenin stepped from his car, a group of workers carried him into what had formerly been known as the Tsar's Room and had now become the People's Room. There a committee of members of the Petrograd Soviet welcomed him and requested that he work with them to defend the revolution. But Lenin made no attempt to reply to his fellow revolutionaries. Instead, he turned to address the crowd, his harsh voice resonating across the room. "The hour is not far off," he proclaimed, "when . . . the people will turn their weapons against their capitalist exploiters. The Russian Revolution, achieved by you, has opened a new epoch. Long live the world-wide Socialist Revolution!"[1]

On April 16, 1917, the Bolsheviks were but one of several left-wing Russian political parties vying for popular support in the turmoil that followed the abdication of the Tsar Nicholas II. Their leader, V. I. Lenin, had been in exile in Western Europe for most of the previous 17 years. A few weeks earlier, the German wartime government, hoping to destabilize the new Russian regime, had arranged for his return to his homeland. The railway coach in which Lenin and 32 other Russian exiles traveled was kept locked as it crossed Germany, and there was no passport control; hence the later references to the "sealed" train. After crossing to Sweden by ship, the party continued on by rail. As Lenin approached the Finnish border, he learned that his followers, led by Stalin and Kamenev, had decided to participate in the new Provisional Government, in strict violation of his own instructions.

Lenin's coldness to the members of the Petrograd Soviet, who shared power with the Provisional Government, was deliberate, as would soon become clear. From the station, he was taken to the Bolshevik headquarters at the palace of Kshesinskaya. There he again addressed the crowd waiting outside and withdrew to the salon where the leaders of his party were gathered to greet him. He sat listening to their speeches, a faint smile on his face. Then he rose to his feet and violently lashed out at them. There would be no support for the Provisional Government. The party must work for the complete overthrow of the capitalist system, together with revolutionaries in other countries.[2] Lenin's followers were abashed, but they had little choice. Either they accepted his leadership unquestioningly or their party would lose the only man capable of leading them to power.

Russia itself seemed most inhospitable terrain for a party leader attempting to communicate a radically new message to the less-favored groups in society. The country, sprawling across two continents, was the least densely populated of any in the West. Its adult illiteracy rate was the highest in Europe.[3] In addition, its population was to a great extent rural, isolated from developments in the cities. Even the urban residents were largely cut off from one another and from the rest of Europe. In a country of 174 million inhabitants, there were only some 230,000 telephones in 1913 and no long distance lines between cities.[4]

Yet, paradoxically, it was from the Russian capital, initially in Petrograd, but subsequently in Moscow, that the new technologies for mass control were first successfully applied. Moreover, it was by the small and initially divided Bolshevik party that these techniques were introduced. By November of 1917 (October by the old Russian calendar), in one of the most exceptional reversals of fortune in history, Lenin had united his party and used it to overthrow the Provisional Government and seize power in Russia. Over the following decade, having changed its name to the Communist Party, his movement would succeed for the first time in managing an industrial economy in which the means of production were collectively owned.

THE FIRST PERMANENT REVOLUTION

The October Revolution was not the first occasion on which a group dedicated to the establishment of a new social order had assumed power in a state. The Jacobins in France in 1793, the liberals and nationalists in a number of European states in 1848, and the *communards* in Paris in 1872 had all ousted existing regimes and substituted distinctly different forms of government. However, in each case, the revolutionary groups were themselves subsequently overthrown by coalitions of more conservative interests. What is striking about the Leninist revolution is that it survived not only a bitter civil war but also a disastrous collapse of the economy and the subsequent death of its leader (in 1924). Indeed, from the early 1920s until the late 1980s, there was no serious internal challenge to the rule of the Communist Party in Russia.

How did the Bolsheviks manage to capture and maintain centralized control over the Russian society and economy? The most frequent explanation of their success is circumstantial, based on a power vacuum that supposedly existed in Russia for a few months in the summer and fall of 1917. The collapse of the tsarist regime was so complete and the power of the succeeding Provisional Government so weakened by the dual regime it shared with the workers' council or Soviet of the capital that any organized group could have seized control.[5] In evaluating this position, however, one should remember that the hot potato of power in Russia had burned the hands of several other groups before it was seized by the Bolsheviks. Why were the latter able to hold on where the others had failed?

Another set of arguments is based on the personality of Lenin, particularly his organizing ability and his astute political judgment. His party was the most tightly disciplined of all the groups struggling for power in the period leading up to November 1917. Moreover, the political platform Lenin chose was ideally suited to Russian public opinion in the final months of the Provisional Government. Russia was exhausted from three years of war, most of its resources were still controlled by a small aristocratic class, and its production and distribution system was in disarray. In this setting, Lenin's slogan, "Peace, land, and food," carried to all corners of the country by a dedicated group of revolutionaries, was bound to arouse strong popular support.[6]

One problem with this position is that by the summer of 1917 the Bolsheviks had become an open mass party. Moreover, it was a movement that Lenin had increasing difficulty in controlling. During the "July Days," when a crowd of soldiers and workers carrying banners with Bolshevik slogans arrived at party headquarters, Lenin was caught unprepared and refused to encourage violent action.[7] As for his ability to sense what the people wanted, his policy on land reform had been borrowed intact from the larger Socialist Revolutionary Party. Even the "peace" plank, the one original element in the Bolshevik program, was unpopular among many Russian nationalists. Two months before the October Revolution, as the German armies approached Petrograd, Lenin himself decided to hedge on his previous position. (Note that since the Julian calendar used in Russia until 1918 had fallen 13 days behind the Gregorian calendar used in Western Europe, what the Russians call the "October" revolution actually occurred in November.) He promised "truly revolutionary" war if the Germans refused to accept his peace conditions.[8] A further problem for the great-person model is that Lenin was not alone: other political leaders – Mussolini, Hitler, and Franco – had equal success in establishing exceptionally authoritarian regimes shortly after this period.

Were the Bolsheviks then simply one example of a more general phenomenon? One of the most provocative explanations for the accomplishments of Lenin and other authoritarian leaders of this period is that their success was due to the introduction of a new form of government – totalitarianism.[9] According to this point of view, the new type of regime was based on the related phenomena of propaganda – the use of public communications to influence political values[10] – and terror – the absence of legal constraints on state power.[11] The essential features of this organizational innovation were, it has been argued, developed by the Russian Communists in the key period between 1917 and 1921.[12]

In assessing this position, one must ask whether the concepts of propaganda and terror constituted anything essentially new. In the past, religious organizations, notably the Catholic Church, had succeeded in imposing tight controls on the circulation of information. Moreover, absolutist regimes such as that of the first Russian Tsar, Ivan IV (the Terrible, 1530–84), had practiced mass purges in order to eliminate dissent. Even if one admits that the degree of control over public communication and the degree of repression were exceptional under the Communists, these policies did not necessarily guarantee consent for the regime that used them, as Nicholas II had discovered. The totalitarian model fails to explain the degree of support that the Soviet regime maintained under even the most difficult conditions.

The Guns-versus-Butter Dilemma

To understand the success of Soviet communism, it is necessary to know how the Russian state itself arose. Across the northern part of the Eurasian land mass east of the Baltic sea, there are few important natural barriers to military movement. The key to controlling this vast territory is a relatively small and habitable area around Moscow, where the Volga, Don, Dnieper, and West Dvina rivers have their headwaters (see figure 7.1). From there, outward expansion to the Black Sea, the Caspian Sea, the Baltic Sea and, via a tributary of the Volga, the Ural mountains is possible – indeed, with gunpowder technology, inevitable.[13] It was from this strategic point that the Grand Dukes of Muscovy began their campaigns of conquest in the fifteenth century, in the process assuming the title of caesar or tsar. Although by the last quarter of the nineteenth century, the Russian rulers had moved their capital to St Petersburg on the Baltic Sea, their control of the Moscow region enabled them to dominate an empire stretching from Finland and Poland in the west to Vladivostok on the Sea of Japan in the east. This territory they ruled in absolutist fashion, with little tolerance for political dissent.

The tsars' claim that absolutist rule was the optimal form of government for Russia could be justified as long as they were able to maintain internal peace in this vast territory while leaving the population enough income for its own subsistence. In other words, the viability of the tsarist regime, like that of governments elsewhere, depended in the final analysis on its capacity to provide both guns and butter to its people. Under the rule of Muscovy, for the first time in history the inhabitants of this region experienced a period of peace, free from nomad invasions. During the decades prior to the First World War, with the exception of a short period in 1904–5, the tsars proved surprisingly successful in providing both protection and the direction required to encourage the modernization of their economy. However, this state intervention put a heavy strain on public finances.

Extensive industrialization began in Russia a century after its commencement in Britain and a half-century after its appearance in France and Germany. This delay in the emergence of manufacturing had a number of implications. Once growth began, it was extremely rapid. Industrial output rose at over 5 percent per year in the last quarter of the nineteenth century.[14] Because of the evolution of technology in favor of capital-intensive production characterized by considerable scale economies, Russian establishments were much larger and economic power therefore more concentrated than in Britain at the same stage of industrialization. Most important, perhaps, was the fact that the new manufacturing technologies placed heavy demands on society to invest in social infrastructure. In addition to roads and ports, railroads and electric generating capacity, along with housing for uprooted workers, were all required on a scale that exceeded that experienced by other European countries.

Elsewhere in Europe, industrialization in the late nineteenth century had permitted rapid increases in per-capita income levels. In Russia, however, in part because of the small initial industrial base, total output (manufacturing plus agriculture and services) grew much less rapidly than manufacturing production. From 1870 to the First World War, total output rose at only 2.5 percent per year. At the same time, Russia's population grew more rapidly than that of other European countries. During the half-century from 1860 to 1913, the annual rate of demographic growth averaged 1.6 percent, compared to 1.2 percent in Germany and England. Owing to the magic of compound interest, the 74 million Russians of the earlier year had become 174 million by the eve of the First World War. As a result, in per-capita terms, Russian income rose at an annual rate of only 0.9 percent in the half-century prior to the First World War.[15] It should be noted, however, that this rate was not significantly below those experienced by England and Germany during their initial decades of industrialization.

Pressure on the Internal Margin

Russia's delayed industrialization also had important implications for the internal margin of the state; that is, for the division between the public and private sectors. The capital requirements for the new capital-intensive industries tended to exceed the savings that could be generated by Russia's own private sector. Foreign direct investment was therefore required on a large scale. For example, by 1916, the mining sector was 91 percent foreign-owned, while 50 percent of the total capital in chemicals was in non-Russian hands.[16]

Even with heavy foreign involvement, however, the private sector in Russia played a smaller part in financing social infrastructure investments than it had in England, France and Germany. By 1912, Russia had built over 70,000 km of railroad, but only after extensive participation by the state. Some two-thirds of the railway network were government-owned.[17] In addition, public agencies provided credit to other industrial sectors. Coming on top of increasingly heavy spending requirements for defense, these additional demands placed a great strain on the finances of the state.

Compared with other European countries at this time, Russia's fiscal system was still quite primitive. In 1912, 88 percent of government revenues came from indirect taxes – that is, levies on transactions rather than on income. Even the structure of indirect taxes showed a lack of diversification. Roughly one-third of revenues came from tariffs on foreign trade. Indeed, Russia had the most highly protected economy in Europe, with import duties representing some 40 percent of the value of total imports. Another third of public revenues came from the state vodka monopoly. Excise taxes on sugar, tea, matches, kerosene, and other products accounted for most of the remaining state revenues.[18] It should be noted that those taxed most heavily were urban consumers, the peasants managing to escape most of the burden of indirect taxes; there is little evidence to support the notion that the peasants suffered unduly from taxation. Moreover, a relatively small part of the total fiscal burden fell on incomes from land and industrial capital.

As a result of these structural weaknesses in the tax system, public revenues failed to keep pace with spending needs. The government was able to meet its financial requirements only by selling interest-bearing bonds outside the country. In 1895, some 30 percent of government debt was held abroad; by 1913, this share had grown to almost one-half.[19] Total foreign investment in Russia in 1914 amounted to almost 8 billion rubles, of which some 6 billion rubles were loans to the state and municipalities.[20] Even if one takes into account the 1.5 billion rubles that Russians had invested abroad, net foreign indebtedness had still reached the level of roughly four times annual export receipts. Nevertheless, the financing of this debt remained well within Russia's capabilities – at least in time of peace.

Blocked Expansion of the External Margin

The growing strain on Russia's public finances occurred at a time when the state's geographical boundary or external margin was also coming under increased pressure. Like the generations of autocrats that had preceded them, the nineteenth-century Russian tsars continued to harbor hopes for even further territorial gains. The two most promising directions of expansion were south-west into the Balkans and south-east into Manchuria. In each case, there was a decaying power long past its prime that appeared incapable of offering strong resistance. The Ottoman dynasty of Turkey in the west and the Manchu (Ch'ing) dynasty of China in the east were each having too much difficulty putting down internal rebellions to be able to defend their borders effectively.

Unfortunately for the tsars, in each region there was also an upstart rival nation prepared to contest Russia's ambitions. In the west, the new German Empire allied itself secretly in 1879 with Austria, Russia's rival in the Balkans. Russia responded in 1890 by forming a secret alliance with France, which Britain subsequently joined. Then in the east, a further setback occurred. The newly modernized Japanese state succeeded in destroying the tsar's fleet and inflicting heavy losses on Russian armies in the Russo-Japanese war of 1904–5. The upshot was that Russia found its plans for expansion blocked both in the east and in the west for the first time in 400 years.

Germany rubbed salt into Russia's wounds in 1909 when she backed Austria's seizure of the former Turkish province of Bosnia. Too weak from the recent war with Japan to contemplate resisting, Russia was forced to withdraw its support for the rival claims of Serbia. It was in the Bosnian capital of Sarajevo five years later that a Serbian terrorist assassinated the Austrian Archduke Franz Ferdinand – an event that provoked an ultimatum from Austria to Russia's Serbian ally. By this time, however, Russia had recovered sufficiently to be able to contemplate supporting her interests in the Balkans by force.

Russia's military calculations in 1914 were straightforward. While her allies, France and England, held down the bulk of German forces in the west, she planned to attack Germany immediately from the rear while simultaneously assaulting Austria. On each front, Russia's great numerical superiority should be enough for victory. Thus when Austria declared war on Serbia on July 28, Russia immediately mobilized. Anxious to bring the war to a rapid end before their opponents' greater numbers could be brought to bear, Germany and Austria quickly declared war on Russia and France. Russia in turn declared war and proceeded to russify the name of her capital, changing it to Petrograd.

The Tsarist Army

As a continental power with limited access to the world's oceans and few natural barriers against external attack, Russia depended for her survival on the strength of her army. In terms of numbers of men, it was by far the largest military force in Europe. With a standing army of 1.4 million soldiers and reserves of 3.1 million in July 1914, Russia had a total of 4.5 million soldiers available for immediate duty. A further 2 million soldiers would be mobilized by the end of the year.[21] By the end of 1916, Russia would have thrown 15 million men into the conflict.[22]

The immediate problem was to find arms and ammunition for these troops. Russia's steel output was greater than that of France, but her production of shells was much lower.[23] Although Russia had 4.6 million rifles on hand, her factories were able to manufacture only 278,000 additional weapons by the end of 1914.[24] When Turkey finally decided to enter the war on the side of the central powers in October 1914, the situation became critical. With the Dardanelles closed and Sweden restricting arms shipments through the Baltic, Russia could be supplied only by Vladivostok or Archangel.[25] In the first quarter of 1915, Russian units received only one-fifth of their minimum needs of shells.[26]

In 1914, Russia managed to take stiff punishment from Germany without crumbling while at the same time making gains at the expense of the Turks and Austrians. However, the following spring, with the battle in the west stalemated, the central powers decided to make an all-out effort to knock Russia out of the war. In May 1915, the German and Austrian armies launched a massive offensive against Russian Poland. Because of the shortage of weapons, many of the defenders were unarmed. Soldiers had to wait for a comrade to fall so that they could take up his rifle.[27] Inevitably, the Russian forces were pushed back, until by December 1915 all of Poland and Lithuania had been surrendered. Yet the front had held and the German–Austrian advance ground to a halt. Meanwhile, the tsar had decided to take personal command of the European front.

By 1916 the Russian army's supply of arms had improved. A new railroad to Murmansk on the Arctic coast, along with double-tracking of the line to Archangel and much of the Trans-Siberian line, permitted an increased flow of imported weapons. At the same time, Russian industry had doubled its production of rifles and tripled its output of machine-guns.[28] In June, General Brusilov launched what was to be Russia's most successful operation of the war, attacking Austrian forces in Galicia (now a part of southern Poland and the western Ukraine). The offensive was finally stopped only in September, when German units were rushed from the west to shore up the battered Austrians.

In short, the first two and a half years of the war demonstrated that when properly equipped, the Russian army was more than a match for either the Turks or the Austrians. The record showed that only German units could consistently defeat Russian troops in the field. However, not enough German divisions could be spared from the western front to deliver the knock-out blow to an enemy whose capacity to withdraw and replenish lost forces seemed inexhaustible.

The Tsarist Secret Police

The more populous a state, the more likely it is that its enemies will be within rather than outside its borders. Since the Russian Empire's population placed it at the upper end of the size spectrum of states, its leaders necessarily gave considerable attention to police actions. One area of administration in which the regime of the tsars had innovated was in the control of internal political dissent. In March 1881, a revolutionary terrorist group, People's Will, assassinated the Tsar Alexander II. A few months later, under the new Tsar Alexander III (1881–1894), the Ministry of the Interior established special police units to combat political crime in St Petersburg, Moscow, and Warsaw. From the official designation of these Protective Sections (*okhrannyye otdeleniya*) came the name used for the tsarist political police over the following decades – the Okhrana.[29]

Under a statute decreed in the same year, the police were granted virtually unlimited powers of summary arrest and detention. Although these powers were in principle temporary, they in fact remained in force until the fall of the regime.[30] In 1887 the Okhrana intercepted a letter that revealed a plot to assassinate the new tsar. One of those arrested and executed for his part in this attempt was a revolutionary named Alexander Ulyanov. Ulyanov's younger brother, Vladimir Ilyich, who was later to take the political cover-name of Lenin, vowed to take vengeance on the authorities for this act.[31] As the resistance to the tsar mounted, the Okhrana's resources and powers were extended. During the first years of the twentieth century, it established units in many of the largest towns. One of its most refined techniques was the infiltration of revolutionary movements and provocation of their members into attempting illegal acts, whereupon they would be arrested.[32] There is some evidence that at about this time Stalin may have acted as an Okhrana agent.[33]

Under the administrative techniques used by the tsarist authorities, it was not always possible to maintain control over the activities of the political police nor to coordinate their activities with those of other enforcement agencies. In 1903, a strike by Okhrana-sponsored unions in Odessa got out of control and had to be suppressed by the regular police.[34] And in 1905, workers in St Petersburg belonging to a movement led by a police agent, Father George Gapon, appealed to Tsar Nicholas II after some of their fellow workers were fired. On Sunday January 22, they marched peacefully on the Winter Palace. There, upon orders from the tsar's uncle, regular troops fired on the marchers, killing at least 150 of them in an incident known as "Bloody Sunday."[35] The massacre sparked a wave of revolution that was only calmed in the fall of 1905 when the tsar promised a constitution and elected assembly. Even so, the following three years saw a wave of political assassinations and summary arrests and executions.

The effectiveness of a political surveillance agency such as the Okhrana depends on its access to information and the way in which it channels that information to those who make decisions. The tsarist secret police relied on a vast network of informers whose activities were coordinated in St Petersburg. There, in the Identity Section, were kept half a million forms, in tens of thousands of files. Forty thousand of these files concerned "secret collaborators" of the regime.[36] In the 1890s, the Okhrana began to take photographs and fingerprints of arrested political dissidents.[37]

On the eve of the First World War, due in no small part to the effectiveness of its police system, the tsarist regime appeared to be in firm control of the country. Early in 1914, however, a decision was made whose effect was to deprive the surveillance agency of some of its most critical information. The Okhrana had previously established a network of police informers within the armed forces to report secretly on the political reliability of the soldiers, sailors, and officers. In an attempt to improve morale as international tensions built up, the regime decided to forbid espionage within the military. As long as developments on the front were favorable, this decision may well have led to a more positive attitude on the part of the troops. However, as unrest mounted within the armed forces in 1916 and early 1917, the authorities were virtually powerless to control it.[38]

The Tsarist Fiscal Bureaucracy

Ultimately, the capacity of the Russian state both to protect its people and assure their economic survival depended on the success of its fiscal bureaucracy in extracting resources from the civilian population. However, tax collection was not simply a matter of deciding how much money was needed and fixing the corresponding tax rates. The regime had to assure that revenues were actually collected and that the amount received was spent on the appropriate services.

Two possible problems could arise. One was incompetence: an official could neglect to carry out his assigned task. The other was corruption: the public servant could confiscate a part or all of the sum collected for his own personal use. To prevent these two problems, there was really only one effective solution. The officials had to be monitored by a second group of administrators – supervisors who made sure that the first group acted as they were supposed to do. In addition, the monitors themselves had to be watched to assure that they did not collude with those being supervised.

Now it is not difficult to see that the more information the supervisors have about what their subjects are doing, the better they will be able to monitor them. What then determines the amount of information available to the supervisor? One factor, obviously, is distance. The farther the supervisor or the information he needs has to travel to and from the capital and the point of tax collection, the greater its cost and the poorer its quality will be. Another factor is the speed at which a message or its bearer is able to travel. The more recent the information, the greater its value as an input in monitoring.

One of the challenges of administering a territory as large as Russia is the immense distances involved. For example, the 1830 km between St Petersburg and Odessa represent well over twice the distance from Paris to Marseille, over three times the distance from Berlin to Munich, and six times the distance from London to Manchester. In the nineteenth century, prior to the completion of the railway network, Russia's vast area made it virtually impossible to monitor the behavior of remote officials effectively. A constant problem of the central authorities was that business piled up in provincial offices without any action being taken. As numerous committees discovered, the amount of work done seemed to have little to do with the number of public servants or the amount they were paid.[39] The regime tried to compensate for this lack of control over distant officials by centralizing decisions as much as possible in St Petersburg. The result was that proposals by provincial governors then accumulated on the desks of minor functionaries in the offices of the capital's ministries.[40]

As might be expected, corruption was rife – indeed, corruption was a way of life – at all levels of the Russian public bureaucracy. In 1853, it was discovered that the manager of a committee that distributed public funds to wounded veterans of the Napoleonic Wars had embezzled 1.2 million rubles. Unfortunately, by the time the crime was discovered, the money had been spent and the man was deceased.[41] Public servants at lower levels used their positions to extract payments in cash or in kind from the local population. Since appeal of administrative decisions was bound to be a long and uncertain process, provincial officials were able to tyrannize their subject populations.[42]

Inefficiency and corruption help explain the primitive and rigid structure of the Russian fiscal system. Government revenues came almost entirely from payments to the state in exchange for the right to make a limited number of types of transactions. Two-thirds of Russia's sea-going trade passed through the Baltic ports. Thus by placing a small number of closely watched officials at these entry points, the government could extract a steady flow of tribute. What better place for a capital than St Petersburg, at the head of the Baltic, through which 90 percent of Russia's sea trade passed?[43] It was here in 1712 that Peter the Great had moved the capital from Moscow as part of his program to open the country to European influence.

In the immediate prewar years, the tsarist fiscal system was able to provide for the government's needs thanks to plentiful supplies of foreign credit. With the beginning of the First World War, however, this situation changed dramatically. Access to Europe's capital markets was sharply curtailed. In addition, with the entrances to the Baltic and the Black seas blocked, customs duties on foreign trade were reduced to a trickle. A final serious blow to Russia's fiscal equilibrium was self-inflicted. In August 1914, as a sacrifice to help further the war effort, the regime announced the prohibition of the sale of alcohol. In so doing, it deprived itself of its most important revenue source. The bulk of war expenditures would be financed by the selling of bonds locally and by the printing of money.

In short, while the tsars managed to maintain control over Russia until 1914, their country's entry into the war brought to light a glaring weakness of their regime. In the end, it was the system's inability to finance both guns and butter that was to bring about its downfall. Largely because of inadequate internal communications, the tsarist bureaucracy was unable to extract enough tribute from its subjects to pay for both the social expenditures of a modern state and the requirements of a prolonged war. If the war had ended in the summer of 1916, the regime could probably have survived – at least temporarily. However, by the end of that year, as the fighting continued, the Russian monarchy was hurtling deeper and deeper into a fiscal black hole from which there would be no escape.

THE INSTRUMENTS OF MASS CONTROL

While the tsarist regime was foundering, its allies and its principal enemy were demonstrating some of the components of a possible solution to the dilemma of guns versus butter. The war that had broken out in the summer of 1914 had been expected to last a few months. Yet as 1917 began, the conflict was well into its third year, with no end in sight. One of the principal reasons for the intensity and the length of the combat was the enhanced fiscal capacity of the modern state. In Germany, over the period from 1881 to 1913, government expenditure had increased from 10 to 18 percent of GNP. During the first two years of the war, this figure rose even more sharply, as new direct taxes were levied.[44] Finally, under "war socialism" established by Ludendorff at the end of 1916, government control was extended to almost all sectors of the German economy.[45] Although no national accounts statistics are available for Germany in this period, it is indicative that even in Britain in 1917, public spending represented 57 percent of GNP.[46] The corresponding German figure was almost certainly higher.

These developments did not escape the attention of an exiled Russian party leader who was determined to create a new kind of government in his home country. The same instruments used by the Western European powers to mobilize large numbers of people and prolong their war efforts could also be applied to control a state in times of peace.

Direct Mass Communication

With the invention of printing and the appearance of the first newspapers in the early seventeenth century, an effective means of reaching large numbers of people became available. Unlike the Catholic Church's network of churches and seminaries, the new medium was *direct:* a newspaper editor could reach his readers without having his message decoded by a chain of intermediaries. As a result, communication was fast: the speed of diffusion was limited only by the swiftness of transport. In less than a day, people in an urban area could be informed of the latest developments.

Yet, by the early nineteenth century, principally because of their high cost, newspapers reached only a small fraction of the total population of even the most advanced western countries. One problem was the labor required to compose a page of type; that is, the cost of the first copy. Manual typesetting allowed only 1,500 pieces of type to be set per hour. The other difficulty was the speed at which the first page could be reproduced; that is, the cost of actual printing. Hand-operated presses could produce only 250 sheets per hour. In 1815, *The Times* of London had a circulation of 5,000 and a price per copy of seven pence.

A major breakthrough occurred at mid-century with the development of the rotary press. In 1844, Richard Hoe in the United States invented a press in which the type was set on a rotating cylinder. The new system permitted speeds of 8,000 copies per hour. However, because the type tended to fall out of the cylinder, the system was subject to frequent breakdowns. Then in the 1850s a way was found to apply stereotypy – the reproduction of set type – to the rotary press. A pasteboard impression of the original typeform was injected with lead alloy. The result was a curved plate that could be set into a cylindrical frame, with no individual pieces of type to work loose. The following decade saw a great expansion in journalism, including the founding of London's first penny newspaper, *The Daily Telegraph.* In 1870, with 240,000 copies sold daily, it was the paper with the largest circulation in the world.

It was at the end of the nineteenth century that the newspaper finally reached maturity as a mass medium. The introduction of electric printing presses in 1884 yielded a further acceleration in printing rates. At about the same time, a German-born American immigrant, Ottmar Mergenthaler, developed the Linotype machine, a device that integrated the different operations involved in typesetting so as to produce whole lines of cast type.

The new machine permitted 5,000 to 7,000 pieces of complete type to be set per hour. By the following decade, it became possible to print hundreds of thousands of cut and folded newspapers in a few hours. In 1896, Alfred Harmsworth founded the *Daily Mail* which sold at one halfpenny. By the turn of the century, his paper reached a circulation of one million: the mass audience had been created.

The capacity of the mass newspaper to generate social change was considerable throughout Western Europe. However, as in other areas of technology, Russia lagged behind other western countries. With its 1910 population of 170 million, including 70 million for whom Russian was the first language, the country represented a vast potential market. Yet prior to the late nineteenth century, there was no means of circulating information rapidly among the general population – or even among those living in the cities and towns. In 1883 there were but 80 newspapers in all of Russia, only a few of which appeared in printings as large as 20,000. Moreover, from 1865 precensorship was applied to all publications except the major papers of Moscow and St Petersburg. In contrast, in the United States with a similar population, there were 850 newspapers in 1880. With the exception of the Civil War period, there was no censorship in America to impede the flow of information. By the turn of the century, the new printing technology had reached Russia: there were several papers with a circulation exceeding 100,000. After the 1905 revolution, precensorship was abolished. In 1908, a new paper, *Kopeika* (Penny paper) appeared and was published in printings of hundreds of thousands until 1917. By 1913, the total number of newspapers in Russia had risen to 1,158.[47]

The innovations in communications appear to have set off a chain of repercussions across Europe. As the cost of reproducing information fell, it became advantageous to extend the ability to read and write to an increasing share of the community. But with the spread of literacy, the economic gains to belonging to a national communications networks increased, thereby raising each individual's willingness to pay taxes to national states. With greater resources that could be allocated to the control of territory, many states began to find their existing boundaries too confining. International tensions rose.

The impact of the mass-circulation press as a medium for the distribution of homogeneous information to vast numbers of people became evident in all European countries in the years prior to the First World War. In Germany, the popular newspapers were *"plus royaliste que le roi,"* demanding that the Hohenzollern government stand up to British attempts to prevent their nation from assuming its rightful place on the world stage. The British popular press behaved in similar fashion, preparing its readers for the inevitable conflict with Germany.[48] When war finally broke out across Europe, it was greeted with unprecedented enthusiasm throughout the belligerent states.[49]

In Russia, as elsewhere in Europe in the summer of 1914, there was a wave of patriotic outbursts among the workers. All parties but Lenin's Bolsheviks either approved the government's war credits or abstained from voting.[50] Over the following year, there was a sharp decline in the number of industrial disputes. In the more advanced states, a greater willingness to pay taxes was quickly reflected in higher levels of tax receipts. How could a backward country like Russia assure that an increased desire to contribute to the collectivity was translated into greater resources at the state's disposal?

Interactive Remote Monitoring

The power of a bureaucracy invariably depends upon the extent of returns to scale. In the case of the armed forces, it is the effect of numbers on the ability to destroy that is important. In the case of a fiscal bureaucracy, however, the scale economies are in the processing of information. What counts is the ability of higher levels of administration to monitor the behavior of officials at lower levels. The better the information of superiors with regard to the actions of their agents, the more efficient the bureaucracy will be.

The introduction of the telegraph in the middle decades of the nineteenth century had accelerated the flow of small amounts of information. In the military domain, where the outcome of a battle could hinge on the rapid transmission of a single command, it had a major impact. However, in civilian applications in the public sector, there were few occasions where the acceleration permitted by the telegraph was very important.

The telegraph had a number of drawbacks as a communications device within a hierarchy. One problem was that it was not confidential. Since every message had to pass by two skilled telegraph operators, it was difficult to keep a communication secret. For these reasons, a person might hesitate before sending confidential information by wire. Moreover, unlike a handwritten letter or an oral message, the telegraph did not permit verification of the sender's identity. To be sure, codification could be used for classified information, but only at the expense of delaying communication. Perhaps the principal difficulty with the telegraph as a communications device within a hierarchy was that it was not interactive. As a result, most messages continued to be handwritten when a quick response was not required or oral when rapid feedback was important.

Four decades after the invention of the telegraph, there came a new electric device that promised to overcome these difficulties. On February 14, 1876, in New York, Alexander Bell filed an application for a patent for "an improvement in telegraphy." The following month he successfully transmitted spoken words by electric current for the first time. By the end of the year, he had developed a transmitter that used a piece of iron on a vibrating steel diaphragm to vary the current flowing through a coil. A similar device at the other end of the line converted the current into sound. Commercial production began in 1877.

Use of the new device expanded rapidly, in part at the expense of the telegraph. Whereas the printing telegraph could transmit at 60 words per minute, the telephone operated at 150–200 words per minute. Moreover, as Bell advertised, his telephone required no intermediary.[51] Most important, however, the telephone was interactive. Questions were answered at virtually the same speed as in normal speech, even though the participants might be separated by many kilometers. By 1887 there were 150,000 telephones in the United States, 26,000 in the United Kingdom, 26,000 in Germany but only 7,000 in Russia. Long-distance communications for distances up to 1,900 km, the distance from Boston to Chicago were possible from 1893. But it was not until 1915, in the United States, that the use of the vacuum tube for amplification permitted voice signals to be transmitted commercially across a continent.

Despite its slow start, Russia eventually came to recognize the importance of adequate telephone networks. The regime granted local monopolies in Moscow and Warsaw to two Swedish firms in return for a percentage of their total revenues.[52] In the three years preceding the First World War, the number of telephones doubled, reaching a total of 231,000 in 1913.[53] Nevertheless, there were few telephones outside the three main cities, and there were no long-distance links between the individual municipal systems.

McLuhan argued that the effect of the telephone was to weaken hierarchical structures: since the caller demanded of his interlocutor only that he be informed, the device cut across hierarchical structures.[54] It is indeed quite possible that there was some disintermediation that resulted from use of the telephone: rather than calling upon a section head for information, the director of a bureaucracy might communicate directly with those in lower echelons. However, by reducing the asymmetry of information between layers in a hierarchy in this way, the telephone permitted the principal better to monitor the behavior of those who worked under him. An improvement in the ability to supervise would in turn strengthen the power of the principal over his subordinates.

The monitoring of remote officials requires not only an interactive means of exchanging information, but also a convenient way to store that information. It is not coincidental that at the same time that Bell was working on voice transmission, others were trying to find a means of reducing the cost of making permanent records. The first to succeed was an American printer, Christopher Latham Sholes. In 1868, with an associate, Carlos Glidden, Sholes received a patent for what was in effect a personal printing machine. In 1873, their patent was bought by the Remington Arms Company, which had a modern factory in New York originally built to make guns during the American Civil War. The first commercial shipments of the Remington typewriter were made the following year.[55]

Although until 1878 the typewriter could print capital letters only, it had several important advantages over handwriting. It was more legible, it was much faster, and it allowed a greater number of carbon copies to be made of an original document. It did not take long to develop machines capable of typing the Russian Cyrillic alphabet. Some of these were quickly put to use by the Okhrana to help organize its rapidly growing network of agents.[56] By the First World War, Russia was well supplied with typewriters imported from the United States and Germany.[57]

An Exclusionist Ideology

To hold power successfully, a regime requires an ideology: it needs a set of rules of behavior which if followed by all of its members favors the extension of its power. In the case of a revolutionary group aspiring for power, such an ideology must be something more than "*à bas l'ancien régime,*" for once the existing structures have been destroyed they must be replaced. Socialist thought as developed by Saint-Simon, Marx, Lassalle, and other nineteenth-century writers, suffered from this weakness. Although these thinkers called for the abolition of individual property rights and therefore the overturning of existing power structures, they offered few guidelines as to how a socialist state might be organized. Even more important, they provided little indication of how the transition would occur and what the role of socialist groups should be during this intermediate period. Whether by evolution or by revolution, most socialists believed the transition to socialism to be inevitable; the details of the interim period were unimportant.

From his studies of the histories of previous revolutionary movements and, more particularly, his experience with dissident groups in Russia in the 1890s, Lenin realized that a successful revolution was unlikely to occur spontaneously. Following a line of thought developed three decades earlier by the Russian revolutionary S. G. Nechayev, he argued in his 1902 monograph, *What Is to Be Done?*, that the workers alone would never evolve beyond a trade-union consciousness. The workers' struggle could succeed only if a "party of a new type," a revolutionary elite, took the lead in organizing the struggle. Members of this elite must be "professional revolutionaries" trained in Marxist theory.[58]

There was an important corollary to this thesis of the role of a revolutionary elite. If the workers could attain their legitimate rights only by aligning themselves behind such a group, then any alternative center of power must necessarily be opposed to the rights of the majority and must therefore be fought. Now the idea that "those who are not for us are against us," is probably as old as the first human social groupings. However, it had never previously been combined with a social theory as powerful as that of Marx. Any action taken by the elite to oppose or repress alternative viewpoints could therefore be justified as a historical necessity. In his 1902 monograph, for example, Lenin scornfully rejected the need for "playing at democracy" within the Russian revolutionary movement. According to Lenin, "an organization of real revolutionaries will stop at nothing to rid itself of an undesirable member."[59]

In amending Marx in this manner, Lenin had made an important innovation. He had developed what might be termed an *exclusionist* ideology; that is, a set of ideas that justifies the existence of a single power center and the rejection of all other competing claims. The approach of Marxist theory was essentially positive: changes in industrial technology – the mode of production – would lead to changes in the social and political superstructure. Lenin's modification added a crucial normative element that would make Marx's prophecies self-fulfilling: workers should unite behind a professional elite to overcome any alternative center of power.

A characteristic that distinguished Lenin from other political leaders in prerevolutionary Russia was his unwillingness to compromise with other political groups or with the regimes in power. In the short run, his intransigence cost him support and weakened the revolutionary cause. In 1903, for example, the Marxist Russian Social-Democratic Party split into two factions over Lenin's attempts to dominate the editorial board of the party newspaper, *Iskra*. Lenin and his followers in the "Bolshevik" (majority) group defeated the "Menshevik" (minority) faction (which included Trotsky until 1917) on a vote to reduce the size of the editorial board. Soon after, however, Lenin lost control of the newspaper to the Mensheviks. To take another example, in 1914 after the declaration of war, Lenin directed the Bolshevik delegates to the Duma, the legislative assembly, to urge Russian workers to fight against their own government rather than against the official enemy. As a result, the five Bolshevik deputies were arrested and later sent to Siberia. In the longer run, however, Lenin's hard line proved profitable. By the time of the final showdown in the late summer of 1917, his party had acquired a distinct image. All the other groups had weakened themselves by compromising in favor of policies that had proved unsuccessful.

The Revolutionary Elite as Monitoring Agency

Lenin's interest in *What Is to Be Done?* was not confined to theoretical questions. As an aspiring political leader, he was also concerned with how to reach the rapidly growing Russian proletariat with his ideas. It will be remembered that in 1902 mass-circulation newspapers had only begun to appear in Russia. However, there were a number of examples of the new journalistic medium in Western Europe, where he had been traveling. Even at this early date, Lenin clearly understood the potential of the newspaper both as a device for unifying his organization and as a means of mobilizing the workers for the revolutionary cause.[60] He argued that the "newspaper would become part of an enormous pair of smith's bellows that would fan every spark of class struggle and popular indignation into a general conflagration."[61]

During the last months of the 1905 revolution, in November and December, Lenin's group put out its own newspaper, *Novaia zhizn'*, until the government clamped down on the socialist press. Another publication, *Zvezda*, started in 1910 as a joint venture between Mensheviks and Bolsheviks, was gradually taken over by the latter. In May 1912, a new Bolshevik daily paper, *Pravda*, appeared for the first time with a press run of 20,000–40,000 copies. Over the next two years, it was closed down nine times but reappeared eight times under a new name.[62]

Yet the revolutionary movement, in Lenin's opinion, needed more than a consistent ideological foundation and a means of disseminating these ideas to the general population. It required also a disciplined political organization, "capable of combining all the forces and of leading the movement not only in name but in deed, i.e. an organization that will be ready at any moment to support every protest and every outbreak."[63] In describing his objective, he used the analogy of workers building a house, likening the party structure to "a staff of experienced bricklayers who had learned to work so well together that they could place their bricks exactly where they were required without a guiding line."[64]

With regard to the party organization, there is a point that is not discussed specifically in the 1902 monograph but that cannot have escaped Lenin's attention. Once the revolution had succeeded, Lenin's bricklayers, who had previously devoted their efforts to political agitation would be assigned a second task. To assure that the new state was governed in accord with socialist principles, the regime would need a monitoring body and the party would play this role. In the prerevolutionary period, he saw the newspaper as not only a vehicle for propaganda but also as a channel for assuring unity within the party on a national scale.[65] What he did not yet realize, perhaps, was that once his movement had come to power, he would need some more effective means of assuring unity than the right to edit articles submitted to the party newspaper.

Lenin's monograph has been called "perhaps the most significant single document in the history of modern communism."[66] It is arguably even more – the political equivalent of the formula for gunpowder. In effect, it is the first recipe for producing a new type of state – one in which all efforts of the individual would be subordinated to the needs of society as a whole, as interpreted by a dedicated governing elite. This result would be brought about by vigorous shaking of the explosive mixture of *exclusionist* ideology, direct mass communication, and interactive remote monitoring of individual behavior.

THE LENINIST REVOLUTION

The Events of February

During the year 1916, while Russia's military situation improved, living conditions for the civilian population deteriorated sharply, particularly in the cities. In part, the problem was a breakdown of internal transport, due to a shortage of skilled workers and the conversion of railway repair shops to military production. By the end of 1916, one-fifth of the railway locomotives was out of service. Most of those remaining were commandeered by the military system to maintain arms production and imports and keep supplies moving to the front.[67] In part, the difficulties in the cities were caused by increasing shortages of manufactured consumer goods. Some 40 percent of urban workers had been conscripted into the armed forces, and much of the production of the remaining laborers was channeled into the military effort.

Yet as long as food supplies to the urban population could be maintained, the regime managed to keep its hold over the cities. Since the outbreak of the war, the authorities had applied a tight control over the expression of dissent. *Pravda* and other revolutionary publications had been closed at the outset and not allowed to reopen.[68] Any attempt to organize demonstrations against the regime had been severely repressed. The urban police force in Petrograd numbered 3,500 and was supplemented by 3,200 mounted Cossacks trained to control crowds with whips. Finally, there was the Petrograd garrison of regular soldiers, numbering some 180,000 troops, including 99,000 men in guards battalions to back up the police units.[69]

Until 1916, the peasants had been willing to exchange their produce for paper money. Much of this currency the peasants hoarded, planning to spend it when conditions improved. By the end of 1916, however, they began to realize that there was little chance of being able to convert these notes into manufactured goods at prewar prices. Accordingly, not only did they stop hoarding, but also they began to dishoard on a large scale.[70] Supplies of food to the cities dropped and the rate of inflation, which had until then been moderate, began to accelerate. Between December 1916 and February 1917, the price of bread rose by 15 percent, potatoes by 25 percent and sausage by 50 percent.[71]

The usual response of an authoritarian regime to accelerating inflation is to fix prices. In the case of grain, the tsarist authorities had imposed compulsory purchase of a proportion of farm production at official prices during 1916.[72] Since these prices were lower than the production costs of many farmers, the predictable result was food shortages. By the beginning of March 1917, people in the capital were lining up all night in long bread queues.[73] On March 8, International Women's Day, female workers in the textile district marched into the streets crying, "Bread!" For the first time, the Cossacks refused to charge the crowds. Over the following days, the marches and demonstrations increased in size.

On March 12, 1917, troops who the previous day had been ordered to fire on the crowds mutinied, shooting any officers who tried to enforce discipline. By the evening, one-third of the entire Petrograd garrison had joined the insurrection.[74] As the uprising within the armed forces spread, two new political bodies that were to share power over the coming months were formed. One was a Provisional Committee of center and left-wing members of the Duma. The other was a workers' council, the Petrograd Soviet, modeled on a similar group set up during the 1905 revolution and made up of delegates chosen by factory committees. The revolt of the Petrograd garrison and the formation of the two new governing bodies fell on February 27 under the Old Style calendar; consequently, the events were known as the February Revolution.

Over the following days, the two bodies worked out an agreement whereby the Soviet would support a Provisional Government headed by Prince Georgii Lvov that would hold power until a constituent assembly could be called to prepare a new constitution. Meanwhile, the railway stations and arms depots of the capital had been taken over by the revolutionary crowd of workers and soldiers. In the military units around the capital, discipline broke down completely. The Petrograd Soviet issued "Order No. 1" decreeing the election of committees within military and naval units and placing these units under control of the Soviet. Fearing that the revolution would spread to troops outside the capital, the army General Staff decided to support the Duma politicians. On March 15, they confronted Nicholas II with telegrams from his commanders on the five fronts urging him to resign. The tsar had little choice but to abdicate.[75]

What had gone wrong for the government of Nicholas II? How could a regime that controlled the army, the police, and the means of mass communication possibly fall from power? As the sequence of events makes clear, one factor was the failure of its administrative machine to match the spending power of its military rivals. In peacetime, the Romanov regime had been hard put to meet the requirements of industrializing the immense territories it had conquered. Nevertheless, with the help of foreign capital, its bureaucracy had been able to extract sufficient fiscal revenues to finance the needed social infrastructure. With the war, however, the Russian government lost most of its existing revenue sources while at the same time facing an enemy capable of concentrating virtually its entire economy behind its military effort.

Another difficulty for the tsarist regime was that its official ideology of loyalty to a hereditary aristocracy proved inadequate as a guideline for individual behavior. Why should the citizen obey a regime dedicated to protecting the wealth of 1 or 2 percent of the population? (The census of 1897 indicated that the hereditary nobility numbered 1.2 million out of a total population of 115 million.)[76] As the aristocracy itself lost power to a rising group of merchants, industrialists, and professionals, former rules of behavior became increasingly irrelevant. Yet the regime was unable to provide a consistent substitute ideology. When the crisis of March 1917 occurred, there was no underlying pool of public support upon which it could draw. Thus its collapse was astonishingly rapid and utterly final.

The lesson of the February Revolution was clear: in an era of mass communications, a regime lacking an effective means of monitoring its bureaucracy, relying on censorship but having no consistent ideology itself, could not hope to remain in power.

The Weaknesses of the Provisional Government

In July 1917, when the socialist Aleksandr Kerensky replaced Prince Lvov as prime minister, the Provisional Government still commanded the backing of most elements of Russian society. However, two months later, despite the change of leadership, the regime had managed to lose almost all of its initial support. Its weakness is sometimes attributed to its decision to pursue the war.[77] However, previous revolutionary regimes had managed to channel the feelings of nationalism released by a successful revolution into acts of patriotism. For example, the revolts of the English Parliament and the French National Assembly against their respective monarchs had been followed by periods of external expansion. Why did the tsar's overthrow not enable his former opponents to unite behind the new government and drive the enemy from Russian soil?

Another explanation that is often given for the Provisional Government's lack of support is the dualistic administration that it shared with the Petrograd Soviet. But why did the new regime not act to trim the Soviet's influence once it had seized power? The inability of a government to assure for itself a monopoly of power is surely a symptom rather than a cause of its weakness.

As an interim body that had not been chosen by its citizens, the Provisional Government lacked any claim to represent the general population. It, like the regime of the Romanovs, was simply another authoritarian administration and therefore had to stand or fall according to its success in satisfying the demands and controlling the behavior of its subjects. Under the new communications technologies, an autocratic regime could not hope to retain power unless certain basic conditions were fulfilled. To what extent did the Provisional Government satisfy the conditions for viable authoritarian rule?

One of these conditions was an ideology, a set of accepted rules of behavior that individuals consider to be in their own interest and that when acted upon contributes to maintaining the regime in power. In a cabinet change on May 18, five socialists including Kerensky entered the Provisional Government. However, many of their fellow revolutionaries considered their participation in the government a betrayal of the workers' and peasants' cause. In the face of unauthorized land seizures by the peasants, the authorities' attitude was ambiguous. While many in the government were sympathetic to the peasants' claims, they felt that they had neither the mandate nor the resources to embark on a full-scale land reform program.[78] As a result, the only claim that the regime could make for popular support was that it would supervise elections for its successor, which would then deal with problems such as land reform. Yet as the months passed, the popular vote was delayed again and again. It was not until the fall of 1917 that the date of the elections was finally fixed for November 25.

Another necessary attribute which the Provisional Government lacked was control over the mass communications media. One of the conditions imposed by the Petrograd Soviet in exchange for its support was freedom of speech. Accordingly, censorship was abolished on March 17, 1917.[79] The field was then open to opponents of the regime to distribute freely arguments for its overthrow.

Finally, authoritarian control of a modern state requires a means of monitoring the state's employees and its citizens. The tax authorities must be closely supervised to assure that revenues are collected. In addition, some means of identifying and suppressing internal opposition to the regime is necessary. With regard to taxation, the Provisional Government was if anything even less successful than its predecessor. State expenses were financed by the printing of money. As for control of dissent, after the

February Revolution the tsarist secret police, the Okhrana, had been disbanded.[80] Between March and November, there was no officially constituted political police organization. Political surveillance was assigned to a small and understaffed unit of the army.[81] Lacking the requirements for power in the age of mass communications, the Provisional Government could not hope to survive.

The Bolshevik Coup d'État

If the terrain in Petrograd following the February Revolution was unfavorable to the Provisional Government, it was ideal for sowing the seeds of an alternative authoritarian form of government. When Lenin stepped off the train in the Finland Station in April, he brought with him a political program that he had been honing during almost two decades in exile, in anticipation of just such a situation. This program contained precisely the elements that the Provisional Government lacked: a consistent ideology, a communications vehicle for diffusing this message and a hierarchically structured monitoring body.

At the heart of Lenin's political program was an *exclusionist* ideology – a consistent justification for rejecting any authority but that of his Bolshevik party. In his "April theses," he simplified his ideas, creating a powerful, simple message that could be diffused to large masses of workers and peasants. There should be no support whatsoever for the Provisional Government. It should be replaced by a "republic of soviets of workers', soldiers', and peasants' deputies" in which all land would be nationalized. Soldiers should refuse to fight and instead fraternize with their supposed enemies. These points were summed up succinctly in the two Bolshevik slogans, "All power to the soviets" and "Peace, land, and bread" that were circulated widely in the following months.[82]

Of prime importance to the Bolsheviks in the political struggle that lay ahead was the diffusion of this political message. However, as the other left-wing parties had similar programs to sell, competition was fierce. Vying for the workers' support were the Menshevik publication, *Rabochaia gazeta* (Workers' newspaper), and the Socialist Revolutionary *Delo naroda* (The people's cause). By June there was also an Anarchist–Communist press devoted to the elimination of all governments.[83] One problem for the Bolsheviks was that neither the party nor the potential readers it wanted to reach could afford to pay for an "educational" campaign on the scale that was required. To the rescue came the Germans, who were understandably interested in the fortunes of a group pledged to take Russia out of the war. The first issue of the revived *Pravda* appeared on March 18. It was printed in 100,000 copies and distributed free of charge.[84]

The final requirement for seizure of power was a means of coordinating and monitoring large numbers of people. Events in July showed that Lenin had still not mastered the practical details of managing the political movement he had created. A major Russian military offensive in Galicia (southern Poland and the western Ukraine) launched in June failed disastrously. On July 16 soldiers from the Bolshevik-dominated First Machine-Gun Regiment revolted and were backed by many Bolshevik rank and file members. The Provisional Government responded by calling in loyalist regiments and by releasing information linking the Bolsheviks to the Germans.[85] Faced with very probable defeat, Lenin refused to encourage the protesters, and the uprising, known as the "July Days," quickly collapsed.

For the Bolsheviks, the immediate consequences of the abortive July revolt were negative. The Provisional Government decided that the moment had come to crack down on its most serious opponents and sent loyalist soldiers to smash the *Pravda* plant. Trotsky and many leading Bolshevik leaders were imprisoned. Lenin avoided arrest only by going into hiding, eventually taking refuge in Finland. However, events were moving inexorably in the Bolsheviks' favor. Inflation accelerated further and food shortages became chronic. By August, prices of dairy products, which were not controlled, were five times their prewar level. The price of bread, which was controlled, was only three times its level of 1914; however, there was less and less of it to be found. In August, the general bread ration in Petrograd was cut to one-half of its March level.[86]

Until the end of the summer of 1917, the Provisional Government had managed to retain the loyalty of the front-line troops. However, on September 9, Kerensky dismissed the commander of the armed forces, General Kornilov, whom he accused of plotting to overthrow the regime. The latter responded by sending troops to take over the capital, having informed them that the Provisional Government was threatened by a Bolshevik uprising. These soldiers were met by thousands of organized workers and peasants who told them that they were being used by counter-revolutionary forces to unseat the government. When the troops refused to advance, the attempted coup failed.[87] During the following weeks, many officers suspected of sympathy with Kornilov were arrested and executed by their troops. The result was virtually to destroy what little cohesion remained in the Russian army.[88] Kerensky had won the showdown but was now left without a formally constituted force capable of defending his government.

As economic conditions worsened and the Provisional Government proved unable to correct the situation, the Bolsheviks made an all-out drive for popular support. Barely a week after *Pravda* was closed, the Petrograd party organization began publishing a new paper, *Rabochii i soldat* (Worker and soldier). During the following three months, the number of daily publications published by the party would rise to 25, with a total circulation of 600,000.[89] A critical point was reached on September 13, when the Bolsheviks gained a majority for the first time in the Petrograd Soviet. On September 18, they also attained a majority within the Moscow Soviet.[90] Even though his party's strength among the vast Russian peasantry was slight, Lenin could now present himself as the representative of the people. Even more important, since the primary loyalty of the Petrograd garrison was to the Soviet, his followers now controlled the only military force in the capital.

During the preceding months the Mensheviks and Socialist Revolutionaries who had dominated the Petrograd Soviet had refused to exercise real political power. Believing in the inevitability of a proletarian revolution for which the February "bourgeois" revolution was a necessary precondition, they had seen no need to precipitate events. Lenin, however, had no such reserves. As he had made clear a decade and a half earlier in *What Is to Be Done?*, he believed that such a revolution could only occur under the leadership of a professional elite. The moment to set events in motion had now come. By October 23, he was back in Petrograd – disguised with a wig and clean-shaven – to convince his followers that it was time to act.

With the Petrograd Soviet now in Bolshevik hands, it was simply a matter of finding the most appropriate moment to direct the garrison troops to seize power. The chairman of the Soviet, Leon Trotsky, had recently been admitted to the Bolshevik Party. On November 1, under Trotsky's direction, the Soviet formed a Military Revolutionary Committee to protect the capital against attacks being "openly prepared by . . . Kornilovites."[91] The Bolsheviks now waited for an occasion to present itself. During the night of November 5–6, Kerensky used military cadets to raid the two main Bolshevik newspapers. Lenin could now claim the need to act in order to protect the revolution.

On the morning of the following day, November 7, regiments loyal to the Bolsheviks, aided by sailors from the Baltic fleet, took over the railroad stations and public services. As other military units stationed in the capital remained neutral, the government had no troops to support it. The coup d'état was virtually bloodless.[92] Within two months, local Bolshevik groups of workers and soldiers had seized power in the name of the soviets in most of the other cities and towns of European Russia. Lenin's task was then to protect his gains against the inevitable reaction from those opposed to Bolshevik rule. Over the coming months, his main concern would be with internal opposition in the Russian cities. He would then turn to the countryside where the struggle between the regime and its opponents would be the subject of a bitter two-year civil war.

The Monopolization of Mass Communications

As a revolutionary himself, Lenin realized that his first task must be to cut off communication from rival political groups to the general population. On the day of the coup, the presses of the liberal *Russkaia volia* were seized. Over the following two days, the Military Revolutionary Committee sent troops to occupy all papers opposed to the new regime – both the "bourgeois" press and socialist newspapers. On November 9, the new Council of People's Commissars, *Sovnarkom,* issued a decree concerning the press. Any paper advocating resistance to the regime or guilty of "slanderous misstatements of facts" could be closed "temporarily."[93]

Representatives of the country's workers' councils had been meeting in the Second Congress of Soviets since the day of the coup. On November 17, the non-Bolshevik members of the Central Executive Committee of the Congress protested against the continuation of the press restrictions. However, the Bolsheviks used their majority to impose a resolution maintaining the restrictions and authorizing the regime to confiscate private presses and stocks of newsprint.[94]

It took several more weeks before the systematic suppression of non-Bolshevik publications could be organized. At the end of December 1917, the Commissariat of Justice decided to set up revolutionary tribunals for dealing with violations of the press regulations. In the meantime, the Cheka – the new Bolshevik secret police – had been granted the power to arrest enemies of the regime. Many of their targets were the editors of non-Bolshevik publications. By the spring of 1918, the leading Menshevik paper was closed down, as were other moderate socialist publications.[95] And finally in the summer of 1918 even the Left Socialist Revolutionary newspapers were silenced. Thirty presses had been confiscated by the end of 1917 and 90 by the end of the following year.[96]

By the fall of 1918 the Communist regime had obtained a monopoly over the principal means of direct mass communication, the newspaper. It used this new power to blanket the cities with a stream of messages, all presenting the same ideological viewpoint. By the end of 1918, total circulation of Communist newspapers had risen tenfold with respect to the eve of the October Revolution.[97] The circulation of *Pravda* reached 120,000. The organ of the Petrograd Soviet, *Izvestia* (News), now under Bolshevik control, appeared in 1918 in press runs of 300,000 to 400,000 depending on the availability of newsprint.[98]

Outside the cities, press distribution was spotty. One of the most frequent complaints of local committees was the difficulty of obtaining newspapers in the villages.[99] As the civil war reached its height, more and more of the regime's publishing resources were directed toward the army and toward soldiers fighting for the enemy. In 1919, there were 170 publications put out by various military units.[100]

THE ROLE OF THE COMMUNIST PARTY

A crucial factor in the fall of both the tsarist monarchy and the Provisional Government had been the inability of these regimes to monitor their public employees effectively. As a result of slacking by officials and outright corruption, the tsarist regime had been obliged to concentrate its tax system on a few easily monitored revenue sources which unfortunately had dried up with the coming of the war. Lenin, of course, faced the same problem; however, his difficulties were compounded by his dependence on former tsarist officials whose loyalty to the Communist regime was questionable: as late as 1929, 37 percent of the personnel of the finance ministry and 29 percent of that of the labor ministry were former tsarist officials.[101]

Lenin's solution to this problem was to introduce a dualistic structure into Russian administration. Parallel to the traditional hierarchy of scribes and supervisors developed 5,000 years earlier by the Sumerians, Lenin introduced a second hierarchy of party members.[102] At the time of the February Revolution, total party membership had been about 40,000. However, by January 1918 the party had 115,000 militants and was still growing rapidly.[103] Formerly, the primary responsibility of these members had been to spread the party's message and to stand up and be counted when votes were taken. Now they would perform the vital function of monitoring the state bureaucracy.

To assure that the decisions of the two hierarchies were coordinated, Lenin made sure that they intersected at the summit. The Congress of Soviets elected an all-Bolshevik "Council of People's Commissars," *Sovnarkom*, to run the state bureaucracy. Its leading members – Lenin, Trotsky, and Stalin – also controlled the Central Committee of the Bolshevik party and its policy committee, the *politburo*, established in 1919.[104] Key posts in the civil bureaucracy were also reserved for Communists. When political judgment was critical, party members themselves would be assigned to positions in the bureaucracy. If positions called for technical competence that the movement could not supply, non-party members would be appointed, but with Bolsheviks to oversee their decisions.

The key to the success of the new bureaucracy was the greatly increased upward flow of information that it promised to produce. All party members within a given organization would be called upon to monitor their comrades, signalling any deviations from the official position. The party leadership took pains to assure that there would always be multiple channels for this upward flow.[105] The Leninist solution to the monitoring problem was, of course, extremely costly in terms of human resources devoted to surveillance. It required in effect a doubling of the bureaucracy's monitoring personnel. It was also inefficient in that intervention by political appointees often resulted in the taking of inappropriate decisions. The key question, however, was not economic efficiency but whether the system could be made to work. Would the Bolshevik government be able to hold onto power where the monarchy, the liberals, the socialists, and the army had all failed? Would the new state be able both to defend itself and assure the means of subsistence to its population?

To a great extent, the success of the party as monitoring agency would depend on the efficiency of the communications system by which information was transmitted upward. No previous authoritarian regime had been able to maintain such an elaborate system of surveillance of its personnel in a bureaucracy of this size. Nevertheless, there was an example of a state with a more limited surveillance system aimed primarily at identifying opponents of the regime. This state was, of course, tsarist Russia and its monitoring agency, the Okhrana. Could the methods of organization used by the Okhrana now be employed for economic as well as political ends? In the first decade of the century, the Okhrana had encountered difficulties in coordinating the activities of its various subunits. Despite the typewriter and urban telephone service, its local units had remained largely autonomous. Between 1905 and 1917, the number of telephones in Russia had increased. However, they remained linked into local networks with no long distance service. In the summer of 1917, for example, communication between Kerensky in Petrograd and Kornilov at Staff General Headquarters at Mogilev 600 km to the south had been by printing telegraph.[106]

By 1921, the Communist Party had grown to almost three-quarters of a million members. With the regime now in command of the military situation, the time had come to concentrate on converting the party to the monitoring of the economy. Requirements for party membership were tightened and the size of the movement cut back to 532,000 members.[107] At the same time, the regime set about establishing a telephone system that would allow it to communicate orally with its dual bureaucracy. During the 1920s the main concern was to link the major urban areas. By 1929, the number of telephones had risen by one-half to reach a total of 330,000.[108]

The Monopolization of Political Power

With control of the means of communication and the party as an agency to monitor the bureaucracy, Russia could now dispense with political competition used by other western countries to maintain administrative efficiency. Even the limited political debate permitted in the last years of the tsarist government was suppressed.

Although the regime of the tsars had been exceptionally repressive by the standards of other European countries, the number of persons it actually executed for political crimes remained quite small. During the decade of expanded police activity in the 1880s subsequent to the assassination of Alexander II, the death sentence for crimes against the state was carried out only 17 times.[109] Lenin, a dedicated revolutionary and brother of a would-be assassin of the tsar, was allowed access to books in his St Petersburg cell when arrested in 1895. He was subsequently sent to a relatively comfortable exile in southern Siberia and allowed to complete his manuscript *The Development of Capitalism in Russia.*[110] Even in the three years that followed the abortive 1905 revolution, the number of executions of political prisoners remained moderate by twentieth-century standards. From August 1906 until the end of 1909, some 6,000 people were put to death for political offenses.[111] However, this was a period in which enemies of the regime were assassinating large numbers of tsarist officials: in the relatively quiet year of 1908, 1,800 officials were killed and 2,083 wounded in terrorist attacks.[112] Why were the authorities so lenient, at least by twentieth-century standards, with those dedicated to the overthrow of their regime? One possible explanation was that since the Romanov regime justified its existence by divine right, it felt compelled to adhere to Judeo-Christian ethical standards, which condemned violence except in self-defense.

Lenin did not allow himself to be bound by such obsolete moral constraints. In accord with the thesis he presented in *What Is to Be Done?*, there could be only one legitimate representative of the people's interests. Any alternative organization threatened to weaken the struggle for the victory of the majority class. Bolshevik political theory therefore justified any measures necessary to eliminate political competition.

At the moment of the Bolshevik coup, there were several other political groups that constituted possible rivals for power. On the right were the supporters of the former tsar and his family, who were imprisoned in Ekaterinburg (now Sverdlovsk) in the Urals. In the center were the Constitutional Democrats (Kadets), a party formed in 1905 by liberals who favored a pluralistic regime. On the left were two other socialist parties. The Socialist Revolutionaries were non-Marxist socialists whose support lay mainly in the provinces. They were ardent advocates of land reform. In the Second Congress of Soviets that met for the first time on November 7, 1917, the day of Lenin's coup, the party split on whether to support the Bolsheviks. The Left Socialist Revolutionaries decided to back Lenin, while the orthodox members of the party walked out in protest against the armed insurrection.[113] Also on the left were the Marxist Mensheviks, who had split with Lenin in 1903 and who called themselves the Russian Social-Democratic Labor Party. Finally, on the far left were the Anarchists.

An indication of the approximate support for each of these formations came on November 25 when, despite the Bolshevik coup, elections were held for the Constituent Assembly. Of the 703 deputies elected, 380 were regular Socialist Revolutionaries, 39 Left Socialist Revolutionaries, 168 Bolsheviks, 18 Mensheviks, 17 Kadets and Rightists, 4 Popular Socialists and 77 minority-group representatives. The Bolsheviks received most of the votes cast in the larger cities, but in the smaller towns and the countryside the Socialist Revolutionaries received enough support to give them an overall majority in the Assembly.[114] Lenin found himself confronted by an elected majority who, with the exception of the Left Socialist Revolutionaries, all opposed his seizure of power. Further opposition came from anarchists and other groups outside the electoral system. Faced with this array of enemies, how was he to maintain his tenuous hold over the state apparatus? The answer was soon to become clear to all.

During the first days after the October Revolution, security in the capital was in the hands of the Military Revolutionary Committee. On November 21, the Central Executive Committee of the Soviets approved the formation of a special unit, the Committee for Struggle against the Counter-Revolution, to deal specifically with political and economic crimes.[115] The proposition had been presented by Felix Dzerzhinsky, a Bolshevik of noble Polish origin with two decades of experience in fighting against the Okhrana. On December 11, the regime cracked down on the leaders of the Kadets, who had called for the Constituent Assembly to meet. They were arrested and put on trial as "the party of the people's enemies."[116]

The principal shortcoming of the Committee for Struggle against the Counter-Revolution as an instrument for controlling dissent was that it depended on the unwieldy 91-member Central Executive Committee made up of 62 Bolsheviks and 29 Left Socialist Revolutionaries elected by the Second Congress of Soviets. Accordingly on December 20, Lenin and his colleagues approved the formation of a new body that would be responsible to the compact *Sovnarkom,* the Bolshevik–Left Socialist Revolutionary coalition cabinet. This agency, the All-Russian Extraordinary Commission for Combating Counter-Revolution and Sabotage became known by the initial letters of the first two words of its name in Russian – the Cheka. This was the beginning of the Bolshevik secret police, under the direction of Dzerzhinsky.

The Constituent Assembly finally met on January 18, 1918. Immediately the Bolsheviks and their Left Socialist Revolutionary allies submitted a proposal that the Assembly limit its own powers to a largely symbolic examination of the organization of a socialist society. When this declaration was defeated, the coalition partners walked out. The following day, the Bolshevik Red Guard militia refused to admit the remaining delegates and the Constituent Assembly came to an end.

One of the major points in the Bolshevik program was the negotiation of peace with the central powers. Talks with the Germans began in December 1917, but the final conditions were not approved by the Central Committee until two months later. Since the Russian army had virtually ceased to exist and any attempt to restore it would probably have caused the overthrow of the Communist regime, the Germans were virtually able to dictate terms. Under the Treaty of Brest-Litovsk of March 3, 1918, Russia was forced to give up all claims to Finland, Lithuania, Poland, and the Ukraine. She lost a quarter of her population and a third of her agricultural production.[117] Since Petrograd was now dangerously close to the border, it was decided to move the capital to Moscow.

Lenin counted on the eventual overthrow of the German government by an international revolution to undo the brutal terms of the treaty. However, the Left Socialist Revolutionaries were not convinced. They resigned from the coalition in protest against the peace conditions. In July one of their members assassinated the new German ambassador to Moscow. On August 30 a Socialist Revolutionary Party member, Fanya Kaplan, wounded Lenin in an assassination attempt, while a colleague fatally shot Uritsky, the head of the Petrograd Cheka.

One of Lenin's first acts on taking power the previous fall had been to abolish capital punishment. However, there is evidence that as early as the following February, the Cheka had been shooting some of its prisoners without trial.[118] The number of victims had risen steadily over the following months as the regime sought to combat opposition from the Anarchists. By June of 1918, Lenin had experienced second thoughts about the death penalty and reinstated it.[119] On the night of July 16–17, the former tsar and his family had been executed. The assassination of Uritsky and the attempt against Lenin now provided the opportunity for the application of violence on an unprecedented scale.

The first victims of the Red Terror that Dzerzhinsky unleashed in the late summer and fall of 1918 were the Socialist Revolutionaries, the main opposition party. On September 3, an *Izvestia* article revealed that over 500 people had been shot in Petrograd in reprisal for the attacks on Lenin and Uritsky.[120] Over the following months, terror was applied on a broad scale against potential enemies of the revolution. In addition to socialists and any peasants who resisted attempts to confiscate their grain, the Cheka attacked the non-socialist former middle class, professionals, former landowners, and army officers.[121] According to official figures, the total number of prisoners executed by the Cheka was 6,300 in 1918 and 2,089 in the first seven months of 1919.[122] However, unofficial estimates place the toll considerably higher. From 1918 to 1922, it is estimated that 140,000 people were executed – roughly ten times the figure for the last half-century of tsarist rule.[123]

During the summer of 1918, the Cheka established special detention centers, separate from the prisons, for political crimes. Originally these concentration camps were used simply to isolate prisoners from the general population until their cases could be dealt with. However, as economic conditions worsened, it was decided that mass executions were a wasteful means of dealing with opponents of the regime. Accordingly, in a resolution of February 1919, Dzerzhinsky introduced forced labor to replace the death sentence for most political prisoners.[124]

By 1920, the only remaining political opponents of the regime were the fellow Marxist members of the Menshevik party. Over the previous two years, their influence had been rising, particularly in the trade-union movement. Finally, in the first months of 1921, Lenin decided to clamp down on his party's only organized rivals. All Menshevik-dominated trade-union associations were shut down and replaced by Communist organizations. Some 2,000 Menshevik members, including all of the party leadership, were arrested. Although a few of the most prominent leaders were later allowed to emigrate, most of those arrested were sentenced to forced labor.[125]

Restoring the State's External Margin

As Lenin picked off internal opposition groups one by one, it became clear that only a military defeat could remove him from power. The spring of the year 1918 found the Communists (the new name for the Bolshevik party) in control of most of the cities of Russia. However, the Russia they ruled was considerably smaller than that held by the tsars. The Treaty of Brest-Litovsk had forced the Soviet regime to abandon its claims to Finland, Lithuania, Poland, and the Ukraine. Moreover, the Communists' hold over the Russian countryside was at best tenuous. While the peasants favored the policy of nationalization of land that Lenin had borrowed from the Socialist Revolutionaries, they opposed the confiscation of food practiced by bands of Communists sent out from the cities.

The return of good weather in the spring of 1918 allowed the regime's opponents to prepare organized military resistance. The White armies grouped themselves on the periphery of Russian territory, where they could be supplied by the British and French, who were understandably anxious to bring Russia back into the war on the Allied side. The strongest of these groups was that of General Anton Denikin, a Kadet and a former tsarist officer of no particular ability. The forces of Denikin's Volunteer Army were concentrated in the lands to the north-east of the Black Sea. To the north of Denikin, farther up the Don river, the Don Cossacks also opposed Communist rule.

As the spring progressed, other areas of opposition to the Communists developed around Samara (now Kubyshev) on a tributary of the Volga, and across the Urals in western Siberia. Initially, Socialist Revolutionaries played a leading role in these uprisings. But by November the eastern territories had come under the effective dictatorship of Admiral Alexander Kolchak. As a former tsarist naval officer, Kolchak was totally lacking in experience in land warfare. Nevertheless, the other White generals eventually recognized him as "Supreme Ruler." With the armistice of November 1918, the strategic interest of Russia to the Allied powers declined considerably. Nevertheless, the British and French continued to support the White armies of Denikin and Kolchak. In addition, the British offered their help to General Yudenich who had organized an army in Estonia and to General Eugene Miller who had assumed power in the north in Archangel.

Despite the array of forces lined up against them, the Communists had a number of advantages in their favor. One was the discipline of their troops. The events of the year 1917 had virtually destroyed the Russian army as a fighting force. After Brest-Litovsk, Trotsky, the new war commissar, set to organizing a new Red Army made up of conscripted workers and peasants, along with almost 50,000 officers from the old army.[126] To monitor the armed forces, the Cheka set up a Special Department, the *Osobye Otdel*. Dzerzhinsky directed that members of this department be established down to the platoon level, where they would assure the political loyalty of the troops and guard against poor military performance.[127]

As the civil war was essentially a struggle for the support of the Russian peasantry, another important factor was the Communist ideology and the organizational structure used to diffuse it.[128] On the first day of his regime, Lenin had published a Decree on Land abolishing private property in land. In addition, to attract the regional ethnic minorities to their cause, the Communists promised a federation of equal nations. Since most of the rural population was illiterate, the newspaper was not an effective means of reaching the countryside. Therefore the Communists took their position to the rural people by using thousands of trained agitators who made use of traveling agit-trains and even a steamer.[129] These trains were soon equipped with motion picture projectors which projected newsreels and a new type of short political film, the *agitka*, the cinematographic equivalent of the poster.[130]

The conservative forces behind the Whites had no consistent platform to offer to the peasants and no such vehicle to distribute it. Their policies on land reform were vague and contradictory. Moreover, the fervent Russian nationalism of Denikin and Kolchak made their relations with the Ukrainian, Cossacks, and Caucasian peoples difficult.[131] There was in fact little to unite the opposition forces except their common fear of the Communists.

Another factor favoring Lenin's regime was Russian geography. Control of Moscow permitted access to river systems leading outward into all parts of European Russia. As long as the Communists held the region around their new capital, they had a strategic advantage over their adversaries. Operating along interior lines, they could shift their forces from one theater to another relatively easily. Communications among the White armies, in contrast, were always tenuous. Operating on the periphery, they lacked an industrial base and were dependent on the irregular arrival of supplies from abroad.

In October 1919, despite these difficulties, it appeared that the White armies might succeed in their objectives. General Yudenich's forces were only a few kilometers from Petrograd. At the same time, White advance guards of General Denikin had advanced from the Ukraine to Tula, within striking distance of Moscow. However, the White armies were overextended, having outrun their supplies of arms and reinforcements. Outnumbered, Denikin and Yudenich were pushed back by fresh assaults of the Red forces. Meanwhile, in the east, the Red armies were driving Kolchak's forces back into Siberia. In November, Omsk fell. By the spring of 1920, the civil war was virtually over, with the Reds in control of most of the former tsarist territory except for Finland, Poland, and the Baltic states.

The final episodes in the determination of the external margin of the Russian state in Europe prior to the Second World War were played out during 1920 and 1921. In Poland, now an independent country as a result of the Versailles Treaty, Joseph Pilsudski, a former socialist, had established a nationalist regime determined to re-establish the country's eighteenth-century frontiers. In the summer of 1920, with Allied help, he was able to rout the Red Army. The Soviet regime had little choice but to accept a greatly enlarged and independent Polish state on its western borders. Under the terms of the Treaty of Riga of 1921, many White Russians and Ukrainians found themselves under Polish rule.

Although the Communists were humiliated by this defeat, the armistice with Poland left them free to mop up the opposition that remained in the remote corners of their territory. The final White armies in the Crimea were defeated, and the states of Armenia and Georgia occupied. By the spring of 1921, with the exception of the Amur region in the far east and Bukhara on the Afghanistan border, the Russian civil war was over. At the end of 1922, all the territories held by the Communists were formally united as the Union of Soviet Socialist Republics.

The State's Internal Margin under "War Communism"

It was the inability of the tsarist regime and the Provisional Government to match the fiscal capacity of the other western states that had ultimately led to their overthrow. The question now was whether the Communists could succeed where their predecessors had failed. Lenin himself believed that he had only to adopt the administrative system created by the war leaders in Germany and apply it to his own country.[132] However, there were important differences between Germany and Russia. One factor was the overall size of the economy to be controlled: Russia's population was twice that of Germany. Another was the territory to be administered: Russia's total area was 50 times greater than that of Germany. Most important was the communications system for transmitting information within the state bureaucracy. Russia at the beginning of the war had fewer than a quarter of a million telephones and virtually no long-distance service. Germany, in contrast, had over five times as many telephones and over a million kilometers of long-distance lines.[133]

Lenin's original intention was to create a highly centralized administration centered in the capital. Soon after the formation of the Soviet cabinet, *Sovnarkom,* he began signing nationalization orders. On November 27, 1917, he proposed the preparation of a plan for demobilization to direct the conversion of the economy from war to peace.[134] On December 14, 1917, a new agency, the Supreme Economic Council (VSNK$_H$), was created to direct economic activity for the nation as a whole.[135] All nationalized firms were organized into *glavki* or main departments of this Council.[136] A short time later, the banks were seized by the regime. Finally in June 1918, as the country slid into civil war, the Soviet government announced the nationalization without compensation of all major industries.

The management of a centralized economy requires a steady flow of detailed information; however, the Bolshevik leaders had virtually no means of acquiring such data. As a result, Lenin's orders for demobilization created chaos. At the Obukhov and Putilov works in Petrograd, for example, equipment for arms production was broken up or sold during the initial demobilization. Consequently, when civil war broke out in the summer of 1918, Russia's production capacity for military output was far below its level of the previous year.[137] Similarly, the authorities seriously underestimated the extent of the spontaneous wave of nationalizations by workers' groups in the initial months of the revolution. Since most of the worker-expropriated plants were small and located in rural areas, they could not be integrated effectively into the *glavki* system.[138]

In late December 1917, shortly before setting up the *glavki,* the government had also authorized the creation of *sovnarkhozy:* regional and district industrial councils, under the jurisdiction of the corresponding soviets or workers' councils that constituted the local governing bodies.[139] The stage was thus set for conflicting attempts to control individual firms, with one set of directives coming from the centralized *glavki* and another from the decentralized *sovnarkhozy*. During the course of the years 1918 and 1919, as the military situation deteriorated, the economic crisis of the regime also worsened. The leadership responded by increased attempts to centralize power. The authority of existing *glavki* was strengthened and new ones were created. Some 50 agencies depended on the Supreme Economic Council.[140] The result of this type of state intervention could only be an increasing loss of control: one condensed-milk plant with fewer than 15 employees was responsible to six different authorities, two at the central level and four at the regional or district level.[141] Finally, at the end of 1919, the Seventh Congress of Soviets decided that glavkism had become excessive and moved to restore the power of the local boards. Over the following year, most of the *glavki* were dissolved, until by the beginning of 1921 only 16 of the industry boards remained in existence.

The net result of the first three years of Communist rule was that although all land and all industrial firms had been nationalized, the Russian economy had yet to be brought under centralized governmental direction, as Lenin had intended. To the extent that state coordination existed, it occurred at the level of the individual urban regions under the local councils. In practice, industry operated largely on an unstructured basis, through the informal links that had arisen at the level of individual establishments. In the countryside, state control was virtually non-existent. With the abolition of private land-holdings, the disparities between the amounts of land held by individual peasants had been greatly reduced. However, Lenin's attempts to organize Committees of Poor Peasants analogous to the workers' soviets had failed and had been abandoned in 1918.[142] In 1920 crops failed, and the food that was produced could be distributed only with great difficulty because of a breakdown of the transportation system.[143]

The Russian economy touched its nadir in 1921. In that year industrial production fell to 31 percent of its 1913 level. Output of steel, cement, and sugar were barely 5 percent of prewar production.[144] Even in agriculture, the sector least disrupted by the transition to socialism, output was only 60 percent of the 1913 level.[145] Moreover, the Communists had still not found a means of raising tax revenues effectively. The budget deficit represented 83 percent of state expenditures. Since almost all public spending was financed by the printing of money, inflation was out of control. During the year 1921, prices rose at an average rate of 26 percent per month.[146]

Conditions in the cities and in the countryside in 1921 were much more severe than those that had brought about the fall of the tsar and the Provisional Government in 1917. Industrial output was less than one-half the level of the revolutionary year, while agricultural production was barely two-thirds as great. The rate of inflation had jumped dramatically. In 1921–2 more people died from hunger and epidemics than had been killed in the First World War and the civil war combined.[147] Yet apart from a revolt of the sailors of the Kronstadt naval base near Petrograd, the Communists' control over all but the most remote regions of their country met no serious challenge. The answer can only be that despite their administrative errors the Communists had mastered the new instruments of mass control in the political and military spheres. The time had now come to apply them to the Russian economy.

The Internal Margin under the New Economic Policy

In March 1921, at the end of the Tenth Congress of Soviets, Lenin introduced a series of measures that became known as the New Economic Policy (NEP).[148] Compulsory confiscation of food from the peasants was replaced by a tax in kind, set a year later at 10 percent of production.[149] Private entrepreneurship was reintroduced for small-scale production and retail trade. Foreign investors were invited to participate in "concessions" in certain sectors of the economy. Although the state retained "the commanding heights," nationalized industries were reorganized into sectoral and regional trusts.[150] The New Economic Policy has been described as an "abandonment" of the Communist regime's initial policy of state control over the economy.[151] It has also been referred to as having "decentralized" control of industry.[152] Among many party members, it was criticized as a retreat from the objective of a socialist society.[153] In actual fact, the NEP was none of these.

The NEP increased rather than decreased effective state control over industry. Indeed, Lenin himself seems to have considered this policy a return to the correct position that he had been forced to abandon three years earlier under the pressure of war.[154] Despite the nationalization of all but a small percentage of industrial enterprises in 1917 and 1918, the state agencies had proven unable to harmonize the activities of even the largest firms. Coordination was achieved in haphazard fashion by bilateral bargaining between individual producers and their clients.[155] Under the NEP, with the nationalized industries organized into trusts or industrial holding companies, the government was able for the first time to monitor the activities of all but the smallest firms. The trusts were to be of two types. One category, trusts for firms producing metal, fuel, or munitions, was placed under the direction of state agencies. All other trusts, such as those for firms producing consumer goods, were given financial and commercial independence.[156] They could set prices and sign contracts for their production. Aside from an allocation for reserves, any profits the trusts made belonged to the state. By the summer of 1923, 478 of these trusts had been formed.[157]

Rather than leading to decentralization, the NEP from its inception saw an ever-increasing centralization of the administration of industry. It will be remembered that at the beginning of 1921 the only effective control of manufacturing was at a purely local level. Under the new trust system, this situation quickly changed. The trusts created for the key sectors of the economy were centrally administered bodies of the *glavki* type, except that they had no powers to impose their authority on third parties. Unlike the *glavki*, however, the new industrial groupings proved to be effective means of coordinating large numbers of workers. Further concentration of power occurred over the course of 1922 and 1923, as most trusts grouped themselves into a small number of "syndicates" to coordinate pricing, storage, and financing.[158]

If anything, the trusts were too successful. Supplied with generous state credit from the banking system, they raised their prices at will and generated large profits. To no small extent, these profits came at the expense of the peasants. As agricultural production rebounded in 1922 and 1923, the rise of farm prices lagged behind that of industrial prices. The result was known as the "scissors crisis." By October of 1923, the ratio of the prices of industrial goods to those of agricultural goods had risen to three times its prewar level.[159] The solution to this crisis demonstrated the state's capacity to intervene effectively in the economy at the national level. The State Bank cut back sharply on the credit it offered to the industrial sector. In addition, maximum selling prices began to be set by a new agency, the Committee for Internal Trade. Finally, in certain industries, foreign manufactured goods were imported and sold at prices lower than those charged by the state syndicates.[160] By October of 1924, the ratio of industrial goods to agricultural goods prices had fallen back to 1.5 times the 1913 level.[161]

Was the New Economic Policy a retreat from socialism as its critics argued? Despite the policy change, by 1923, the private sector accounted for only 12.5 percent of industrial employment and 5 percent of output. Moreover, since the average number of employees per private establishment was only two, this sector comprised for the most part firms that had never been brought under effective state control, even at the local level.[162] As for foreign investments, there were only a few cases where concessions were actually granted, mostly in the area of foreign trade rather than production.[163] Even in agriculture, the new tax in kind represented the first successful effort by the Russian state to seize the agricultural surplus for industrial development.

Finally, this period saw the first successful introduction of socialist planning at a national level. In February 1921, a State Planning Commission (Gosplan) was set up.[164] During the period from 1921 to 1924, planning was primarily passive: it involved the preparation of forecasts of future economic developments.[165] However, the work accomplished during this period would provide the basis for the more active setting of targets that was to characterize the next phase of Soviet development.[166]

The results of the New Economic Policy were striking. By 1925, inflation was under control. The following year, Russian national income for the first time exceeded its prewar level. Agricultural output was 18 percent higher than in 1913. Despite the disruptions of the initial years of the revolution, industrial production in 1926 had almost rebounded to its prewar level and over the following years it would shoot ahead rapidly.[167] In short, during the first half-decade of the 1920s, there occurred the first successful attempt to extend state control into virtually all activities within a large urbanized society. The extension of this program to cover the rural sector had already been indicated as the next step by Lenin and would be carried out by his successor, Joseph Stalin.

THE PARADOX EXPLAINED

Why was it that the introduction of modern techniques for mass communication should have had their greatest impact in Russia, the most backward region of Europe, where they were least accessible to the general population? One factor was precisely the delay with which the new technologies were applied in Russia. The country's lag behind the rest of Europe in the creation of powerful mass information networks put the state under such great external pressure that extreme measures could be justified.

In Western Europe, the electric motor, combined with the rotary press and the Linotype machine, produced a sharp drop in newspaper publishing costs that permitted the formation of the first mass audience. At the same time, the telephone and the typewriter increased the number of people whose behavior could be monitored by a single individual. With large numbers of people simultaneously expressing similar desires for increased state spending, and the appearance of a means to administer such spending efficiently, previous limits to the size of the public sector were no longer binding.

Despite their success in extending their territorial borders into the far corners of the world, the governments of nineteenth-century Western European states controlled only a small fraction of their nations' resources. In the early 1870s, for example, government spending represented less than 10 percent of total income in Germany and the United Kingdom. With the introduction of new communications technologies, however, the situation outside Russia changed. Over the following three decades, the public share climbed steadily in most Western European countries, reaching 15 percent in England and Germany by the beginning of the twentieth century.[168] The First World War saw a further jump in government spending, as Britain, France, and Germany all succeeded in diverting a third or more of their output to the public sector. With each major western power in possession of greater fiscal resources, it was inevitable that one or more states would attempt to extend their political boundaries.

Russia could not isolate itself from these developments; however, there was a significant delay before their effects began to be felt. Mass-circulation newspapers appeared for the first time in Russia in the five years preceding the First World War. Although urban telephone networks also expanded rapidly in this period, the evolution of the country's telecommunications system lagged far behind that of Western Europe. The number of telephones per capita remained well below the levels of other industrialized countries. Moreover, in part because of the eccentric position of the capital, St Petersburg, and the great distances that separated this city from the rest of the country, Russia failed to develop a network of long-distance telephone communications prior to the First World War.

With no effective means of monitoring its far-flung bureaucracy, Russia was unable to tax income from industrial production or agriculture effectively. The Russian fiscal system therefore failed to keep pace with developments in Western Europe. The result was a precarious balance between the level of public spending required to hold the vast territory together and the tax receipts that the state bureaucracy could extract from its subjects. With Russia's entry into the war, the problem became critical. The tsarist government lost its two most important sources of revenues – import duties and taxes on alcohol. The eventual refusal of peasants to accept the banknotes printed to finance increased military spending meant that the regime could no longer provide both guns and butter to its people. When the authorities chose arms production over food, an uprising by the capital's civilian population aided by the local garrison brought down Tsar Nicholas II. Similar problems six months later cost the following Provisional Government its popular support.

How could Russia defend its territory from more advanced predator states having enormous public resources at their disposal? Russia's geography permitted a force that held the Moscow region to control a vast area across eastern Europe and northern Asia. It was Lenin who devised a way for a backward agricultural state with limited internal communications to capture the resources needed to defend itself. His system made use of the mass-circulation newspaper, along with other propaganda devices such as agitators, films, and posters, as vehicles for reaching millions of people rapidly with a single, identical message. The content of this message was a powerful new ideology that justified the suppression of political competition.

Lenin's system also included a means of maintaining administrative effectiveness in the absence of the information-intensive political and economic competition that characterized other European states. He discovered a way to use Russia's limited supply of the new means of interpersonal communications – the telephone and typewriter combination – to establish effective administrative control over the vast Russian empire. In effect, Lenin substituted labor for information. Since the latter was scarce, it would be reserved for a monitoring elite – the Communist Party – a duplicate organizational hierarchy that would supervise the conventional bureaucracy.

During the first three years after the October Revolution, Lenin concentrated on establishing his monopoly of power in the political and military domains. The effects on the external margin of the state were remarkable. The Bolshevik party began its reign in 1917 barely in control over the cities of European Russia. However, by 1921, of the tsars' former empire, only Finland, the Baltic states, and Poland lay outside the Communists' zone of influence. Within two decades, even these limits would be overcome.

With all opposition eliminated, Lenin then spent the last three years of his life setting up the monitoring system that would permit the state to function effectively. By the end of the year of his death, 1924, Russia had virtually recovered from the ravages of invasion and civil war. The country was poised for a period of rapid industrial expansion that would continue throughout the years of the Great Depression, when the western economies were foundering. Russia had expanded the internal margin of the state – the power of the hierarchy over the individual – to an extent never previously attained.

NOTES

1 David Shub, *Lenin* (The New American Library, 1948), p. 107.
2 Ibid., p. 108.
3 Carlo M. Cipolla, *Literacy and Development in the West* (Penguin, 1969), p. 114.
4 S. P. Turin, *The USSR: An Economic and Social Survey*, 3rd edn (Methuen, 1948), p. 36.
5 William R. Corson and Robert T. Crowley, *The New KGB: Engine of Soviet Power* (William Morrow, 1986), p. 34.
6 Sheila Fitzpatrick, *The Russian Revolution* (Oxford University Press, 1982), p. 44.
7 Ibid., p. 51.

8 Robert Payne, *The Life and Death of Lenin* (Simon and Schuster, 1964), p. 356.

9 Hannah Arendt, *The Origins of Totalitarianism* (Harcourt, Brace, Jovanovich, 1951), ch. 9.

10 Jacques Ellul, *Histoire de la propagande* (Presses universitaires de France, 1967), ch. 1.

11 Carl J. Friedrich and Zbigniew Brzezinski, *Totalitarianism, Dictatorship and Autocracy*, 2nd edn (Praeger, 1965), p. 129.

12 Richard Lowenthal, *The Impact of the Russian Revolution* 1917–67 (Oxford University Press, 1967), pp. 35–6.

13 W. H. Parker, *An Historical Geography of Russia* (Aldine, 1968), p. 20.

14 Roger Munting, *The Economic Development of the USSR* (Croom Helm, 1982), p. 32.

15 Angus Maddison, *Economic Growth in Japan and the USSR* (Norton, 1969), p. 92.

16 Parker, *An Historical Geography of Russia*, p. 300.

17 Munting, *The Economic Development of the USSR*, p. 33.

18 Ibid., pp. 34–5.

19 Ibid., p. 34.

20 Maddison, *Economic Growth in Japan and the USSR*, p. 91.

21 Hugh Seton-Watson, *The Russian Empire*, 1801–1917 (Clarendon Press, 1967), pp. 699–700.

22 Munting, *The Economic Development of the USSR*, p. 40.

23 Brian Bond, *War and Society in Europe*, 1870–1970 (Fontana, 1984), p. 110.

24 Seton-Watson, *The Russian Empire*, p. 700.

25 Ibid., p. 705.

26 Bond, *War and Society in Europe*, p. 110.

27 Seton-Watson, *The Russian Empire*, p. 709.

28 Ibid., p. 719.

29 Ronald Hingley, *The Russian Secret Police* (Hutchinson and Co., 1970), p. 72.

30 Ibid.

31 Ibid., p. 78.

32 Maurice Laporte, *Histoire de l'Okhrana* (Payot, 1935), p. 19–21.

33 Hingley, *The Russian Secret Police*, p. 107.

34 Ibid., p. 89.

35 Bertram D. Wolfe, *Revolution and Reality: Essays on the Origin and Fate of the Soviet System* (University of North Carolina Press, 1981), pp. 47–8.

36 Laporte, *Histoire de l'Okhrana*, p. 30.

37 Hingley, *The Russian Secret Police*, p. 87.

38 Ibid., p. 108.

39 Seton-Watson, *The Russian Empire*, p. 209.

40 Ibid., p. 210.

41 Ibid., p. 211.

42 Ibid.

43 Parker, *An Historical Geography of Russia*, p. 180.

44 Carolyn Webber and Aaron Wildavsky, *A History of Taxation and Expenditure in the Western World* (Simon and Schuster, 1986), p. 353.

45 Bond, *War and Society in Europe*, p. 118.

46 Webber and Wildavsky, *A History of Taxation and Expenditure*, p. 440.

47 Peter Kenez, *The Birth of the Propaganda State: Soviet Methods of Mass Mobilization* 1917–1929 (Cambridge University Press, 1985), pp. 21–4.

48 Bond, *War and Society in Europe*, p. 76.

49 Ibid., p. 96.

50 Seton-Watson, *The Russian Empire*, p. 699.

51 Ibid., p. 53.

52 Parker, *An Historical Geography of Russia,* p. 300; H. N. Casson, *The History of the Telephone,* (A. C. McClurg, 1910), p. 260.
53 Ibid.; Turin, *The USSR,* p. 36.
54 Marshall McLuhan, *Understanding Media: The Extensions of Man* (McGraw Hill, 1964), p. 271.
55 Wilfred A. Beeching, *Century of the Typewriter* (Heinemann, 1974), p. 32.
56 Laporte, *Histoire de l'Okhrana,* p. 19.
57 Beeching, *Century of the Typewriter,* p. 37.
58 V. I. Lenin, *What Is to Be Done?* (Foreign Language Press, Peking, 1975), p. 152.
59 Ibid., pp. 172–3.
60 Mark W. Hopkins, *Mass Media in the Soviet Union* (Praeger, 1970), p. 62.
61 Lenin, *What Is to Be Done?* p. 210.
62 Kenez, *The Birth of the Propaganda State,* p. 27.
63 Lenin, *What Is to Be Done?* p. 198.
64 Ibid., p. 202.
65 Ibid., pp. 206–7.
66 Seton-Watson, *The Russian Empire,* p. 562.
67 Maurice Dobb, *Soviet Economic Development since* 1917, 6th edn (Routledge and Kegan Paul, 1966), p. 70.
68 Kenez, *The Birth of the Propaganda State,* p. 28.
69 Leonard Schapiro, *The Russian Revolutions of* 1917 (Basic Books, 1984), pp. 36, 43.
70 Dobb, *Soviet Economic Development,* pp. 71–2.
71 Schapiro, *The Russian Revolutions,* p. 35.
72 Dobb, *Soviet Economic Development,* p. 73.
73 Ibid., p. 72.
74 Schapiro, *The Russian Revolutions,* p. 43.
75 Ibid., p. 53.
76 Seton-Watson, *The Russian Empire,* pp. 534–5.
77 Schapiro, *The Russian Revolutions,* p. 50.
78 Ibid., pp. 66–7.
79 Kenez, *The Birth of the Propaganda State,* p. 29.
80 Hingley, *The Russian Secret Police,* p. 111.
81 Ibid., p. 115.
82 Fitzpatrick, *The Russian Revolution,* p. 44.
83 Schapiro, *The Russian Revolutions,* p. 77.
84 Kenez, *The Birth of the Propaganda State,* pp. 30–1.
85 Schapiro, *The Russian Revolutions,* p. 83.
86 Dobb, *Soviet Economic Development,* p. 73.
87 Schapiro, *The Russian Revolutions,* p. 115.
88 Ibid., p. 118.
89 Kenez, *The Birth of the Propaganda State,* pp. 34–5.
90 Fitzpatrick, *The Russian Revolution,* p. 54.
91 Schapiro, *The Russian Revolutions,* pp. 130–1.
92 Ibid., p. 132.
93 Kenez, *The Birth of the Propaganda State,* p. 38.
94 Ibid., p. 40.
95 Ibid., p. 41.
96 Ibid., p. 44.
97 Ibid.
98 Ibid., p. 45.
99 Ibid.

100 Ibid., p. 46.
101 Edward Hallett Carr, *Socialism in One Country* 1924–1926, vol. 1 (Macmillan, 1958), p. 117.
102 Derek J. R. Scott, *Russian Political Institutions*, 2nd edn (Praeger, 1961), p. 136.
103 Ibid., p. 158.
104 Ibid., p. 143.
105 Raymond A. Bauer, Alex Inkeles, and Clyde Kluckhohn, *How the Soviet System Works* (Harvard University Press, 1964), p. 42.
106 Schapiro, *The Russian Revolutions*, p. 111.
107 Scott, *Russian Political Institutions*, pp. 159–60.
108 Harry Schwartz, *Russia's Soviet Economy*, 2nd edn (Prentice-Hall, 1954), p. 423.
109 Hingley, *The Russian Secret Police*, p. 78.
110 Ibid., p. 84.
111 Ibid., pp. 101–2.
112 Fitzpatrick, *The Russian Revolution*, p. 29.
113 Donald W. Treadgold, *Twentieth Century Russia*, 3rd edn (Rand McNally, 1972), p. 149.
114 Ibid., p. 157.
115 Schapiro, *The Russian Revolutions*, p. 138.
116 Ibid., p. 147.
117 Ibid., p. 170.
118 Leonard Schapiro, *The Communist Party of the Soviet Union*, 2nd edn (Random House, 1971), p. 266; Hingley, *The Russian Secret Police*, p. 120.
119 Ibid., p. 122.
120 Ibid., p. 124.
121 Ibid., p. 129.
122 Edward Hallett Carr, *Socialism in One Country* 1924–1926, vol. 2 (Macmillan, 1959), p. 425.
123 Schapiro, *The Russian Revolutions*, p. 187.
124 Carr, *Socialism in One Country*, vol. 2., p. 425.
125 Schapiro, *The Russian Revolutions*, p. 190.
126 Treadgold, *Twentieth Century Russia*, p. 163.
127 Corson and Crowley, *The New KGB*, pp. 39–40.
128 Kenez, *The Birth of the Propaganda State*, p. 3.
129 Richard Taylor, *Film Propaganda: Soviet Russia and Nazi Germany* (Croom-Helm, 1979), p. 49.
130 Richard Taylor, "A medium for the masses: agitation in the Soviet Civil War," *Soviet Studies*, 22 (April 1971), p. 569.
131 Treadgold, *Twentieth Century Russia*, pp. 185–6.
132 Thomas F. Remington, *Building Socialism in Bolshevik Russia* (University of Pittsburgh Press, 1984), p. 51.
133 *Brockhaus Enzyklopädie* (F.A. Brockhaus, Wiesbaden, 1968), vol. 6, p. 173.
134 Remington, *Building Socialism in Bolshevik Russia*, p. 54.
135 Treadgold, *Twentieth Century Russia*, p. 160.
136 Ibid., p. 164.
137 Remington, *Building Socialism in Bolshevik Russia*, p. 54.
138 Ibid., pp. 57–9.
139 Ibid., p. 63 .
140 Ibid., p. 69.
141 Ibid., p. 70.
142 Treadgold, *Twentieth Century Russia*, p. 198.
143 K. Leites, *Recent Economic Developments in Russia* (Clarendon, 1922), p. 216.

144 Raymond Hutchings, *Soviet Economic Development* (Blackwell, 1971), p. 36.
145 Roger A. Clarke, *Soviet Economic Facts 1917–1970* (John Wiley and Sons, 1972), p. 10.
146 Schwartz, *Russia's Soviet Economy*, p. 471–2.
147 Fitzpatrick, *The Russian Revolution*, p. 85.
148 Schapiro, *The Russian Revolutions*, p. 198.
149 Treadgold, *Twentieth Century Russia*, p. 200.
150 Alec Nove, *An Economic History of the USSR* (Penguin, 1969), pp. 85, 97.
151 Fitzpatrick, *The Russian Revolution*, p. 87.
152 Dobb, *Soviet Economic Development*, p. 132.
153 Schapiro, *The Russian Revolutions*, p. 203.
154 Alec Nove, *Political Economy and Soviet Socialism* (George Allen and Unwin, 1979), pp. 78–9.
155 Remington, *Building Socialism in Bolshevik Russia*, p. 55.
156 Dobb, *Soviet Economic Development*, p. 132.
157 Ibid., p. 135.
158 Ibid., pp. 158–60.
159 Ibid., p. 175.
160 Ibid., p. 173.
161 Ibid., p. 175.
162 Ibid., p. 142.
163 Ibid.
164 Hutchings, *Soviet Economic Development*, p. 37.
165 Ibid., p. 49.
166 Munting, *The Economic Development of the USSR*, p. 49.
167 Clarke, *Soviet Economic Facts*, p. 8.
168 Clive Trebilcock, *The Industrialization of the Continental Powers, 1780–1914* (Longman, 1981), p. 87.

8

The Atomization of America

Between the middle and the end of the 1970s, there occurred a decline in the global power of the United States and a deterioration in the situation of the majority of American citizens. These developments coincided with a sharp fall in corporate tax receipts as a share of the country's total income. The American corporation itself was undergoing a crisis with downsizing and plant closings. The underlying cause of these developments appears to have been technological. In the early 1960s, the complexity of integrated electronic circuits began to double every year, driving down the cost of information manipulation, transmission, and storage. The traditional American multidivisional corporation proved inappropriate for the new technologies. However, in the process of overtaking the US, Japanese firms developed a new form of organization. Smaller, flatter, and more flexible than the American behemoths, the new lattice-form corporation is incapable of generating the tax revenues of its predecessors. It is at the leading edge of a trend toward more atomistic social structures.

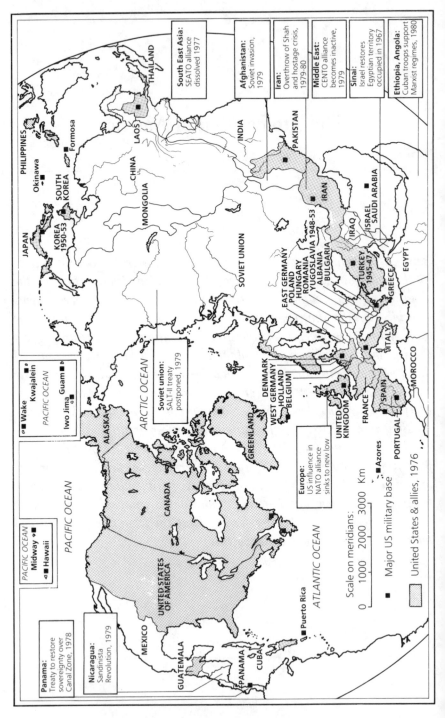

Panama:
Treaty to restore sovereignty over Canal Zone, 1978

Nicaragua:
Sandinista Revolution, 1979

PACIFIC OCEAN
Midway ○■
○◁■ Hawaii

PACIFIC OCEAN
○ Wake
Kwajalein ○
Iwo Jima ○ ■ Guam ᵇ

Soviet union:
SALT-II treaty postponed, 1979

Europe:
US influence in NATO alliance sinks to new low

South East Asia:
SEATO alliance dissolved 1977

Afghanistan:
Soviet invasion, 1979

Iran:
Overthrow of Shah and hostage crisis, 1979-80

Middle East:
CENTO alliance becomes inactive, 1979

Sinai:
Israel restores Egyptian territory occupied in 1967

Ethiopia, Angola:
Cuban troops support Marxist regimes, 1980

PHILIPPINES
Formosa
Okinawa
SOUTH KOREA
KOREA 1950-53
JAPAN
THAILAND
LAOS
CHINA
INDIA
PAKISTAN
MONGOLIA
SOVIET UNION
IRAN
SAUDI ARABIA
ISRAEL
IRAQ
TURKEY 1945-47
GREECE
EGYPT
EAST GERMANY
POLAND
HUNGARY
ROMANIA
YUGOSLAVIA 1948-53
ALBANIA
BULGARIA
ITALY
SPAIN
FRANCE
UNITED KINGDOM
PORTUGAL
MOROCCO
Azores
DENMARK
WEST GERMANY
HOLLAND
BELGIUM
GREENLAND
ARCTIC OCEAN
ALASKA
CANADA
UNITED STATES OF AMERICA
MEXICO
GUATEMALA
PANAMA
CUBA
Puerto Rica
ATLANTIC OCEAN
PACIFIC OCEAN

Scale on meridians:
0 1000 2000 3000 Km

■ Major US military base

United States & allies, 1976

Figure 8.1   The American Empire, 1976–80: pressure without and within.
(*Source: The Times Atlas of World History*, 1984, pp. 292–3.)

The debate was held in Cleveland, a decaying steel-making city on the shores of Lake Erie. Although only a thousand spectators were present in the convention center, over 100 million others watched by television as retired ABC news commentator Howard K. Smith introduced the candidates. Most viewers were curious to have a close look at the Republican challenger, Ronald Reagan, who was noted for his extreme right-wing views. With the 1980 elections only a week away, many voters still had serious reservations about the competence of the former screen actor and California governor compared to that of his opponent, the Democratic incumbent, Jimmy Carter. Reagan held a slight lead in the polls, but his initial advance had been weakening as the campaign drew to a close.

The questions, posed by a panel of journalists, covered a range of domestic and international issues. In his replies, President Carter steadfastly defended his administration, supporting his position with a barrage of statistics. Oil imports had been cut by 25 percent; nine million new jobs had been added, 1.3 million for blacks and another million for those who spoke Spanish; $43 billion would be spent over the next ten years to rebuild transportation systems. Attacking his opponent, Carter repeated a charge made during the primary campaign by Reagan's running mate, George Bush, that the former governor was proposing voodoo economics. He went on to accuse Reagan of wanting to discard the Strategic Arms Limitation Treaty (SALT II) – "a dangerous and disturbing thing" to do. However, the President appeared tired and nervous, his makeup giving him a gray appearance.

Ronald Reagan, at 69, was 15 years older than the President, but his dark hair, tanned face and ease before the cameras gave an impression of youth, vigor, and confidence. Avoiding statistics, he stated his ideas calmly and simply. Why was it inflationary for people to spend their own money but not for the President to spend it for them? He would negotiate with the Soviets a reduction in nuclear weapons "to the point that neither one of us represents a threat to the other."

In many respects, the televised debate between the 1980 presidential candidates echoed a confrontation that took place almost two centuries earlier between two of the country's "founding fathers." Like Reagan, Thomas Jefferson, the author of the Declaration of Independence and the country's third president (1801–9), favored an atomistic society with "a minimum of government and governing." His opponent, Alexander Hamilton, one of the principal authors of the country's constitution, advocated a strong central government. Although Hamilton himself was killed in a duel by a member of Jefferson's party, his ideas eventually predominated. The century prior to the Cleveland debate had witnessed a relentless strengthening of the power of the American state over its citizens, particularly under the more recent presidents of Jimmy Carter's Democratic party.

Finally, each candidate was given a chance to make his closing comments. Jimmy Carter fumbled, thanking the people of Cleveland and Ohio "for these last few hours of my life." He then concluded by making a plea to the individual undecided voters whose support was essential if he were to close the gap that separated him from Reagan in the polls. With Carter out of the debate, Reagan coolly unleashed the attack he had rehearsed with Republican Representative David Stockman in the garage of his rented Virginia estate. Looking directly into the television camera, he suggested that next Tuesday in the voting booth, people should ask themselves, "Are you better off than you were four years ago? Is it easier for you to go and buy things in the stores than it was four years ago? Is there more or less unemployment in the country than there was four years ago? Is America as respected throughout the world as it was? Do you feel that our security is as safe, that we're as strong as we were four years ago?"

In his final remarks, Reagan seemed to touch a sensitive nerve in the American public. Although many experts later gave the debate to Carter on points, a sampling poll done for CBS showed that by a margin of 44 percent to 36, the public felt Reagan had won. The following Tuesday, the poll results were confirmed, as Reagan went on to win a landslide victory. He captured 51 percent of the popular vote to Carter's 41 percent (independent presidential candidate John Anderson won 7 percent of the vote), and 44 states to Carter's six. Evidently, in late 1980, large numbers of American voters did feel that they were worse off than they had been four years earlier. What had happened and why?

THE HIGH-WATER MARK

In the year 1976, the United States was celebrating the bicentennial of its declaration of independence from Britain. Having finally extricated itself from the quagmire of Vietnam and recovered from the scandal of Watergate, the country was basking in a period of peace, prosperity – and power. Despite its recent military setbacks, America's influence was immense around the globe (see figure 8.1). With its 48 mainland states plus Alaska, Hawaii, and the capital district, the United States was the most populous and prosperous of the nations in the western hemisphere. In the Caribbean, it held the island of Puerto Rico, an associated commonwealth won as booty in the Spanish–American war of 1898, along with the US Virgin Islands, purchased from Denmark in 1917. To the south-west, in the

Pacific, the United States had acquired further bits of territory over the preceding century. The Americans held Samoa, Guam, Wake Island, the Trust Territory of the Pacific Islands, and other islands.

Within its own hemisphere, the US was the dominant power. It controlled a strategic area on the isthmus joining North and South America – the Panama Canal Zone. Early in the twentieth century, in return for American support for its separation from Colombia, Panama had granted the United States sovereignty "in perpetuity" over a 16 km wide strip to be used for the construction of a canal. The waterway itself had been completed in 1914. Over the following decades, with its massive territorial and economic presence, the US had succeeded in virtually excluding other major powers from its own hemisphere. Only in Cuba, where the leaders of a 1959 revolution had set up a socialist government favorable to the Soviet Union, did a hostile power have an ally within the region. That virus appeared to have been successfully isolated, the pro-Marxist regime in Chile having been overthrown by a US-backed military coup in 1973.

In addition to its territorial possessions, the United States maintained large numbers of troops in foreign bases around the world through treaties with its allies. Under the North Atlantic Treaty Organization (NATO), the US had over a quarter of a million soldiers stationed in Europe, most of them in the German Federal Republic. In Asia, the largest concentration of American troops was in South Korea, where the US maintained a full division with 30,000 men. America's ambitions had been checked in 1975 when its South Vietnamese ally, no longer supported by US troops, was overrun by soldiers backed by North Vietnam. However, in geopolitical terms, the forging of new political ties with the People's Republic of China, begun with President Richard Nixon's Peking visit in 1972, more than compensated for this defeat. The death of Mao Tse-Tung in September of 1976 left open the possibility of a further strengthening of Sino-American relations.

Another area of US strength was the Middle East. Egypt, the region's most populous state, had broken its former links with the Soviet Union and was known to favor closer ties with the West. The other three strongest powers of the region – Israel, Turkey, and Iran – were US allies. In Iran, Muhammad Reza Shah Pahlevi was using his windfall petroleum revenues from the first oil crisis to convert his country into the superpower of the Persian Gulf. Indeed, the Shah was one of the most important foreign customers of the US arms industry.

Throughout this vast zone of American influence – the "free world" – US corporations had acquired an economic presence that complemented their country's military power. In Canada, Europe, Latin America, and Asia, American capital combined with local labor and resources. Trees were cut down, minerals extracted, and cars, computers, and thousands of other products assembled according to instructions from managers located thousands of kilometers away in the United States.

The State of the Union

If America was able to make its presence felt abroad, from the Philippines to Greenland, it could do no less within its own territorial boundaries. One of the criteria of success of a modern state is its ability to maintain stable prices while assuring that its workers are fully employed. The American economy had barely been grazed when the Arab petroleum-exporting states had ordered a boycott of oil shipments to the US in October 1973. The annual rate of inflation had flared up briefly to a postwar high of 13 percent in 1974. By 1976, however, price increases had fallen below 6 percent a year. During the recession that followed the oil crisis, unemployment in the United States had also shot up – to a postwar record of almost 8 percent of the labor force in 1975. By the time of the 1976 elections, however, the employment situation had improved: fewer than 7 percent of the labor force were looking for work.

Another measure of a modern state's success in controlling its own territory is the extent to which it is able to assure a minimum level of public services for its citizens. Although the United States had originally been a rural society, by 1976 seven out of ten Americans lived in cities. These cities were linked by highway and air networks that together constituted a model for the rest of the world. As in other industrialized countries, rail service had difficulty surviving without public subsidies. In 1970, the United States had followed the European example, setting up a federal agency to control virtually all inter-city passenger service by rail. And in 1976 Congress had intervened to consolidate six bankrupt freight railroads in the north-east into the Conrail system.

The postwar period had seen the flight of the more prosperous white residents from the cores of most urban areas. However, massive federal grants to states and cities assured that minimum standards in education, health, and housing were nevertheless maintained. Greatly expanded by Democratic President Lyndon Johnson in the 1960s under the title of the Great Society, these programs had been continued under his Republican successors, Richard Nixon and Gerald Ford.

Public investment plays a key role in reducing the costs of private exchanges. For example, without government-financed road networks and port facilities, it becomes extremely costly to transport goods. It was therefore disturbing that in the country as a whole, the fraction of total Gross National Product allocated to public works had fallen from 2.3 percent to

1.6 percent in the decade prior to the 1976 elections.[1] Action would eventually have to be taken to avoid the collapse of roads and bridges and the decay of the mass-transit systems of the major cities. Yet this was a long-term problem: because of the long life of such installations, few people had yet been seriously inconvenienced by deterioration of the nation's capital stock.

One cause of concern for most Americans who lived in cities was the rapid rise in violent crime. In part because of a steady increase in the share of the total population in the age group 15–24 years, crime rates had been climbing steeply. Yet here a combination of social spending and additional funds for law enforcement finally seemed to be showing results. The robbery rate had declined for the previous two years. At the same time, the rate of other violent crime (murder, rape, and assault) seemed to be stabilizing. In 1976, for the first time in many years, the number of violent crimes other than robbery increased at a rate no greater than that of the population as a whole. There were further grounds for optimism in the cities. For several years, the total number of arrests for violations involving hard drugs had declined. Opium, cocaine, and synthetic narcotics remained a social problem – particularly in the largest cities – but one that appeared at last to be being brought within acceptable limits.

The Fiscal Boundary

To control this vast territory, both within and outside its own borders, the American state required an unprecedented flow of public resources. The United States is a federation: under the constitution of 1787, the founding states ceded limited fiscal powers to a common central authority. Until the beginning of the twentieth century, state and local governments still held the lion's share of total fiscal powers. However, in 1909, the federal administration began to levy a tax on corporate profits, and in 1913 a constitutional amendment gave it similar powers with respect to personal incomes. Since the rates set on these taxes were initially low, by the eve of the Great Depression, state and local governments still collected two of every three dollars paid in taxes. But during the 1930s and early 1940s, the federal authority greatly expanded its revenue base, primarily by raising the rates of taxation on personal income and on corporate profits. By 1941, three out of five tax dollars were collected by the central government.

With a government revenue structure based on flexible income taxes levied at the federal level in place, the stage was set for a rapid rise in taxes as a share of America's total income. From 11 percent in 1929, the public share of income rose to 22 percent in 1949. By 1976, after a further quarter-century of tax increases, one dollar out of every three in the country's total income was captured in taxes levied by governments at one level or another.

Guns or Butter?

The choice between military and social objectives in the spending of public revenues – guns versus butter – is a difficult one for any society. In the case of a world power, the complexity is heightened by the realization that its decisions will affect those of both its allies and its enemies. To protect its borders and maintain its influence outside its own territory, the United States had built up a strong military force. At the height of the Vietnam War in 1967, defense spending represented close to 10 percent of GNP and almost half the total federal budget. Since 1940, the greater part of military manpower requirements had been filled by conscription. Then in 1973, as America withdrew from the fighting in south-east Asia, the country returned to a volunteer army. By the 1976 presidential elections, the defense share of GNP had been halved, to about 5 percent. Nevertheless, there were still over two million men and women in uniform.

As military spending was cut back in the 1970s, attention turned increasingly to improving the level of public services offered across the nation. The most important spending responsibilities in education, transportation, and urban renewal remained with the lower levels of government. Since the primary taxing powers lay in the hands of the central administration, transfers from the federal to state and local governments were necessary. The share of grants-in-aid in total income provides a rough measure of the country's commitment to controlling the territory within its boundaries. Over the previous decade, federal grants to lower levels of government had risen extremely rapidly – from under 2 percent of GNP in 1967 to 3.4 percent a decade later. In 1976, these grants to the states and cities represented almost one-quarter of their total revenue sources. During this period, then, Americans had made a deliberate decision for butter over guns.

Over most of the decade that preceded the bicentennial, total government expenditures had risen in line with tax receipts. However, the recession of 1974–5 had caused enormous increases in transfer payments to the unemployed and to those needing social assistance. At the same time, the growth of tax receipts ground to a temporary halt. The result, inevitably, was a sharp increase in the federal deficit, which reached 4.9 percent of GNP in 1975 and remained at a disturbingly high 3.2 percent in 1976. However, due to the fiscal conservatism of earlier years, interest payments on the public debt still represented under 7 percent of federal expenditures. There was confidence that once steady growth got under way again, the deficit could be cut back, as it had been in the past.

The American Corporation

One of the keys to the success of the United States was a uniquely American organizational innovation: the modern corporation. This institution had been developed gradually over the previous hundred years. In the mid-nineteenth century, American railroad owners had been compelled to grapple with the problem of coordinating the movements of people and equipment spread over enormous distances, traveling at speeds far greater than those previously known. The solution they discovered was a separation of management into two distinct subgroups – line and staff. Managers on the line were responsible for giving orders to employees; in doing so, they followed standards established by staff executives.[2] In addition, geographical divisions were set up headed by supervisors with the authority to make day-to-day decisions.[3]

A further development occurred in the 1920s as the multidivisional or "M-form" corporation, to use Oliver Williamson's terminology, began to replace the existing unitary or "U-form" structure in the largest firms.[4] Alfred Chandler has shown how as the corporation grew, adding multiple products and services, centralized managers became overwhelmed by the complexity of the decisions to be made.[5] The solution, discovered at about the same time by General Motors and Dupont, was to create semi-autonomous operating divisions organized by product, brand, or geography. A central corporate staff then set objectives and allocated resources among divisions.

The multinational corporation, an organizational model that American firms began to use extensively in the 1950s, was an extension of the basic M-form structure across national boundaries.[6] Authority was delegated to the managers of foreign subsidiaries, who were free to make their own decisions provided that they adhered to objectives set out for the organization as a whole and remained within the limits of the resources allocated to them by the central administration. In the 1950s and 1960s, American firms used the multinational corporation structure as a device for transferring technology abroad. In 1976, US foreign assets in the form of direct investments outweighed foreign direct investments in the US by a ratio of more than four to one.

A country's balance of payments on current account measures its sales of goods and services to the rest of the world less its foreign purchases. In the bicentennial year, the United States current account was in surplus, as it had been in most years of the twentieth century. The country was therefore a net exporter of capital to the rest of the world. Although the trade balance, which measures merchandise transactions alone, showed a slight deficit in 1976, there was no apparent cause for alarm: a year earlier there had been a trade surplus of roughly the same magnitude.

PRESSURE ON THE BORDERS

During the four years of the presidency of Jimmy Carter, the first major cracks began to appear in this edifice of American power. One indication was a decline in the territorial presence of the United States and its allies on several fronts around the world. In some cases, the losses were the result of deliberate policy decisions, while in others they were due to events beyond American control.

In the case of the Panama Canal Zone, the loss was deliberate. In 1977, the US administration negotiated a treaty with Panama under which it would turn the Canal Zone over to the Panamanians in stages between 1979 and the end of the century. The treaty was strongly opposed by most Republican and by some Democratic Senators. Ronald Reagan, campaigning already for the next presidential elections, commented on a radio program carried by 500 stations, "You know, giving up the Canal itself might be a better deal if we could throw in the State Department."[7] Polls showed the American public sharply divided, many agreeing with Senator S. I. Hayakawa: "It's ours, we stole it fair and square."[8] The treaty nevertheless passed the Senate in 1978 and came into effect the following year.

A second territorial setback for the United States in Central America was unexpected. In Nicaragua, the Somoza family had been in power since 1936. For nearly two decades, their regime had been engaged in conflicts with guerrillas of the Sandinista National Liberation Front, who operated from bases in neighboring Costa Rica and Honduras. In July 1979, following seven weeks of heavy fighting, the dictatorship was overthrown. The United States, which had stationed troops in the country from 1912 to 1933, refused to intervene. The new regime appointed a cabinet of 18 members drawn from various political and professional groups. However, it also quickly established close ties with Cuba. When the cabinet resigned in December "to confirm, substitute, or relocate according to the convenience and necessities of the Sandinista revolutionary process," it became clear that the dominance of the United States within its own hemisphere had been seriously undermined.

In the Middle East, a major source of tension was the border between America's ally, Israel, and neighboring Egypt. After its victory in the Six-

Day War of 1967, Israel had occupied Egyptian territory in the Sinai peninsula. However, now that Egypt had cut its ties with the Soviet Union, there was less reason for the US to support Israel over this issue. Accordingly, in 1978, President Carter invited the leaders of the two countries to meet with him at his retreat in Camp David to negotiate an end to the dispute. The following year, Israel and Egypt signed a treaty under which Egyptian sovereignty over the Sinai peninsula was restored. Peace had been preserved, but the strategic position of America's ally had been weakened. Should Egypt fall into the hands of an extremist regime, Israel's loss of the desert buffer zone could prove costly.

Another attempt by President Carter to reduce American defense commitments did not yield even a qualified success. In 1972, Strategic Arms Limitation Talks between the USA and the Soviet Union had led to the signing of a treaty (SALT I) that forbade the installation of antiballistic missiles and limited offensive nuclear weapons. A second treaty (SALT II) was negotiated by the Carter administration. However, in December 1979, the Soviet Union ordered troops into Afghanistan to support a new pro-Soviet regime recently installed by a military coup. Senate ratification of the SALT II treaty was therefore shelved indefinitely. The period of *détente* in relations between the United States and the Soviet Union was over. And a country that had formerly been neutral was being incorporated into the ring of satellite states that surrounded the Soviet Union.

Within the NATO alliance, the abrasive anti-Communism of Carter's national secutiry advisor, Zbigniew Brzezinski, alienated the representatives of several countries. The Europeans looked less and less to America for leadership in their foreign relations.[9] Meanwhile, on the Continent, a defeated former enemy had recovered much of its lost economic power. Symbolically, the value of the West German Deutschmark rose relative to that of the US dollar throughout the 1970s. In a 1972 treaty, East and West Germany had agreed to recognize each other's sovereignty; since then, economic and political relations between the two states had been continually improving. Financially and economically, the Germans were beginning to challenge America for the position of dominance in Europe.

Elsewhere in the world, there were further setbacks for American power during the Carter administration. During the 1950s, the United States and its western allies had encouraged the formation of regional alliances in Asia to block Communist expansion. In 1977, the Southeast Asia Treaty Organization (SEATO), which included Pakistan, the Philippines and Thailand, was formally dissolved. And in 1979 the Central Treaty Organization (CENTO) whose Asian members were Iran, Turkey, and Pakistan, became inactive. Meanwhile, in Africa, Cuba was sending troops to Africa to support the Marxist regimes of Ethiopia and Angola.

The Iran Hostage Crisis

More than any other event, it was the seizing of the staff of the American embassy in Teheran that symbolized to the world the new weakness of the United States. To comprehend this event, it is necessary to have some understanding of the conditions under which the Shah of Iran was overthrown. In January 1978, Iran's tightly controlled press published an attack on one of the Shah's bitterest opponents, Ruhollah Khomeini.[10] An ayatollah, the highest rank of priests among the Shiite Muslims, Khomenei was at that time living in exile in the holy city of Najef in Iraq. The article accused him of having colluded with Communists and landlords to oppose the Shah's land reform programs.

In Iran's religious center, Qom, 5,000 of Khomeini's supporters assembled to protest against the article. They were met by the Shah's police, who opened fire with automatic weapons, killing dozens and injuring many more. In the Islamic religion, the fortieth day after a death is reserved for mourning. Accordingly, 40 days after the initial protest, there were new demonstrations – and more killings. This cycle of violence was repeated on a wider and wider scale over the following months.

Khomeini made use of the latest technology to bypass the regime's control over the mass media. Dialing directly by telephone from a new residence outside Paris, he called for the overthrow of the Shah. His messages were recorded on cassette, copied and distributed rapidly from mosque to mosque. In this way, a medieval institution combined with solid-state technology to nullify the instruments of mass control. In November, Khomeini was able to initiate a general strike whose effect was to shut off the flow of oil production, the source of the regime's wealth.

The Shah, who had been treated secretly for cancer for six years, seemed at a loss to devise an effective response.[11] Over the following two months, as kerosene for heating and gasoline for transport became increasingly scarce, Iran's economy ground to a halt. Again and again there were bloody clashes between demonstrators and the police and army. Finally, on January 16, 1979, with the country in chaos and no alternative remaining, the Shah took the controls of his Boeing 707 and flew off into exile in Egypt.

Two weeks later, the Ayatollah Khomeini returned from Europe to set up a new Islamic republic in Iran. However, he remained implacably opposed to his country's former ruler. In October 1979, the Shah, who was now seriously ill in Mexico, requested permission to enter the United States for medical treatment. Well aware of the attitude of the Khomeini government, Carter argued with his advisers and cabinet that the request should be denied. Finally, however, he gave in to his Secretary of State and his National Security Adviser, who favored admitting the Shah on "humanitarian" grounds.[12]

On this occasion, the President would have been better to follow his first instincts. Several days later, on November 4, 1979, the guards at the US embassy in Teheran were overwhelmed by a mob of "demonstrators" who took the American staff of over 60 people hostage. Although negotiations with the Iranians were quickly initiated, work was also begun on a plan to free the hostages by force if necessary. Five months later, with the negotiations going nowhere, Carter overruled his own Secretary of State to order the rescue mission to proceed.

On the night of April 24, 1980, eight aging Sea Stallion helicopters took off from the deck of the US navy carrier *Nimitz* sailing in the Gulf of Oman off the southern coast of Iran. They carried a group of 90 commandos from the Pentagon's anti-terrorist Blue Light unit who were to break into the embassy and rescue the hostages. Two helicopters broke down en route, but the force proceeded with the remaining six. At a desert rendezvous point south of Teheran, it was discovered that an additional helicopter had mechanical problems and could not continue. The mission was aborted. However, as one of the helicopters attempted to refuel at the beginning of the return flight, it collided with a C-130 transport. Eight servicemen were killed.

The aborted rescue mission was a humiliation for the United States. In Teheran, the Iranians displayed the charred remains of the dead American soldiers before foreign television cameras at the US embassy. However, negotiations for the release of the hostages continued. On the Sunday before the November 1980 elections the Iranian parliament met to discuss conditions for resolving the crisis. Unfortunately, the conditions announced were such that no immediate release was likely: Iran called for the US to unfreeze Iranian assets, abandon its financial claims against Iran, help return the fortune of the late Shah, and agree not to intervene in its internal affairs. Two days later, the American public took out its frustrations on its own leaders, voting the Carter administration out of office.

Internal Disarray

If American power was on the wane on a number of fronts around the world, what could be said about the state's control over the territory lying within its own borders? In 1979, the disturbances in the Iranian oil industry caused a severe drop in world petroleum output. Intervention by the Energy Department, created by President Carter two years earlier, served only to aggravate the crisis. Energy price controls caused domestic producers to hold back production. As a result, there were lineups for gasoline that extended for blocks in many cities. As if shortages were not enough, consumer prices increased by almost 14 percent in 1980 – a rate greater than that of the period of the first oil shock. Meanwhile, with a slowdown in production, unemployment crept up to 7 percent.

In the cities, there were further problems. After a lull in the mid-1970s, violent crime rates had begun to climb rapidly. The year 1980 saw a record number of 23,040 murders in the United States, an increase of 23 percent over the 1976 figure.[13] Assaults and robberies were also up sharply. One apparent cause for optimism was that the number of arrests for drug abuse violations fell from 1976 to 1980. However, this relief was to be short-lived: two years later, in 1982, owing to a rapid increase in use of cocaine, the number of narcotics arrests would also begin to soar.[14]

Even more seriously for the long-term, the rate of investment in social infrastructure had continued to decline. In the last two years of the Carter administration, capital outlays for public works were about 1.2 percent of GNP – barely one-half the rate of a decade earlier.[15] Without the necessary investments in roads, bridges, mass transit, and airports, people would face greater delays in traveling and in sending goods. Economic productivity would fall. Moreover, without increases in equipment for supplying clean water and disposing of wastes, the quality of life would deteriorate across the country.

The Fiscal Boundary

The external and internal crises of the Carter administration coincided with a breakdown in the economy's ability to generate additional tax revenues. After rising steadily for four decades, tax receipts as a proportion of total income had failed to grow in the 1970s. The government share of total income, including Social Security contributions, had stalled at slightly over 30 percent of GNP.

One of the principal problems for governments at all levels in the United States was to tax capital. Since the 1960s, corporate income tax receipts as a share of the country's total income had fallen sharply. Revenues from this source declined from 4.4 percent of GNP in 1968 to 3.1 percent in 1980.[16] Other forms of taxes paid by corporations had also fallen relative to GNP. To a certain extent this shortfall could be offset by raises in tax rates on other transactions or forms of income; in particular, by higher rates on personal incomes. However, there was a danger that such tax increases could be counterproductive in terms of revenue generation. The higher the rates levied on personal income, the greater the incentive for individuals to avoid payment, either by changing their place of residence, by increasing their leisure, or by hiding their income from the authorities. From the beginning of its mandate, therefore, the Carter administration found itself in an increasingly tight revenue bind. Tax rates could not be raised, yet the deficit had to be trimmed and unemployment lowered.

Something had to give. During the first two years of his mandate, Carter persuaded Congress to further cut the growth of defense spending. In 1978, the military budget as a share of GNP fell to a postwar low of 4.8 percent.[17] The difficulty with this strategy was that it collided head-on with the conversion to an all-volunteer army. To pay competitive wages, it was necessary to devote nearly half the defense budget to personnel costs. Even then, it remained difficult to hire and retain first-class soldiers and officers.

One result of the budgetary restrictions imposed on the Pentagon was a shortage of qualified manpower. Another equally serious difficulty was the procurement and maintenance of modern equipment. Probably both of these factors help explain the disastrous outcome of the attempt to rescue the American hostages in Iran in April 1980. Ironically, in 1979, the United States had begun to rearm, the Senate having insisted upon a substantial rise in defense spending in return for supporting the strategic arms limitation treaty (SALT II) with the Soviet Union.[18] In 1980, with the collapse of *détente* following the Soviet military intervention in Afghanistan, Congress approved further large increases in the Pentagon's budget.

Another possible way out of the fiscal bind was to cut grants to lower levels of government. Initially, Carter's intentions had been quite the opposite. From 1975 to 1977, federal grants to states and municipalities had remained flat, at 3.5 percent of GNP.[19] In January 1978, the Carter administration released the first budget that it had prepared in its entirety. In the "liberal" tradition of his Democratic predecessors, F. D. Roosevelt, H. S. Truman, J. F. Kennedy, and L. B. Johnson, Carter proposed an ambitious program of social legislation. The welfare system would be reformed, new funds would be allocated to rebuild the cities, and the first steps would be taken to establish a national health insurance system.

These ambitious plans fell victim to growing voter revolt against high levels of taxation. On June 6, 1978, by a wide margin, the voters of California approved Proposition 13, an amendment to the state constitution that sharply restricted the powers of municipalities to levy property taxes. Over the following months, the proposals for new social programs were allowed to die in Congress. In 1979, the level of federal grants-in-aid fell relative to GNP, reversing a process that dated back to the years immediately after the Korean War.[20]

It may be seen that the Carter administration reacted to the slowdown in the growth of tax revenues by cutting back on the amounts devoted to territorial control. Cuts in defense spending reduced US capacity to intervene around the world to protect its foreign interests. At the same time, reductions in transfers to states and municipalities relative to income would make it increasingly difficult to assure minimum standards in public services across the country. In effect, these two types of cutbacks constituted a withdrawal of the American government from territory that it had previously been committed to controlling – both outside and within its own borders.

Despite these cutbacks in spending, the three levels of government combined to run up a huge total budgetary deficit. The federal budget remained disturbingly in disequilibrium in the late 1970s. From 1970 to 1980, federal government assets actually grew faster than liabilities; however, the greater part of this growth consisted of appreciating values of illiquid land, buildings, and equipment that could not readily be turned into cash to finance current expenditures.[21] The Carter presidency was the first since the Second World War not to have experienced a budget surplus in any of its four years in power.[22] As a result, when an economic slowdown occurred in 1980, there was little room for fiscal maneuvering. The administration reacted too little and too late to prevent unemployment from reaching 7 percent in a year in which it was seeking a renewal of its mandate.

A factor even more worrying for the long term was the American balance of payments. For three years in a row from 1977 to 1979, the US current account was in deficit. This meant that the United States, for the first time in a century, was systematically borrowing from the rest of the world. The major problem was the trade balance. For four consecutive years, the United States imported far more goods than it exported. Even the recession of 1980 did not cut the country's voracious appetite for foreign goods sufficiently to produce a trade surplus.

Corporate Blight

If the receipts from corporate taxation failed to keep pace with income growth in the 1970s, an important question arises. Why were business tax rates not increased to compensate for this revenue loss? The simplest answer is that the American firm was in no condition to support additional taxes. The success of a new organizational form – the modern corporation – had been one of the key factors explaining the rise to dominance of the United States during the second century of its existence. It follows that any weakening of the position of the American corporation as an institution was equally a threat to the global position of the United States.

At some point in the early 1970s, the American corporate sector began to encounter difficulties. One indication appears in statistics of the growth of employment in the largest manufacturing firms. For over a century, the trend had been to ever-larger production units. Whether through internal growth or mergers, corporations had raised their scale of production, increasing their market shares in their own industries, protecting themselves by moving into related sectors that supplied raw materials and parts or distributed the finished product. For most of the 1960s, almost all of the growth in US manufacturing employment was accounted for by the largest firms, those employing 500 workers or more.[23] Even when slower growth came, during the first Nixon administration (1967–72), employment in large firms continued to rise, while the number of workers in small and medium firms declined.

Then during the middle years of the 1970s (1972–7) a change began to occur. Employment in large corporations continued to grow. However, the number of workers in small and medium firms also began to rise sharply. During the subsequent decade, this relative decline of the big corporation became absolute. While employment in small firms increased at an unprecedented rate, the number of jobs in large companies actually declined from 1977 to 1986.[24] Corporations now found it profitable to spin off divisions outside their principal line of activity. And if management did not act fast enough, corporate raiders with access to large pools of borrowed funds would seize a controlling interest and sell off individual subsidiaries to pay back their creditors.

Something more was occurring than a simple change in the optimal scale of the corporation. Over the previous century, as American firms had expanded, their financial requirements had outstripped the risk capital available to the entrepreneurs who owned them. Accordingly, to obtain additional equity funds, firms had made increasing use of stock markets. In return for a share of profits, the wider public provided the additional risk capital necessary to finance increases in the scale of production. Beginning in 1978, however, the use of the stock market to finance business expansion declined. In that year, net issues of corporate equity in the United States were negative: firms retired existing shares in an amount that exceeded their issues of new equity. This pattern was repeated in 1979, 1984, and 1985.[25] It was as if American capitalism were on the retreat.

There is evidence that the US corporation as an institution was itself coming under attack from alternative methods of organizing production. Until the early 1970s, foreign direct investment assets in the United States amounted to only 1 percent of the country's GNP. Beginning in 1973, however, this percentage began to rise, as European and Japanese firms increased their stake in the US economy. By 1980 the assets of foreign direct investors had risen to 3 percent of GNP. By 1987, the percentage would double again, reaching a level almost as great as that of US direct investment assets abroad.[26]

All three trends – firm downsizing, net stock retirement, and the penetration of foreign capital – indicate that a fundamental change was occurring in economic organization in the United States.

TOWARD AN ATOMISTIC SOCIETY

The problems of the United States in the late 1970s had been building up over a number of years. The loss of territory controlled by the nation, the deterioration of life in its cities, the disappearance of the country's traditional trade and budget surpluses, and the crisis of the corporation were all evident from the 1960s on. As early as 1965, US corporate profits began to be squeezed.[27] However, it was not until the last two years of the Carter presidency that these issues generated crises sufficient to capture the headlines. What had gone wrong?

Carter himself attributed his administration's troubles to bad luck. In his memoires, he referred to "an almost unbelievable series of crises" during the final 14 months of his mandate.[28] Indeed, at first glance, the Iran hostage incident, the budget deficit, the rise in urban violence, and the trend toward corporate downsizing would seem to be unrelated events. Yet it is the ability to avoid crises wherever possible and to deal with them effectively when necessary that constitutes leadership. The Carter administration has been accused of aimless "drift," of reacting to individual crises without any overall vision.[29] Were America's problems simply a result of poor leadership? By avoiding Jimmy Carter's errors, might Teddy Kennedy or Gerald Ford have been able to keep America on a steadier course?

Many would doubt that the problems of the United States were due to chance or to the errors of a single man. Indeed, the continuation of America's fiscal and balance of payments problems during the presidency of Ronald Reagan suggest that the problem was something more basic. Citing historical evidence since the Middle Ages of causality running from economic to military power, the historian Paul Kennedy suggested that there was a deeper cause for the decline of American might. The foreign policy difficulties of the United States, he argued, were due to "imperial overstretch."[30] In the 1980s, America's global military obligations had not changed in a quarter-century, despite a decline in the country's share of world GNP and manufacturing production.[31]

Kennedy's analysis is in effect, a life-cycle model. Like previous models of this type proposed by Spengler, Toynbee and, more recently, Olson, it suggests that a country resembles a living organism, going through phases of growth, maturity, and decline.[32] The American state had had its day; it was time for power to be transferred to its more dynamic successors. If this approach is correct, then changes in countries' fortunes should be uncorrelated. At any given moment, states will be in various phases of their life cycles. Those in the early stages of their cycle will be expanding, while those at a later phase will be contracting. Overextension will characterize states in the final stages of the cycle, when the costs of holding earlier territorial acquisitions outstrip a society's declining economic resources.

Do individual states go through such independent life-cycles? Perhaps, but they seem to do so within a broader pattern. In the seventeenth century, for example, the global expansions of the Netherlands, France, and England were correlated. Similarly, the imperialist wave of the second half of the nineteenth century touched almost all of the major European powers simultaneously. In the middle decades of this century, the expansions of the spheres of influence of the three superpowers – the Soviet Union, the USA, and China – were similarly timed. Recent declines in their external prestige and internal cohesion also seem to be more than coincidental.

The fortunes of individual countries would appear to be decided, at least in part, by an underlying current that determines whether at any one time the size of the representative state is increasing or decreasing. At any particular moment, the surface available for settlement on each continent is more or less fixed. Therefore, during a period in which the *representative* state is growing, there must be some states in decline. In this way, one may explain the historical examples of fall from dominance studied by Kennedy up to the mid-twentieth century. From the end of the Middle Ages until the middle of the twentieth century, the current of change would appear to have been flowing in the direction of larger states.

Yet the declines of Spain, France, or Britain in earlier periods are intrinsically different from the current tendencies toward the breakdown of centralized power in the United States, the Soviet Union and, despite short-term reversals, the People's Republic of China. At present, there is no larger country that threatens to take the place of these declining imperial powers. Indeed, the current situation is somewhat similar to that of the Roman and Han empires in the third century AD in that the largest states are threatened with decomposition.

Even this parallel is incomplete. The transition to less centralized political units over the first few centuries of the Christian era was accompanied by increasing militarization and rising tax levels. However, the tendency since the beginning of the 1970s has been (with the exception of the Reagan administration in the US) toward *declines* in defense spending and great pressure to lower tax levels. At the same time, the web of social policy has begun to unravel, and corporate production units have been breaking into smaller and smaller elements. In effect, the most recent trends point toward an increasingly atomistic society. To understand them, one must examine why, despite growing average wealth, tax receipts have stopped rising relative to income.

Taxes and the Corporation

What have tax receipts to do with the decline of states? In a recent study, Margaret Levi proposed the hypothesis that, "the history of state revenue production is the history of the evolution of the state."[33] She attempted to verify this affirmation with a detailed study of four historical examples: Republican Rome, late medieval England and France, eighteenth-century Britain, and twentieth-century Australia. In each case, the essential question was the extent to which a ruler could extract tax revenue from his country's population. The evidence she presented supports the view that the state is an organization designed to maximize the fiscal revenues of a ruling individual or group. The organization's success depends on its ability to extract tax receipts without destroying its sources of income.

The remarkable economic and military expansion of the United States during the second century of its existence was based in large part on the efficiency of an American innovation – the corporation. Indeed, to explain the rise and recent decline of US power, one need only link Levi's model of the state as a tax-fueled engine to Chandler's vision of the corporation as source of organizational efficiency gains. Over the first half of the twentieth century, as the American corporation became the world economy's major creator of new ideas for raising productivity, it could be taxed increasingly heavily without threatening its ability to compete. The crumbling of American power in the 1970s coincided with a crisis in this same organization. Were the macro-developments at the level of the society related to the micro-developments in the health of the corporation, and if so how?

In the 1970s, as nominal rates of interest rose with inflation, corporations were able to use increasing interest deductions to reduce their taxable income. For given corporate profit tax rates, then, receipts from business taxes fell relative to US total income. To some extent, these revenue losses would be offset by higher taxes paid by those who received interest payments. Increasingly, however, US debt came to be held by non-residents who paid a withholding tax rate that was lower than the corporate rate. Moreover, to the extent that debt-holders themselves were taxed on nominal rather than real interest rates, saving was discouraged. By the end of the 1970s, there were irresistible pressures to lower the top personal income tax rates in order to avoid this problem.

Another development in the 1970s further weakened the capacity of

American governments to levy taxes on holders of capital. Under the US fiscal system, the income earned by equity capital is taxed twice: once by corporate profits taxes; then, if it is distributed as dividends to shareholders, through taxes on personal income. Alternatively, if after-tax earnings are retained by the firm, its shareholders will pay capital gains taxes on the increased value of their shares. In the late 1970s, American corporations began massive repurchases of their own stock. Increasingly, they financed themselves by borrowing rather than by raising risk capital. Since interest payments by corporations are tax-deductible, the resulting increase in corporate debt relative to equity constituted an additional weakening in the taxation of holders of capital.

There are many different ways to measure debt–equity ratios.[34] When tangible assets are valued at their replacement cost, corporate debt equity ratios remain relatively constant over time. However, it is more likely that corporations base their dividend policies on the book value of their net worth than on asset replacement cost: a sudden rise in the cost of replacing a firm's plant and equipment is unlikely to result in a more generous dividend. If equity is measured by book value, there is a substantial rise over time in the overall corporate debt–equity ratio, which changed from 0.98 in 1966 to 1.53 in 1980.[35]

Congress and state legislatures could have compensated for this revenue loss by increasing tax rates, by changing allowable deductions, or by finding alternative ways of taxing capital. Instead, a federal tax-cut bill passed in 1978 raised the amount of capital gains that could be sheltered from income taxes. At the same time, the federal corporate income tax rate was cut from 48 percent to 46 percent. Taxation was nevertheless a major issue in the 1980 election, Reagan promising to further cut taxes if elected. The late 1970s also saw the beginning of intense competition among states and municipalities to attract foreign investors. Far from raising their rates of taxation on corporations, lower levels of government in the United States were actually subsidizing new business investments. If the American state was in difficulty in the late 1970s, it was because the principal source of its revenue growth – the corporation – was in the midst of a crisis.

The Miniaturization Revolution

The origin of the drama lies in a change in the way of making one of the simplest of devices – a switch. Everyone is familiar with the way in which a household electrical switch may be used for turning a light on or off. What may not be quite so obvious is that such a device can also store information. Suppose that when the switch is off, it is assigned the value zero and when it is on, the value one. Then to learn what information is stored, all that is required is to check the status of the device.

Since any number may be written as a sequence of zeros or ones – that is, in binary form – with enough switches it is possible in this way to record any numerical information. Moreover, if one has a code for translating the letters of the alphabet into zeros and ones, one can use a series of switches to record a word, a sentence or even an encyclopedia. In fact, any information – from an image in color to the sound of a piano key – may be broken down into a sequence of zeros and ones and recorded. This form of data, broken up into separate numerical units, is known as digital information. The application of switches is not limited to storage. They may also be used to perform calculations and logical operations.

Household electrical switches are sufficiently slow and expensive that few people would prefer using them to even the most cumbersome forms of writing, such as the cuneiform script developed by the Sumerians. However, if it were possible to increase the speed and reduce the cost of switches sufficiently, at some point people would begin to prefer digital to manual calculation and digital information storage to writing or printing.

The problem was to find a fast, low-cost switch. The first commercial computers produced in the 1950s used vacuum tubes; however, these devices were slow, expensive and unreliable. In terms of conduction of electricity, there are substances called semiconductors that are halfway between conductors and insulators. Examples of such compounds are gallium arsenide and aluminum phosphide. They can be made to conduct either very little – a state assigned the value zero – or very greatly – a state assigned the value one. Packaged into an electronic component called a transistor, semiconductors thus made possible switches that were faster and cheaper than mechanical or vacuum-tube devices.

It was in the 1950s that the crucial development occurred. The transistor had been invented at Bell Labs in 1948. The home town of one of its three inventors, William Shockley, was in Palo Alto, California. In 1955, he returned to this town in the Santa Clara valley south of San Francisco to establish his own firm.[36] Then in 1957, eight of his senior employees left his company in turn to found a new firm, Fairchild Semiconductor. In 1959, a technological breakthrough at Fairchild and another American firm, Texas Instruments, permitted many semiconductor switches to be imprinted on a tiny chip measuring four millimeters square.[37] The new device became known as the *integrated circuit*. The chip itself was made of silicon, the principal ingredient in ordinary beach sand. By 1969, there were no fewer than 25 semiconductor firms in the Santa Clara area, which became known as Silicon Valley.

The integrated circuit made possible a new generation of large computers, typified by IBM's 360 series, launched in 1964. Six models of computers, differing primarily in memory capacity, were all able to share the same programmed instructions (software). Whereas the two preceding generations of data processors had been based on vacuum tubes and individual transistors respectively, with magnetic cores for memories, the third generation was based on integrated circuits.[38] The new computers were faster, more dependable and less expensive than their predecessors.

Solid-state technology also permitted a new type of data processor, smaller, less expensive, tougher, and able to function under a wider range of temperature and humidity levels than the mainframes produced by IBM. Digital Equipment Corporation launched the first of these minicomputers in 1960.[39] By the late 1960s, the company's success with this product and its successors had attracted other entrants into what had become the fastest-growing sector of the computer industry. Another development made possible by the integrated circuit was use of the remote terminal. Users at some distance from the computer could contact it directly rather than sending information to be centrally processed; that is, they could do their computing "on-line." Input and output were handled by a cathode ray tube linked to a keyboard.

Initially, integrated circuits were expensive; moreover, the rigidity of their design meant that each was able to do only a very specialized task. The heart of a large computer is its central processing unit, which performs all calculations and logical operations, in addition to controlling other functions such as storage, input, and output. In the case of IBM mainframes, this unit required hundreds or thousands of individual chips, each designed to perform a particular function.

In 1971, Marcian "Ted" Hoff, an engineer at a small semiconductor firm named Intel, designed a single chip that contained the entire central processing unit of a simple computer. At first, these microprocessor chips were used to run watches and calculators. It was not long, however, before the first microcomputer built around an Intel microprocessor chip was put on the market: the 1975 Altair sold in kit form for under $500. In 1977, Steven Jobs and Steven Wozniak formed a new company, Apple Corporation, to produce Apple II microcomputers.[40]

The Decentralization of Decision-making

The introduction of the first commercial computers in the 1950s had favored large firms. Companies big enough to be able to absorb the overhead expense of setting up a data-processing system could greatly reduce the cost of acquiring financial information about each of their divisions. Computers also lowered the expense of paying suppliers and employees and keeping track of sales. Initially, the computer also served to centralize decision-making. Data would be compiled on sheets within each subunit of the corporation and then be sent to the central mainframe for processing in batches. Operating at head office, close to the top of the firm's organization chart, the computer service department would have direct access to senior management. Central managers would therefore remain well-informed about the firm's recent activities, and allocate resources on the basis of very recent performance data.[41]

With the third generation of computers based on integrated circuits, the trend toward centralization slowed. After 1965, increased use of the remote terminal served to offset this centripetal tendency. Departments located at some distance from the computer, but linked to it by telephone or cable, could now have access to its services directly without having to send information to a central site to be processed.

As low-cost minicomputers came into wide use in the 1970s, decentralization could be carried a step further. The individual branch or department could now do its own data processing without passing through a central facility. Since the minicomputer was able to function in the harsh environment of the laboratory or factory, it was possible to lower sharply the cost of producing the first model of a new product. The optimal scale of production therefore declined.

The minicomputer also had an effect on middle management. Standardized programs made redundant whole layers of personnel previously responsible for filtering information on its way from top to bottom in the organizational hierarchy. Thus decentralized decision-making became possible. Indeed, it became essential. If large firms were to continue to compete successfully against smaller rivals they would be required to devolve the powers of central management to subordinate levels – the hierarchy would have to be flattened.

Did Decentralization Require Downsizing?

In the United States, decentralization took the form of downsizing the corporation. By the late 1970s a trend toward smaller firms was under way. Employees were laid off, plants were closed or consolidated, and divisions were spun off as separate corporate units. Was this downsizing a sign of success in the adaptation of the firm to new technologies? If so, it should have been accompanied by vigorous growth of the corporate sector as a whole. Although each firm had fewer employees, an even more rapid increase in the number of firms would have indicated that downsizing was simply a response to a decrease in the optimal scale of the firm.

Overall statistics for US manufacturing show that this was not the case. From 1977 to 1986, the number of firms increased just enough to offset the decline in the number of employees per firm. Overall manufacturing employment changed very little over the decade. Another indication is provided by security issues. During its century of rapid expansion, the American corporation had acquired risk capital by emitting stock, most of it through stock exchanges. The volume of net equity issues therefore provides a measure of the state of health of the corporate sector. In 1978, American corporations began to be net purchasers of their own stock. The principal explanation would appear to be the low market evaluation of the prospects. With shares selling for well under the replacement value of the underlying assets, firms could increase per-share profits by stock repurchases. This process accelerated during the 1980s.

Direct investment statistics support this evidence of weakness in the US corporate sector. If US firms had been those most successful in absorbing the new technologies, their direct investments in the rest of the world should have continued to rise rapidly. Instead, throughout the 1970s, US direct investment abroad stagnated. Since American firms tended to reinvest most of their foreign earnings overseas, US assets abroad kept pace with GNP. However, the phase of global expansion of the American corporation was over. Beginning in 1981, the overseas assets of US firms actually began to fall relative to the country's GNP.

During this same period, foreign investments in the United States started to rise sharply as a proportion of US GNP. Had foreign firms managed to downsize more effectively? The evidence from Japan reveals that firms in that country firms were able to decentralize without losing the advantages of large scale. Many of the largest Japanese corporations are in effect alliances of hundreds of individual firms. Hitachi Ltd comprises some 600 companies, of which 27 have issued their own publicly trade shares. Matsushita Electric Industrial Co. is made up of 161 consolidated corporations.[42]

Rather than an optimal response to a new technology, the observed downsizing seems to have been an indication of weakness on the part of US firms. Unable to decentralize effectively, they had little choice but to break up if they were to survive. American business practices with their emphasis on the individual entrepreneur and a rigid hierarchy of power were inappropriate for a period in which decisions were becoming so complex that a collective approach, with contributions from many areas of expertise, was essential.

Downsizing and specialization had obvious advantages in bringing decision-makers closer to the production level. But they also had disadvantages. The pool of experienced workers and managers that could be drawn on for new projects without the start-up cost of hiring someone from outside shrank. Complementarities that cut across industry boundaries were much more difficult to achieve. For example, no American firm has successfully integrated computers and telecommunications or aircraft and automobiles. The capacity to finance long-term industrial research also diminishes with the scale of the organization.

As the firm's size shrinks, survival increasingly becomes a gamble rather than a controlled risk. If managers happen to choose correctly, their companies can become extraordinarily successful – for a time, at least. However, when their choices are inappropriate, their firms' very existence can be threatened. In 1979, the third year of Jimmy Carter's mandate, the number-three American car-maker was on the verge of bankruptcy. At the beginning of the 1970s, Chrysler had held 16.1 percent of the US automobile market, but by 1979, its share had fallen to only 9.6 percent.[43] One of the company's problems was its failure to produce enough fuel-efficient cars in the period following the energy crisis of 1973–4. Moreover, its entire product line was plagued with quality defects.

Chrysler's reaction to its problems was to downsize. Unable to meet government fuel-economy standards, the firm dropped its line of trucks in 1976.[44] In 1978, Chrysler sold its subsidiaries outside North America in order to raise capital for investments at home. It then left the leasing business, where it had been losing money. When gasoline shortages in the US began in the spring of 1979, following a fall in Iran's oil production, the company's sales of large cars plummeted. Two years previously, Chrysler had launched its own front-wheel-drive small cars, the Omni and Horizon. The new models were selling well, but the company could not meet the demand. The firm had unwisely decided not to produce its own motors for the small cars. Under an agreement signed with Volkswagenwerk AG, Chrysler was limited to a supply of 300,000 engines a year .[45]

By the summer of 1979, Chrysler's inventories of unsold cars had climbed to a level equivalent to a half-year of sales. In September of that year, Chrysler's chief executive officer, John Riccardo, resigned, turning power over to former Ford president Lee A. Iacocca. For the first nine months of 1979, Chrysler was in the red to the tune of $722 million – more money than any American firm had lost previously. Desperately short of cash, it turned to Congress for a loan guarantee of $1.5 billion.

THE RISING SUN

While Chrysler was downsizing, one of its competitors was upsizing. In that same month of September 1979, a motorcycle plant began production in Marysville, Ohio. It turned out an 1100 cc motorcycle that was soon being exported to 24 countries in Europe and other parts of the world.[46]

However, this was not an American success story: the new plant belonged to a Japanese firm, Honda Motor, and represented the first manufacturing investment by the Japanese motor-vehicle industry in the United States. In December 1979, Honda executives took the further decision to build a car plant on a site adjacent to the motorcycle facilities at Marysville. The new factory would produce the phenomenally successful compact Accord model using American labor.

Many reasons have been offered for the success of Japanese corporations. It has been suggested that their industrial performance has been due to the government's policy of protecting the domestic market from imports of consumption goods.[47] Protection, it might be thought, allows local producers to attain the scale economies necessary for low-cost exporting to the rest of the world. However, other large developing countries such as India and Brazil have carried out similar policies of trade restriction with meager results. In the case of Honda, isolation from world competition probably delayed the firm's development. It was only when co-founder Soichiro Honda traveled to Europe in 1954 that he discovered German and Italian motorcycles that were three times more powerful than his own with the same displacement.[48]

Another explanation offered for Japan's success is its government's industrial strategy emphasizing centralized coordination of the development of new technologies.[49] In practice, state intervention has probably hindered the growth of the private sector. In the early 1960s, for example, the Ministry of International Trade and Industry (MITI) tried to prevent new firms from coming into the Japanese automobile industry, fearing that excessive competition would hurt the country's chance of overtaking the American major producers.[50] Had this policy been successful, it would have prevented one of the most striking examples of successful entry into an established industry – that of Honda Motor, a motorcycle producer, into the car industry.

Japanese firms, it has been said, have increased their shares of world markets on the basis of borrowed, copied, or stolen technology.[51] There are documented cases of copying of American know-how by Japanese producers.[52] However, while stolen technology may help explain the sales growth of some Japanese firms in their own domestic market, it cannot explain the country's success in foreign markets, such as the United States or Europe, where patent rights are generally vigorously enforced. Japan's first successful penetration in foreign motor-vehicle markets – the Honda Super Cub motorbike – was based on a light-weight 50 cc engine that put out a remarkable 4.5 horsepower and was developed entirely by Honda's engineers. Similarly, in 1971 Honda developed a fuel-efficient low-pollution automobile engine, the CVCC. The Japanese motor was the first to meet the US emission control standards for 1975.[53] Nor was Honda an exception. Since the 1970s, Japan has spent a higher proportion of its GNP on non-military research and development than the United States.[54]

Production as Information Transformation

If it was not by protecting their home market, by coordinating industrial strategy, or by copying foreign technology that Japanese firms bettered their foreign rivals, how did they succeed and why? A possible answer lies in their nation's response to humiliation. After opening their market partially to trade under threat of blockade from US Admiral Perry's "black ships" in 1853, the Japanese resolved to acquire western technology. Brenner has suggested that a fall in the relative income of an individual or a group will lead to increased effort to regain the lost status.[55] Throughout the century that followed the restoration of the Meiji emperor in 1868, the Japanese were determined to overtake the West.[56] To catch up in a race, one who starts later must run faster than those in the lead. It is in part this situation of the successful overtaker that explains the performance of Japan.

With their defeat in the Second World War, the Japanese suffered an additional humiliation. Their efforts were then redoubled: to avoid such a situation in the future, they must build an economy that was stronger than that of any potential rival. During the next two decades, therefore, the pace of change in the country accelerated, as the need for reconstruction was added to the longer-term goal of catching up. It was during the first decade and a half after the Second World War that something dramatic occurred. In the process of transforming their economy, Japanese companies developed a new form of organization devoted to rapid change. When the miniaturization revolution began in the 1960s, these new-style firms were the ones best placed to take advantage of it.

There were historical precedents for such institutional transformation while catching up. In latter decades of the nineteenth century, Germany and the United States both strove to overtake the industrial leader, Britain. In each country, technological institutes were set up to train engineers for applied research. Leading firms in the two nations also established industrial research labs.[57] In doing so, both countries were setting up specialized institutions designed to change the information used in the production process.

Traditionally, economists have viewed production as the combination of capital, labor, and raw materials using a given recipe or technology. This approach is justified when technology is constant or changes only occasionally and by small, discrete jumps. Until the mid-twentieth century, observers could perhaps be excused for assuming that at any time the amount of information was fixed. Such a theoretical approach was in keeping with the discontinuous way in which research was applied to production.

What happens, however, when the recipe itself is constantly changing? The integrated circuit was invented in 1959. Five years later, Gordon E. Moore, an engineer at Fairchild Semiconductor noted that the complexity of an electronic chip, as measured by the number of components it contained, tended to double every year. The costs of integrated circuits have consequently steadily decreased – by approximately 30 percent a year since 1973.[58] Because each circuit element of a chip can contain one bit of data – in the form of a zero or a one – the result has been a steady fall in the cost of storing information.

A redefinition of the concept of production becomes necessary. An alternative to the fixed-recipe approach is to view information – that is, the recipe itself – as a variable input in the production process. Data about consumer tastes, about the technical characteristics of different materials and processes, about the skills of individual workers are gathered together. They are then transformed in combination with raw materials and with the participation of effort from machines and workers. The result is more information – a computer program, a film, a story, a song, new instructions for making, using and repairing – and sometimes a physical object (a good) or a change in an object (a service). Production then converts information, objects, and services into other information, objects, and services. The point made here is different from the more familiar observation that information production is itself becoming an important activity that may be distinguished from other productive efforts.[59] Rather, it is that information transformation is increasingly becoming inseparable from other activities.

As production becomes increasingly a question of information transformation, decision-making becomes more complex. The skills of many specialists – engineers, computer programmers, accountants, advertising copy people, and market researchers – are required to convert today's knowledge into the information one wishes to have tomorrow. Another implication is that change will occur faster. When information storage is expensive, a new recipe will be embodied in hand-drawn designs, skilled craftsmen, and specifically conceived equipment. It may take many years to design and test the plans for a new product such as a car engine. However, if designs are conceived and verified, and equipment retooled simply by modifications to the code in a computer's memory, change can occur extremely rapidly.

It is this revolution in information handling that explains the crisis in the American corporation in the 1970s. The M-form (multidivisional) firm, with its centralized research staff and separate line divisions for production was well-suited to the pattern of innovation of the first three-quarters of the twentieth century. At a typical moment goods would be being produced according to a uniform design, with a volume high enough to permit scale economies unattainable by competing firms in other countries. From time to time, the research staff would develop a new product or process. The production process would then be punctuated by a brief period of change before settling back into a new routine. Once the technology for a given product had become standardized, it could be exported, first to other industrialized countries and eventually to the world's low-wage regions.

As the complexity of production and the rate of change increased in the 1970s, this form of organization became increasingly inadequate. Those responsible for introducing new information were too far removed from those who were doing the actual production to be able to intervene quickly and effectively. To reduce the distance between thinkers and doers – that is to decentralize decision-making – many American firms had no choice but to break up. Multi-product conglomerates went back to basics, selling off unprofitable divisions. American industry on the whole entered upon a period of retrenchment, with a slowdown in productivity growth and employment.

The L-form Corporation

Meanwhile, the form of organization developed by the Japanese to rebuild their economy with technology borrowed from the West proved to be ideally suited to the accelerated pace of change and the increased complexity of decisions of the miniaturization revolution. To catch up, Japanese managers converted their entire organization into what might be called a lattice, a network in which information was generated, distributed, and stored. There are four essential components of the L-form (lattice) corporation: goals, incentives, feedback, and participation.

Although the M-form firm generally had an implicit objective – for example, maximizing per-share profits – it was rarely explicit and seldom one with which all members of the organization could identify. Workers, for example, would be unlikely to be strongly motivated to raise the profits available for shareholder dividends. In contrast, managers of the L-form firm fixed an objective that was generally accepted by all workers. In 1954, for example, Honda Motor set as its goal the winning of the Tourist Trophy race for motorcycles held each year on the Isle of Man. To the firm's workers, most of whom were young, such a goal was highly appealing. In its first year of European competition, 1959, the company placed sixth, seventh and eighth in the 125 cc class, and won the manufacturing team prize. Two years later, the firm took the first five positions in both the 125 cc and the 250 cc classes.[60]

The organization also requires a system of incentives to motivate individuals to work toward the common goal. Each member of the firm must feel that his individual contribution is valued. In the M-form corporation, the worker was traditionally paid his wage based on the number of hours he had worked. He could be fired or laid off with little notice. In contrast, in the largest Japanese corporations, there is for most workers an implicit guarantee of lifetime employment. Thus they are confident that they will receive part of the long-term gains from their own efforts. Their short-term collective efforts are also rewarded. Although hourly rates are low, particularly for young workers, Japanese firms distribute a substantial share of their profits in the form of bonuses to their employees. In 1979, the average annual bonuses for white-collar university graduates employed in manufacturing amounted to over five months of salary. Bonuses to blue-collar workers in the transport equipment industry were over three months of salary.[61]

Feedback about the extent to which the firm's objectives are being met is also an essential element of the L-form corporation. Under the multi-divisional form, managers often tend to let problems accumulate until they become crises. For example, inventories of parts, goods in process or unsold output impose a cost to the corporation. As in the case of Chrysler in 1979, excessive inventories are in effect an error message, to be avoided if possible. Starting with Toyota in the 1930s, Japanese firms were the first to develop the "just-in-time" system of manufacturing, whereby stocks of parts and goods in process are minimized by precise scheduling of production.[62]

Japanese companies also pay great attention to the quality of their product, taking corrective measures when necessary to avoid defects. Rather than rely on specialized monitoring staff, the firm expects each worker to be his own quality inspector. During the first days of assembly of Honda dirt-bikes in Ohio, a worker neglected to put a check mark on the fuel cocks indicating that a rubber sealant ring had been properly installed. An engineer from Japan who spotted this lapse in company methods had the worker take apart 75 motorcycles to verify the sealant ring. No defect was found, but the message was effectively transmitted. Only when the quality of these dirt bikes was satisfactory did Honda allow assembly of its deluxe touring motorcycle to begin.[63]

Training of workers to make sure that they keep abreast of the constantly evolving technology is another type of feedback loop within the L-type corporation. In preparing for motorcycle production in Ohio, Honda assigned five Japanese engineers to supervise 16 American workers. The new employees spent two weeks just to learn the proper use of tools. For a further two weeks they assembled and disassembled ten motorcycles each day. Only then were they given specific job assignments. Cross-training of this type permitted every worker to be able to perform the jobs of each of his co-workers. Many of the American employees were subsequently flown to Japan for further training in welding, painting, and assembly.[64]

The final aspect of the alternative organizational form is participation. The traditional corporation is organized as a layered pyramid. Within the pyramid, it has been suggested, there is an invisible boundary separating those who make decisions from those who execute them.[65] Above the line are white-collar staff who are required to apply discretion in their work within the limits of established rules and to communicate in written form, as typified in Weber's model of bureaucracy. Below the line are those who perform specialized, manual, repetitive tasks in accord with the principals of the American management engineer F.W. Taylor. Essentially, management contributes virtually all informational input within a rigid hierarchical structure, whereas labor provides only physical services with minimal informational content.

The L-form corporation modifies this participation structure in a number of ways, flattening the organizational pyramid, and multiplying the possible channels of communication. In part, the leveling is symbolic, involving managers' wearing company uniforms and eating with workers in the firm's cafeteria. However, the changes also involve questions of substance. Employees in Japanese manufacturing plants originated the idea of quality circles to discuss ways of improving production and working conditions. Roughly half of all Japan's manufacturing workers are involved in such groups.[66] Employees are also encouraged individually to make suggestions for improving productivity. In 1981, for example, 300,000 suggestions were made by Honda workers, some 90 percent being accepted.[67]

In the traditional M-form corporation, communication lines tend to be vertical, with orders coming from above and the response from below. As a result, horizontal dialogue between individuals at the same level and diagonal interaction between levels and across divisions is effectively stifled. Japanese firms have developed novel ways of opening these other communication channels. Honda, for example, has created nodes of communication throughout the corporate lattice with its expert system, formally instituted in 1968. Staff and line workers are classified into four levels according to their expertise, with no limit being placed on the total number of experts.[68] When a new plant is being considered, or when non-routine production problems arise, the firm can call on these experts to come up with a solution outside the formal corporate structure.

Communication within the organization is not achieved without cost. In

1972, Sony opened a plant in San Diego, California, to assembly its new Trinitron television sets for the US market. American managers, used to taking decisions on their own, found that they had to participate in what seemed like endless meetings. Discussions continued until a consensus was reached, the Japanese participants being anxious to avoid confrontations in which someone would lose face. Yet the advantages of this approach are considerable. All those who are affected by a decision share the same information and understand why the decision is taken. As a result, implementation can proceed swiftly with a minimum of resistance.[69] With improved communication between management and workers, there is less need for a formal organization to serve as an intermediary. Accordingly, American unions have generally been frustrated in their attempt to unionize the US plants of Japanese firms.

The flattening of the organization chart to encourage participation is particularly important in research, where layers of bureaucracy in a large M-form corporation serve to stifle originality. In applied research and development, Japanese firms were pioneers, developing methods of producing new ideas quickly. For example, in 1960, Honda set up an autonomous research and development center outside of the corporate structure.[70] Engineers in the Honda R & D Co. Ltd. could propose their own research themes, working alone subject to adequate supervision. Alternatively, groups were formed as required to work on specific problems. Within these groups, more than one possible approach was taken, so that alternative results could be compared and the most appropriate method chosen.

A final means of simplifying command structures is by substituting market decisions for those taken within a hierarchy. Japanese firms tend to do considerably more subcontracting than their American counterparts. In 1975, purchased parts represented 73 percent of total component costs in the Japanese automobile industry, compared with under 60 percent in the US.[71]

The Shoot-out

The first major engagements between the alternative forms of organization in technology-intensive industries occurred in the 1970s. Initial skirmishes in the production of black and white television sets had ended in favor of the Japanese producers. To compete, US firms moved their production abroad: by 1972, imports accounted for 62 percent of monochrome television sets sold in the US.[72] The fighting then moved on to color models. In 1966, the American firm, Motorola, had been the first to build a prototype solid-state color television set – one in which all vacuum tubes except the picture tube had been replaced by integrated circuits. However, three years later, it was not Motorola but the Japanese firm, Hitachi, that had launched the first commercial solid-state color television sets. Between 1970 and 1976, the Japanese share of the US color-television market climbed from 17 percent to 45 percent.[73] Unable to compete profitably with the Japanese, Motorola sold its television division in 1974 to Matsushita, producer of electronic products bearing the Panasonic label.[74]

Then in the mid-1970s, the American automobile industry became the target of the Japanese attack. As the decade started, this was the most important industrial sector in the US. In 1970, motor vehicles and parts producers accounted for 5 percent of all manufacturing jobs. American firms with their foreign subsidiaries dominated the world automobile market. They had beaten back the attacks of European producers by putting out their own fuel-efficient small cars. Between 1970 and 1976, the fall in the value of the US dollar measured in foreign currencies would allow Detroit to keep its share of the home market despite the oil crisis of 1973–4.[75]

During the subsequent period from 1976 to 1980, however, Detroit's dominant position collapsed, the import share doubling from 14.7 to 28.2 percent of total US new-car registrations.[76] By the decade's end, Japan alone accounted for 80 percent of these imports. With domestic automobile production 25 percent below its trend, US producers were beginning to hurt. The bloodletting would continue until 1981, when the Japanese auto manufacturers, faced with the threat of quota legislation in the US Congress, agreed to "voluntary" export restrictions to the United States.

Although seven different Japanese firms were exporting over a dozen car designs to the United States by the beginning of the Carter presidency, one model more than any other symbolized the threat to American industry. In the summer of 1976, Honda released the Accord on the US market. With its advanced aluminum sideways-mounted engine, five-speed transmission, front-wheel drive, independent suspension, disc brakes, and radial tires, the new model was technically far in advance of any American small car.[77] It also embodied electronic refinements such as a dashboard warning panel for unlatched doors and warning lights for low fuel, and indicators for tire rotation and oil change.[78]

For the American consumer, the choice between the caretakingly designed and assembled Honda Accord and trouble-prone domestic cars, such as the Volare and Aspen offered by Chrysler, was clear. For the American big three, the implications were also obvious. Immediately the various divisions of domestic car manufacturers bought up virtually all the available Accords in the Detroit area.[79] Fourteen years later, however, they had still not come up with a successful copy of this model.

A Japanese Empire?

The dust jacket of Paul Kennedy's book, *The Rise and Fall of the Great Powers*, shows two men stepping down from a structure supported by a globe, one carrying a British flag and the other an American flag. A third figure carrying a Japanese flag scrambles to take their place at the top. Will the successive British and American empires be followed by a period of Japanese hegemony, as the image suggests? An age of Japanese military dominance seems unlikely. Unique among history's pretenders to a position of world dominance, Japan, under its US-imposed constitution, has virtually no offensive military capacity. Nevertheless, it might be argued that the absence of a strike force is actually an advantage, since it permits almost all the country's resources to be directed toward increasing its economic power.

Yet to predict an economic empire of the rising sun – in the sense of a small number of people in a few giant Japanese interlocked corporations (*zaibatsus*) making decisions that determine the activities of millions of people around the world – is to misunderstand the nature of integrated-circuit technology. Most importantly, the new techniques do not favor bigness. The optimal scale of the lattice-type corporation based on information transformation is smaller than that of the multidivisional-type corporation devoted to mass production of goods with a standard technology. In the United States, industrialization was accompanied by increasing concentration. As the Japanese economy has grown, however, concentration in many sectors has decreased. For example, Sony and Honda, two firms that have had the most impact outside their own country, were new entrants that started outside the existing industrial power structure. In its respective industry, neither firm has achieved nor seems likely to achieve the dominance that General Motors, IBM or Boeing experienced prior to 1975. By adopting similar management systems, previously established Japanese corporations such as Toyota or Matsushita and later entrants have prevented these innovators from capturing a commanding market share.

Since the minimum optimum scale of firm has fallen, it has become easier for companies outside the leading country to compete effectively. By using management methods similar to those developed in Japan, European firms such as Volvo have been able to defend their places in export markets. Recently in the US, Ford, Motorola, and other firms have succeeded in raising their product quality while reducing unit labor requirements. Other US firms such as Dow and 3M have developed effective new procedures for decentralizing corporate decision-making and research. In East Asia, firms in countries such as South Korea, with wages lower than those of Japan, have been able to break into the automobile and consumer-electronics industries, challenging the Japanese abroad. Finally, Japan itself does not have the resources to achieve technological dominance in virtually all sectors, as the United States did in the 1950s. In communications technology, small and medium computers, chemicals, pharmaceutical products, and aviation, Japanese firms have failed to overtake their European or American counterparts.

In their postwar export drive, the strategy of Japanese corporations has been to keep prices low in order to generate volume and increase market share. Such a strategy, with its low profit margins, would be highly vulnerable to any tax increases on the part of the home government. However, without a domestic industrial base to provide a vast flow of tax revenues, Japan would be unable to convert its technological leadership into military dominance. If this argument holds for Japan, it also applies to each of the other blocs that constitute its potential rivals. In the 1980s, governments around the world were compelled to cut taxes and apply heavy doses of subsidies to keep their corporate sectors viable. Heavy taxation of capital – the essential element for military expansion – was certain to lead to economic decline. The implication is clear: the revolution launched by the introduction of the integrated circuit means the end of empire.

A UNIQUE OCCURRENCE

Between the middle and the end of the 1970s, signs of decline in the global power of the American state became evident to even the most myopic of observers. In Central America came the loss of sovereignty over the Panama Canal Zone and the victory of the Sandinistas in Nicaragua; in the Middle East, the overthrow of the Shah of Iran and the withdrawal of Israel from the Sinai; elsewhere in Asia, the Soviet invasion of Afghanistan and the collapse of the CENTO and SEATO alliances; in Africa, the support of Cuban troops for Marxist regimes opposed to US interests. This change in the status of a superpower was symbolized most vividly by the inability of the American administration to intervene effectively to assure the release of its own embassy personnel in Teheran, where they were held captive for 14 months.

Internally, the situation of the majority of American citizens began to deteriorate. Inflation and unemployment hit postwar highs. Mortgage rates skyrocketed. At the same time, the cities were hit by an ever-swelling wave of violent crime. As real wages of workers fell while profits and rents increased, the income gap between rich and poor began to widen. Another problem was that the country started to import more goods than it exported.

The US balance of payments slipped systematically into the red: for the first time in the century, America was borrowing abroad.

The decline in power abroad came after a decade of cutbacks in defense expenditures as a share of national income. With the switch to a volunteer army, an increasing share of what remained in the defense budget was eaten up by salaries. Equipment expenditures were trimmed to the bone, as the mechanical failures during the abortive attempt to free the Iran hostages illustrated. The Carter administration was also the first in a half-century to cut back in federal aid to states and local governments as a share of total income.

Although no single factor can explain all of these developments, many can be attributed to a slower growth in the total tax receipts of federal, state, and local governments that began around 1970. As spending require-ments continued to increase as rapidly as before, large budget deficits became inevitable. Indeed the process of deterioration accelerated, as each year's deficits added to the cost of debt servicing. The Carter administration was the first since the Second World War not to be able to generate a single year's budget surplus.

The slowdown in tax growth was due in large part to a fall in corporate tax receipts as a share of the country's total income. Although, technically, rising corporate interest deductions explain most of this revenue shortfall, the question of why governments did not seek ways to make firms pay more taxes remains. Based on available evidence, the most plausible answer is that the American corporation itself was going through a crisis. Overall manufacturing employment in the United States ceased to grow in the decade after 1976. Small firms survived, but total employment in large firms – which employed two workers out of three – fell sharply. Additional taxation would have further endangered jobs that were already threatened by firm downsizing and by plant closings and consolidations.

Ironically, the American corporation was itself the creator of the shock that was threatening its very existence. In 1959, engineers at Intel and Texas Instruments had discovered a way of imprinting many electronic switches on a tiny piece of silicon. As the technology evolved, the capacity of these integrated circuits tended to double every year, driving down the cost of information manipulation, transmission, and storage. Increasingly, as integrated circuits were adopted throughout manufacturing industry, production became a matter of transforming information. Goods and ser-vices were the by-products of this transformation process.

Because of the US corporation's rigid channels of communication and its overly centralized power structure, decision-makers were too distant from actual production to intervene effectively in a transformation process that was continually changing. The trend to smaller size that became evident after 1970 is not a sign of successful absorption of the new processes. Rather it represents a survival reflex, necessary to avoid disaster. Unable to manage rapid change, firms sold off money-losing divisions in order to improve their profitability. In effect, they were achieving decentralization of decision-making through downsizing.

During the two decades after the Second World War, Japanese firms were struggling to catch up with their rivals in the country that had defeated them. In the process of overtaking they succeeded in developing a new form of corporate organization. The L-form (lattice) corporation was the result. Although on paper, its organization chart resembled that of an American firm, decisions were made in a radically different way. Instead of a hierarchy in which higher dominated lower and bigger smaller, Japanese firms moved toward consensus-type management. Those with expertise related to the issue at hand would share their information and collectively reach a solution.

There appears to be a maximum size beyond which this information sharing is no longer efficient. Thus the largest Japanese corporations remain considerably smaller than American firms of the preceding generation. Unable to dominate their industries, they are confronted with an unprecedented degree of competition both at home and abroad. To remain competitive, they must cut their profit margins on sales to a minimum, relying on large volume to generate the income to finance further productivity gains. To remain viable, their foreign competitors must follow suit.

These new technological conditions spell the end to empire – both economic and military. Individual firms are no longer able to dominate their industries on a global scale, as occurred during the decades of American pre-eminence. In addition, medium-sized firms lacking monopoly power in their industries and with strong foreign competition cannot afford to pay high levels of taxes. Nor can the mass of the industrialized countries' workers, increasingly exposed to competition from foreign labor that may be either cheaper or more productive. Yet without massive flows of fiscal revenues, military dominance of large territories is not possible.

Why had America's prestige and economic strength declined during the presidency of Jimmy Carter? Although few American voters realized it, the answer to Reagan's challenge in the televised debate of 1980 was right before their eyes. Almost all of the hundred million viewers were watching the candidates on television sets that incorporated the technology of the integrated circuit, invented by American firms two decades earlier. And most of these screens bore the labels of Japanese firms that had succeeded in developing a new type of organization, designed for the efficient transformation of information, and ideally suited to the new techniques.

For the first time in history, a dominant technology favorable both to smaller political units and to governments that intervened less in the lives of their citizens had been introduced. In the future, people would find themselves increasingly left to their own resources, dependent on what they could obtain for themselves by selling their services in the marketplace. It had taken two centuries, but Thomas Jefferson's vision of a society of atomistic competitors was finally beginning to be realized. For the power of the centralized state over the American people, it was not the end but only the beginning of the end.

NOTES

1 Business Week, August 7, 1989, p. 18.
2 Alfred D. Chandler, Jr, *The Visible Hand: The Managerial Revolution in American Business* (Belknap Press, 1977), pp. 105–6.
3 Ibid., p. 102.
4 Oliver Williamson, *Economic Organization: Firms, Markets and Policy Control* (Wheatsheaf, 1986), p. 151.
5 Alfred D. Chandler, Jr, *Strategy and Structure: Chapters in the History of the Industrial Enterprise* (MIT Press, 1962), pp. 295–7.
6 Williamson, *Economic Organization*, p. 159.
7 Ronnie Dugger, *On Reagan: The Man and his Presidency* (McGraw-Hill, 1983), p. 273.
8 *The Economist*, April 15, 1989, p. 43.
9 Joseph Conlin, *The American Past: A Survey of American History* (Harcourt, Brace, Jovanovich, 1984), p. 850.
10 William H. Forbis, *Fall of the Peacock Throne: The Story of Iran* (Harper and Row, 1980), pp. 3–9.
11 Hamilton Jordan, *Crisis: The Last Year of the Carter Presidency* (G.P. Putnam's Sons, 1982), p. 31.
12 Ibid., pp. 31–2.
13 Federal Bureau of Investigation, *Crime in the United States. Unified Crime Reports*, 1982, p. 43, table 2.
14 Ibid., 1976, p. 173, 1980, p. 191, and 1982, p. 167.
15 *Business Week*, August 7, 1989, p. 18.
16 Economic Report of the President, 1989, pp. 308, 402.
17 Ibid., pp. 308, 403.
18 Congressional Quarterly Inc., *Budgeting for America* (Washington, 1982), p. 127.
19 *Economic Report of the President*, 1989, pp. 308, 402.
20 Ibid.
21 Robert Eisner, *How Real is the Federal Deficit?* (The Free Press, 1986), pp. 29–30.
22 *Economic Report of the President*, 1989, pp. 308, 403.
23 Small Business Administration, *The State of Small Business*, 1984, p. 162.
24 Ibid., 1984, p. 162, and 1988, p. 62.
25 Paul Bennett, Anne de Melogue, and Andrew Silver, "Corporate debt-equity ratios," *Federal Reserve Bank of New York Quarterly Review*, 10 (1985), p. 46.
26 *Economic Report of the President*, 1989, pp. 308, 429.
27 Bennett Harrison and Barry Bluestone, *The Great U-Turn: Corporate Restructuring and the Polarizing of America* (Basic Books, 1988).
28 Jimmy Carter, *Keeping Faith: Memoires of a President* (Bantam, 1982), p. 7.
29 Conlin, *The American Past*, p. 849.
30 Paul Kennedy, *The Rise and Fall of the Great Powers* (Random House, 1987), p. 515.

31 Ibid., p. 521.
32 Oswald Spengler, *The Decline of the West* (Allen and Unwin, 1926); Arnold J. Toynbee, *A Study of History*, revised and abridged (Oxford University Press, 1972); Mancur Olson, *The Rise and Decline of Nations* (Yale University Press, 1982).
33 Margaret Levi, *Of Rule and Revenue* (University of California Press, 1988), p. 1.
34 See Bennett et al., "Corporate debt-equity ratios."
35 Small Business Administration, *The State of Small Business*, p. 225.
36 Ernest Braun and Stuart Macdonald, *Revolution in Miniature* (Cambridge University Press, 1978), p. 124.
37 Tom Forester, *The Story of the Information Technology Revolution* (MIT Press, 1987), p. 20.
38 Thomas H. Athey and Robert W. Zmud, *Introduction to Computers and Information Systems*, 2nd edn (Scott, Foresman and Co., 1988), pp. A-8, A-9.
39 Ibid., p. A-6.
40 Ibid., p. A-10.
41 Christopher Rowe, *People and Chips: The Human Implications of Information Technology* (Paradigm, 1986), p. 91.
42 *Business Week*, March 27, 1989, p. 94.
43 Paul Miesing, "The Chrysler Corporation Loan Guarantee Act of 1979," in *Organization Policy and Strategic Management: Text and Cases*, ed. James M. Higgins (The Dryden Press, 1983), p. 737.
44 Ibid., p. 746.
45 Ibid.
46 Tetsuo Sakiya, *Honda Motor: The Men, the Management, the Machines* (Kodansha International Ltd, Tokyo, 1982), p. 210.
47 Charles H. Ferguson, "America's high-tech decline," *Foreign Policy*, 74 (1989), p. 129.
48 Sakiya, *Honda Motor*, p. 111.
49 Ferguson, "America's high-tech decline," p. 129.
50 Sakiya, *Honda Motor*, pp. 136–7.
51 Ferguson, "America's high-tech decline," p. 129.
52 Clyde V. Prestowitz, *Trading Places: How We Allowed Japan to Take the Lead* (Basic Books, 1988), p. 84.
53 Sakiya, *Honda Motor*, p. 182.
54 *The Economist*, May 20, 1989, p. 91.
55 Reuven Brenner, *History – The Human Gamble* (University of Chicago Press, 1983).
56 Prestowitz, *Trading Places*, pp. 7–9.
57 D. S. L. Cardwell, *Technology, Science and History* (Heinemann, 1972), pp. 215–20.
58 Forester, *Information Technology Revolution*, p. 27.
59 Ernst Braun, *Wayward Technology* (Greenwood Press, 1984), p. 214.
60 Sakiya, *Honda Motor*, p. 115
61 Ibid., p. 194.
62 Susumu Watanabe, "Micro-electronics and employment in the Japanese automobile industry," World Employment Programme Research Working Paper, International Labour Office, Geneva, 1984, p. 7.
63 Robert L. Shook, *Honda: An American Success Story* (Prentice-Hall, 1988), pp. 114–15.
64 Ibid., pp. 48–9.
65 Rowe, *People and Chips*, p. 104.
66 Sakiya, *Honda Motor*, p. 208.
67 Ibid., p. 207.
68 Ibid., p. 177.
69 Nick Lyons, *The Sony Vision* (Crown Publishers, 1976), pp. 176–7.

70 Sakiya, *Honda Motor*, p. 170.
71 Watanabe, "Micro-electronics and employment," p. 6.
72 Prestowitz, *Trading Places*, p. 201.
73 Ibid.
74 Ibid., p. 202.
75 C. S. Chang, *The Japanese Auto Industry and the US Market* (Praeger, 1981), p. 204.
76 *World Motor Vehicle Data*, 1981 edition, p. 27.
77 Brock Yates, *The Decline and Fall of the American Automobile Industry* (Empire Books, 1983), pp. 37–8.
78 Ibid., p. 41.
79 Ibid., p. 42.

Conclusion

Historical change appears to have its origins in innovations that alter the optimal scale of organizations. By modifying the efficiency of either the state's military organization or its fiscal bureaucracy, new weapons and informational technologies change the optimal tax rate and territorial boundaries. Conflict among or within states then leads to new patterns of territorial boundaries and modifications in the degree of government intervention. There are four possible types of innovation – centralizing, liberalizing, feudalizing, and atomizing – each with a characteristic effect on state borders and tax levels. Overall, there has been a trend toward larger political units, accompanied by a cycle of expansion and contraction in the importance of the public sector within each state. At present, atomizing innovations in information technology are threatening the fiscal equilibrium and territorial integrity of the largest and most heterogeneous states.

East German Communist Party Secretary Erich Honecker predicted that it would last for a century.[1] The 3 m high wall, built of concrete blocks and topped by barbed wire, stretched for 45 km along the border separating East from West Berlin. Its construction had begun, unannounced by the East German government, over an August weekend in 1961. Designed to keep citizens of the German Democratic Republic from fleeing toward higher living standards and greater political freedom in the West, it had been quite successful: only a few thousand had managed to escape over the years since its completion. But by late September 1989, a way had been found to circumvent the barrier and its chain-link extensions along the boundary with West Germany. Weekly, thousands of East Germans were passing through the newly opened frontier between Hungary and Austria.

To stem the flow of refugees, the East Berlin regime stopped issuing visas for travel to Hungary. Thousands of East Germans desiring to emigrate then began to seek refuge in the West German embassy in Prague. In early October, special trains were organized to take them to the West. As the trains passed through Dresden, thousands of local residents battled with police in an attempt to get aboard. At the same time, regular Monday street demonstrations in favor of greater political freedom began in Leipzig, to the south-west of Berlin. Each week they attracted larger numbers of people.

Meanwhile, in other eastern European countries, events were also moving at a rapid pace. On June 4, the opposition Solidarity movement in Poland won all but one of the contested seats in parliamentary elections. In August, it went on to form the first non-communist government in Eastern Europe in four decades. On October 7, the Hungarian communist party, under reform leadership, voted to change its name to the Hungarian Socialist Party. It promised free elections. Elsewhere, however, in Czechoslovakia, Bulgaria, and Romania, where strong leaders showed no hesitation in using their police to crush dissent, the situation remained relatively calm.

In East Germany too, the crisis seemed to call for a display of power. Honecker argued with his fellow party leaders to order the police to use "all available force" to clear the streets.[2] But his colleagues, led by Egon Krenz, the *politburo* member responsible for youth and internal security, disagreed.[3] Instead, on October 18, they forced Honecker out of office, and Krenz took over as government leader. Nevertheless, the exodus through Czechoslovakia and Hungary continued, at rates that now reached 300 people an hour. Since the beginning of the year, East Germany had lost almost a quarter of a million people, most of them young and well-educated.[4] Despite the leadership change, the Monday demonstrations in Leipzig grew in size. On November 6, the protest attracted half a million marchers. Three days later, with the economy suffering from the disruptions, the authorities finally decided to compromise. Krenz promised that at some unspecified date in the future, free elections would be held. A spokesman for the government also announced that beginning the following day, East Germans would be free to cross into West Germany without special permission, at any time and for as long as they chose.

Shortly before midnight on Thursday November 9, 1989, East Berlin border guards swung open the gates of the crossings to the West. Under blazing floodlights, thousands of citizens from both sides of the city swarmed around and onto the wall, shouting and tooting horns. With hammers and chisels, ropes and chains, they began the task of destroying the hated barrier. In the following days, the authorities would send in cranes to continue the task of demolition. But the opening of the gates only served to accelerate the growing crisis in East Germany. A month later Krenz himself would be forced to resign to make way for a caretaker regime that would prepare for free elections in the coming year.

The Berlin wall had lasted 28 bitter years. Its fall was a signal to dissidents across Eastern Europe. In late November, there were massive demonstrations against Communism in the streets of the Czechoslovakian capital, Prague. There, on December 10, President Gustav Husak, who had held power with Soviet backing since the spring of 1968, resigned. By the year's end, authoritarian leaders would also be thrown out of office – whether peacefully or by force – in Bulgaria and Romania. Even in the Soviet Union, where Mikhail Gorbachev had been directing a gradual economic and political liberalization, the situation began to get out of hand. Dissidents in the newly elected Congress of People's Deputies started to attack the KGB, while nationalist movements in the constituent republics challenged not only one another but also the power of the central authorities.

To err in forecasting is, alas, human, and Erich Honecker was not alone. Over the past few centuries, there have been numerous attempts to predict society's future by extrapolation from current trends. Few have been successful. In 1948, for example, an English socialist writer named Eric Blair finished a manuscript in which he made a bold prediction in the form of a novel. Disturbed by an apparent world-wide convergence toward greater government control of society, he suggested that within a few decades the world might be divided into a small number of all-invasive superstates. Maintaining total control over information, the leaders of these states would keep their citizens in a situation of constant dependence. Blair found the title of his novel by twisting the last two digits of the current year. *Nineteen Eighty-four*, which he published the following year under his pen name of George Orwell, has shocked new generations of readers ever since.

Because Orwell died of tuberculosis in 1950, he did not live to see the extent to which his predictions would be realized. Orwell himself intended his novel as a picture of what "could arrive" rather than what necessarily would happen.[5] In fact, however, his projections turned out to be far wide of the mark. Whereas Orwell had foreseen generalized totalitarianism, the year 1984 brought clear signs that state power was in retreat around the globe. It saw the re-election in the United States of Ronald Reagan, a president committed to reducing the government's intervention into the lives of its citizens. In the Soviet Union, the same year witnessed the rising power of Mikhail Gorbachev as heir apparent to the ailing Konstantin Chernenko. Chosen General Secretary the following year, Gorbachev would begin to dismantle the cumbersome apparatus of the Communist Party. In Orwell's own country in 1984, Margaret Thatcher had just won a landslide victory she would interpret as a mandate to demolish the welfare state. The assassination of Indira Gandhi in India permitted the transfer of power to her son Rajiv, who would begin to introduce liberalizing reforms. And in China, the regime of Deng Xiaoping announced a major shift away from central planning and partial movement toward a free-market system.

Orwell's forecasting error, like that of Honecker, illustrates the danger of predicting society's future by projecting a continuation of current trends. An unforeseen shock such as the electronics revolution of the most recent decades can totally change the direction in which states are evolving. A similar fate may well fall to the current generation's predictions of the marvels of an "information society."[6] Yet while the shocks themselves may be difficult to foresee ahead of time, their consequences may nevertheless fall into a common pattern. A given type of disturbance might have predictable consequences, leading to characteristic changes in the size and structure of states. By evaluating the probability of each type of shock, one could then proceed to assess the likelihood of different future outcomes.

THREE CLASSES OF EVENTS

Is it possible to detect a consistent pattern in the events of the past? As one sifts through the historical evidence, three types of records recur time and again. One class of recorded events consists of innovations in informational and military technology that have altered the optimal scale of organizations. Another set of recorded events is made up of changes in contractual relations among individuals. A final group of records comprises changes in the territorial boundaries of states and in their internal structure.

The inventions that have transformed the optimal scale of organizations have been few. In the case of information processing techniques, the innovations that have had the greatest impact on scale economies have probably been writing, printing, the mass media, and the integrated circuit. Each altered the optimal scale of social networks for the exchange of information. As for military innovations, returns to scale changed most remarkably with the introduction of metal weapons, heavy cavalry, artillery, and the railway and telegraph. In each case, there occurred a sharp change in the optimal size of military formations.

Major transformations in contractual relations have also been relatively rare. In the non-military sphere, the emergence of the first bureaucracies was a key event. The formation of world-wide commodity and financial markets was another. Yet a further occurrence was the establishment of disciplined political parties claiming an exclusive right to represent the state's citizens. Finally, the lattice-form corporation oriented to the transformation of information is the most recent major occurrence.

Among military relationships, the appearance of the first infantry armies was a critical development. The transition to more loosely structured cavalry forces was a second key event. The addition of an artillery corps devoted to the development and application of new technologies marked a further transformation. Still another major organizational change was the emergence of the general staff, able to coordinate the movements of individual spatially separated armies.

Modifications of territorial boundaries and tax levels have been extremely numerous. Yet systematic changes in the size of states in general and in the importance of their public sectors have been relatively infrequent. Prior to writing, the typical political units in the lower Tigris and Euphrates valleys in southern Iraq were small, largely self-sufficient agricultural settlements, the largest of which comprised fewer than 2,000 people (see chapter 1). These communities appear to have been governed by a general assembly of all adult free men. Most land was held by individual families. However, by the time of the first cuneiform records of the Sumerian civilization at the end of the fourth millennium BC, the size and structure of political units in this region had changed dramatically. The first cities, reaching over 10,000 inhabitants, had appeared. Each of these "temple-states" was administered by a hierarchy of priests and scribes who organized teams of workers to maintain the irrigation canals and cultivate an important share of the agricultural land. In a brief period, communities had increased in size and become more centralized.

Over the middle centuries of the third millennium BC, with the introduction of bronze weapons, the tendency in Sumer was to larger political units. The many small autonomous temple communities gradually gave way to a dozen contiguous territorial states. Finally, around 2340 BC, after prolonged interstate warfare, the Semitic leader, Sargon the Great, established an empire that extended over much of present-day Iraq (see chapter 2). During this same period, there is evidence of a decline in the power of the temple over resource allocation. In the Sumerian territorial states, records of transfers of private property in land, along with markets for the voluntary exchange of goods, appear for the first time around 2500 BC. This trend toward larger political units and enhanced use of markets continued until the beginning of the Christian era.

Throughout the first millennium AD, there occurred a decline in the size of the typical state and an increase in its degree of centralization. During the middle decades of the third century AD, centralized power collapsed in the Roman empire (as it did in China). In part, the problem was barbarian attacks; however, an additional difficulty was renewed challenges to imperial authority from provincial commanders. By the time of Constantine (reigned 310–37), Rome's territorial integrity had been re-established from Britain in the north-west to Syria and Egypt in the south-east. However, the state's *nominal* boundaries had been restored only by a switch to a defense-in-depth strategy that moved the empire's *effective* borders inward (see chapter 3). Simultaneously, effective tax rates rose sharply. These two trends continued over the next six centuries, until by the end of the millennium the Roman empire (renamed Byzantine) had shrunk to little more than present-day Greece and Turkey. Over the same period, the rise of feudal institutions left only a small amount of Western Europe's resources to be allocated by the market.

Beginning in the second quarter of the fifteenth century, there was a renewed tendency toward larger, less centralized states. It was during this period that Charles VII, followed by his son and grandson, stripped away the powers of the nobility who had dominated France at the beginning of the century. By the last decade of the fifteenth century, royal power extended throughout the French hexagon. As for taxes, real peacetime royal tax revenues per capita were probably slightly higher under Charles VIII in 1490 than under his great-grandfather, Charles VI in 1413 (see chapter 4). However, total taxes as a share of income almost certainly declined between the beginning and the end of the fifteenth century. A comparison of the change from feudal duchy to Renaissance kingdom therefore shows a shift to a larger, less-centralized social organizations.

In the seventeenth and eighteenth centuries, a new type of political unit emerged in Western Europe – the nation state. This latest political form was based on widespread literacy in the vernacular: the nation state was essentially a network of individuals able to receive and send messages in a standardized written version of a spoken language. For a brief half-century, the Dutch were the masters of a globe-spanning economy centered in Amsterdam. Then, for the following century and a half, England and France vied with each other for global dominance. The seventeenth and eighteenth centuries also saw sharp rises in tax rates across Western Europe, as rulers and legislatures found that they could extract more revenues from their citizens without causing them to leave the new national information networks (see chapter 5). To take the most striking example, in 1648 the tiny United Provinces of the Netherlands were able to maintain an army of 55,000 men, almost three times the size of the force under Charles VII of mighty France at the end of the Hundred Years War. In 1695, the typical Dutch household paid over a third of its income in taxes.

The second and third quarters of the nineteenth century witnessed an expansion of territorial boundaries, accompanied by a decrease in the tax share of income. The 1850s and 1860s saw three major series of wars in which the authority of a central regime was asserted over regional powers. In the Italian Wars of Independence, France aided its ally, Sardinia (Piedmont) against Austria in the key battles leading to Italian unification. Prussia, in three wars against Denmark, Austria, and France, managed to unite the smaller German states under its leadership (see chapter 6). Finally, the Union side in the American Civil War put down a revolt by the southern states and extended its control across the North American continent. As for tax rates, the middle years of the nineteenth century marked the low point for tariffs, which constituted the most important revenue source in most countries.

In the decades preceding the First World War, most Western European states substantially increased their average tax rates. These public revenues were then used to finance territorial expansion. Taxes as a share of income doubled in Germany and rose sharply in England, largely to finance military spending (see chapter 7). This was also a period of renewed European imperial conquest in Africa and Asia. Isolated from competing networks, the United States did not attempt to expand its influence outside of the Americas and the Pacific basin prior to 1940. Over the following two decades, however, the public share in the US rose, while the territory dominated by the state was extended around the globe.

Since 1970, the largest states have encountered increasing difficulties in controlling their territory and in financing their public expenditures. The United States has been unable to maintain its previous global military commitments while at the same time assuring a uniform public presence throughout its own internal territory (see chapter 8). In the Soviet system, outbreaks of inter-ethnic violence and resistance to central control in the constituent republics and allied states show corresponding weaknesses. At the same time, pressure for deregulation and intense opposition to tax increases in the United States, accompanied by a retreat from central planning in the Soviet Union, show that state intervention in the economy has also encountered increased resistance in both countries.

THE DIRECTION OF CAUSALITY

It is one thing to be able to group events into classes. But it is another thing entirely to go beyond taxonomy to suggest directions of causality. What are the links, if any, between the key informational and military innovations, changes in contractual relationships, and modifications in the size and structure of states? One possible means of answering this question is by a priori reasoning. Such an approach works best in examining the link between innovations and types of interpersonal contracts. In each historical case, the most plausible explanation is that it was the innovation that led to new types of contractual arrangements. Thus it was undoubtedly writing that permitted extended hierarchies rather than layers of bureaucrats who developed a means of coding information. Similarly, it was metal weapons that enabled differentiated military hierarchies to arise rather than large infantry armies that issued orders for developing new types of weapons. A similar analysis applies to the other key innovations.

Establishing the link between each pair of innovation and organizational changes on the one hand and the observed transformations in social structure on the other is more difficult. In many cases, causality could go in either direction. For example, while it may well be writing that permitted complex societies to emerge, it appears just as plausible that the first cities arose due to demographic pressure and that writing was developed to provide a means of better organizing large settlements. Similarly, increases in military scale economies may have made larger states possible, or it could be that extended political units required larger armies and therefore developed the appropriate technologies.

An alternative method of establishing causality is to examine the chronological sequence of events. Knowing that time moves in only one direction, one may conclude that a later event cannot be the cause of an earlier one. In most of the historical examples of transformations in the structure of society, there is some means of establishing the sequence of events. The order of developments is most difficult to establish in the earliest example. Uruk's initial spurt of growth, to a population of 10,000 people, coincided with the development of writing. However, it should be noted that its further rapid growth into a city of over 40,000 people occurred in a period of four centuries following this innovation.[7] Moreover, there are strong reasons for rejecting the principal alternative explanation of the appearance of cities – demographic pressure. Settlements as large as 1,000–2,000 inhabitants had existed in the Middle East for four millennia prior to the discovery of writing.[8] There was therefore more than enough time for population pressure to have led to larger political units if other conditions had permitted.

In each of the seven other cases, the timing of events is less open to question. Bronze weapons were found in Sumerian graves dating from two centuries earlier than the empire of Sargon the Great.[9] Similarly, horses large enough and strong enough to carry armor both for themselves and their riders were first encountered by the Romans at Carrhae in 53 BC, two centuries before the first serious pressures on the imperial borders. In the late medieval period, the crucial improvements in artillery – in particular, iron-reinforced and cast-iron projectiles – were developed and introduced into France prior to the consolidation of royal power in the 1440s and 1450s.[10]

In modern times, the appearance of a flourishing printing industry publishing in the Flemish–Dutch vernacular took place in the sixteenth century; that is, before the development of a Dutch nation state in the period from 1600 to 1650. The nineteenth-century example is also unambiguous. An initial attempt to form a Prussian-led union of German states failed in 1850, when Prussia backed down rather than face probable defeat at the hands of Austria. The completion of the principal pieces of the German rail and telegraph networks in the 1850s and 1860s permitted the envelopment strategy that provided Prussia the margin of victory at Sadowa in 1866, the largest battle in history up to that time. The chronology was similar in the cases of Italy and the United States.

The mass-circulation newspaper was introduced at the end of the nineteenth century in Europe and North America and in the decade before the First World War in Russia. Using their own presses and those seized from their opponents, the Bolsheviks established the most complete monopoly over the circulation of information that had been seen to that time. Successful state control of production and extension of the state's borders occurred in the following decades. In the United States, the first major increases in non-military spending as a share of GNP occurred somewhat later, in the 1930s, subsequent to the introduction of radio. The emergence of that country as a world power came in the 1940s.

Finally, although integrated electronics methods were developed in the 1940s and 1950s, their widespread use in large numbers of products first occurred in the 1970s. The recent resistance to American and Soviet state intervention, whether military or economic, clearly followed this innovation.

Historical change therefore appears to have its origins in innovations that alter the optimal scale of organizations. Once introduced, these new technologies lead to the emergence of new types of contractual relationships. Conflict among or within states then generates new patterns of borders and variations in the degree of government intervention.

Table 9.1   Effects of innovations on the size and tax level of states.

Innovation	Date	Change in scale economies		Change in political units	
		Informational	Military	Size	Tax level
Centralizing innovations					
Writing	~3100	Increase	—	Increase	Increase
Printing	1650	Increase	—	Increase	Increase
Mass media	1900	Increase	—	Increase	Increase
Liberalizing innovations					
Bronze arms	~2700	—	Increase	Increase	Decrease
Artillery	1440	—	Increase	Increase	Decrease
Railroad	1825	—	Increase	Increase	Decrease
Feudalizing innovation					
Heavy cavalry	~50	—	Decrease	Decrease	Increase
Atomizing innovation					
Integrated circuit	1959	Decrease	—	Decrease	Decrease

~ BC.

A PATTERN OF HISTORY

With the direction of causality suggested, it becomes possible to explore for possible regularities in recorded events. Since the beginning of the historical period, there have been four major changes in information-processing technology (see Table 9.1). Three of these – writing, printing, and mass media – have involved increases in scale economies. However, the last and most recent innovation, the integrated circuit, appears to have lowered the returns to scale in information processing. There have also been four major changes in military technology. Metal arms, artillery, and the railroad–telegraph combination each increased the size of the optimal armed force. However, the introduction of heavy cavalry reduced the returns to greater organizational size in military operations.

In all, then, there have been four types of technological shocks to social organization. Moreover, each of these types of innovation has had a distinctive effect on the structure of the typical state. One type of shock has increased the scale economies of information processing The historical examples – writing, printing, and the mass media – have each led to larger states with higher tax levels. Since such a change transferred political power from smaller to larger jurisdictions and economic power from private to public hands, it might be referred to as a *centralizing* innovation. Innovations of this type have been one of the dominant forces in history, accounting for the rise of the first cities, the nation state, and the modern totalitarian and welfare states.

Another type of innovation has increased the returns to scale in the application of military force. Historical examples of such shocks have been the introduction of metal weapons, artillery, and the railroad and telegraph. When these new technologies were applied, there was a tendency toward larger political units within which market forces were given a freer reign. Accordingly these shocks might be termed *liberalizing* innovations. They too have played an important role in history, accounting for the rise of commercial empires in ancient times, the emergence of large unrestricted trading zones in the kingdoms of Renaissance Europe and free-trade among industrial countries in the mid-nineteenth century.

Yet another category of new technology has reduced the scale economies of applying organized violence. There has been only one important historical example of such a shock: the introduction of heavy cavalry in the first millennium of the Christian era. This type of innovation tends to reduce the optimal size of states, while at the same time increasing the degree of public control over the actions of individuals. In reference to the small custom-dominated political units of medieval Europe, it might be referred to as a *feudalizing* innovation. Despite the relative rarity of this category of event, it has left a lasting impression on human memory. To this day, the fall of the Roman Empire remains an inexhaustible theme for historical discussion.

A final type of innovation tends to produce smaller political units in which the individual is left to depend more on his own resources. Although there have been no previous examples of such a shock, changes in this direction appear to have been occurring in many countries in recent years. As the effect is to break up the previous mass societies of the era of the all-encompassing state into smaller, less-invasive communities, this type of innovation might be called *atomizing* change. Rare though it has been historically, it is likely to be the dominant theme of social change until well into the twenty-first century.

On the whole, over the course of history, there has been a tendency toward larger units of political organization. Six of the eight key innovations have tended to increase the size of the typical state. Only in the period of the dark ages and in the most recent decade has the tendency of humans to cluster into ever-larger territorial groupings been checked. However, there has been no corresponding trend in the degree of centralization of decision-making. Four innovations have increased the public sector's share of income, while four have reduced it. It is interesting to note that each successive innovation has reversed the direction of change in the degree of centralization. For example, the present period represents a phase of withdrawal of the state from economic intervention after almost a century of increasing public control.

In short, the historical record indicates a systematic pattern in which technological shocks generate changes in the size and structure of states. Although the shocks themselves may not be predictable, each type of innovation has a characteristic effect on borders and tax levels. Overall, there has been a trend toward larger states, accompanied by a cycle of expansion and contraction in the importance of the public sector within each political unit.

THE PATTERN EXPLAINED

How might the observed pattern of changes in the size and structure of political units be explained? Why is it that the position of the typical state's borders and the relative size of its public sector have tended to change simultaneously over the course of history? Why have such transformations tended to follow the introduction of new technologies for processing information and applying violence? Why do the changes in social organization vary systematically with the type of technological shocks? It is time to offer a possible explanation for the crises that have shaped our history.

To answer these questions, it is necessary to have some understanding of the nature of a state. From the mightiest empire to the tiniest principality, the basic characteristics of the state are the same. In a community in an isolated region, for example, members of some households may wish to hire employees to patrol their land in order to discourage theft and assault. Those families that do not contribute nevertheless benefit from their neighbors' spending. But the non-participation of some community members reduces the total amount of resources available to provide the service. There will therefore be a strong incentive for the organizers to force all households to contribute. Additional employees will be hired to collect the contributions from all community members. The result is in effect a state – an organization that holds an exclusive right to collect revenues from all households by force or threat of force and to use these funds to provide services collectively.

A public organization must be able to generate non-voluntary contributions in order to encourage productive effort on the part of its employees; in other words, it must have the power to tax. And it must be able to punish when there is evidence of malfeasance; that is, it must have the power to apply force. Since collecting tax revenues and applying force are specialized activities, most historical states have assigned each of these tasks to a distinct hierarchical structure. The generation of rewards is the role of the fiscal bureaucracy, while the imposition of punishment is the role of the police–military apparatus. Both hierarchies are responsible to the decision-making individual or group in the community. This decision-maker or ruler is in effect the principal in a set of contractual relations with the state's employees.

The leading group in a community may discover that the revenues it can raise through taxation exceed the total wage bill of its public employees. If the organizers are able to appropriate this surplus, they will have a powerful incentive to extend their service to neighboring communities. By controlling additional territory they can increase the total surplus above the cost of providing public services. For this reason, there will be a tendency for a state to attempt to expand outward.

No political unit has yet managed to dominate the world's surface in its entirety. What is it that sets a territorial limit to a state's power? The ability of the principal to monitor each fiscal agent's effort – either directly, or indirectly, through supervisors' reports – will tend to diminish with the number of agents or with distance. As a result, the net tax receipts received by the principal from each additional unit of territory he controls will decline as the state expands. A similar problem of control arises in the principal's contracts with spatially distributed soldiers. Here again there will be a loss of control with distance as the state expands. As a result, the cost of obtaining the minimum military effort required to keep each additional unit of territory controlled will increase with the distance of that unit from the capital.

How large will the typical state be in terms of population or area? How intervening will it be in terms of the share of total income that will be extracted in taxes to be used for collective rather than individual purposes? It is plausible to suppose that the dominant group or principal in the state will tend to maximize the surplus of tax revenues that remains after the tax collectors and the security employees have been paid. The principal will therefore attempt to enlarge the state until the tax revenues from an additional unit of territory are just equal to the additional cost of administering it. For any smaller state, there would remain an incentive for the principal to expand his domain, since the net revenue from additional territory would be greater than the cost of holding it. However, beyond a certain point, additional territory would no longer pay its upkeep cost. The wise ruler will not attempt to hold such land.

With the nature of the state defined, it is possible to examine the crises that it is likely to undergo. Innovations that alter the contractual relations between the ruler or principal and the public employees or agents will affect both the size and structure of the state. The proportion of a society's resources allocated by the government may serve as a measure of the degree of centralization. For example, a low level of taxes implies that allocation decisions are made by individuals through decentralized market transactions, whereas a high level of taxes implies considerable centralization in resource allocation. The principal–agent approach then suggests an explanation for the effects of each of the four possible types of innovation.

An innovation that increases the scale economies of information processing raises the gains to the individual from interacting with the other members of the society. It therefore permits the state to raise levels of taxation without causing individuals to move away. The resulting increase in revenues then permits the acquisition of additional territory. This type of *centralizing* innovation will lead to larger states with higher average tax levels, as the historical examples of the introduction of writing, printing, and the mass media illustrate.

A discovery that raises the returns to scale in the application of violence lowers the cost of controlling territory. The state can therefore simultaneously cut tax rates and shift its borders outward. Expansion continues until tax receipts from the last unit of territory just cover the cost of controlling it. Consequently, there will be a tendency toward larger, more liberal states in which the market plays a greater role in allocating resources. The *liberalizing* effect on the state of the introduction of metal weapons, artillery, and the railroad and telegraph may be explained in this way.

There has been only one historical example of a decrease in the scale economies of military control; however, its effect was profound. Such a change tends to raise the cost of controlling territory. The state must therefore raise tax rates. To do so, however, it must also shift its boundaries inward so that its fiscal bureaucracy may be more closely controlled. The borders contract toward the capital until tax receipts from the most distant unit of territory again just cover the cost of controlling it. Consequently, there will be a tendency toward smaller, less liberal states, with the market playing a diminished role in allocating resources. A *feudalizing* shock of this type occurred with the introduction of heavy cavalry in the first millennium AD.

The current period seems to be the only important case in history of a shock that reduces the returns to scale in information processing. This type of innovation lowers the gains to the individual from interacting with the other members of society. It therefore requires the state to lower levels of taxation in order to prevent individuals from moving away. The resulting decrease in revenues necessitates the abandonment of marginal territory whose control becomes too expensive. This kind of shock therefore leads to smaller states in which the government plays a reduced role. The introduction and development of the integrated circuit appear to be having an *atomizing* effect on societies around the world.

In short, systematic changes in the size of states and their levels of taxation may be explained as the result of innovations in the technology of information and violence. By altering the efficiency of either a society's military organization or its fiscal administration, new technologies change the optimal tax rate and the territorial boundaries of the typical state.

WHERE ARE WE GOING?

As the examples of Erich Honeker and George Orwell illustrate, it is extremely hazardous to attempt to predict the future evolution of society. Even if one is astute enough to detect the current trend, there is a danger that at any moment it may be upset by a new innovation. Ironically, the transistor – the innovation that was to reverse the 500 year tendency toward more centralized information processing – was invented in 1948, the year in which the manuscript for *Nineteen Eighty-four* was completed.

It is probably safe to predict that the current wave of change toward reduced informational scale economies (an *atomizing* innovation) that began around 1960 has yet to play itself out. If so, one might predict several further decades of continued pressure on large states and on their fiscal equilibrium. The current massive budget deficits of the United States, the Soviet Union, and the People's Republic of China will not disappear overnight. Nor will it become easier for their rulers to counter the centrifugal forces threatening to divide these superstates into smaller, more manageable entities. Other large multi-ethnic states such as India, Canada, Yugoslavia, and Ethiopia will also be threatened with decomposition.

One often hears that the states of Europe are about to unite to form a tightly knit federation such as the United States or the Soviet Union. It is precisely the opposite that is likely to occur. The three superpowers risk breaking up to form squabbling clusters of smaller states on the European pattern. Second-order powers such as Japan and Germany that have been held within sub-optimal borders for almost a half-century will be the principal beneficiaries of this tendency. Their influence will continue to expand into the void created by the territorial retreat of the largest states. Elsewhere in the world, local powers that have heretofore been kept in check by the threat of superpower intervention will be tempted to satisfy their territorial ambitions.

What type of different innovation might the next wave bring? There are three possible candidates: an increase in informational scale economies, or an increase or decrease in military scale economies (*centralizing, liberalizing,* or *feudalizing* innovations respectively). Since each type of change is perfectly plausible, it is perhaps foolhardy to attempt to choose among them. Nevertheless, forced to select, one might examine the pattern of previous events. Suppose, for example, that both the trend and the cycle detected in the historical pattern of innovation and social change were to persist. The implications are clear. The dominant trend has been toward larger political units. Therefore, at some point, the current difficulties of the largest states would begin to ease. As for the cycle, if the alternation between contraction and expansion of the public sector persists, the next shock should bring an increase in the willingness to pay taxes. The resulting increase in public revenues would permit control of additional territory by a single state.

The type of shock that would bring about an increase in both the size of the state and the importance of its public sector is an increase in informational scale economies (a *centralizing* innovation). At present, an increasingly important limiting factor in determining the size of organizations appears to be the creative capacity of the human brain. Since it is difficult for two individuals to innovate together, the current tendency is to bring more and more information to the individual creator. Standardized computer programs and ever more powerful workstations and microcomputers allow her or him to work independently of support staff. As the pace of change has picked up, the individuality of the creative process has been the driving force in reducing the scale of the organization. Small firms have been able to innovate more effectively than larger ones.

Should it be possible for more powerful groupings of creativity to be formed, however, the current trend toward small-scale activity could be reversed. Networks of larger scale within which information could be exchanged and enhanced rapidly could then be established. The productivity gains from such networks would permit higher tax levels, since individuals would be willing to pay more to avoid foregoing access to the information generated. Increased taxes could then finance larger political units.

As a first step, the computer could be used as an intermediary to enhance cross-fertilization among individuals. Already there are developments in this direction. At American companies such as Ford, Northrop, and Lockheed, shared data bases permit individual problem-solving skills to be integrated. Computer-aided design and engineering permit what is known as concurrent engineering, in which both the product and the production process are developed simultaneously.[11]

Progressively, however, the human input in the creative process is likely to be reduced. With developments in artificial intelligence, the computer will be able to substitute for an ever-greater range of human functions. In

1950, the mathematician A. M. Turing predicted that by the year 2,000 computers would be able to imitate human intelligence perfectly.[12] Although this prediction is unlikely to be realized, over the next century the goal of a thinking machine will be approached if not actually attained. Since computers can interact much more efficiently than humans, the existing limits to the scale of creativity may then gradually be overcome.

If this tendency toward large-scale organizations based on artificial intelligence should materialize, society may well move in the direction predicted by George Orwell in *Nineteen Eighty-four*. With ever-larger information networks, small states will become increasingly unviable. Seizing the rents from their information systems, the largest states will be able to expand their borders, much as Prussia did within the German *Bund* in the nineteenth century. By threatening their small neighbors with economic isolation or, perhaps, unpleasant environmental spillovers, the largest political units would be able to absorb the smaller ones.

The role to be assigned to humans within a computer-integrated society remains problematic. During previous periods of increases in informational scale economies – the rise of the city, the nation state, and the welfare state – people gained security only at the expense of greater government intervention into their private lives. As developments in artificial intelligence permit the integration of ever-larger networks of machines, such developments could recur on an even greater scale than in the past. The world predicted by Honecker and Orwell may yet come to pass.

NOTES

1 *Time*, November 20, 1989, p. 27.
2 *Time*, January 1, 1990, p. 28.
3 *Time*, October 30, 1989, p. 47.
4 *Time*, November 20, 1989, p. 26.
5 Quoted in Jenni Calder, *Animal Farm and Nineteen Eighty-Four* (Open University Press, 1987), p. 95.
6 For a review of this literature, see Christopher Rowe, *People and Chips: The Human Implications of Information Technology* (Paradigm, 1986).
7 Robert McC. Adams, *Heartland of Cities* (University of Chicago Press, 1981), p. 85.
8 Arther Ferrill, *The Origins of War* (Thames and Hudson, 1985), p. 28.
9 P. R. S. Moorey, "The archaeological evidence for metallurgy and related technologies in Mesopotamia, c.5500–2100 BC," *Iraq*, 44 (1982), p. 29.
10 H. Dubled, "L'artillerie royale française à l'époque de Charles VII et au début du règne de Louis XI (1437–1469): les frères Bureau," *Sciences et techniques de l'armement*, 50 (1976), p. 579.
11 *Business Week, Innovation in America*, 1989, p. 146.
12 David Bolter, *Turing's Man: Western Culture in the Computer Age* (University of North Carolina Press, 1984), p. 12.

Bibliography

Adams, Robert McC., *The Evolution of Urban Society*, Aldine, Chicago, 1966.

Adams, Robert McC., *Heartland of Cities*, University of Chicago Press, Chicago, 1981.

Adams, Robert McC., "Mesopotamian social evolution: old outlooks, new goals," in *On the Evolution of Complex Societies*, ed. Timothy Earle, Undena, Malibu, 1984.

Addington, Larry H., *The Patterns of War since the Eighteenth Century*, Indiana University Press, Bloomington, 1984.

Allmand, Christopher, *The Hundred Years War: England and France at War c.* 1300–1450, Cambridge University Press, Cambridge, 1988.

Altheim, Franz, *Le déclin du monde antique: examen des causes de la décadence*, Payot, Paris, 1953.

Andic, Suphan and Jindrich Veverka, "The growth of government expenditures in Germany since unification," *Finanzarchiv*, 23 (1964), pp. 169–278.

Andreski, Stanislav, *Military Organization and Society*, University of California Press, Berkeley, 1968.

Arendt, Hannah, *The Origins of Totalitarianism*, Harcourt, Brace, Jovanovich, New York, 1951.

Athey, Thomas H. and Robert W. Zmud, *Introduction to Computers and Information Systems*, 2nd edn, Scott, Foresman and Co., Glenview, 1988.

Aymard, Maurice, "Introduction," in *Dutch Capitalism and World Capitalism*, ed. M. Aymard, Cambridge University Press, Cambridge, 1982.

Bailey, Anthony, *The Low Countries*, American Heritage, New York, 1972.

Barbour, Violet, *Capitalism in Amsterdam in the Seventeenth Century*, Johns Hopkins, Baltimore, 1950.

Bauer, Raymond A., Alex Inkeles, and Clyde Kluckhohn, *How the Soviet System Works*, Harvard University Press, Cambridge, Mass., 1964.

Bean, Richard, "War and the birth of the nation state," *Journal of Economic History*, 33 (1973), pp. 203–21.

Beeching, Wilfred A., *Century of the Typewriter*, Heinemann, London, 1974.

Bell, Daniel, *The Coming of Post-Industrial Society*, Basic Books, New York, 1973.

Beniger, James R., *The Control Revolution: Technological and Economic Origins of the Information Society*, Harvard University Press, Cambridge, 1986.

Bennett, Paul, Anne de Melogue, and Andrew Silver, "Corporate debt–equity ratios," *Federal Reserve Bank of New York Quarterly Review*, 10 (1985), pp. 46–8.

Bernardi, Aurelio, "The economic problems of the Roman Empire at the time of its decline," in *The Economic Decline of Empires*, ed. Carlo M. Cipolla, Methuen, London, 1970, pp. 16–83.

Blackbourn, David and Geoff Eley, *The Peculiarities of German History*, Oxford University Press, Oxford, 1984.

Blum, Ulrich and Leonard Dudley, "A spatial approach to structural change: the making of the French hexagon," *Journal of Economic History*, 49 (1989), pp. 657–76.

Bolter, David, *Turing's Man: Western Culture in the Computer Age*, University of North Carolina Press, Chapel Hill, 1984.

Bond, Brian, *War and Society in Europe, 1870–1970*, Fontana, London, 1984.

Boorstin, Daniel, *The Discoverers*, Vintage, New York, 1983.

Boserup, Ester, *Population and Technological Change: A Study of Long-Term Trends*, University of Chicago Press, Chicago, 1981.

Bottéro, Jean, "The first Semitic empire," in *The Near East: The Early Civilizations*, eds J. Bottéro, E. Cassin, and J. Vercoutter, Weidenfeld and Nicolson, London, 1967, pp. 91–132.

Boxer, C. R., *The Dutch Seaborne Empire 1600–1800*, Hutchinson, London, 1965.

Braudel, Fernand, *Civilization and Capitalism: 15th–18th Century*, vol. 1, *The Structures of Everyday Life*, vol. 2, *The Wheels of Commerce*, vol. 3, *The Perspective of the World*, Harper and Row, New York, 1981–4.

Braudel, Fernand, "Profits et bilan de plus d'un demi-millénaire," in *Histoire économique et sociale de la France*, vol. IV, part 3, *Années 1950 à nos jours*, eds Fernand Braudel and E. Labrousse, Presses universitaires de France, Paris, 1977, pp. 1–8.

Braun, Ernest and Stuart Macdonald, *Revolution in Miniature*, Cambridge University Press, Cambridge, 1978.

Braun, Ernst, *Wayward Technology*, Greenwood Press, Westport, Conn., 1984.

Brenner, Reuven, *History – The Human Gamble*, University of Chicago Press, Chicago, 1983.

Brinton, Crane, John B. Christopher, Robert Lee Wolff and Robin W. Winks, *A History of Civilization*, 6th edn, 2 vols, Prentice-Hall, Englewood Cliffs, NJ, 1984.

Brockhaus Enzyklopädie, F. A. Brockhaus, Wiesbaden, 1968.

Brunner, Heinrich, "Der Reiterdienst and die Anfänge des Lehnwesens," *Zeitschrift der Savigny-Stiftung für Rechtsgeschichte, Germanistische Abteilung*, 8 (1887), pp. 1–38.

Butler, Pierce, *The Origins of Printing in Europe*, University of Chicago Press, Chicago, 1940.

Butzer, Karl W., *Early Hydraulic Civilization in Egypt: A Study in Cultural Ecology*, University of Chicago Press, Chicago, 1976.

Calder, Jenni, *Animal Farm and Nineteen Eighty-Four*, Open University Press, Milton Keynes, 1987.

Calleo, David, *The German Problem Reconsidered,* Cambridge University Press, Cambridge, 1978.

Cardwell, D. S. L., *Technology, Science and History,* Heinemann, London, 1972.

Carneiro, Robert L., "Theory of the origins of the state," *Science,* 169 (1970), pp. 733–8.

Carr, Edward Hallett, *Socialism in One Country* 1924–1926, 2 vols, Macmillan, London, 1958–9.

Carr, William, *A History of Germany* 1815–1945, Edward Arnold, London, 1969.

Carter, Jimmy, *Keeping Faith: Memoires of a President,* Bantam, New York, 1982.

Casson, Herbert N., *The History of the Telephone,* A. C. McClurg, Chicago, 1910.

Chandler, Alfred D., Jr, *Strategy and Structure: Chapters in the History of the Industrial Enterprise,* MIT Press, Cambridge, Mass., 1962.

Chandler, Alfred D., Jr, *The Visible Hand: The Managerial Revolution in American Business,* Belknap Press, Cambridge, Mass., 1977.

Chang, C. S., *The Japanese Auto Industry and the US Market,* Praeger, New York, 1981.

Chappell, Warren, *A Short History of the Printed Word,* Nonpareil Books, Boston, 1970.

Childe, V. Gordon, "The urban revolution," *Town Planning Review,* 21 (1950), pp. 3–17.

Church, William F., "France," in *National Consciousness, History and Political Culture in Early-Modern Europe,* ed. Orest Ranum, Johns Hopkins, Baltimore, 1975, pp. 43–66.

Cipolla, Carlo M., *The Economic History of World Population,* rev. edn, Penguin, Harmondsworth, 1964.

Cipolla, Carlo M., *Guns, Sails and Empires,* Pantheon, New York, 1965.

Cipolla, Carlo M., *Literacy and Development in the West,* Penguin, Harmondsworth, 1969.

Clarke, Roger A., *Soviet Economic Facts* 1917–1970, John Wiley and Sons, New York, 1972.

Clausewitz, Carl von, *On War,* tr. J. J. Graham, 3 vols, Routledge and Kegan Paul, London, 1956.

Clough, Shepard B., *The Rise and Fall of Civilization: An Inquiry into the Relationship between Economic Development and Civilization,* Columbia University Press, New York, 1951.

Congressional Quarterly Inc., *Budgeting for America,* Washington, 1982.

Conlin, Joseph, *The American Past: A Survey of American History,* Harcourt, Brace, Jovanovich, New York, 1984.

Contamine, Philippe, "La France à la fin du XVe siècle: pour un état des questions," in *La France à la fin du XVe siècle,* eds B. Chevalier and P. Contamine, Paris, Centre national de recherche scientifique, 1985, pp. 1–12.

Contamine, Philippe, *Guerre, état et société à la fin du moyen âge. Étude sur les armées des rois de France,* 1337–1494, Mouton, Paris, 1972.

Contamine, Philippe, *War in the Middle Ages,* Blackwell, Oxford, 1984.

Corson, William R. and Robert T. Crowley, *The New KGB: Engine of Soviet Power,* William Morrow, New York, 1986.

Cottrell, Leonard, *The Anvil of Civilization*, New American Library, New York, 1957.

Dahrendorf, Ralf, *Society and Democracy in Germany*, Doubleday, New York, 1967.

Darko, E. "Influences touraniennes sur l'évolution de l'art militaire des Grecs, Romains et Byzantins," *Byzantion*, 12 (1937), pp. 119–47.

Daumas, Maurice, *Histoire générale des techniques*, vol. II, *Les premières étapes du machinisme*, Presses universitaires de France, Paris, 1965.

David, Paul, *Technological Choice, Innovation and Economic Growth*, Cambridge University Press, London, 1975.

Demandt, Alexander, *Der Fall Roms*, C. H. Beck, Munich, 1984.

De Vries, Jan, *The Economy of Europe in an Age of Crisis*, Cambridge University Press, Cambridge, 1976.

Dillard, Dudley, *Economic Development of the North Atlantic Community*, Prentice-Hall, Englewood Cliffs, NJ, 1967.

Diringer, David, *Writing*, Praeger, New York, 1962.

Dobb, Maurice, *Soviet Economic Development since 1917*, 6th edn, Routledge and Kegan Paul, London, 1966.

Dubled, H., "L'artillerie royale française à l'époque de Charles VII et au début du règne de Louis XI (1437–1469): les frères Bureau," *Sciences et techniques de l'armement*, 50 (1976), pp. 555–637.

Dubois, Henri, "Le commerce de la France au temps de Louis XI: expansion ou défensive?," in *La France à la fin du XVe siècle*, eds B. Chevalier and P. Contamine, Centre national de recherche scientifique, Paris, 1985, pp. 15–29.

Dugger, Ronnie, *On Reagan: The Man and his Presidency*, McGraw-Hill, New York, 1983.

Duncan, T. Bentley, "Niels Steensgaard and the Europe–Asia trade of the early seventeenth century," *Journal of Modern History*, 47 (1975), pp. 512–18.

Dupuy, R. Ernest and Trevor N. Dupuy, *The Encyclopedia of Military History from 3500 BC to the Present*, 2nd edn, Harper and Row, New York, 1986.

Economic Report of the President, Washington, 1989.

Edwards, John, *Language, Society and Identity*, Blackwell, Oxford, 1985.

Edzard, Dietz Otto, "The Early Dynastic period," in *The Near East: The Early Civilizations*, eds J. Bottéro, E. Cassin, and J. Vercoutter, Weidenfeld and Nicolson, London, 1967, pp. 52–90.

Eggenberger, David, *An Encyclopedia of Battles*, 2nd edn, Dover, New York, 1985.

Ehrenberg, Richard, *Capital and Finance in the Age of the Renaissance*, Jonathan Cape, London, 1928.

Eisenstein, Elizabeth L., *The Printing Press as an Agent of Change*, Cambridge University Press, Cambridge, 1979.

Eisner, Robert, *How Real is the Federal Deficit?* The Free Press, New York, 1986.

Ellul, Jacques, *Histoire de la propagande*, Presses universitaires de France, Paris, 1967.

Faden, Arnold M., *Economics of Time and Space*, Iowa State University Press, Ames, 1977.

Falkenstein, Adam, "The prehistory and protohistory of Western Asia," in *The Near East: The Early Civilizations*, eds J. Bottéro, E. Cassin, and J. Vercoutter, Weidenfeld and Nicolson, London, 1967, pp. 1–51.

Favier, Jean, *La guerre de cent ans,* Fayard, Paris, 1980.

Federal Bureau of Investigation, *Crime in the United States. Unified Crime Reports,* Washington, 1976, 1980, 1982.

Ferguson, Charles H., "America's high-tech decline," *Foreign Policy,* 74 (1989), pp. 123–44.

Ferrill, Arther, *The Fall of the Roman Empire,* Thames and Hudson, London, 1986.

Ferrill, Arther, *The Origins of War,* Thames and Hudson, London, 1985.

Fitzpatrick, Sheila, *The Russian Revolution,* Oxford University Press, Oxford, 1982.

Forbis, William H., *Fall of the Peacock Throne: The Story of Iran,* Harper and Row, New York, 1980.

Forester, Tom, *The Story of the Information Technology Revolution,* MIT Press, Cambridge, Mass., 1987.

Fox, E. W., *History in Geographic Perspective: The Other France,* Norton, New York, 1971.

Friedman, David, "A theory of the size and shape of nations," *Journal of Political Economy,* 85 (1977), pp. 59–78.

Friedrich Carl J. and Zbigniew Brzezinski, *Totalitarianism, Dictatorship and Autocracy,* 2nd edn, Praeger, New York, 1965.

Fryde, E. B. and M. M. Fryde, "Public credit with special reference to North-Western Europe," in *The Cambridge Economic History of Europe,* vol. III, *Economic Organization and Policies in the Middle Ages,* eds M. M. Postan, E. E. Rich, and E. Miller, Cambridge University Press, Cambridge, 1971, pp. 430–553.

Gadd, C. J., "The cities of Babylonia," in *The Cambridge Ancient History,* 3rd edn, vol. I, part 2, *Early History of the Middle East,* eds I. E. S. Edwards, C. J. Gadd and N. G. L. Hammond, Cambridge University Press, Cambridge, 1971, pp. 93–144.

Gaier, Claude, *L'industrie et le commerce des armes dans les anciennes principautés belges du XIIIme à la fin du XVme siècle,* Les belles lettres, Paris, 1973.

Gallery, John Andrew, "Town planning and community structure," in *Biblioteca Mesopotamica,* no. 4, *The Legacy of Sumer,* ed. Denise Schmandt-Besserat, Undena, Malibu, 1976, pp. 70–7.

Gaussin, Pierre-Roger, *Louis XI: Un roi entre deux mondes,* Nizet, Paris, 1976.

Gelb, Ignace J., *A Study of Writing,* University of Chicago Press, Chicago, 1963.

Geyl, Pieter, *The Netherlands in the Seventeenth Century,* part 1, 1609–1648, Ernest Benn, London, 1961.

Gibbon, Edward, *The History of the Decline and Fall of the Roman Empire,* Peter Fenelon Collier, New York, 1899.

Gibson, McGuire, "By stage and cycle to Sumer," in *Biblioteca Mesopotamica,* vol. 4, *The Legacy of Sumer,* ed. Denise Schmandt-Besserat, Undena, Malibu, 1976, pp. 51–8.

Goerlitz, Walter, *History of the German General Staff,* Westview Press, Boulder, 1985.

Goody, Jack and Ian Watt, "The consequences of literacy," in *Literacy in Traditional Societies,* ed. J. Goody, Cambridge University Press, Cambridge, 1968, pp. 27–68.

Goody, Jack, *The Domestication of the Savage Mind,* Cambridge University Press, Cambridge, 1977.

Hargrove, Edwin C., *Jimmy Carter as President: Leadership and the Politics of the Public Good.* Louisiana State University Press, Baton Rouge, La, 1988.

Harrison, Bennett and Barry Bluestone, *The Great U-Turn: Corporate Restructuring and the Polarizing of America,* Basic Books, New York, 1988.

Henderson, W. O., *The Rise of German Industrial Power,* Temple Smith, London, 1975.

Herre, Franz, *Moltke, der Mann und sein Jahrhundert,* Deutsche Verlag-Anstalt, Stuttgart, 1984.

Hertz, Frederick, *The German Public Mind in the Nineteenth Century,* Rowman and Littlefield, Totowa, NJ, 1975.

Hingley, Ronald, *The Russian Secret Police,* Hutchinson and Co., London, 1970.

Hirsch, Rudolf, *Printing Selling and Reading,* 2nd printing, Otto Harrassowitz, Wiesbaden, 1974.

Hogg, O. F. G., *Artillery: Its Origin, Heyday and Decline,* Hurst, London, 1970.

Hopkins, Mark W., *Mass Media in the Soviet Union,* Praeger, New York, 1970.

Howard, Michael, *War in European History,* Oxford University Press, Oxford, 1976.

Huizinga, J. H., *Dutch Civilization in the Seventeenth Century,* Collins, London, 1968.

Humble, Richard, *Warfare in the Ancient World,* Cassell, London, 1980.

Hurstfield, J., "Social structure, office holding and politics, chiefly in Western Europe," in *The New Cambridge Modern History,* vol. 3, *The Counter-Reformation and Price Revolution,* ed. R. B. Wernham, Cambridge University Press, Cambridge, 1968, pp. 126–48.

Hutchings, Raymond, *Soviet Economic Development,* Blackwell, Oxford, 1971.

Hyma, Albert, "Calvinism and capitalism in the Netherlands, 1555–1700," *Journal of Modern History,* 10 (1938), pp. 325–43.

Innis, Harold A., *The Bias of Communication,* University of Toronto Press, Toronto, 1951.

Innis, Harold A., *Empire and Communications,* Clarendon, Oxford, 1950.

Isaac, Benjamin, *The Limits of Empire: The Roman Army in the East,* Clarendon, Oxford, 1990.

Jacobsen, Thorkild, *Toward the Image of Tammuz and Other Essays on Mesopotamian History and Culture,* ed. William L. Moran, Harvard University Press, Cambridge, 1970.

Jones, A. H. M., *The Later Roman Empire 284–602,* Blackwell, Oxford, 1964.

Jones, A. H. M., *The Roman Economy,* Blackwell, Oxford, 1974.

Jordan, Hamilton, *Crisis: The Last Year of the Carter Presidency,* G. P. Putnam's Sons, New York, 1982.

Kenez, Peter, *The Birth of the Propaganda State: Soviet Methods of Mass Mobilization 1917–1929,* Cambridge University Press, Cambridge, 1985.

Kennedy, Paul, *The Rise and Fall of the Great Powers,* Random House, New York, 1987.

Kirby, Richard S., Sidney Withington, Arthur B. Darling, and Frederick G. Kilgour, *Engineering in History,* McGraw-Hill, New York, 1956.

Kitchen, Martin, *The Political Economy of Germany 1815–1914,* Croom Helm, London, 1978.

Kossmann, "The Low Countries," in *The New Cambridge Modern History*, vol. 4, ed. J. P. Cooper, Cambridge University Press, Cambridge, 1970, pp. 359–84.

Kramer, Samuel Noah, *The Sumerians: Their History, Culture and Character*, University of Chicago Press, Chicago, 1963.

Kraus, Antje, *Quellen zur Bevölkerungs-, Sozial- und Wirtschaftsstatistik Deutschlands 1815–1875*, Band I, Harald Boldt Verlag, Boppard am Rhein, 1980.

Lamberg-Karlovsky, C. C., "The economic world of Sumer," in *Biblioteca Mesopotamica, vol. 4, The Legacy of Sumer*, ed. Denise Schmandt-Besserat, Undena, Malibu, 1976, pp. 59–68.

Landes, David S., *The Unbound Prometheus*, Cambridge University Press, Cambridge, 1969.

Lansing, Elizabeth, *The Sumerians: Inventors and Builders*, McGraw-Hill, New York, 1971.

Laporte, Maurice, *Histoire de l'Okhrana*, Payot, Paris, 1935.

Larsen, Mogens Trolle, "The tradition of empire in Mesopotamia," in *Mesopotamia, vol. 7, Power and Propaganda: A Symposium on Ancient Empires*, ed. M. T. Larsen, Akademisk Forlag, Copenhagen, 1979, pp. 75–103.

Lee, W. R., "Tax structure and economic growth in Germany (1750–1850)," *Journal of European Economic History*, 4 (1975), pp. 153–78.

Leites, K., *Recent Economic Developments in Russia*, Clarendon, Oxford, 1922.

Lenin, V. I., *What Is to Be Done?*, Foreign Language Press, Peking, 1975.

Le Roy Ladurie, Emmanuel, "Les masses profondes: la paysannerie," in *Histoire économique et sociale de la France*, vol. 1, part 2, *Paysannerie et croissance*, eds Fernand Braudel and E. Labrousse, Presses universitaires de France, Paris, 1977.

Levi, Margaret, *Of Rule and Revenue*, University of California Press, Berkeley, 1988.

Lloyd, Seton, *The Archaeology of Mesopotamia*, Thames and Hudson, London, 1978.

Lloyd, Seton, *Foundations in the Dust*, Thames and Hudson, New York, 1980.

Loftus, William Kennett, *Travels and Researches in Chaldaea and Susiana*, Gregg International Publishers, Westmead, Eng., 1971.

Lösch, August, *The Economics of Location*, Yale University Press, New Haven, 1954.

Lot, Ferdinand, *L'art militaire et les armées au moyen âge en Europe et dans le proche orient*, vol. 2, Payot, Paris, 1946.

Lowenthal, Richard, *The Impact of the Russian Revolution 1917–67*, Oxford University Press, Oxford, 1967.

Lucas, A. and J. R. Harris, *Ancient Egyptian Materials and Industries*, Edward Arnold, London, 1962.

Luttwak, Edward N., *The Grand Strategy of the Roman Empire from the First Century AD to the Third*, Johns Hopkins, Baltimore, 1976.

Lyons, Nick, *The Sony Vision*, Crown Publishers, New York, 1976.

Maddison, Angus, *Economic Growth in Japan and the USSR*, Norton, New York, 1969.

Masselman, George, "Dutch colonial policy in the seventeenth century," *Journal of Economic History*, 21 (1961), pp. 455–68.

McLuhan, Marshall, *The Gutenberg Galaxy: The Making of Typographic Man*, University of Toronto Press, Toronto, 1962.

McLuhan, Marshall, *Understanding Media: The Extensions of Man*, McGraw-Hill, New York, 1964.

McNeill, William H., *Mythistory and Other Essays*, University of Chicago Press, Chicago, 1986.

McNeill, William H., *Plagues and Peoples*, University of Chicago Press, Chicago, 1976.

McNeill, William H., *The Pursuit of Power: Technology, Armed Force and Society since* AD 1000, University of Chicago Press, Chicago, 1982.

McNeill, William H., *The Rise of the West: A History of the Human Community*, University of Chicago Press, Chicago, 1963.

Miesing, Paul, "The Chrysler Corporation Loan Guarantee Act of 1979," in *Organization Policy and Strategic Management: Text and Cases*, ed. James M. Higgins, The Dryden Press, Chicago, 1983, pp. 737–58.

Millar, Fergus, *The Roman Empire and its Neighbours*, 2nd edn, Holmes and Meier, New York, 1981.

Mokyr, Joel, *Industrialization in the Low Countries, 1795–1850*, Yale University Press, New Haven, 1976.

Montgomery of Alamein, Field Marshall Viscount, *A History of Warfare*, Collins, London, 1968.

Moorey, P. R. S., "The archaeological evidence for metallurgy and related technologies in Mesopotamia, c. 5500–2100 BC," *Iraq* (1982), 44, pp. 13–38.

Moscati, Sabatino, *The Face of the Ancient Orient*, Routledge and Kegan Paul, London, 1960.

Mueller, Dennis C., *Public Choice II*, Cambridge University Press, Cambridge, 1989.

Mumford, Lewis, *The City in History*, Harcourt, Brace and World, New York, 1961.

Munting, Roger, *The Economic Development of the USSR*, Croom Helm, London, 1982.

Nelson, Richard R., *Understanding Technical Change as an Evolutionary Process*, North-Holland, Amsterdam, 1987.

Nelson, Richard R. and Sidney G. Winter, *An Evolutionary Theory of Economic Change*, Harvard University Press, Cambridge, Mass., 1982.

Nipperdey, Thomas, *Deutsche Geschichte 1800–1866*, Beck, Munich, 1983.

North, Douglass C., *Institutions, Institutional Change and Economic Performance*, Cambridge University Press, Cambridge, 1990.

North, Douglass C., *Structure and Change in Economic History*, Norton, New York, 1981.

North, Douglass C. and Robert Paul Thomas, *The Rise of the Western World: A New Economic History*, Cambridge University Press, Cambridge, 1973.

Nove, Alec, *An Economic History of the USSR*, Penguin, London, 1969.

Nove, Alec, *Political Economy and Soviet Socialism*, George Allen and Unwin, London, 1979.

Olson, Mancur, *The Rise and Decline of Nations*, Yale University Press, New Haven, 1982.

Olson, Mancur, "Toward a more general theory of government structure," *American Economic Review, Papers and Proceedings*, 76 (May 1986), pp. 120–5.

Oppenheim, A. Leo, *Ancient Mesopotamia: Portrait of a Dead Civilization*, University of Chicago Press, Chicago, 1964.

Oppenheim, A. Leo, "A bird's-eye view of Mesopotamian economic history," in *Trade and Market in the Early Empires*, eds K. Polanyi, C. M. Arensberg and H. W. Pearson, The Free Press, New York, 1957, pp. 27–37.

Parker, W. H., *An Historical Geography of Russia*, Aldine, Chicago, 1968.

Parsons, Talcott, *Societies: Evolutionary and Comparative Perspectives*, Prentice-Hall, Englewood Cliffs, NJ, 1966.

Partington, J. R., *A History of Greek Fire and Gunpowder*, Heffer, Cambridge, 1960.

Payne, Robert, *The Life and Death of Lenin*, Simon and Schuster, New York, 1964.

Perkins, J. A., "Fiscal policy and economic development in XIXth century Germany," *Journal of European Economic History*, 13 (1984), pp. 311–44.

Petit-Dutaillis, Charles, *Charles VII, Louis XI et les premières années de Charles VIII (1422–1492)*, Tallandier, Paris, 1981.

Pirenne, Henri, *Medieval Cities: Their Origins and the Revival of Trade*, Princeton University Press, Princeton, NJ, 1925.

Pirenne, Jacques, *Civilisations antiques*, Albin Michel, Paris, 1951.

Plumb, J. H., "Introduction," in *The Dutch Seaborne Empire 1600–1800*, by C. R. Boxer, Hutchinson, London, 1965, pp. xiii-xxvi.

Pocock, John, "England," in *National Consciousness, History and Political Culture in Early-Modern Europe*, ed. Orest Ranum, Johns Hopkins, Baltimore, 1975, pp. 98–117.

Polanyi, Karl, "Marketless trading in Hammurabi's time," in *Trade and Markets in the Early Empires*, eds K. Polanyi, C. M. Arensberg, and H. W. Pearson, The Free Press, Glencoe, 1957.

Powell, Marvin A., "Sumerian merchants and the problem of profit," *Iraq*, 23 (1977), pp. 23–9.

Prestowitz, Clyde V., *Trading Places: How We Allowed Japan to Take the Lead*, Basic Books, New York, 1988.

Ramm, Agatha, *Germany 1789–1919*, Methuen, London, 1967.

Remington, Thomas F., *Building Socialism in Bolshevik Russia*, University of Pittsburgh Press, Pittsburgh, 1984.

Ringgren, Helmer, *Religions of the Ancient Near East*, tr. John Sturdy, The Westminster Press, Philadelphia, 1973.

Roorda, D. J., "The ruling classes in Holland in the seventeenth century," in *Britain and the Netherlands*, vol. 2, eds J. S. Bromley and E. H. Kossmann, J. B. Wolters, Groningen, 1964, pp. 109–32.

Rosenberg, Hans, *Bureaucracy, Aristocracy and Autocracy: The Prussian Experience 1660–1815*, Harvard University Press, Cambridge, Mass., 1958.

Rostovtzeff, Michael I., *Social and Economic History of the Roman Empire*, 2nd edn, 2 vols, Oxford University Press, London, 1957.

Rowe, Christopher, *People and Chips: The Human Implications of Information Technology*, Paradigm, London, 1986.

Ruffle, John, *The Egyptians: An Introduction to Egyptian Archaeology*, Cornell University Press, Ithaca, 1977.

Sakiya, Tetsuo, *Honda Motor: The Men, the Management, the Machines*, Kodansha International Ltd, Tokyo, 1982.

Sanders, William T., "Pre-industrial demography and social evolution," in *On the Evolution of Complex Societies*, ed. Timothy Earle, Undena, Malibu, 1984, pp. 7–39.

Schapiro, Leonard, *The Communist Party of the Soviet Union*, 2nd edn, Random House, New York, 1971.

Schapiro, Leonard, *The Russian Revolutions of* 1917, Basic Books, New York, 1984.

Schmandt-Besserat, Denise, "An archaic recording system and the origins of writing," *Syro-Mesopotamian Studies*, 1 (1977), pp. 2–30.

Schmandt-Besserat, Denise, "The origins of writing, an archaeologist's perspective," *Written Communication*, 3 (1986), pp. 31–45.

Schwartz, Harry, *Russia's Soviet Economy*, 2nd edn, Prentice-Hall, New York, 1954.

Scott, Derek J. R., *Russian Political Institutions*, 2nd edn, Praeger, New York, 1961.

Seton-Watson, Hugh, *Nations and States*, Methuen, London, 1977.

Seton-Watson, Hugh, *The Russian Empire, 1801–1917*, Clarendon Press, Oxford, 1967.

Shook, Robert L., *Honda: An American Success Story*, Prentice-Hall, New York, 1988.

Showalter, Dennis E., *Railroads and Rifles*, Archon, Hamden, Conn., 1976.

Shub, David, *Lenin*, The New American Library, New York, 1948.

Simon, Walter M., *Germany in the Age of Bismarck*, George Allen and Unwin, London, 1968.

Skinner, G. William, "The structure of Chinese history," *Journal of Asian Studies*, 44 (1985), pp. 271–92.

Slicher van Bath, Bernard Hendrik, "The economic situation in the Dutch Republic during the seventeenth century," in *Dutch Capitalism and World Capitalism*, ed. M. Aymard, Cambridge University Press, Cambridge, 1982, pp. 23–35.

Small Business Administration, *The State of Small Business*, Washington, 1984.

Spengler, Oswald, *The Decline of the West*, Allen and Unwin, London, 1926.

Steensgaard, Niels, *The Asian Trade Revolution of the Seventeenth Century*, University of Chicago Press, Chicago, 1973.

Steensgaard, Niels, "The Dutch East India Company as an institutional innovation," in *Dutch Capitalism and World Capitalism*, ed. M. Aymard, Cambridge University Press, Cambridge, 1982, pp. 235–57.

Steinberg, S. H., *Five Hundred Years of Printing*, Penguin, Harmondsworth, 1955.

Strachan, Hew, *European Armies and the Conduct of War*, George Allen and Unwin, London, 1983.

Strayer, Joseph R., *On the Medieval Origins of the Modern State*, Princeton University Press, Princeton, NJ, 1970.

Supple, Barry, "The nature of enterprise," in *The Cambridge Economic History of Europe*, vol. 5, *The Economic Organisation of Early Modern Europe*, eds E. E. Rich and C. H. Wilson, Cambridge University Press, Cambridge, 1977, pp. 436–43.

Taylor, Richard, *Film Propaganda: Soviet Russia and Nazi Germany*, Croom-Helm, London, 1979.

Taylor, Richard, "A medium for the masses: agitation in the Soviet Civil War," *Soviet Studies*, 22 (1971), pp. 562–74.

Thompson, E. A., "Early Germanic warfare," *Past and Present*, 14 (1958), pp. 2–27.

Tilly, Charles, *Coercion, Capital and European States*, Blackwell, Oxford, 1990.

Tilly, R. H., "Capital formation in Germany in the nineteenth century," in *The Cambridge Economic History of Europe*, vol. 7, *The Industrial Economies: Capital, Labour and Enterprise*, eds P. Mathias and M. M. Postan, Cambridge University Press, Cambridge, 1978, pp. 382–441.

Todd, Malcolm, *The Northern Barbarians*, Hutchinson, London, 1975.

Toffler, Alvin, *The Third Wave*, William Morrow and Co., New York, 1980.

Toffler, Alvin, *Powershifts*, Bantam, New York, 1990.

Toynbee, Arnold, *Mankind and Mother Earth: A Narrative History of the World*, Oxford University Press, London, 1976.

Toynbee, Arnold J., *A Study of History*, revised and abridged, Oxford University Press, London, 1972.

Treadgold, Donald W., *Twentieth Century Russia*, 3rd edn, Rand McNally, Chicago, 1972.

Trebilcock, Clive, *The Industrialization of the Continental Powers* 1780–1914, Longman, London, 1981.

Trevor-Roper, H. R., "Religion, the Reformation and social change," *Historical Studies*, 4 (1961), pp. 19–29.

Tuchman, Barbara W., *A Distant Mirror: The Calamitous 14th Century*, Ballantine, New York, 1978.

Turin, S. P., *The USSR: An Economic and Social Survey*, 3rd edn, London, Methuen, 1948.

Usher, A. P., "The general course of wheat prices in France: 1350–1788," *Review of Economics and Statistics*, 12 (1930), pp. 162–7.

Van der Wee, Herman, "Monetary, credit and banking systems," in *The Cambridge Economic History of Europe*, vol. 5, *The Economic Organisation of Early Modern Europe*, eds E. E. Rich and C. H. Wilson, Cambridge University Press, Cambridge, 1977, pp. 290–392.

Van Houtte, Jan A., *An Economic History of the Low Countries* 800–1800, Weidenfeld and Nicolson, London, 1977.

Van Houtte, Jan A., and Leon Van Buyten, "The Low Countries," in *An Introduction to the Sources of European Economic History* 1500–1800, eds Charles Wilson and Geoffrey Parker, Cornell University Press, Ithaca, 1977, pp. 81–114.

Wallerstein, Immanuel, *The Modern World System II: Mercantilism and the Consolidation of the European World-Economy*, 1600–1750, Academic Press, New York, 1980.

Watanabe, Susumu, "Micro-electronics and employment in the Japanese automobile industry," World Employment Programme Research Working Paper, International Labour Office, Geneva, 1984.

Watkins, Trevor, "Sumerian weapons, warfare and warriors," *Sumer*, 39 (1983), pp. 100–2.

Webber, Carolyn and Aaron Wildavsky, *A History of Taxation and Expenditure in the Western World*, Simon and Schuster, New York, 1986.

Weber, Max, *The Protestant Ethic and the Spirit of Capitalism*, George Allen and Unwin, London, 1930.

Weber, Max, *The Theory of Social and Economic Organization*, The Free Press, New York, 1964.

Westenholz, Aage, "The Old Akkadian Empire in contemporary opinion," in *Mesopotamia*, vol. 7, *Power and Propaganda: A Symposium on Ancient Empires*, ed. M. T. Larsen, Akademisk Forlag, Copenhagen, 1979, pp. 107–24.

White, Lynn, Jr, *Medieval Technology and Social Change*, Oxford University Press, Oxford, 1964.

Williamson, Oliver, *Economic Organization: Firms, Markets and Policy Control*, Wheatsheaf, Brighton, 1986.

Wilson, Charles, *The Dutch Republic and the Civilization of the Seventeenth Century*, McGraw-Hill, New York, 1968.

Wilson, Charles, *Economic History and the Historian*, Weidenfeld and Nicolson, London, 1969.

Wilson, Charles, *The Transformation of Europe*, 1558–1648, University of California Press, Berkeley, 1976.

Wittfogel, Karl A., *Oriental Despotism: A Comparative Study of Total Power*, Yale University Press, New Haven, 1957.

Wolfe, Bertram D., *Revolution and Reality: Essays on the Origin and Fate of the Soviet System*, University of North Carolina Press, Chapel Hill, 1981.

Wolfe, Martin, *The Fiscal System of Renaissance France*, Yale University Press, New Haven, 1972.

World Motor Vehicle Data, 1981 edition.

Yadin, Yigael, *The Art of Warfare in Biblical Lands in the Light of Archaeological Study*, McGraw-Hill, New York, 1963.

Yates, Brock, *The Decline and Fall of the American Automobile Industry*, Empire Books, New York, 1983.

Zumthor, Paul, *La vie quotidienne en Hollande au temps de Rembrandt*, Hachette, Paris, 1959.

Suggested Reading

Those who enjoy the search for cause and effect in historical events may wish to pursue further some of the ideas explored in this study. With a few exceptions, the references below are limited to recent books available in English. (For other sources, including articles in scholarly journals, please refer to the detailed notes to each chapter.) There are three types of references that are of interest: first, general studies of historical change; second, inquiries into the evolution of communications or military technology; and third, research on the developments that occurred within the eight individual historical periods selected for this book.

General Studies of Historical Change

The pioneering study of cyclical change in past and present civilizations is Oswald Spengler's *The Decline of the West* (1916–20, translated into English in 1926). Arnold J. Toynbee's *A Study of History* (1934–61), available in abridged form in a 1972 volume, adds a good measure of Anglo-Saxon reserve to Spengler's pessimism. William H. McNeill's *The Rise of the West* (1963) emphasizes the considerable degree of interaction among the world's main cultural regions. His *Plagues and Peoples* (1976) suggests provocatively that micro-organisms may be responsible for the fall of major civilizations in the past. Focusing on the modern period of history, Paul Kennedy in *The Rise and Fall of the Great Powers* (1987) offers an alternative explanation for such declines: namely, the tendency for expanding powers to overextend themselves during periods when their opposition is weak. However, Charles Tilly in *Coercion, Capital and European States* (1990) argues that no single model can account for the diversity in state structures to be found in Europe over the past millennium.

The economic historian Douglass C. North has gone over the same historical material searching for economic explanations for changing political structures. In *The Rise of the Western World: A New Economic History* (1973, written with Robert Paul Thomas), *Structure and Change in Economic History* (1981) and *Institutions, Institutional Change and Economic Performance* (1990), he has emphasized the importance of institutions that create the incentives to exchange and to innovate. Mancur Olson's *The Rise and Decline of Nations* (1982) argues that over time the privileges accumulated by interest groups within a society may distort these incentives, thereby precipitating economic decline.

Inquiries into the Evolution of Communications or Military Technology

Two of the earliest studies of the link between communications technology and social structures are *Empire and Communications* (1950) and *The Bias of Communication* (1951) by Harold A. Innis. His ideas were extended and popularized by Marshall McLuhan in *The Gutenberg Galaxy: The Making of Typographic Man* (1962) and *Understanding Media: The Extensions of Man* (1964). Two key studies of literacy – the ability to send and receive written communications – are Carlo M. Cipolla's *Literacy and Development in the West* (1969) and Jack Goody's *The Domestication of the Savage Mind* (1977). Recently, Alvin Toffler in *The Third Wave* (1980) and *Powershifts* (1990) has speculated on the social effects of new electronic technologies.

With regard to military technology, the most comprehensive source is undoubtedly *The Encyclopedia of Military History from 3500 BC to the Present* (2nd edn, 1986) by R. Ernest Dupuy and Trevor N. Dupuy. The evolution of military techniques in antiquity is well covered by Richard Humble in *Warfare in the Ancient World* (1980) and by Arther Ferrill in *The Origins of War* (1985). The political repercussions of the evolution of military techniques over the past millennium are compellingly traced by William H. McNeill in *The Pursuit of Power: Technology, Armed Force and Society since AD 1000* (1982). For the most recent centuries, Michael Howard's *War in European History* (1976), Larry H. Addington's *The Patterns of War since the Eighteenth Century* (1984) and Brian Bond's *War and Society in Europe, 1870–1970* (1984) are to be recommended.

Research on Developments within Individual Historical Periods

Sumer   The development of writing in Sumer is explained by Ignace J. Gelb in *A Study of Writing* (1963). The principal archaeological discoveries in Mesopotamia and their implications for our understanding of the first urban societies are vividly described by Samuel Noah Kramer in *The Sumerians: Their History, Culture and Character* (1963). Recent assessments of developments in Mesopotamia during the protohistoric period may be found in articles by Robert McC. Adams and William T. Sanders in *On the Evolution of Complex Societies*, edited by Timothy Earle (1984). For details of how the the first cities appeared in Sumer, see Robert McC. Adams' *Heartland of Cities* (1981).

Akkad   The classic study of the development of weapons in the Fertile Crescent is Yigael Yadin's *The Art of Warfare in Biblical Lands in the Light of Archaeological Study* (1963). The outbreak of warfare among the cities of Sumer and the construction of the Akkadian empire are outlined in C. J. Gadd's article in *The Cambridge Ancient History*, vol. I, part 2 (1971). Studies by Adam Falkenstein, Dietz Otto Edzard and Jean Bottéro in *The Near East: The Early Civilizations*, edited by J. Bottéro, E. Cassin, and J. Vercoutter (1967) provide additional details on this period. Articles by Mogens Trolle Larsen and Aage Westenholz in *Mesopotamia*, vol. 7, *Power and Propaganda: A Symposium on Ancient Empires* (1979), edited by M. T. Larsen, suggest that the Akkadian state represented a new form of social organization.

The Later Roman Empire　Edward N. Luttwak has written a detailed account of the evolution of military techniques in the Roman Empire in *The Grand Strategy of the Roman Empire from the First Century* AD *to the Third* (1976). Arther Ferrill in *The Fall of the Roman Empire* (1986) shows how military decisions taken in the fourth century fatally weakened the Roman Empire in the West. That there was any overall strategy behind these developments is however contested by Benjamin Isaac in *The Limits of Empire: The Roman Army in the East* (1990). For information on the history and economy of imperial Rome in its final centuries, *The Later Roman Empire* 284–602 (1964) and *The Roman Economy* (1974) by A. H. M. Jones are to be recommended.

Fifteenth-century France　The rapid developments in European military technology during the late Middle Ages are portrayed in Philippe Contamine's *War in the Middle Ages* (1984). The implications of war for the French fiscal system are analyzed by Martin Wolfe in *The Fiscal System of Renaissance France* (1972). For an account of the Hundred Years War from the French viewpoint, the reader should consult Jean Favier's *La guerre de cent ans* (1980). In English, a recent study by Christopher Allmand, *The Hundred Years War: England and France at War c.*1300–*c.*1450 (1988), places these events in their military and social context.

The United Provinces of the Netherlands　The innovations in printing in the fifteenth century are described by S. H. Steinberg in *Five Hundred Years of Printing* (1955). Their social impact in the sixteenth century is the subject of Elizabeth L. Eisenstein's *The Printing Press as an Agent of Change* (1979). Charles Wilson's *The Dutch Republic and the Civilization of the Seventeenth Century* (1968) and *The Transformation of Europe, 1558–1648* (1976) present the social developments that occurred in the Netherlands in the late sixteenth and early seventeenth centuries and place them in their European context. The rise of the first true multinational corporation is studied by Niels Steensgaard in *The Asian Trade Revolution of the Seventeenth Century* (1973).

The Unification of Germany　Dennis E. Showalter in *Railroads and Rifles* (1976) examines developments in military technology and organization in Prussia during the decades leading up to German unification. The historical details of this period are described by Agatha Ramm in *Germany 1789–1919* (1967) and by William Carr in *A History of Germany 1815–1945* (1969). For an analysis of the changing economic role of the Prussian State, see W. O. Henderson, *The Rise of German Industrial Power* (1975).

The Russian Revolution　The roles played by newspapers, film, and posters in Russian society before and after the 1917 revolutions are set out by Peter Kenez in *The Birth of the Propaganda State: Soviet Methods of Mass Mobilization* 1917–1929 (1985). For the historical details, Sheila Fitzpatrick's *The Russian Revolution* (1982) and Leonard Schapiro's *The Russian Revolutions of* 1917 (1984) make compelling reading. The restructuring of the Russian economy initiated under Lenin is analyzed by Alec Nove in *An Economic History of the USSR* (1969) and Thomas F. Remington in *Building Socialism in Bolshevik Russia* (1984).

The Carter Presidency   Tom Forester's *The Story of the Information Technology Revolution* (1987) provides a clear description of recent developments in microelectronics technology. Christopher Rowe *People and Chips: The Human Implications of Information Technology* (1986) explores the implications of these innovations for social organization. Of the many studies of American and Japanese corporations, Tetsuo Sakiya's *Honda Motor: The Men, the Management, the Machines,* (1982) and Brock Yates's *The Decline and Fall of the American Automobile Industry* (1983), with their focus on the late 1970s, are particularly interesting. For the people and events of Jimmy Carter's presidency, one should consult Edwin C. Hargrove's *Jimmy Carter as President: Leadership and the Politics of the Public Good* (1988).

General Index

Italic numbers, such as *48,* indicate that maps or illustrations appear on that page.

Name Index